The
BUSINESS OF MARTYRDOM

The
BUSINESS OF MARTYRDOM

A History of
Suicide Bombing

Jeffrey William Lewis

Naval Institute Press
Annapolis, Maryland

Naval Institute Press
291 Wood Road
Annapolis, MD 21402

Library of Congress Cataloging-in-Publication Data
Lewis, Jeffrey W.
  The business of martyrdom : a history of suicide bombing / Jeffrey W. Lewis.
    p. cm.
  Includes bibliographical references and index.
  ISBN 978-1-61251-051-4 (hbk. : alk. paper) — ISBN 978-1-61251-097-2 (e-book) 1. Suicide bombings—History. 2. Suicide bombers—History. 3. Terrorism—History. I. Title.
  HV6431.L493 2012
  363.32509—dc23

                                                                        2011044682

♾ This paper meets the requirements of ANSI/NISO z39.48-1992 (Permanence of Paper).
Printed in the United States of America.

20 19 18 17 16 15 14 13 12   9 8 7 6 5 4 3 2 1
First printing

For Tasha, Kaia, and Sammi

CONTENTS

FIGURES AND TABLES

FIGURES

TABLES

ACKNOWLEDGMENTS

The Business of Martyrdom: A History of Suicide Bombing views the phenomenon of suicide attacks through the lens of technology. It was motivated by the confluence of my ongoing interest in the relationship between humans and technology, particularly the boundaries between people and machines, and the worldwide increase in suicide operations in the early 2000s. Shortly after the al Qaeda attacks of 9/11, I was given the challenge of teaching courses on terrorism, technology, and national security issues in Ohio State University's Undergraduate International Studies Program. At that time, relatively little had been written about suicide bombing. As researchers from a variety of backgrounds began filling in this gap, it became clear that despite the technological metaphors used for suicide bombing, few of them were prepared to accept the idea of suicide bombers as literal "smart bombs." My decision to pursue this study was therefore born of a desire to analyze this new and puzzling phenomenon within a well-established framework in order to provide a perspective and context that seemed to be lacking, despite wave after wave of books and articles about it. Along the way I benefited enormously from the new scholarship and from many of the researchers who produced it, particularly the empirical psychological studies and field-work that have provided the evidence upon which my argument rests. This book is therefore both a synthesis of recent scholarship as well as a technological interpretation of suicide bombing.

Since the intellectual roots of this study go deep, I have accumulated a great many personal and professional debts, which it is an honor and a pleasure finally to acknowledge. I must draw special attention to John C. Burnham and Alan Beyerchen of the Ohio State University Department of History for their ongoing support throughout my academic career. Both have served as intellectual sounding boards throughout the writing of this book and have patiently read through numerous drafts. I hope that their influence is readily discernable on the pages that follow. I must also thank the faculty, staff, and students of Ohio State's Undergraduate International Studies Program. Anthony Mughan, the director, has created an intellectual environment in which I have had an enviable degree of freedom to develop as a teacher and a researcher. The IS staff—Karlene Foster, Richard Meltz, and Elizabeth Langford—have supported me in innumerable ways over the past decade, making the completion of this book that much easier. Since my position in the International Studies Program is that of a teacher, it should come as no surprise that many of the ideas in this book originated in the classroom and that I therefore owe an unusually great deal of thanks to my many excellent students over the years.

Support for this research was provided by the Department of Homeland Security through the National Consortium for the Study of Terrorism and Responses to Terrorism (START) (grant number N00140510629). Any opinions, findings, and conclusions or recommendations in this document are those of the author and do not necessarily reflect the views of the Department of Homeland Security. At the START Center, Director Gary LaFree, Kathleen Smarick, Katherine Worboys-Izsak, Gary Ackerman, Victor Asal, Laura Dugan, and Jeffrey Bale provided encouragement and ideas as I began to conceptualize the manuscript during a postdoctoral fellowship for the 2007–2008 academic year. Mia Bloom and Clark McCauley offered excellent advice and read portions of the manuscript as well. The final product is much stronger thanks to their attention.

In 2006 I participated in the Summer Workshop on Teaching about Terrorism (SWOTT), hosted by the University of Georgia, where I first met many of the scholars who would have an impact on the final manuscript. David Rapoport showed an interest in this project at an early stage and was the first to publish the ideas that would form part of Chapter 8, "The Business of Martyrdom." Anonymous readers at the journals *Terrorism and Political Violence* and *Dynamics of Asymmetric Conflict* provided valuable criticism on early versions of some of the chapters. I also benefited from critical reviews of the entire manuscript by readers at the Naval Institute Press as well as several other publishers. While I have not been able to accommodate all of their suggestions, their feedback strengthened the rigor of the argument and the quality of the writing.

My editor at the Naval Institute Press, Adam Kane, was supportive, pragmatic, and clear, making the publication of my first book smooth and relatively trauma free. *The Business of Genocide,* by my colleague Michael Thad Allen, provided some of the ideas for my own book and was also the inspiration for the title. Monsignor Frank Lane helped me to understand the relationship between authenticity and martyrdom. This relationship became an integral part of the book's argument, and I cannot imagine having comprehended it fully without Father Lane's unique mix of decency, humility, and intellectual rigor.

To the many others that I have not named but who also assisted in the development of this book over the years, I offer a collective and sincere thank you. Any mistakes or errors of interpretation that remain are entirely my responsibility.

To my wife, Karen, I owe thanks on a professional and personal level. As a colleague she read and critiqued the entire manuscript, cleaned up the writing, and improved the tables and figures. My personal debt to her is immeasurable, for without her, nothing that I value highly today—my marriage, my family, my home, and my career—would have been possible. As both my family and this book grew, our children's grandparents—my mother, Marcia Marquis, and my in-laws, Edward and Elizabeth Keefer—provided a support network without which I could never have managed to be both an author and a father. Finally, my deepest thanks go to my daughters—Natasha, Kaia, and Samantha—who have made me happier and prouder than I have ever been. I dedicate this book to them.

A NOTE ON PROPER NAMES

Much of this study deals with the Arabic-speaking world. There is no universally accepted means for transliterating Arabic into English, so names of prominent individuals and organizations have entered the English language with a sometimes bewildering number of different spellings. Since I am not an Arabic speaker, I cannot attest to the virtues of one system of transliteration as opposed to another. Therefore, for purposes of clarity, I have chosen what I believe to be the most commonly used and recognizable spellings of important names—for example, al Qaeda, rather than al-Qa'ida; Osama bin Laden, rather than Usama bin Ladin; Shiite rather than Shi'ite or Shia; and Hizballah, rather than Hezbollah or Hizbullah— to cite the most prominent examples. I have done this with the hopes of making the text more accessible to readers. These spellings are used consistently in my writing, but alternative spellings in direct quotations and book and article titles have been properly retained.

The
BUSINESS OF MARTYRDOM

INTRODUCTION
The Human Use of Human Beings

*The simplest method of obtaining target discrimination
is through its recognition by intelligence.*[1]

—National Defense Research Council, 1946

*But in truth there is no difference between their [American
and Israeli] attacks and ours. Both of us have one thing in common—
to annihilate the enemy. The rest is mere logistics and differences in
techniques. Whether one attacks by planes or by car bombs the objective is
the same. Who is to say that they are better or more civilized just
because they use twentieth-century equipment? Who decides that it
is more right or correct or even more acceptable to kill one's
enemy by warplanes rather than car bombs?*[2]

—"Hassan," Hizballah member

TACTICAL MARTYRDOM

The impact of the September 11, 2001, al Qaeda attacks on the United
States extended beyond their physical and financial effects. They shred-
ded Americans' confidence about their security and left behind a sense of
vulnerability not seen in the United States since the tensest moments of
the Cold War. In the months and years after the attacks, another factor
added to the psychological toll—frustration at the failure of U.S. intel-

ligence services to have anticipated the attack or to intercept the attackers beforehand. The frustration was well-founded in some respects. The FBI and CIA had the information they needed to disrupt the plot, yet because of a lack of vision, interagency mistrust, and poor leadership they were unable to make effective use of it.

In other respects, the failure to anticipate 9/11 is understandable because the operation was designed to exploit blind spots in the collective thinking of the U.S. security community. The attacks completely rewrote the rules of airliner hijacking. Previously, hijackings had been theatrical affairs in which the hijackers traded power over their hostages' lives for concessions in a ruthless kind of negotiation.[3] The September 11 hijackings, however, were about aircraft, not people; in fact, the passengers were potential liabilities, rather than assets, as demonstrated by the resistance of the passengers on United Flight 93 and their success in stopping the hijackers from reaching their destination. The goal of the hijackings was to reprogram the guidance systems of the airliners so that they could be used as massive cruise missiles. To direct these missiles at their targets, the hijackers installed their own control systems—pilots who had been trained in the specific task of crashing the airliners into buildings. Since the security measures extant at the time had been established on the assumption that the lives of passengers were more valuable to hijackers than the aircraft, they proved to be ineffective for this fundamentally different kind of attack.

The September 11 attacks therefore had more in common with the United States' arsenal of precision-guided munitions than with the history of aviation terrorism, a fact noted by two experts on the "precision revolution" in air-delivered weapons. Soon after 9/11, Michael Russell Rip and James M. Hasik wrote, "The two attacks in New York displayed pinpoint accuracy against targets only half a city block wide. This sort of precision is otherwise attainable only with laser, electro-optical, or satellite guidance."[4] Prior to the al Qaeda operation, this sentence probably would have read "such precision is *only* attainable" with the systems they reference.

After 9/11, it is essential to think more broadly about technology and to recognize the attacks on that day as having employed a fundamentally different form of guidance technology in which computation and decision making were performed by individuals instead of computers. From such a perspective, the pilots of the four diverted aircraft were not "normal" hijackers carrying out an agreed upon tactic; nor did they "use" the aircraft to attack the United States. Rather, they were the control elements of a weapon system whose destruction was a necessary and anticipated consequence of a successful mission, as is the fate of a precision-guided munition (PGM) produced by a technologically advanced state. Also like a PGM, the entire system—consisting of aircraft, hijackers, and pilots—was used by actors who were not physically present, in the case of 9/11 the al Qaeda leadership that had planned and directed the mission.

This basic relationship—the use of human beings by other human beings—is the defining characteristic of suicide bombing. Horror at the brutal results of suicide attacks and an almost lurid fascination with the mental state of the individuals who commit such violence have tended to deflect attention away from this relationship, but it is the constant presence of "use," more than any other factor, that has made suicide bombing problematic to analyze in terms of previously accepted understandings of self-sacrificial violence. For example, suicide bombers have typically been understood within their communities and their sponsoring organizations to be martyrs in the traditional sense of the word—that is, individuals who willingly sacrifice their lives on behalf of a cause. The willingness of such individuals to give their lives, in turn, has the strategic effect of validating the cause and the organizations that fight for it.

At the same time, however, suicide bombing differs appreciably from martyrdom as conventionally understood because historically martyrs have for the most part accepted suffering for themselves without inflicting harm upon others. The power of martyrdom lies in the willingness of the individual to suffer, even unto death, which stems from the martyr's certainty in his or her beliefs and a sense that to compromise those beliefs would be a worse alternative than death. Since suicide bombing by its nature inflicts harm, often grievous, indiscriminate harm, many analysts strongly believe that suicide bombing cannot be understood in terms of martyrdom. To reconcile these two understandings of suicide bombing, one must shift attention away from individual bombers and toward the organizational element that uses them.

The presence of users in suicide bombing confirms that it is indeed different from most historical instances of martyrdom, but the fact that the bombers are often willing to die on behalf of others suggests some overlap with the classical martyr's willingness to die for a cause. It is therefore proffered here that suicide bombing be understood as a new type of martyrdom—that is, "tactical martyrdom." Suicide bombing can still generate the strategic, legitimizing power of classical martyrdom, but with an added dimension. By allowing organizations to control what would otherwise be an individual act, suicide bombing makes "martyrdom" predictable and usable, thereby contributing significantly to the power of militant groups by providing them with intelligent guidance systems for their weapons.

Tactical martyrdom is therefore different from most traditional understandings of martyrdom. This does not necessarily imply the opposite, however, which would be that suicide attacks are the same as individual suicides. Certainly, many suicide attackers appear to have been motivated by despair, fatalism, or even self-aggrandizement, making their choice selfish and therefore similar to that of typical suicides. At the same time, the social dimension of the violence is consistent with the history of martyrdom in different cultural traditions. Suicide bombers therefore do not fit readily into the categories of martyrdom or individual suicide. Instead, to understand suicide bombing, it is more appropriate to think of lethal self-violence in terms of a spectrum stretching from individual, selfish suicide to classical martyrdom on behalf of others, with today's tactical martyrs falling somewhere in between. Depending on individual motivations, some may fall closer to the ideal of classical martyrdom, some may fall closer to individual suicide, but few can be easily pigeon-holed into either extreme. In this sense tactical martyrdom is not exactly martyrdom and is not exactly suicide, but something different— the human use of human self-sacrifice.

A NEW APPROACH FOR UNDERSTANDING SUICIDE BOMBING

For more than three decades, suicide bombers have been used by a host of extremist groups in increasingly diverse and innovative ways. In 2004 such bombers carried out at least 102 attacks, successfully striking targets in Afghanistan, Iraq, Israel, Turkey, Uzbekistan, and elsewhere. The final toll for 2005 was more than 300 suicide bombings, resulting in 3,171

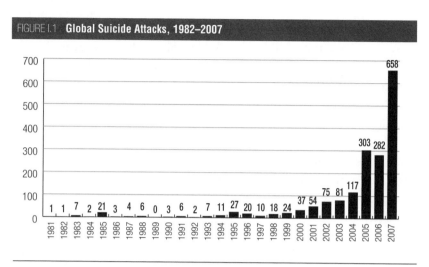

FIGURE I.1 **Global Suicide Attacks, 1982–2007**

Source: Robin Wright, "Since 2001, a Dramatic Increase in Suicide Bombings," *Washington Post,* April 18, 2008.

fatalities. According to the *Washington Post*, the total number of suicide attacks globally declined in 2006, to 282, but then more than doubled in 2007, to 658 operations (see Figure I.1).[5]

Even as suicide bombing became a significant global security problem it remained difficult to analyze. Since few people understand why an individual would choose to kill him- or herself while indiscriminately killing others, the psychology of the individual suicide bomber attracted a disproportionate share of public fascination and scholarly attention after the phenomenon became a regular occurrence in the 1980s. This focus on the mindset of individual bombers precluded understanding the organizational character of suicide bombing for many years. In particular, the issues of agency and use were often mistakenly attributed to the bombers or their cultures rather than their sponsoring organizations.

As suicide bombing became more common in the first decade of the current millennium, the frequency and ingenuity with which organizations trained and utilized their followers prompted rethinking, and in the early 2000s a scholarly consensus on the centrality of organizational control of suicide bombing took shape. In 2004 Bruce Hoffman and Gordon McCormick articulated this consensus in terms that evoke technological processes of manufacturing. They wrote, "Although suicide attacks often appear to be the actions of deranged individuals, with rare exceptions they are seldom the product of an individualized choice. They are almost always the product of an organizational process designed to transform otherwise normal individuals into agents of self-destruction."[6]

The addition of analysis of the organizational component reveals suicide bombing to be a process that operates simultaneously on three levels: that of the individual bomber, the culture that supports the bomber and bombing, and the organizations that make and use the bombers. Of significance, the psychology and therefore rationality of suicide bombing varies depending upon the level of analysis. Although scholars have demonstrated that there can be a rational motivation for the use of suicide bombing at the group level, this same logic is often completely missing when one examines the desires and motivations of the individual bombers. What is needed at this point is an integrated approach that encompasses all three levels as well as the simultaneous presence of rational and irrational motivations that exist within suicide bombing.[7]

Although numerous books and articles have been published on suicide bombing, scholars remain tentative when addressing the subject. The most common metaphor used to describe the suicide attacker is that of a smart bomb. For example, Bruce Hoffman writes that suicide bombers are "the ultimate smart bomb," and Mohammed Hafez suggests that suicide bombers "are perhaps the smartest [bombs] ever invented."[8] Still, in spite of the smart bomb metaphor, most observers continue to regard suicide bombing as a tactic—a pattern of behavior that is particularly lethal and tends to be used when all others have failed, perhaps, but still a tactic.[9]

This designation remains incomplete at best because it only takes into account the act of lethal self-violence carried out by the bomber (or bombers) against his or her targets. This designation does not address the numerous factors at the individual, organizational, and cultural levels that make suicide bombing possible. In short, calling suicide bombing a tactic describes how suicide bombers are used but does nothing to explain how and why they are made, or why some groups use them well, some poorly, and others not at all. It may have been appropriate when overall understanding of the phenomenon was poorer, but given the current state of knowledge, a more complex explanatory framework is necessary.[10] *The Business of Martyrdom: A History of Suicide Bombing* provides such a framework by integrating recent empirical research on the organizational character of suicide bombing to push the insight of the smart bomb metaphor to its logical conclusion by arguing that tactical martyrdom is a form of technology that is consistent with—and understandable in terms of—other technological systems.

The Business of Martyrdom is a historical analysis of the technology of suicide bombing that traces its invention and reinvention, diffusion, and transformation at the hands of its users. A historical approach is necessary because suicide bombing has changed significantly over the past three decades. The more recent studies of it are structured thematically, rather than historically, and thus fail to present a consistent, chronologically organized narrative. The thematic approach reveals an underlying but unwarranted assumption—that one explanation for suicide bombing can be applied to a broad range of cultures and societies with minimal modification. Suicide bombing, however, is a dynamic process that takes on some of the characteristics of the cultures employing it yet also has some common elements observable across societies. The suicide bombing of the 1980s was similar to but not the same as the suicide bombing of the 2000s, so to try to approach the subject as if they were indeed identical poses significant problems for any analysis.[11]

This book provides a fluid explanatory mechanism, that of the technological system, to account for suicide bombing's dynamic character without sacrificing analytical rigor or the possibility of comparative analysis. Technologies, properly understood, are processes that integrate behavior, thinking, and physical materials and transform them into goods or services of greater utility. Understanding suicide bombing historically as a technological system takes into consideration the haphazard, contingent process by which such bombing began and also offers a plausible explanation for its diversity and diffusion. The spread of technologies is never uniform or homogeneous; instead, societies embrace or reject specific technologies depending on how a technology allows them to solve problems consistent with their values and norms. In all cases, the same basic technology will vary from region to region as the different cultures adapt it to their own standards and expectations. Each cultural manifestation of a particular technology is thus a hybrid of general and specific characteristics.

"Their" Answer

In July 2001 FBI agent Ken Williams filed an electronic memo with his superiors in which he suggested that Osama bin Laden was making a sustained effort to send his followers to the United States to learn to fly commercial airliners at civil aviation colleges. The memo was based on fieldwork through which Williams had determined that an unusual number of individuals who were of "investigative interest" to the bureau had registered for flight schools in Arizona.[12] In the aftermath of the 9/11 attacks, this report appeared to be prophetic, prompting inquiries into exactly why the FBI had not acted on the so-called Phoenix memo. The bureau's defense was that the memo had been little more than a hunch; Williams himself had not thought about hijacking, but that al Qaeda was planning a long-term infiltration of the civil aviation industry. Thus, even when presented with this information, the U.S. intelligence community was unable to anticipate the nature of the threat posed by passenger aircraft being used as weapons, despite the fact that al Qaeda had already made repeated use of suicide bombers for its most spectacular attacks. In its evaluation of the situation, the National Commission on Terrorist Attacks upon the United States (the 9/11 Commission) attributed this lack of foresight to an overall lack of imagination on the part of intelligence agencies when dealing with the threat of terrorism.[13] This explanation is only partially true.

Analysts did indeed have difficulty imagining something along the lines of the 9/11 attacks, but this does not imply that they were not applying their imaginations to the world of terrorism and mass-casualty attacks. Indeed, their imaginations were running wild, but down all the wrong paths. Since the second Bill Clinton administration, analysts had been certain that terrorists were on the verge of carrying out mass-casualty attacks using so-called weapons of mass destruction—nuclear, biological, and chemical weapons. This obsession became so deeply ingrained in the thinking of the security community that analysts could no longer imagine the use of any other type of weapon for such a scenario. Timothy Naftali writes that as of 2001, "No one assumed that al Qaeda would press forward with a mass casualty event that required only conventional weapons."[14]

Analysts in the U.S. security community tended to be locked into a mode of thinking that equated military power, and therefore security, with technology. They defined technology in terms of material devices independent of human context and understood "high" technology to be more expensive, more complex, and inherently more effective than older systems.[15] Analysts therefore projected their own thinking and biases regarding technology onto their adversaries, imagining that terrorist groups, like states, would need complex technologies to carry out high-consequence operations. Less-complex technologies, in contrast, were assumed to be less effective. The 9/11 attacks proved these assumptions wrong.

Because security officials tended to think of technology in terms of devices rather than people, they could not recognize suicide attackers as a form of guidance technology since physically there is little resemblance between a human suicide attacker and precision-guided munitions. Nevertheless, both systems perform an identical task: they both allow human intelligence to affect delivery and detonation of an explosive interactively in real time. In technology, how well a particular system does a given job is the yardstick that matters, not whether different approaches to the same job resemble one another.[16]

In recent decades, the U.S. government has invested billions of dollars in a host of artificial intelligence systems to replicate human powers of cognition. None of these systems will ever be mistaken for a person, but all have been created specifically for the purpose of performing human cognitive tasks, and thus from a technological perspective are potentially equivalent to humans in certain contexts. For example, research into artificial intelligence sponsored by the Department of Defense has led to the creation of autonomous vehicles that can navigate unfamiliar terrain without ongoing human guidance in order to remove military personnel from combat zones and therefore from harm.

Although the capabilities and durability of these prototypes remained severely limited, the use of machines to replace certain human capacities was by the early 2000s commonplace on the battlefields of Iraq and Afghanistan. Most of the robots and drones used by U.S. combat troops are not entirely autonomous because they are remotely linked to human operators. Nonetheless, they reflect a culturally specific approach to modern combat that stems from a societal aversion to casualties in warfare. Instead of being the inevitable result of scientific progress, the developments of robots and other automated systems in this scenario were choices.

In the words of U.S. Navy researcher Bart Everett, "To me, the robot is our answer to the suicide bomber."[17]

It is ironic that robots represent "our" answer to suicide bombing since suicide bombing itself was originally "their" answer to the high-technology systems deployed by Western nations and their allies during the Cold War and afterward. Indeed, most groups have expressed this notion to justify the use of suicide bombers. In the context of the Israeli-Palestinian struggle, a member of Hamas' Izz al-Din al-Qassam Brigades told the journalist Nasra Hassan, "We do not have tanks or rockets, but we have something superior—our exploding Islamic human bombs. In place of a nuclear arsenal, we are proud of our arsenal of believers."[18] In an expression of the same sentiment, signs were posted at one point in classrooms at al-Najah University in Nablus and the Islamic University of Gaza that read, "Israel has nuclear bombs, we have human bombs."[19]

Technology—whether "their" answer or "our" answer—is a physical manifestation of cultural values.[20] When a technologically advanced state employs its most sophisticated weapons, it is not only carrying out military operations but also legitimizing its society's value systems. Airpower in particular has come to be nearly synonymous with Western military might, not only because it allows states that employ it to project force with relatively little chance of harm to its personnel, but also because the technically sophisticated platforms of modern airpower are understood by their users to be evidence of a superior educational, research, and manufacturing capability. From this perspective, weapons are embodiments of progress.[21] Their use affirms the perceived superiority of the culture that produced them and is therefore a form of psychological as well as physical warfare.

The situation is similar to suicide bombing's tactical martyrs. Suicide bombers represent much more than a desperate effort to "throw bodies" at the technologically advanced forces of their adversaries. Their use allows an organization to invert roles, empowering themselves by portraying the mechanized forces of their adversaries as efforts to substitute machines for such human values as courage, faith, and willingness of the individual to sacrifice for the community. A senior Hizballah official wrote that one purpose of "martyrdom" operations was to expose "the Israeli soldier as one who hides in the safety of his military machines, afraid of direct military conflict." When the journalist Barbara Victor asked a group of Palestinian children why they were not afraid of the Israelis, one replied, "Because Israeli soldiers are cowards. They have tanks and guns. They hide behind their big machines."[22]

Technology Practice

The psychological impact of airpower is so similar to the psychological impact of suicide bombing that from this perspective a discussion of both types of bombings as forms of technology is intuitive. However, the tendency to understand technology in material terms that hampered analysts prior to 9/11 seems also to have obscured the actual nature of suicide bombing. This general tendency in Western society has had the unfortunate effect of divorcing an understanding of technology from its human context.[23]

From a historical perspective, however, equating technology with physical devices is relatively recent in comparison with a much longer tradition of understanding technology as knowledge. The root of the word stems from the Greek *tekhne,* meaning "art," "craft," or "skill." For centuries people understood technology as knowledge or doing, which was perfectly sensible since throughout much of human history the tools and devices at hand really were relatively simple, and it was human skill that made them useful. By the nineteenth century, European users of the term still emphasized descriptions of or teaching about the arts, especially the practical arts. By the turn of the twentieth century, this meaning began to change somewhat, and Europeans took to differentiating between "technique," meaning procedures of working with material culture, including engineering, and "technology," the study of such activities.[24]

In the twentieth century, as tools and machines became progressively more complex, and more important, as human skill was transferred to machines as a consequence of mechanization and automation, machines came to be seen as technology whose purpose was to replace rather than to complement human skill. Despite advances in machinery, automation, and control, however, the abilities of machines remained task specific and limited vis-à-vis human flexibility and creativity. Seeing machines as the sum total of technology therefore restricted dramatically how people thought about technology.[25]

There is, however, a well-established tradition in which technology is understood much more broadly. Leaders in the business world often define technology as an activity or a mode of problem solving that involves the mutual interaction of ideas and material devices. Peter Drucker, an iconic figure in the study of business management, drew upon comparisons with human biology to conclude that technology was about human activity, not physical things.[26] Joel Mokyr began his highly regarded analysis of the modern information economy by writing, "Simply put, technology is knowledge, even if not all knowledge is technological." He continued, "Hence useful knowledge . . . deals with natural phenomena that potentially lend themselves to manipulation, such as artifacts, materials, energy, and living beings."[27] Taking this understanding even further, Thomas Hughes defined technology as "the *effort* to organize the world for problem solving so that goods and services can be invented, developed, produced, and used."[28] This definition holds that much of technology—i.e., people and ideas—is intangible.

Everett M. Rogers, in *Diffusion of Innovations,* one of the most widely read texts about technological innovation in the business world, took a similar approach. Rogers' definition of technology incorporates Hughes' insight that technology is an idea or process, but also recognizes another important theme for the current analysis—control. Rogers argues, "A *technology* is a design for instrumental action that reduces the uncertainty in the cause-effect relationships involved in achieving a desired outcome."[29] This short definition links what technology is (i.e., ideas) with what technology is for (i.e., solving problems). In other words, technology solves problems by conferring some level of control over a given situation on its users.

In the early 1980s, the historian Arnold Pacey published a schematic representation for an expanded, dynamic understanding of technology. He defined technology as an interactive complex consisting of three factors: a technical aspect, composed of the actual physical devices and skills used to do work and solve problems; culture and society, as expressed through goals, values, and ideas; and organizations.[30] Pacey represented these three factors as the vertices of a triangle whose sides represent relationships of mutual communication and feedback. He called this interactive complex technology practice (see Figure I.2).

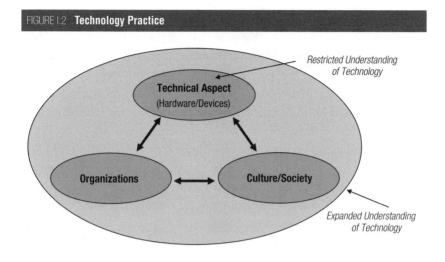

FIGURE I.2 **Technology Practice**

Source: Adapted from Arnold Pacey, *The Culture of Technology* (Cambridge, Mass.: MIT Press, 1983), 6.

The three levels are not hierarchical, but are linked in a simple flat network in which no one factor is privileged over the others. Pacey noted that it would be facile to isolate the top vertex, the technical element, and consider it as technology in its entirety; he cautioned, however, that this would represent a severely restricted understanding. A more complete representation of technology (and thus including suicide bombing, as argued here) must integrate cultures and organizations. He concluded that any definition of technology must include "liveware" as well as hardware and summarized his model as follows: "Technology practice is thus the application of scientific and other knowledge to a practical task by ordered systems that involve people and organizations, living things and machines."[31]

Need, Possibility, and Use

Acknowledging that suicide bombing is a technology allows for a multicausal explanation of the phenomenon that is much more consistent with historical reality than the single-variable explanations that have been offered to this point. Demonstrative of this approach is the popular explanation of suicide bombing advanced by Robert Pape in *Dying to Win* and further developed in *Cutting the Fuse*, co-authored by Pape and James Feldman.[32] Although the two authors acknowledge the importance of multiple factors within the process of suicide bombing, in the end they offer a single-variable explanation for it: foreign occupation. Suicide bombing, they argue, is a strategic approach taken by militant groups for combating occupation by a religiously different power and is usually directed against democracies. They suggest that suicide bombing is best addressed by minimizing the footprint of occupation through an offshore balancing of forces.

This explanation is inconsistent with the complex historical reality of suicide bombing. There are, for example, conspicuous instances in which occupation has not provoked suicide bombing. Furthermore, in recent years suicide bombing has taken place in (or has been carried out by citizens of) countries that have experienced no foreign occupation, and many suicide attacks have not been directed against democracies. Also, governments that have managed to bring a halt to suicide bombing in recent years have done so not by minimizing their presence in contested territories but by intensifying their occupations and defeating their adversaries through brute force. This indicates that rather than being the primary cause of suicide bombing, foreign occupation appears to correlate strongly with the phenomenon for obvious reasons: occupations are often characterized by ethnic or religious differences that facilitate de-humanization and violence on both sides, and the occupying power often possesses greater military power than the occupied people, necessitating and legitimizing any form of resistance no matter how extreme.

Pape's causal mechanism has therefore been greeted skeptically by many analysts familiar with suicide attacks, with Assaf Moghadam being particularly critical. Moghadam has presented a comprehensive analysis of suicide bombing that demonstrates that much of it in recent years has not been part of a national liberation strategy, has not taken place in areas suffering a direct occupation, and has not necessarily targeted democracies.[33] According to Moghadam, the increase in suicide bombing from 2002 through 2007 was driven largely by the global jihadi movement centered around al Qaeda and its affiliated organizations. This movement in turn was driven by an ideology that glorifies self-sacrifice and martyrdom and resulted in a global diffusion of suicide attacks in which militants with an ideological commitment to self-sacrificial violence spread suicide bombing around the world.

Moghadam's analysis takes a multi-causal approach in explaining suicide bombing, emphasizes the importance of radical ideologies in driving the global jihadi movement, and makes a powerful case for understanding recent suicide bombing as being different from older, more localized suicide bombing, but at the same time tends to view ideologies as being fixed rather than changing in response to external stimuli. As Thomas Hegghammer has noted, incarnations of jihadi ideology in the early 1990s produced far fewer suicide bombings than did later periods, so clearly something changed within the movement and within the ideology causing it to shift in emphasis toward self-sacrificial violence. It seems clear that what is needed is an integration of Pape's emphasis on external political and military factors and Moghadam's focus on internal factors, such as ideology.[34]

Approaching suicide bombing as a technological system allows for integrating these explanations through a well-established method (see Figure I.3). Suicide bombing, like all technologies, is the product of interactions between internal cultural factors and external pressures. These interactions constitute the dynamic relationships that connect the vertices of the technology practice triangle. External pressures, such as foreign occupation, create the problems or challenges that a particular culture

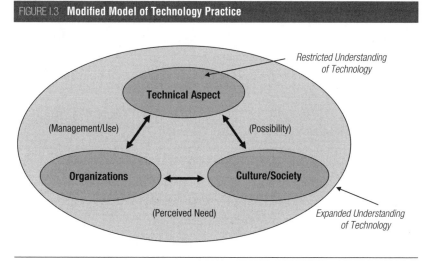

FIGURE I.3 **Modified Model of Technology Practice**

Source: Adapted from Arnold Pacey, *The Culture of Technology* (Cambridge, Mass.: MIT Press, 1983), 6.

hopes to solve; in other words, they create the culturally specific "necessity" for a solution to a problem. The well-known saying "necessity is the mother of invention" describes this driver of innovation but also oversimplifies the matter because technologies satisfy subjective desires more so than they do any universally recognizable objective need.[35] A subtle distinction, perhaps, but grasping that perceived "need," rather than objective need, drives innovation allows for an understanding of why different cultures identify different problems that "need" to be solved.

Possibility encompasses internal factors—ideas, skills, and devices—that a culture has at its disposal for solving a particular problem. Novel technologies do not emerge spontaneously. Instead, they result from the reconfiguration and modification of existing technologies and ideas, so what a culture is capable of achieving in terms of technology depends upon what it has already achieved.[36] The knowledge and devices available to a given culture circumscribe how that culture attempts to solve its problems. For a culture without a manufacturing capability, using conventional cruise missiles is an impossibility; suicide attackers, however, may be a viable option if the culture's ideology views self-sacrifice as admirable.

The interplay of cultural factors and external pressures explains the underlying similarities in the development of suicide bombing by different organizations. The differences in the way groups recruit and deploy their suicide attackers are, however, so significant that they led Mohammed Hafez to suggest that a generalized theory of suicide bombing cannot be proffered.[37] To explain these differences, one must integrate a third factor of technological systems: use. In this context use takes the form of management and training of potential recruits in addition to their deployment in the course of their missions.

Use is an essential element of technology, but the way that differences in use produce significant local variations in the basic, underlying technology is often underappreciated. Different users may use the same technologies differently, but more important, as they use technologies, they change them. Effective users often find new ways to employ old technologies. Use is an opportunity for learning and experimentation, so the world of use is a source of constant innovation and reinvention.[38] A full understanding of suicide bombing therefore must integrate need and possibility as well as use.

Assessing suicide bombing through the modified model of technology practice is therefore relatively straightforward, as the organizations and cultures that promote suicide bombing fit well within the corresponding vertices of the interactive triangle (see Figure I.4). The only major cognitive leap is accepting the replacement of the technical element of the system with the human suicide attacker. Making this substitution allows one to examine the individual psychological motivations of suicide attackers independently of the shared social meanings of the technology present at the organizational and cultural levels. It also allows for an examination of the dynamic relationships between all three vertices.

A Functional Definition of Suicide Bombing

Many analysts hesitate to make a sharp distinction between suicide bombing and other forms of high-risk combat missions. For example, nearly all of them consider the Assassins, a radical sect of Shiite Muslims active circa 1000–1200 CE, to be antecedents of today's suicide bombers because the assassins inevitably faced a high probability of death in carrying out their missions, and many seem to have desired to die. Viewing high-risk attacks as precedents for suicide bombing is problematic for two reasons.

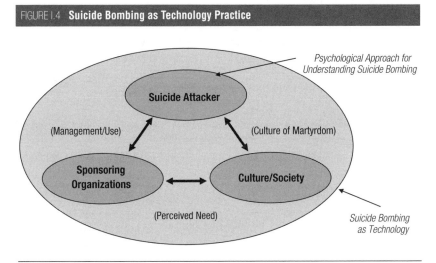

FIGURE I.4   **Suicide Bombing as Technology Practice**

Source: Adapted from Arnold Pacey, *The Culture of Technology* (Cambridge, Mass.: MIT Press, 1983), 6.

First, high-risk operations are common throughout the history of combat. Why not also include the Spartans, who willingly fought to the death at Thermopylae, in the list of historical precursors to suicide bombing? Inevitably any effort to contextualize suicide bombing historically by presenting it as a form of high-risk attack will be either selective and idiosyncratic or so broad as to be of little use. Second, such a genealogy of suicide bombing obscures one of the most important realities of contemporary suicide bombing: the extent to which the circumstances surrounding the death of the individual have moved from the individual to the organization sponsoring the attack. This is a consequence of the introduction of explosives to high-risk missions, which in turn compressed two previously distinct events—the success of the attack and the subsequent death of the attacker—into one inseparable act. By making the death of the individual attacker the objective of the mission, suicide bombing has taken an event that historically was the result of the individual's actions and choices in the highly uncertain realm of combat and made it a certainty predetermined by the mission. This certainty has come at the expense of individual choice during the mission and has necessitated the social and cultural programming that characterizes suicide bombing, which in turn explains why suicide bombing is rarer than high-risk missions.

The definition of suicide bombing offered here is therefore a functional definition based on how the human bomber is used by the organization responsible for his or her attack. Such an emphasis on function presumes that suicide bombers are not agents of violence and should not be considered users of the weapons they direct. Rather, they are agents of control. It is their intelligence—their ability to recognize and respond to the environment in real time, to discriminate, and to make decisions— and not their fighting ability that contributes to the effectiveness of the weapon and to the potential success of the mission. Thus, for the purposes of this book, a suicide attack is defined as follows: an instance of organizationally directed violence that utilizes at least one human being for purposes of weapon guidance and control that necessitates the death of the attacker(s). Suicide bombing, in turn, is the social process through which suicide attackers are made. The term "suicide" is appropriate because in most instances of this type of attack there is conclusive evidence in the form of written or videotaped testimonials that the decision to carry out lethal self-violence was made with the understanding of the attacker and was anticipated by him or her.

"Guidance and control" may or may not include the actual detonation of the device, so the definition also applies to the so-called remote-control martyrs who are used to guide a weapon to a particular location, at which point the weapon is detonated remotely without the consent or anticipation of the bomber. Although technically not suicide, from a functional perspective the two cases are identical. In both instances, human intelligence is used to direct a weapon to a target, and the death of the bomber is necessary and anticipated from the perspective of the user, that is, the sponsoring organization. Since the only factor that differentiates these attacks from suicide bombing more generally is the intent of the bomber, it is difficult to gauge fully the extent of this phenomenon, as such attacks have undoubtedly taken place numerous times since they were first documented in the mid-1980s.[39] These operations make use of human intelligence for tactical purposes, but they are generally understood as being manipulative in the extreme, so they cannot exploit the strategic, legitimizing elements of voluntary self-sacrifice, thus making them less effective and less numerous than "regular" suicide attacks.

The definition of suicide bombing presented here excludes other forms of high-risk attacks, including "no-escape" attacks, in which a person opens fire with the intention of provoking a lethal response and then fights to the death. There are similarities, of course. In the Palestinian context, the attackers, their organizations, and society tend to recognize both forms of attack as belonging to the broader category of *istishhadia*, or martyrdom. Recruitment and preparation for both kinds of missions, including the completion of martyrdom statements and videos, are also similar.[40] Nevertheless, significant differences would appear to require classifying no-escape missions separately. In these types of operations, the death of the attacker is de-coupled from the execution of the attack and is therefore not always necessitated by the attack. In addition, the death of the attacker is not self-inflicted. Although the attacker may well desire death, professing the desire to die and possessing the capability to commit lethal self-violence are two very different mental states. Since the death of the attacker in a no-escape attack is neither required nor self-inflicted, there is a degree of freedom that is not present in suicide bombing.[41]

THE HUMAN USE OF HUMAN BEINGS

Technology and Rationality

The mutual interplay between people, ideas, and devices within technology practice invalidates one of the primary assumptions underlying the above-mentioned simplified definitions of technology as gadgets—that technology is at its heart applied science, i.e., rational, logical knowledge put to use for the purpose of solving problems. It follows from this assumption that technology should be a rational process. For many in the West with a "technology as gadgets" perspective, technology is an inherently progressive means by which scientific knowledge takes physical form and diffuses from the scientific elite to the masses.[42]

This is a powerfully held preconception regarding technology today and is likely to be leveled against the argument that suicide bombing, which many refuse to recognize as being either logical or rational, is a technology. There are two counter-criticisms to this argument. First, there is a brutal logic to suicide bombing when one views the phenomenon from the organizational level. Suicide bombing can, indeed, be rational in power-political terms. Second, technologies are elements of specific human cultures that have no obligation to be rational or logical. That is, the presence of irrational elements in a given system does not disqualify it as a technology and does not preclude the presence of rational elements in the same system.

The complexity of technology practice allows for the possibility that different elements of the same technological system can be simultaneously rational and irrational, rendering any judgment as to the rationality of the entire system problematic. Rational means can be put to the most irrational of ends, and irrational motivations can sometimes lead to rational action.[43] Both occur in suicide bombing. Although there is often logic at the organizational level, the motives of individual bombers vary widely, ranging from the logical—such as securing financial support for family members as a result of carrying out a bombing assignment—to the much more emotional and irrational, including revenge and empowerment. The result of many suicide bombings, the indiscriminate slaughter of noncombatants, suggests that the entire enterprise is irrational, but this brutality can pay off rationally in the form of coercive political power. In a sense, then, both impressions about suicide bombing are correct: it is rational, and it is irrational. Suicide bombers are therefore consistent with weapon technologies more generally, for weapons have always been a fusion of rational utility and irrational cultural, psychological, and aesthetic factors.[44]

The Mechanization of Man

Suicide bombing integrates living and nonliving elements to create a relatively inexpensive weapon that nevertheless is intelligent in the truest sense. This integration of living (including human beings) and nonliving, like the integration of rational and irrational, is common in technological systems. Animals and plants were domesticated and integrated into the large-scale technologies of husbandry and agriculture, which ultimately made settled human existence possible. The use of living things is therefore among the oldest and most significant elements of technology.

Furthermore, throughout history human beings have been included in technological systems so that one group might be exploited and used by another. The most common human use of human beings is slavery. Although its precise form has varied over time and among cultures, slavery—the use of involuntary human labor—is a technology whereby human beings are used by others because of their ability to work, think, or other-wise act on materials and assist in creating goods, products, or services for human consumption. No less a figure than Aristotle stated, "A slave is property with a soul," a "living tool." He compared human slaves to draft animals and concluded that "the use of domestic animals and slaves is about the same; they both lend us their physical efforts to satisfy the needs of existence."[45] The technology of slavery resulted from a mental innovation rather than a physical one—the perception that not all human groups are equal. This mental construct made slavery possible by allowing one group of humans to cast another group as being less than human and therefore making the latter acceptable for use by the former.[46] Once this step was taken, the forced domestication of humans proved to be no more troubling to the conscience of the slaveholder than the domestication of animals had been to the farmer. Slavery has contributed historically to more large-scale construction projects than has any other form of power.

Human mental labor, not just physical labor, can also be exploited in technological systems. For nearly two and a half centuries, from the first recorded use of the term "computer" in 1646 until 1897, the tedious, repetitive calculations known as scientific computation, or as it is called today, data processing, were done by human beings, who were called computers.[47] The *Oxford English Dictionary*'s first definition for "computer" is "One who computes; a calculator, reckoner; *spec.* a person employed to make calculations in an observatory, in surveying, etc." The term was first applied to a mechanical calculating device in 1897. Only in 1946 was the term applied to ENIAC, the first large-scale, general-purpose electronic computer.

By the late 1800s, people were being used as components within extremely sophisticated computational systems. Teams of people served as living calculating machines to carry out the numerical computations increasingly required by scientific and military projects. Managers broke down tasks into discrete steps and then presented these steps to the "computers," who calculated repetitive mathematical computations by hand, eventually providing management with tables of processed data. In the years before electronic computers, human beings interfaced with mechanical devices in an increasingly professionalized and mechanized bureaucracy.[48] By World War II human and machine elements had been integrated into hybrid control systems in which the human and machine elements were both engineered and modified to improve system performance. Harold Hazen, an engineer at the Massachusetts Institute of Technology, summed up this approach in a memo to Warren Weaver, who at that time sat on the National Defense Research Committee: "This whole point of view of course makes the human being . . . nothing more or less than a robot, which, as a matter of fact, is exactly what he is or should be."[49]

By the 1960s, human beings were still being used in sophisticated control and computational systems, but they were increasingly becoming redundant design elements, that is, backups to be used in case the electronic computers failed, not primary computational elements. NASA engineers thought in these terms.[50] Their counterparts in the Soviet Union took this train of thought further, to the point that they began to use machine terms to evaluate potential cosmonauts and to engineer people through conditioning to fit into mechanical systems. A Soviet cybernetics specialist, Igor Polatev, asserted that repetitive training was the key to mechanizing people and thereby avoiding human error. He wrote, "The less his various human abilities are displayed, the more his work resembles the work of an automaton, the less [the human operator] debates and digresses, the better he carries out his task." For their part, Soviet cosmonauts protested the "excessive algorithmization" of their behavior.[51]

A Behavioral Compression Algorithm

The suggestion that suicide bombing is a control technology draws on a long history of the human use of human beings, particularly as data-processing centers in technological systems. Although in many contexts silicon-based electronics or hardware guided by software have innumerable advantages over people, in certain other contexts, human liveware offers a relative advantage. This is especially true in suicide bombing, because by substituting human beings for electronic computers, suicide bombing provides a dramatic increase in efficiency by charging its human computers with tasks for which they are well-suited, such as visual recognition, discrimination, and decision making. Computers are still not very good at these kinds of tasks; a child can easily beat the most sophisticated computer program when it comes to such seemingly simple tasks as the recognition of human faces.[52]

The organizations that deploy suicide attackers restrict the bombers' behavior in significant ways to ensure that they will carry out their missions as planned. Limiting the freedom of the individual involves stripping away alternatives and leaving only a narrow mission scenario as the socially acceptable range of actions for the individual or individuals. This behavioral compression is the true technological innovation of suicide bombing—limiting the behavior of certain human beings so that they can be used reliably by other human beings.

There is ample precedent in which a set of routines transforms the nature or behavior of an agent into a form of technology, even if the set of routines itself is completely immaterial. Brian Arthur cites digital compression algorithms as such a form of technology.[53] The best-known digital compression algorithm is probably the one that produces the MP3 audio file format, which greatly reduces the size of audio files. Such algorithms are a significant part of the technology of digital music and video storage and transmission—without which a huge portion of the consumer electronics market could not exist—yet the algorithms, by their very nature, are completely invisible, executing their operations without altering the content of their subject files in any significant way.

Whereas the purpose of the MP3 algorithm is to compress the size of audio files, the purpose of suicide bombing is to compress the space for behavioral possibilities available to individuals or small groups of individuals. Organizations that deploy suicide attackers have therefore developed behavioral compression algorithms that allow them to influence the actions of some of their followers in a systematic manner. Various groups have developed different algorithms based on their cultures and symbols, but in all cases repetition of a relatively simple message—self-sacrifice for the group—from a number of different and mutually reinforcing sources limits the behavior of the prospective bomber, much as the repetitive training of the Soviet space program was meant to limit and "algorithmize" the behavior of cosmonauts.

The suggestion that suicide bombing is a form of control technology is thus consistent with other instances of the use of humans as control elements in technological systems. Such a turn of events would undoubtedly have horrified Norbert Wiener, one of the founders of cybernetics, an interdisciplinary control science that emerged from World War II antiaircraft fire control systems. For Wiener, any system of control, social or otherwise, that reduced human possibilities by constraining and mechanizing the actions and thoughts of people was to be avoided. In 1950 he wrote, "I wish to devote this book to a protest against this inhuman use of human beings; for in my mind, any use of a human being in which less is demanded of him and less is attributed to him than his full status is a degradation and a waste." He continued, "Those who suffer from a power complex find the mechanization of man a simple way to realize their ambitions." He considered such behavior to be "a rejection of everything that I consider to be of moral worth in the human race."[54]

Wiener's misgivings reflect an apprehension toward technology and the modern world that has been shared by critics on the right and the left of the political spectrum, namely, the fear that technology will reduce humankind into raw material for technological processes and human relationships into transactions. Suicide bombing incorporates both these transformations. Individual recruits form the material basis for guidance and delivery systems for weaponry and are discarded when the weapons fulfill their functions. Individual relationships—with family, community, and deity—are likewise transformed into the programming steps necessary to persuade the bomber to behave in a calculated manner, which by design strips away individual choice and freedom. From this perspective, suicide bombing, used so often by groups that fear and reject the modern world, is a quintessentially modern technology that pushes the disenchanting and de-sacralizing elements of the modern world to their limits.

ABOUT THE BOOK

The Business of Martyrdom: A History of Suicide Bombing consists of three sections that correspond to the life cycle of technological systems—innovation, during which new technologies are developed; diffusion, during which technologies spread and are adapted to new environments; and commodification, during which previously rare technologies see regular use and come to be distinguished in a crowded market through marketing and branding. In the first section, concerning innovation, Chapter 1 analyzes the invention of a primitive form of suicide bombing in Imperial Russia, in particular the cultural, organizational, and technical antecedents that made self-sacrifice potentially useful as a form of control technology. Chapter 2 examines the early history of suicide bombing, focusing on its reemergence in war-torn Lebanon and the role played by revolutionary Iran. Chapter 3 looks at the spread of suicide bombing from the Middle East with an emphasis on the importance of use in shaping the technology in new cultural contexts. Its focus is the independent reinvention of suicide bombing by the Liberation Tigers of Tamil Eelam in their effort to carve an independent state for the Tamil people out of territory currently integrated into Sri Lanka.

In the second section, discussing diffusion, Chapter 4 presents a well-known model of technological diffusion and applies it to the experiences of the Provisional Irish Republican Army and the Workers' Party of Kurdistan, two groups for whom the diffusion of suicide bombing was problematic. Chapters 5 and 6 discuss the diffusion of suicide bombing to the Israeli-Palestinian struggle, an especially important case study because of the quantity of analytical work that has been produced regarding Palestinians' use of the technology. In its early stages, covered in Chapter 5, Palestinian suicide bombing was improvised and inefficient. In the mid-1990s, practice, failure, and the direct transfer of know-how from Hizballah led to the refinement and controlled use of suicide bombing for a political goal. As suicide bombing became more socially acceptable, and as individuals began to seek organizations to assist in their desire to take part in suicide attacks, it became much easier for them to be carried out by small, relatively autonomous groups. This newer organizational dynamic drove the suicide bombing of the second intifada. Local actors and groups initiated these attacks more than centralized organizations did, but the operations conformed in broad terms with the goals and motivations of these larger organizations. The Palestinians therefore provide an illustrative case of the interaction of the top-down and bottom-up dynamics that came to characterize much of global jihadi suicide bombing in the new millennium.

Chapters 7 and 8, in the third section, on commodification, explore a new trend in suicide bombing—its spread from one area to another via the ideology and personnel of the global jihadi movement. The conclusion of *The Business of Martyrdom* examines the reasons for the decline in suicide bombing from 2008 to 2010 by exploring a fundamental tension that emerges through the use of human bombers—reconciling organizations' systematic use of them with the freedom necessary to make martyrdom authentic to a broader audience. The tactical and strategic dimensions of martyrdom are fundamentally at odds with each other, and poor management of this contradiction has made globalized suicide bombing difficult to justify socially and may well have diminished its appeal to groups with a local agenda.

This historical analysis of suicide bombing offers several lessons about technology more generally. First, relatively simple technologies can provide advantages over more sophisticated technologies provided they are integrated into their human, social, and cultural contexts. Second, the effectiveness of a given technology at the tactical level need not necessarily generate strategic advantage. Third, single variable explanations are insufficient for understanding suicide bombing or, indeed, any technology. Instead, technology should be understood as a complex, ongoing process involving people, ideas, and machines.

Part I
INNOVATION

1

MARTYRDOM AS INNOVATION

The Invention of Suicide Bombing
in Imperial Russia

At approximately 2:15 p.m. on Sunday, March 1, 1881, Alexander II, tsar of Russia, was returning to his palace in St. Petersburg after observing the maneuvers of two guard battalions.[1] Alexander had been advised to be cautious, because in 1879 the People's Will (Narodnaya Volya), a revolutionary group, had condemned him to death and had already tried on at least four occasions to kill him. Given several possible routes, the tsar chose at the last minute to return along the Yekaterininsky Canal. On the one hand, this was a fortuitous choice because along an alternative route, the People's Will had painstakingly tunneled under the street and planted a large bomb intended to destroy Alexander's carriage as it passed. Alexander's last-minute decision rendered all of this work useless. Alexander stopped to pay a visit to one of his cousins, and this permitted three members of the People's Will to relocate and implement a secondary plan to kill him with smaller, portable bombs.

A young man named Nikolay Rysakov moved close to the roadway as Alexander's carriage passed and lobbed a small bomb at it. The explosion damaged the carriage and severely injured a young boy and one of the tsar's Cossack guards, both of whom later died from their injuries. Inexplicably, Alexander chose to loiter in the area. He checked on the health of the two injured people and inspected the carriage and the bomb crater. The delay

Portions of this chapter were originally published in Jeffrey Lewis, "Self-Sacrifice as Innovation: The Strategic and Tactical Utility of Martyrdom," *Dynamics of Asymmetric Conflict* 1, no.1 (March 2008), 66–87.

allowed time for another People's Will member, Ignaty Grinevitsky, to take up his position. As the tsar approached to within a couple of paces, Grinevitsky turned and threw his bomb at Alexander's feet. This second explosion severely injured Alexander, who died later that afternoon, as did the bomber.

Although Grinevitsky's attack was not originally intended as an act of self-sacrifice, the assassination of Alexander II provides a snapshot of the multiple factors that led to the emergence of an early form of suicide bombing in Imperial Russia. Grinevitsky's death was a consequence of his decision to control the blast of the bomb by keeping himself and the weapon as closely integrated as possible until its detonation. This mental innovation, which provided a nineteenth-century bomber with a flexible control system for his weapon, resulted from the convergence of two factors that drive technological innovation more generally—perceived need and possibility.

The latter factor, the possibility for self-sacrifice during the course of the mission, came from Grinevitsky's socialization and individual mental preparation for the attack. The culture within the People's Will was such that its members accepted that in opposing the tsar they were accepting the inevitability of their own deaths. Although he did not plan on killing himself, Grinevitsky clearly understood that the mission would probably require his life. The night before the attack, he wrote, "It is my lot to die young, I shall not see our victory, I shall not live one day, one hour in the bright season of our triumph, but I believe that with my death I shall do all that it is my duty to do, and no one in the world can demand more of me."[2]

Grinevitsky's mental preparation to become a martyr for his cause allowed him to improvise and to take his own life during the course of the mission. The pressure that drove him to make this improvisation was the factor of perceived need, for a reliable way to strike at Alexander. Four elaborate bomb plots, five if one includes the undetonated mine from March 1, had already failed. Each of these attempts had taken considerable time and effort, and each had exposed members of the group to possible arrest and execution. In addition, Grinevitsky had just witnessed the failure of Rysakov's attack on Alexander and the subsequent arrest of the bomber (who was executed several days later). It is reasonable to assume that the combination of frustration at the ongoing lack of success and his acceptance of the inevitability of his death persuaded Grinevitsky to carry out his mission in a way that was almost certain to take his own life as well as that of the tsar. Thus, in this unanticipated manner, the technology of suicide bombing first emerged in Imperial Russia.

rinevitsky's decision illustrates the transformation of martyrdom from an individual act into a reliable form of control technology for weaponry. Grinevitsky's form of self-sacrifice, made at the spur of the moment, established a precedent that would eventually become a more regular phenomenon in which the decision to die would be taken away from the individual bomber and conferred upon the leadership of the bomber's organization. Grinevitsky's decision to use his own life in order to kill Alexander was therefore an important innovation that in time would offer a powerful advantage to groups with the capability to exploit their members in a similar manner.

IDEAS AND INNOVATION

Innovation is essentially a messy process of trial and error. Edward Constant describes the process as recursive; it begins with a set of cultural constraints, or foundational knowledge, which bound the possibilities from which the innovation can emerge.[3] Foundational knowledge consists of a set of assumptions on how to approach a specific problem. It can be manifested mentally, in attitudes and ideas, as well as physically, in preexisting tools and devices, the technological antecedents from which new technologies are derived.[4] Individuals and groups working with these antecedents reconfigure them, sort through new possibilities, and devise solutions that seem to fit a particular perceived need, often in an increasingly effective manner. In this way technological solutions can evolve toward a better fit between technology and problem, although this need not always be the case.

In this process of technological evolution, ideas are the drivers for change. Physical tools and devices change as a consequence of these ideas, with new devices being built and new uses being found for older tools thus resulting in new technologies.[5] Since much innovation actually stems from modification of preexisting technologies in use, the power of antecedents and foundational knowledge to constrain the possibilities of innovation cannot be overstated. Individuals and groups with different foundational knowledge bases and different technological antecedents will invariably explore different ways of satisfying their same desires.

Technological Antecedents: Origins of the U.S. Precision Revolution

An example of the sometimes unanticipated means by which technological antecedents and foundational knowledge shape even complex weapon systems is the development of precision-guided munitions (PGMs) by the United States. The acronym PGM is used to differentiate "smart" weapons that are interactively guided to a target after being launched from "dumb" munitions that cannot be directed once fired.[6] These weapons were not the inevitable result of a universal process of progressive technological development, but the consequence of a culturally determined need intersecting with a culturally and historically specific set of technological possibilities. They are weapons of choice, selected by the United States because they solve American problems using American tools and ideas.

Since the 1930s, airpower enthusiasts in the United States had struggled to reconcile the power of aerial bombardment with American ideals of humane warfare. They understood that the American public would never embrace aerial bombing unless it could be assured that bombers could be used with surgical precision to incapacitate the enemy without slaughter.[7] During World War II, however, precision was never achieved, so "strategic bombing" meant full-scale, indiscriminate bombing of population centers. Small-scale tactical use of airpower in the Korean War was often ineffective since hitting such individual targets as bridges, tunnels, and trains required skill beyond the ability of most pilots. These failures, coupled with the preexisting desire to make airpower into a humane weapon, created the need for improved guidance and control, which drove research into PGMs and led to the first generation of interactively guided munitions in the 1960s.

The technological antecedents that allowed these desires to be realized came from an unexpected sector. In the early 1960s, the U.S. military conducted extensive research on lasers as potential weapons; by its own admission, it had been trying to develop "death rays." Because of the specificity of the wavelength of their light, lasers revealed themselves to have a second potential function—as beacons that could allow a weapon to home in on a target in an interactive manner. This secondary function quickly became the foundation for the first generation of precision-guided munitions. These weapons consisted of a laser designator, which illuminated a potential target. Electro-optical sensors on the actual weapon (a modified, old-fashioned "dumb" bomb) would then recognize the laser and guide the projectile toward the illuminated target. The first prototypes were tested in the mid-1960s, and by 1968 laser-guided bombs were being deployed.[8]

The precision munitions utilized to such great effect in the early 1990s during the Persian Gulf War were refinements of this basic technology. They were not without their drawbacks, of course. Smoke, fog, and sandstorms could obscure the laser signature, making use of PGMs weather dependent. In addition, the weapons were not completely autonomous since they demanded ongoing feedback from an illuminating source, which in turn required that a manned platform of some kind remain in the vicinity of the target to provide information for the weapon. In the immediate aftermath of the war, the U.S. Navy and Air Force jointly developed a new class of precision munitions to address these shortcomings.[9]

The new weapons, Joint Direct Attack Munitions (JDAMs), utilize navigational signals from global positioning system (GPS) satellites. A person enters target data into a transmitter, which sends the data to a GPS receiver attached to the weapon. The weapon then compares this information to signals that it receives from GPS satellites, matches the two, and modifies its trajectory after its firing in order to reach the designated target area. Humans set the coordinates and launch the weapon, but from that point on guidance and control are autonomous and self-correcting, even in poor weather, making satellite-guided munitions true "fire and forget" weapons.[10]

As with laser-guided weapons, the basic technology for JDAMs was originally developed for a different purpose and in a different sector. The military initially drove the development of GPS technology for navigational purposes. GPS was used extensively in the Persian Gulf War as a navigational aid. Signals from GPS satellites helped aircraft to positively identify their locations (especially at night) and thus contributed to the overall accuracy of conventional bombing runs. GPS signals, used in conjunction with night-vision gear, also allowed for the precise large-scale coordination of armored attacks twenty-four hours a day and thus increased the maneuverability and sustainability of armored operations. After the war, when the limitations of laser-guided munitions became clear, the concept of targeting was reconsidered a navigational problem. Again, it was a mental leap—reimagining bomb guidance as a navigational problem, similar to the previous leap of reimagining death rays as homing beacons—that allowed a technology developed for an alternative purpose to be used in a different manner and then rapidly applied in this new context.

The technological antecedents (i.e., lasers and GPS) for both types of precision munitions reflect the American propensity during the Cold War and after it to solve security issues through increasing reliance on complex, technologically sophisticated systems. Other groups, lacking these physical resources, have made use of a different kind of cultural antecedent, martyrdom, to allow them to apply human intelligence directly to the problem of weapons guidance and control. For the suicide bombing revolution, the enabling technological antecedent was also a mental one—reimagining the way that martyrdom could be used.

SHAPING POSSIBILITIES: THE UTILITIES OF MARTYRDOM

Martyrdom has been one of the most important but also one of the most difficult factors to analyze in the phenomenon of suicide bombing. Although there is a public understanding of what a martyr is in general terms, individuals who choose to end their own lives do so for their own reasons, which means that martyrdom in practice is also an individual answer to a deeply personal set of issues. This leads to differences between the biographies and testimonies of martyrs more generally and suicide bombers specifically, especially as understood by those outside the bombers' communities.

It is therefore necessary to focus on the use of martyrdom at the organizational level—martyrdom as an element of culture that is used to connect the group to society and to individual recruits. In this sense, martyrdom is a means by which organizations use symbols and rituals to link their operational goals to the much broader expressions of altruism and self-sacrifice that can be found in nearly any community, especially a community whose members feel threatened. This use of martyrdom is intended to provide control over individuals and allow the group to use them with a relatively high degree of assurance that they will perform predetermined tasks, even when that task means killing themselves as well as others. Such control over the individual confers a much greater level of control over the mission and also helps to convince observers in the broader community that the attack is a legitimate form of violence.

Control of this kind should not be considered brainwashing. It is not a one-way street, but a reciprocal process. Martyrdom gives meaning simultaneously to individual deaths and to general causes; the individual dies for a cause, and the cause is legitimized through the blood sacrifice of the individual in a process of mutual feedback. This situation, in turn, allows a group that can make a persuasive claim to represent a cause to shape the general parameters of individual deaths in advance. It is not brainwashing because the prospective bombers are not mindless automatons executing commands against which they have no power to resist. Rather, the bombers accept the general mission parameters (including the necessity of death) while retaining a degree of individual initiative and decision making. It is this combination of reliability and creativity that makes them so dangerous. Martyrdom is therefore the foundational knowledge that allows extremist groups to explore the possibility of suicide bombing.

Martyrdom in History

The word "martyr" derives from the Greek *martus*, which means "witness" or "one who testifies to events that he or she has personally observed." In the early Christian Church, the term initially referred to the Apostles, signifying their personal witness to the public life and teachings of Christ. Since such testimony was fraught with risk in the Roman Empire, the term quickly evolved and began to take on elements of its current generally accepted meaning: one who serves as witness at great personal risk to himself or herself. During the first centuries of the Christian Church, the meaning of the word shifted even more, as the generations with a personal knowledge of Christ passed away. A martyr, or a witness of Christ, then came to mean someone so convinced of the truth of the Christian religion, without having known Christ personally, that he would willingly sacrifice his life rather than deny his faith.[11] In the centuries since, the word has become generally accepted as meaning a fatal act of religious witness.

Martyrdom plays a significant role in most religious traditions. It can serve to validate any number of sacred causes, national or ideological, including those ostensibly secular. The phenomenon of choosing death on behalf of others is common enough that more than a century ago Emile Durkheim categorized it as one of the three major subtypes of suicide. Durkheim called this form of lethal self-violence altruistic suicide and argued that it stems from an incomplete differentiation of the self, or ego, and a correspondingly excessive social integration that causes the individual to see her life as belonging to the group rather than to herself.[12]

According to Durkheim, in cultures in which the rights of individuals are subordinated to the rights and benefit of the group as a whole, social pressure on the individual can become so intense that the individual might feel obligated to sacrifice his or her life on behalf of the group. There could also be cases, however, in which the pressure is less coercive, leaving the individual with the choice of whether or not to die for the group. "Optional altruistic suicide," as Durkheim called this situation, corresponds closely with the more generally accepted definition of martyrdom, the primary difference being that although martyrs choose to die, death is usually inflicted by others. More important, the social impact of optional altruistic suicide is precisely that of martyrdom. While individual suicide, what Durkheim called egoistic suicide, stems from despair, altruistic suicide "on the contrary, springs from hope; for it depends on the belief in beautiful perspectives beyond this life. It even implies enthusiasm and the spur of a faith eagerly seeking satisfaction, affirming itself by acts of extreme energy."[13]

Durkheim acknowledged that while "lower" societies were the "theatre par excellence" of altruistic suicide, it could also be found in more advanced societies. For evidence, he turned to the example of Christian martyrdom. In the following passage, he addresses the difference between lethal self-violence and death at the hands of others:

All those neophytes who without killing themselves, voluntarily allowed their own slaughter, are really suicides. Though they did not kill themselves, they sought death with all their power and behaved so as to make it inevitable. To be suicide, the act from which death must necessarily result need only have been performed by the victim with full knowledge of the facts. Besides, the passionate enthusiasm with which believers in the new religion faced final torture shows that at this moment they had completely discarded their personalities for the idea of which they had become the servants.[14]

Martyrdom was thus a form of the more general phenomenon of altruistic suicide and often was seen as being life-affirming rather than destructive.

Martyrdom as a Legitimizing Force

Martyrs create boundaries. By their very nature, martyrs occur at the intersection of two belief systems. They believe in one system to such an extent that they are willing to die for it; at the same time, they are so opposed to the other system that they are willing to suffer death to defy it.[15] Martyrdom thus serves simultaneously to bind members of one belief system and to set them apart from the believers in another system. It is a powerful organizational tool.

Martyrdom serves such an integrative purpose across a wide range of cultures and societies because it is essentially public. It is an act of witness, but it is always an act of witness that is observable by others, allowing it to build group solidarity and to legitimize a cause.[16] The common theme of individual sacrifice on behalf of others ensures a familiar, ritualized quality to martyrdom; it is a kind of public theater, in which symbolic deaths are played out for the crowd, which makes martyrdom a powerful means by which to build group solidarity.[17] States build such solidarity similarly by solemnly observing public holidays in which citizens are encouraged to venerate those who have sacrificed their lives for the state. The terminology used is not that of martyrdom—often the word "hero" is used rather than "martyr"—but the meaning is the same. It is the heroes who have given their lives for a cause who are typically singled out for respect.[18]

Consensus building via ritual is also important for nonstate actors who cannot define their identities based on generally recognized institutions or borders. The dramatic rituals surrounding martyrdom help to impose coherence on small, fragmented movements that depend on secrecy for survival and on publicity for success. Extremist groups, which deal with matters of life and death, are especially prone to turn to the ritual and symbolism of martyrdom to create group solidarity and validate the sacrifices made by individuals for their communities. Ritualistic celebration of martyrs serves to coordinate the activities of various local groups lacking formal bureaucratic structures, but more important, conveys the impression of greater strength and solidarity and order than might actually exist.

On a practical level, martyrdom justifies the decision to use deadly force on the part of any organization. If one is willing to die for a cause, indeed, if a member of an organization proves this by readily choosing to kill himself for the cause, he demonstrates that the cause, whatever it may be, truly does matter more than life itself. An unwillingness to die invites charges of hypocrisy, discrediting the organization and cause.[19] This is particularly important for nonstate militant groups, for they have elected to take the right to use lethal force into their own hands without formal legal authorization. Sanctification by blood, through martyrdom, serves to legitimize this decision at a level higher than mere legality and is thus all but a requirement for terrorist groups hoping to portray themselves as idealists fighting for a cause.

Constructing Martyrs

Martyrdom is a socially constructed process. Individuals who are willing to die are necessary parts of this process, but alone are insufficient for its success. In addition, the deeds of prospective martyrs must be observed and interpreted by others in order to become a part of public discourse. The martyr, of course, has no control over his or her story after death, so ironically he or she becomes less important in the process of image creation than those who live and cultivate the martyr's image. Michael Barkun calls these cultivators martyrologists. He asserts, "A martyr is not . . . simply a creation of an individual who decides to die in a particular way. It is, rather, a persona that needs to be constructed, and at the least requires the cooperation of martyrologists who present the death in the desired way."[20] Martyrologists make it possible to instrumentalize and then use individual acts of self-sacrifice by creating a narrative and casting individuals in set roles. Whether the individuals actually fit the role is secondary, for in dying they remove themselves from the scene and thus any possibility of spoiling the illusion.

The death of the martyr gives the martyrologist a blank slate with which to work. Within the context of suicide bombing, the martyrologis strives to excel at framing and interpreting acts of individual self-sacrifice. Mohammed Hafez has studied groups in the Palestinian territories and Iraq that utilize suicide bombing and has found noteworthy similarities in the ways that the groups construct their martyrs. He states, "Martyrdom rituals elevate jihad and self-sacrifice into something higher than core beliefs of the faith; they turn them into *performative* traditions and *redemptive* actions through which the faithful express their devotion. . . . In short, they create a culture of martyrdom where none existed previously."[21]

Controlling Circumstances and Choices

It is a profoundly moving event when a soldier sacrifices his life for his comrades—for instance, by using his body to shield them from harm—or an adult sacrifices her life to save that of a child—for example, by throwing herself in front of a car in the process of pushing the child out of the way. The profundity of such acts derives from the individual sacrificing his or her life having had no desire to die. That is, the person sacrifices something precious, his or her life, for something more precious, the life of another. That person's decision is compelled only by the individual sense of what is right.

Such incidents are rare, as they typically result from unusual circumstances and brave choices. The circumstances impose a choice upon the individual to risk his or her life. The choice belongs to the individual, but the decision is imposed. Organizations that use suicide bombers endeavor to capture the essence of such spontaneous acts but cannot simply entrust them to chance. They attempt therefore actively to shape the circumstances surrounding potential bombers in order to guide the choices made by them. That is to say, they try to take a spontaneous, seemingly heroic event and make it predictable, revealing the major difference between suicide bombings and unplanned acts of self-sacrifice.

In a suicide attack, the immediate circumstances surrounding the act of self-sacrifice are not imposed, but rather are chosen. Since individual suicide bombers are not physically constrained by circumstances in the manner discussed above, they must be subjected to psychological constraints that lead them to believe that they are in a situation in which their death is necessary.

These constraints take the form of behavioral algorithms devised by the bombers' sponsoring organizations. In the context of computers, an algorithm is simply an ordered set of instructions written to be understood and executed by a machine. In the context of suicide bombing, organizations create behavioral algorithms by manipulating cultural symbols and narratives to create sets of instructions that influence the behavior of their followers so the organizations can control and use these people with a high degree of reliability. Applying the algorithm leads to the death of an individual, so the entire life of the bomber—all the possibilities that he or she might expect to realize during the course of a full lifetime—must be excluded, compressing the life itself into little more than the execution of a mission-specific set of instructions.

This type of programming takes many forms. It can involve specific rituals meant to bind individuals to a course of action and hold them true to it, as in the case of the videotaped testaments often made by bombers in advance of their missions. It can rely on pressure from family members and religious leaders to encourage young people to sacrifice themselves for their communities. It can also take more passive forms, for example, graffiti, songs, music videos, even textbooks, all of which might alert a child to the glories of martyrdom from a very young age. Such "cultures of martyrdom" have been observed in the most systematic users of suicide bombers: Hizballah in Lebanon, Palestinian Islamists, the Liberation Tigers of Tamil Eelam, and the global jihadi movement. These cultures intentionally make their members familiar, and comfortable, with the idea of self-sacrifice on behalf of the group.

The researcher Ehud Sprinzak has noted that "no organization can create a person's basic readiness to die. The task of recruiters is not to produce but rather to identify this predisposition in candidates and reinforce it."[22] In other words, organizations do not create the individual's *will-*

ingness to die; rather, through ritual and symbolism they enhance the *capacity* of the individual to take his or her own life. Both the individual willingness to die and the organizational willingness to kill are necessary, yet neither is sufficient to the task on its own. Rather, the lethality of suicide bombing emerges from this confluence of individual and organizational motivations.

Circumstances can come together to make this process easier on the part of the organization. In environments of extreme brutality, a prospective bomber might express a sense of fatalism, a conviction that his life is in the hands of his adversary, not his own. In such a situation, perceived choices are already radically curtailed, consisting of dying on the adversary's terms or dying on his own terms. Given such a mindset, suicide bombing is potentially empowering, as it gives control over the means and time of death to the individual as well as confers upon him the power to strike back in retribution.

Taking an act whose power derives from its rareness and making it predictable entails some risk. For example, should the act come to be seen as the imposition of an organizational agenda on an unwilling individual, rather than the free choice of that individual, the legitimizing power of martyrdom could be lost or might boomerang and discredit the responsible organization. Authenticity is essential for the public acceptance of suicide as martyrdom. This is why the use of unwilling proxies or unaware, remote-control martyrs has not been as sustainable as the use of volunteer suicide bombers.

Tactical Martyrdom

The extensive use of martyrdom imagery and ritual to support campaigns of suicide bombing strikes many as inconsistent with the broader history of martyrdom since historical martyrs are often associated with pacifism, or at least passivity, with their deaths being the consequence of the actions of others. Historical martyrs may have been suicides in the sense discussed by Durkheim, but most caused no harm to others while seeking their own deaths. The systematic use of suicide bombers in the recent waves of terrorism has led some to classify this type of violence as offensive martyrdom, or predatory martyrdom, in contrast to the passive, defensive martyrdom of the past.[23]

However, historically the concept of martyrdom has meant various things to different cultures, and in many instances, passivity has given way to a much more aggressive form of martyrdom. St. Francis of Assisi actively sought martyrdom and went out of his way to place his life at risk in the hopes that he would be killed doing God's work.[24] In Islamic history there are numerous instances of "fighting martyrs," who blur the line between active and passive, or offensive and defensive, martyrdom.[25] The overall mutability of martyrdom—its numerous historical manifestations, its social, posthumous construction, and the fact that the feelings of individual martyrs regarding their own deaths are and will always be unknowable—renders contemporary judgments on whether suicide bombing is a legitimate form of it beside the point, for there is no one universally accepted understanding of martyrdom to serve as a baseline for comparison.

There is, however, a common denominator, which is that martyrdom has usually tended to serve a strategic purpose, contributing to the long-term goals of a particular organization or group by asserting the group's values, establishing individual and group identities, and providing the moral justification for killing others. Suicide bombing is unique in that it adds another level of utility to martyrdom and allows it to function at the tactical level as well as at the strategic level. Martyrdom used at the tactical level retains all of these strategic functions but in addition serves as the primary social mechanism through which flexible guidance systems are constructed. It therefore contributes not only to the legitimacy of the group at the strategic level; it also contributes, on the tactical level, to the capabilities of the organization.

DAGGERS, GUNPOWDER, AND DYNAMITE: ALONG THE ROAD TO SUICIDE BOMBING

The Assassins as Historical Precedent?

Systematic analyses of suicide bombing usually trace the phenomenon back to the Assassins, extremist members of a sect of Shiite Muslims known properly as the Ismailis, who operated out of mountainous regions of what is now Iran from approximately 1100 to 1300 CE.[26] As pious Shiites who saw the Sunni Seljuk Turks, who controlled their territory, as heretics, the

Ismailis believed it was their religious duty to resist them, violently when necessary, in order to purify the faith. This in turn motivated the practice for which they have become famous—the murder by dagger of prominent political officials. These bold and seemingly reckless murders ultimately inspired the name by which the Ismailis are more famously remembered. "Assassin" is a corrupted form of the Arabic word *hashishiyyin*, meaning "hashish," implying that the fanaticism of the Ismailis was the result of drug use. Although the use of hallucinogenic drugs by the assassins has been discredited by sound scholarship, the origin and persistence of this particular myth illustrates a significant element of assassin attacks—the ruthless conviction demonstrated by the murderers.

The Ismailis killed by the dagger alone, even when other possibilities were available. The weapon symbolized the conviction of the individual fighter because it necessitated that he engage his victim at close range and therefore minimized the likelihood of a successful escape. Thus, as a consequence of the chosen weapon, the life of the attacker was inevitably at risk, since most of their targets, being individuals of importance, were well guarded. The most striking characteristic of Ismaili political murders, however, was that the attackers often did not even try to escape. After carrying out a successful attack, the killers would sometimes submit to arrest and execution or to immediate death at the hands of enraged bystanders.[27]

These early suicidal missions differed appreciably from those of today's suicide bombers, however, so using the Assassins as historical precedent is questionable. First, although it was necessary for a potential assassin to accept the high probability of death if he undertook a mission, this is not the same as accepting the certainty of death, much less having the will to commit suicide. For an assassin, a suicidal mindset was unnecessary because his death and that of his victim were two acts not necessarily connected. That is to say, after committing the murder, the attacker still had the option of trying to escape. Whether he chose to exercise this option is less important than the fact that he had it, which is an option not available to a suicide bomber. Thus suicide bombing conflates these two discrete events—murder of one's enemy and one's own death—into a single act. All that can be said with certainty is that the assassins' attacks were indeed symbolic, high-risk missions in which demonstrating individual courage and conviction was as important as the physical deed itself. This hardly makes the assassins unique in the history of conflict.[28]

Presenting the Assassins as a precedent for modern suicide bombers draws attention to the common factors of dedication to a cause and acceptance of self-sacrifice, but this is insufficient for understanding suicide bombing fully, since fanaticism and martyrdom are more general phenomena observed innumerable times in the history of conflict. The Assassins used martyrdom for its legitimizing power. The organizations that today deploy suicide bombers use tactical martyrdom as a means to an organizational end. A complete explanation must therefore incorporate the end toward which these would-be martyrs are directed—control.

It is essential for any militant organization waging an armed struggle to maintain control over two things. It must control its people, but it must also be able to control its weaponry, particularly because the power made possible by advances in explosives in the nineteenth century and onward has changed the nature of militant attacks. When the bomb replaced the dagger as the most sensational weapon available to militant groups, it changed the role of the individual in high-profile attacks. Unlike the assassins, individuals in bomb attacks did not cause damage through their own skill or training, but served instead to direct the power of explosives, ensuring that they would detonate in the right place and at the right time: They became agents of control rather than agents of violence.

This transformation came with a cost, since transferring violent agency from the attacker to the weapon necessitated destruction of the weapon during the course of the mission. As a consequence, in most explosive weapon systems, human control agents have been physically separated from the weapon itself in order to provide for their safety. Separating the two components of the system in this manner, however, greatly complicated the issue of control, contributing to numerous extravagant failures over the decades and necessitating extensive preparation. Integrating bomber and bomb offered the potential of overcoming many of these difficulties and providing truly effective, flexible control.

Continuity and Change: Bombs in the History of Terrorism

On December 12, 1867, three members of the Irish nationalist Fenian movement hid 548 pounds of gunpowder in a beer cask, placed it in a wheelbarrow and pushed it to the wall of Clerkenwell prison in London. There, they lit a fuse to the cask and then sought shelter from the explosion. The fuse, however, sputtered and flamed out; two more attempts to light it failed. After that, the fuse was too short to allow the men enough time to seek shelter, so they called off their attack. They returned the next day and were more careful to ensure that the fuse was truly lit before retreating to safety. This time the bomb went off, blasting a hole through the prison wall, damaging nearby houses, and starting fires that spread through nearby slums. Six people were killed by the bomb blast, nine more by the fires and other indirect effects; more than a hundred people were injured, and as many as four hundred houses destroyed or damaged.[29]

After the Fenians began to wage their violent campaign against the British, bombs became the preferred means for individuals and small groups to challenge the power of established states. Analyzing data from the 1960s through the 1980s, Bruce Hoffman found that nearly half of all terrorist incidents had been bombings. The reasons for this dependence were clear. "Bombs," Hoffman wrote, "provide a dramatic, yet fairly easy and often risk-free, means of drawing attention to the terrorists and their causes. Few skills are required to manufacture a crude bomb, surreptitiously plant it, and then be miles away when it explodes." He derived a rough rule of thumb regarding terrorists and their weapon choices that held true through the early 2000s: "the frequency of various types of terrorist attacks decreases in direct proportion to the complexity or sophistication required."[30]

This reliance on a single class of weapons suggests that terrorists are fundamentally conservative when it comes to weapon technologies, preferring to imitate rather than innovate.[31] There is some truth to this suggestion, but it is not the whole story. Terrorists have indeed been conservative in preferring relatively simple, effective technologies, but simplicity does not preclude innovation. In fact, the need to develop more robust and dependable weapons has been a powerful dynamic, driving constant innovation among groups from the Provisional IRA to Iraqi insurgents. Certainly, explosives have improved dramatically, conferring more destructive power upon clandestine organizations than the Fenians had at their disposal. The area in which these groups have demonstrated the greatest ingenuity and sophistication, however, has been in the means by which they deliver and detonate their weapons, that is, the technologies of control.

The Clerkenwell bombing demonstrates that large-scale explosive power has been available to organizations and individuals for more than a century. It also demonstrates, via the failed fuse, that more important than the actual explosive power of the bomb is having the ability to get the bomb to detonate at the desired time and location. This is not a trivial issue; it has been one of the most significant operational constraints facing those who have elected to use bombs. Although bombs are among the simplest of destructive technologies in a relative sense, they are still very demanding to make and use in an absolute sense. The entire process, from manufacture to detonation, requires high levels of explicit knowledge as well as tacit know-how and experience. A mistake anywhere along the way can quite literally be deadly, very often for the bomb maker and his organization, rather than their intended victims.

The People's Will and Dynamite

All of these challenges confronted Russian revolutionaries of the late nineteenth century who would become some of the most enthusiastic advocates of the bomb as a tool of terrorism. For their groups, the technical challenges were difficult to solve since the bomb was a new and unproven technology. Only in 1866 had Alfred Nobel succeeded in harnessing the extraordinary explosive power of nitroglycerine in the stable, safe, and reliable form of dynamite. Approximately twenty times more explosive than black powder, dynamite was quickly venerated within anarchist circles as the breakthrough that would allow the few to challenge the many and thus bring about social justice.[32]

Dynamite became such a powerful symbolic weapon because it tapped into preconceptions regarding technology held by many anarchists. As the powers of the state expanded in the nineteenth and twentieth centuries, those who sought to challenge the state's monopoly on lethal force faced the prospect of being irrelevant in the face of state power. The only possibility for these individuals and groups was to have an impact disproportionate to their numbers.[33] Dynamite proved to be much more challenging to use than they imagined, so those groups that chose to employ it for its symbolic value had to constantly scramble to overcome the operational difficulties of using this new weapon.

Nowhere was this gap between the abstract power of dynamite and actually using it demonstrated more clearly than in the campaign of the People's Will against Alexander II. The People's Will was a radical fragment of a larger reform movement, the Populists, who in the 1870s hoped to stimulate opposition to Alexander by "going to the people" and mobilizing the Russian peasantry.[34] The populist movement failed, however, in part due to the deeply conservative, religious, and superstitious nature of the Russian peasantry. The peasants rejected the university-trained intellectuals who had hoped to inspire them, and as a result the main populist movement, Land and Liberty, split at the end of the 1870s into the Black Repartition, which rejected political violence and went into exile, and the People's Will. An executive committee of twenty people headed the People's Will, whose functional membership consisted of approximately five hundred people. Many more sympathized with the group but were not officially part of the organization.

The leaders of the People's Will embraced the anarchist cult of dynamite for largely symbolic reasons and may well have created more difficulties for themselves than if they had dedicated themselves to simpler weapons, such as pistols. Michael Frolenko, a member of the organization involved in the plot of March 1, 1881, said that the use of dynamite rather than a pistol would send a more powerful message. A pistol "would not have created such an impression. It would have been seen as an ordinary murder, and thus would not have expressed a new stage in the revolutionary movement."[35]

After condemning Alexander to death on August 25, 1879, the People's Will embarked on killing the tsar through numerous elaborate plots utilizing dynamite. All of them failed prior to Grinevitsky's suicidal attack. The fact that the People's Will had excellent bomb makers, dedicated operatives, and high-quality intelligence, and still failed repeatedly demonstrates a fundamental reality of terrorist missions: however many ways there are for them to go right, there are always far more ways for them to go wrong.[36] This puts groups using terror under intense pressure to succeed as often as possible. The only way they can hope to do so is to be "control freaks," eliminating as many extraneous variables as possible so as not to squander opportunities and erode the psychological impact of their attacks.[37] There are two ways to improve control over potential missions. First, reduce uncertainty by utilizing the most reliable weapons, which accounts in the twentieth century for the ongoing popularity of the bomb. Second, as demonstrated by the People's Will, improve control in order to give the group the flexibility necessary to adjust the mission while it is in progress.

Even as they prepared the large, emplaced bomb in early 1881, the bomb makers of the People's Will were also at work on much smaller, portable weapons. Weighing some five or six pounds each and cylindrical in shape, the type of bomb that ultimately killed Alexander consisted of nitroglycerine stabilized by pyroxilin, a form of guncotton, and was much smaller than the huge bombs that had been preferred up to that point.[38] These bombs had a much smaller radius of effect, not much more than a meter, so they had to be positioned with much greater accuracy than larger ones in order to be effective. This necessity posed a dilemma for the bombers: They could ensure their own safety by lobbing the bomb from a distance and accepting a corresponding loss of accuracy, or they could remain in close proximity to the bomb, effectively coupling their ability to determine the precise place of detonation with the explosive power of a small quantity of nitroglycerine to create a nineteenth-century smart bomb. Different bombers made different choices in this regard, and during the course of Russian history, those terrorists who got close enough to risk their own lives were the most successful.

Necessity's Mother

The bomb therefore created the perceived need for the human bomb. Thus the experience of the People's Will and of countless other cases of technological innovation contradict the common wisdom that "necessity is the mother of invention," for invention drives necessity every bit as much if not more than necessity drives invention. The tendency for new technologies to create new needs is so widespread that Jared Diamond, in his classic work *Guns, Germs, and Steel*, suggests turning the popular saying around: invention is actually the mother of necessity. New technologies create new possibilities but at the same time reveal new limitations, which then suggest solution through the application of preexisting technologies and ideas in novel and sometimes unanticipated ways.[39]

In the case of suicide bombing, the limitations of emplaced bombs "necessitated" the invention of portable bombs, which in turn "necessitated" a more accurate guidance and control system, which, given the technological capabilities of the time, was best achieved by exploiting the desire for martyrdom already present among some individuals. One innovation led to the next in the iterative, recursive manner described above, allowing the technology that would eventually become suicide bombing to begin evolving toward a better fit with the problem it was meant to solve—weapon guidance and control.

The Cult of Martyrdom

Although martyrdom is common in the history of conflict, the groups that have made the most extensive use of suicide bombers have possessed an exaggerated sense of the importance of martyrs as role models for revolutionary action. In Russia, such a cult began to emerge in the 1860s. Undoubtedly, one factor was the inflexible, dogmatic means by which the Russian tsars jealously guarded their authority from all perceived threats. Since all forms of political protest, even peaceful expressions, could lead to imprisonment and perhaps death, the educated youth, or intelligentsia, of Russia found themselves in a frustrating situation. The severity of the criminal code meant that in opposing the state they had to consider the possibility that they would be caught and executed. Thus a polarizing kill or be killed mindset took root. Since peaceful reform was not possible, for a number of people violence became the default response.[40]

The dedication toward violent social revolution coincided with a much greater awareness of and fascination with suicide in educated Russian society. Newspapers first began to report suicides with regularity in the 1870s and 1880s, creating an impression that suicide was on the rise.[41] Thus presented, suicide attracted the attention of Russian thinkers and writers, who in turn made suicide an integral part of the revolutionary tradition of late Imperial Russia. Dostoevsky, critical of the revolutionary subculture, parodied the revolutionaries' fascination with suicide in *The Possessed*. As critiqued by Dostoevsky, suicide was the ultimate expression of the revolutionaries' nihilistic obsession with individual freedom and empowerment.[42]

Although the revolutionaries professed to have broken completely with Russian culture and society, they could not help but be influenced by the deeply Christian culture that surrounded them. Revolutionary ideology became for them a form of religious crusade, sometimes articulated in religious and sometimes in secular terminology. For example, Saloman Vittenberg, arrested and tried after one of the first attempts to kill Alexander II, wrote the following to his friends from prison:

> Naturally I do not want to die. To say that I am dying willingly would be a lie. But this fact must not cast a shadow on my faith and on the certainty of my convictions. Remember that the highest example of honour and sacrificial spirit was without doubt shown by the Savior. Yet even he prayed "Take this cup away from me." And so how can I not pray also? And yet I too, like Him, tell myself, "If no other way is possible, if it is necessary that my blood should be shed for the triumph of Socialism, if the move from the present to a better organization can only be made by trampling over our bodies, then let our blood be shed and flow to redeem humanity; let it serve as manure for the soil in which the seeds of Socialism will sprout. Let Socialism triumph and triumph soon. That is my faith."[43]

Despite the revolutionary frame, Vittenberg's narrative was familiar: The social situation was hell; the social equality that the revolutionaries dreamed about was heaven; revolution was the purgatory necessary to purify mankind. Naturally, the revolutionaries became the priests of this new faith.[44] In emulating Christianity, the secular faith of the revolutionaries demanded martyrs.

On April 2, 1879, Alexander Solovyov attempted to assassinate Alexander II by shooting him. After missing, Solovyov apparently tried to commit suicide, but failed, and was arrested and condemned to death. He stated that he had been motivated by the sacrifices of his predecessors: "Like ghosts, the martyrs for the people, who figured in many major political trials and who perished prematurely, pass through my imagination."[45] As noted above, Ignaty Grinevitsky understood that his decision to participate in the plot to kill Alexander likely would necessitate his death. After Alexander's murder, five members of the conspiracy to kill him were also arrested and hanged.[46] Even before their deaths on April 3, 1881, Vera Figner, one of the leaders of the People's Will, penned a letter to the new tsar, Alexander III. She declared that violence would not intimidate the movement. On the contrary, she wrote, "Whole dozens of our leaders have been seized and hanged. They have died with the courage and calmness of martyrs, but the movement has not been suppressed, it has grown and gained strength."[47] Thus, prior to its reinvention as a means of control, a culture of martyrdom had served as a source of legitimacy and identity for Russian revolutionaries for more than a decade.

Suicidal Attacks after Alexander II's Assassination

Since Grinevitsky's decision was improvised and personal, there was no organizational apparatus dedicated to promoting more attacks of a similar nature. In addition, the formal structure of the People's Will was dismantled in the years immediately following Alexander II's murder, although the name and idea of the movement persisted until the end of Alexander III's reign.[48] Shortly after the turn of the century, a broader wave of terrorist violence gripped Russia, during which the use of suicide bombers became a recurring, if not exactly common, element of escalating violence between revolutionaries and the state.

The Party of Socialist Revolutionaries (PSR) was responsible for the bulk of the dynamite attacks between 1902 and 1906. Ideologically, party members grounded themselves among the urban working class and in many ways saw themselves as the heirs of the People's Will.[49] Within the PSR, the Terrorist Brigade—sometimes called the Combat Organization—became an independent unit, with its own membership and financing. Those who carried out the actual murders were, according to the group's bylaws, not subordinate to the political leadership of the organization. Boris Savinkov, leader of the Terrorist Brigade after 1903, recalled, "In accordance with the decision of the Party, the Terrorist Brigade becomes an autonomous organization, based on the principle of strict conspiracy and independence of action and to be devoted exclusively to destructive and terrorist activity."[50] The brigade came to include self-selected adherents of a culture of martyrdom who differed ideologically from the group as a whole. Members of the Terrorist Brigade proudly identified themselves with martyrdom and differentiated themselves from rank-and-file PSR members by their self-proclaimed willingness to die for the cause. Many in the brigade came to view with disdain their comrades who were not as fanatical and in some cases were prone to compromise.[51]

The group launched its first attacks in 1902, using pistols, but was unsuccessful. The following year, Savinkov took control of the brigade and shifted the choice of weaponry to the hand-thrown bomb. The brigade initially targeted several officials, but owing to shortages in manpower and bombs eventually focused its attention on Viacheslav von Plehve, the incoming minister of internal affairs. It faced the same difficulties that had frustrated the People's Will decades earlier: von Plehve was only accessible when he traveled in his carriage, making him a mobile and unpredictable target. The terrorists could only get close enough to kill von Plehve if they were on foot and used small bombs; this meant that the bombs required a high degree of accuracy. Perhaps recalling Grinevitsky's successful attack, one of Savinkov's colleagues, Ivan Kaliayev, suggested a way out of the dilemma:

> There was, of course, the inevitable risk of failing to hit the carriage by striking beyond or short of the aim. Kaliayev, who had kept quiet to this moment, concentrating his attention on Azev's directions, suddenly said: "There is a way of insuring against that."
>
> "How?"
>
> "To throw oneself under the horses' feet." Azev looked at him intently.
>
> "What do you mean, to throw oneself under the horses' feet?"
>
> "Well imagine the carriage coming along. I throw myself with my bomb under the horses. The bomb will either go off, and then the carriage must stop, or it will not explode, the horses will become frightened—again the carriage must come to a halt. It will then be up to the second man to finish the job."
>
> All were silent. Finally Azev said: "But you will be killed."
>
> "Of course." Kaliayev's plan was bold and reckless. It really did guarantee success.[52]

While this appears to be the first case in which self-sacrifice was discussed in a tactical manner, the Terrorist Brigade did not carry out Kaliayev's plan exactly as he conceived it. Instead, Eugene Azev, who was later revealed to be a traitor, steered the group away from this more radical plan and toward their standard practice of having two or three terrorists throw their bombs from a short distance to allow them the possibility of surviving the mission. When the attack was carried out on July 15, 1904, Egor Sazonov succeeded in killing von Plehve, but only by getting so close to von Plehve's carriage that he was wounded by the explosion. He later committed suicide in prison.[53]

Much to Kaliayev's disappointment, Savinkov had only given him a supporting role in the von Plehve operation. In early 1905, however, Savinkov designated Kaliayev as the lead bomber in a more ambitious plan—the plot to assassinate Grand Duke Sergei Alexandrovich, governor general of Moscow. On February 2 the brigade had its opportunity, but Kaliayev aborted the mission at the last minute because the grand duke had children with him in his carriage.

Two nights later they had a second opportunity, but since they did not have the time to plan in advance, only Kaliayev was available to carry out the attack. Savinkov was reluctant, believing that a minimum of two bombers would be necessary to ensure success. Kaliayev was insistent, however, and Savinkov, under pressure to act while the opportunity presented itself, agreed to an improvised attack with Kaliayev as the sole bomber. In his memoirs Savinkov recalled, "I knew Kaliayev. I knew that none of us could be so confident of himself as he. I knew he would hurl the bomb only in the very front of the carriage, and not before, and that he would be master of himself to the end."[54] Clearly it was Kaliayev's demonstrated willingness to kill himself while killing the grand duke that made his superior confident enough to proceed with the mission. Kaliayev's readiness to martyr himself made an otherwise impossible mission possible. Savinkov's memoir may well be the first documented instance of a member of an organization planning to use another member as a suicide attacker.

Kaliayev killed the grand duke by throwing his bomb from approximately four paces away while running full speed toward the carriage. Remarkably, Kaliayev survived the attack. His case is extremely interesting because he demonstrated through his actions the practical utility of having a bomber who is willing to die and in his later writings asserted that his survival had diminished the symbolic and demonstrative aspects of the mission. In a letter from prison he wrote, "To die for one's convictions is but a summons to battle, and no matter how great may be the sacrifices necessary for the destruction of absolutism, I firmly believe that our generation will put an end to it forever." Kaliayev was clearly thinking in both tactical and strategic terms; having achieved a tactical success, he then used his incarceration and trial to complete his martyrdom in order to legitimize his group and the struggle. Upon receiving the death penalty, he challenged his captors: "I rejoice at your verdict. I hope you will have the courage to carry it out as openly and as publicly as I executed the sentence of the Party of Socialists-Revolutionaries. Learn to look the advancing revolution straight in the eye."[55]

Kaliayev's attack is also noteworthy because it demonstrates that the purpose of integrating a person with a bomb is not necessarily to cause maximum or indiscriminate damage, but to allow for control in a more general sense—ensuring that the actual outcome of an attack corresponds with the desired outcome. In contrast to the modern use of suicide bombers, Kaliayev and some of his Russian comrades deliberately sought to limit the consequences of their attacks. Kaliayev was not the only Russian terrorist to risk his own life to prevent indiscriminate casualties, although he is certainly the best remembered and most celebrated.[56] Other Russians, however, showed no such restraint, and the rhetoric of many of them was as bloody-minded as that of today's global jihadis.

The assassination of the grand duke was the most dramatic success during Savinkov's tenure as leader of the Terrorist Brigade. The following year, 1906, the group attempted to kill Vice Admiral F. V. Dubasov, governor general of Moscow, on April 23. The attacker, Boris Vnorovskii, threw his small bomb from close range. Vnorovskii was killed in the attack, as was one of Dubasov's aides, but the admiral escaped with minor injuries. The next month, on May 14, two terrorists sought to kill Lt. Gen. Nepliuev, commander of the Sevastopol' fortress. One of them, sixteen-year-old Nikolai Makarov, threw his bomb under Nepliuev's feet, but the bomb failed to explode. Meanwhile, the bomb carried by his accomplice, Ivan Frolov, detonated accidentally, killing Frolov and six bystanders and injuring thirty-seven others.[57] During the early 1900s, Russian revolutionaries carried out several other attacks that cost bombers their lives.[58] Three members of the Maximalists, the most bloody-minded of the Russian revolutionaries, attempted to kill Prime Minister Peter Stolypin in his villa in August 1906. When stopped by guards, they yelled, "Long live freedom! Long live anarchy!" and detonated the sixteen-pound bombs they were carrying, killing themselves and twenty-seven other people.[59]

CONCLUSION

On the whole, the suicidal and near suicidal missions in Imperial Russia amounted to a tiny percentage of the overall terrorist violence directed against the state, but they were among the most dramatic and memorable. They are significant in the current context because they anticipated the suicide bombing of the late twentieth century in two important ways. First, the missions inevitably required the death of the attacker. Of all the high-profile attacks discussed above, every bomb thrower died as a consequence of his mission, either in the course of the attack, through execution, or by suicide in prison. There was no way of knowing in advance whether their death would result from the mission, but they had little alternative than to assume that they would die, possibly by their own hand. The bombers prepared themselves for this inevitability through indoctrination into a cult of martyrdom that caused them to place an exaggerated importance on self-sacrifice and to make their willingness to die a fundamental element of their identities. Second, the nature of the bombs meant that the terrorists became control elements rather than agents of violence. Martyrdom and self-sacrifice, already components of attacks, quickly became the cultural mechanisms that made the transition of bombers from assassin to control system possible.

There are, however, significant differences between the attacks of the Russian revolutionaries and suicide bombers today. One of the most important is the lack of physical integration between the bomber and the weapon. Kaliayev threw his bomb, allowing him to survive the attack. He was undoubtedly prepared and willing to die, but today's suicide bombers, who strap explosives to their bodies or ride in their vehicular bombs, eliminate the possibility of survival. The complete integration of bomber and bomb has become possible due to portable electronics that allow for much more reliable and covert detonation than fuses or impact.

Even more important, the organizational level characteristic of suicide bombing today did not exist in Imperial Russia. None of the Russian groups developed managerial structures specifically for the purpose of recruiting, indoctrinating, and deploying bombers and then exploiting the public spectacle of their suicide attacks. In Russia, the decision on whether to die, or at least risk death, remained in the hands of the individual bomber throughout the course of the mission rather than with the organization. Since there were so few suicide attackers, and those who survived often ended up killing themselves in prison if they were not executed, it may well be the case that suicide attacks reflected a form of mental pathology.[60] In this sense, Russian suicide bombing remained an improvisational, unsophisticated form of technology.

2

THE WEAPON OF MARTYRDOM

Lebanon, 1981–1985

The weapon of martyrdom is the main and pivotal weapon on which we can rely, one that has proven its effectiveness and that prompts the enemy to reconsider its objectives.[1]

—Naim Qassem, deputy secretary-general of Hizballah

On December 15, 1981, a suicide bomber drove a car packed with explosives into the compound of Iraq's embassy in Beirut. The driver detonated the explosives, causing a massive blast that leveled the building, killed sixty-one people, and injured more than one hundred. Among the dead was Abdul Razzak Lafta, Iraq's ambassador to Lebanon.[2] Several groups claimed responsibility for the attack, but it is now usually attributed to al-Dawa (The Mission, or The Calling). Al-Dawa, a Shiite organization originally formed in the late 1950s in Iraq, had by the late 1970s turned to militancy after being systematically repressed by the Baathist government. In response to al-Dawa operations targeting public officials, Iraqi president Saddam Hussein brutally attacked Shiite clergy in 1980. During the crackdown, the revered Ayatollah Bakr al-Sadr, an influential figure in the founding of al-Dawa, was murdered by Iraqi security forces.[3] Much of al-Dawa's leadership fled the country, primarily settling in Iran and in Lebanon. The 1981 attack was presumably an effort by the remnants of al-Dawa to strike back at the Iraqi government. In any case, in contrast to the sporadic, individual suicide attacks of Imperial Russia, the Beirut bombing signaled the evolution of suicide bombing into a refined, more effective organizational phenomenon, using technology uniquely appropriate for the environment. Within the next two years, five more high-profile suicide bombings in Lebanon would kill hundreds and make Hizballah, a coalition of militant Shiite groups, internationally notorious.

The use of human beings for bomb guidance systems remained unique to the Russian context for years after the decline of the Party of Socialist Revolutionaries there. Then, during World War II, the government of Imperial Japan made the most thorough and systematic use of suicide attackers yet seen, deploying thousands of human bombs between late 1944 and the end of the war in August 1945. During much of the post–World War II era, suicide attacks such as those carried out by the Japanese Kamikaze were rare.[4] It was not until the 1980s and 1990s in revolutionary Iran and later in war-torn Lebanon that factors analogous to those prevailing in wartime Japan created an environment conducive to the manufacture of human bombs. These factors included a grave disparity in military force between combatants, a civilian population under siege, and a culture that had been led to devalue individual lives relative to society as a whole. The leadership of Iran was the most important sponsor of this new technology, and although the Iranian government's role in the use of human bombs was often covert, it nonetheless contributed to their spectacular impact, which in turn facilitated the diffusion of suicide bombing to groups with little or no state support.

"ORGANIC SYSTEMS OF CONTROL"

The Kamikaze

Measured in sheer numbers, the most extensive use of suicide bombers to date was made by the government of Imperial Japan in the last year of World War II. The attackers are usually referred to as the Kamikaze, but Tokkotai, short for Tokubetsu Kogekitai, which means special attack units, is more accurate.[5] In autumn 1944, as the United States established the uncontested superiority of its armed forces over those of Japan, the leadership of Japan decided to unleash a new weapon—explosives-laden aircraft (and to a lesser extent submarines and boats) piloted by humans on one-way missions to inflict as much damage as possible on U.S. naval vessels. The Japanese began sustained use of the Tokkotai in October 1944. More than three thousands pilots would kill themselves in suicide missions before the cessation of hostilities between the United States and Japan in August 1945. The Tokkotai had a powerful psychological impact on U.S. forces, but their operational record was mixed. They could be devastating when they penetrated the Navy's outer defenses, sinking a number of ships, but on the whole, they did not inflict the level of damage envisioned by the Japanese leadership.

The motivating factor in creating these special attack units was the overwhelming disparity between the armed forces of Japan and those of the United States. By mid-1944 the Japanese empire was in full retreat and the civilian population under a state of siege. The Japanese had lost air and naval superiority at the battle of Midway in 1942, and their ability to carry out offensive operations steadily declined thereafter, a process finalized by the destruction of the Japanese navy as an offensive force in the Battle of Leyte Gulf in October 1944. Earlier in 1944 the United States had begun large-scale aerial bombardment of the Japanese mainland. Most important, by that point U.S. submarines had imposed a complete naval blockade on the Japanese islands. Given this disparity in power, the Japanese leadership hoped that relatively small numbers of Tokkotai would be able to sink a disproportionate number of U.S. ships and thus degrade the capacity of the Navy to operate. Japan's military leadership intended for the Tokkotai to have a psychological impact as well, by projecting an image of fanaticism, which, coupled with the tenacity exhibited by Japanese fighters in defending island after island in the Pacific, would make the Americans reconsider an invasion of the Japanese mainland.

The use of the Tokkotai was in no way preordained, although some historians regard them as the inevitable outcome of Japanese fanaticism and militarism. Their production necessitated sustained effort, requiring the Japanese leadership to innovate in a number of areas to make the Tokkotai a viable weapon system. The first attacks utilized regular aircraft deemed to be of little military value and therefore disposable. As the number of missions increased, more aircraft were required of course, so the military began to design and build cheap, stripped-down planes that were little more than flying bombs powered by rockets carrying a nose cone full of explosives. They also designed and built cheap watercraft specifically for suicide missions.[6]

Cost was a major factor in training men for Tokkotai missions. For this reason, the training period for pilots was shortened, and young, relatively inexperienced men were sent to die instead of experienced pilots. Japanese leaders made use of a variety of social and cultural mechanisms to compel these young men to die for the emperor. They drew upon the tradition of ritual suicide as a means of securing honor in the Japanese military as well as elements of Buddhism and state Shinto.[7] Their efforts at cultural programming did not always work, however. Many pilots were drawn from outside the military, including from universities, where students were graduated early so they could participate in the missions. Often, these young men were among the most open-minded and least militaristic in Japanese society and therefore did not always respond enthusiastically to appeals to patriotism and honor. In response, the government reverted to shame, coercion, and devotion to loved ones to impose control over these men so they would behave in the desired manner.

Ironically, the Tokkotai, who today are remembered as the epitome of fanaticism, were sometimes fatalistic young men who saw no realistic alternative to their own deaths and hoped only that their sacrifice would in some way mitigate the most dreadful effects of the war on their families and loved ones. Hayashi Ichizo, who died at the age of twenty-three on April 12, 1945, wrote to his family, "To be honest, I cannot say that the wish to die for the emperor is genuine, coming from my heart. However, it is decided for me that I die for the emperor." Men like him did not subscribe whole-heartedly to the ideology of the Empire, but rather " 'volunteered' to reproduce the ideology *in action* while defying it *in their thoughts.*"[8]

Despite the government's sustained effort to present the suicide missions of the Tokkotai as noble sacrifices for a worthy cause, the entire phenomenon amounted to little more than a failed research and development program. The attacks were neither large enough in number nor destructive enough in capability to have more than a superficial effect on the U.S. Navy. In addition, unlike Kaliayev, who believed that victory was possible, many of the Tokkotai pilots knew they were being used as a last-ditch effort to salvage a cause that had already been lost. Consequently, the attacks seem to have done little to galvanize the morale of the Japanese population as a whole.

The Japanese government used suicide attackers in a slightly different manner than did the Russian revolutionaries, bringing suicide bombing much closer to the form widely used in recent years. In World War II, the individual's decision to die during the course of a suicide attack was subordinated to organizational decision making to make the creation of human bombs more reliable. Furthermore, the Tokkotai were completely integrated into their bombs, leaving no possibility of survival. If death was anticipated and probable for the Russians, it was anticipated and necessary for the conclusion of a Tokkotai mission. Taken together, these two elements—constraining the behavior of individuals so that they would take their own lives and then physically fusing them with a warhead—amount to nothing less than the mechanization of human beings.

Some of the Tokkotai could see precisely what was being done to them. They were not really pilots flying aircraft, but material to be consumed during the course of the mission—disposable control elements for disposable vehicles. Hayashi Tadao, a pilot who died on July 28, 1945, at the age of twenty-four, recorded in his diary, "I do not avoid sacrifice. I do not refuse the sacrifice of myself. However, I cannot tolerate the reduction of the self to nothingness in the process. I cannot approve it. Martyrdom or sacrifice must be done at the height of self-realization. Sacrifice at the end of self-annihilation, the dissolving of the self to nothingness, has no meaning whatsoever." Even more precisely, in a letter written the night before his fatal mission, Uehara Ryoji wrote, "As Special Unit Pilots we turn into machines once we board our airplanes. . . . We become a machine whose function is to manipulate the control-column."[9]

"Organic Target Seeking"

The Japanese were not the first to use training and coercion to turn living beings into guidance systems during World War II. This distinction belongs to the Soviet Union. When Nazi Germany invaded in 1941, leaders in the Soviet army wondered if conditioned-response training in dogs could be used for military advantage. They developed a program of behavioral conditioning in which dogs were trained to seek food under machines, such as tanks and trucks, whose engines were running. The trained dogs were then outfitted with an explosive package, denied food to ensure that they were hungry, and released near German forces. The explosives were attached to a vertical stick that would trigger the bomb if pushed over or bent, as would happen when the dogs went underneath a vehicle. Soviet trainers hoped that the dogs would seek food under German machines, detonating the bombs that they were carrying and disabling mechanized forces. Although the Soviet "mine dogs" reportedly destroyed numerous German vehicles, they were far too unreliable for regular use. The dogs were unable to discriminate between Soviet and German vehicles, for example, and because of the noise of combat many chose to remain near their trainers rather than venture over to the German forces.[10]

During World War II, American researchers also explored the idea of using animals as guidance systems in Project Pigeon, an effort conceived by the behavioral psychologist B. F. Skinner.[11] Prior to the war, Skinner had achieved fame through his research on conditioned response in animals. In 1940, even before the United States became involved in the war, Skinner was imagining ways in which his research could be put to military ends. According to Skinner, he had been observing the collective behavior of a flock of birds when he was struck by a thought: "Suddenly I saw them as 'devices' with excellent vision and extraordinary maneuverability. Could they not guide a missile?"[12]

Over the next few years, Skinner received government funding to try to put this idea into practice. His plan was to familiarize birds with a potential target site and to condition them to peck at an image of it. The trained bird would then be suspended in an air-dropped bomb with a window to allow the bird to see the target. In theory, the bird would then peck its way toward the appropriate area on the viewfinder, and a mechanical apparatus attached to the bird would register the animal's movements and use them to direct the bomb toward the target. Skinner selected pigeons as the guidance systems and began the project on an experimental scale.

Trainers used aerial photographs and food rewards to condition the pigeons to peck toward a specific feature on the New Jersey coast, but the challenges of mechanically linking the animal to the bomb ultimately doomed the effort. Project Pigeon never made it beyond the experimental stage. Skinner was frustrated by what he deemed to be a lack of vision on the part of the U.S. military and by the end of the war admitted that the project had nothing to show for it except some useless apparatus and "a few dozen pigeons with a strange interest in a feature of the New Jersey coast." Efforts by the Army Air Force to use bats as guidance systems for incendiary bombs were similarly unsuccessful and were suspended after the bats accidentally burned down a theater and officers' club at the Carlsbad Army Air Field.[13]

Project Pigeon, like the Tokkotai, deliberately blurred the line between life and machine. Toward the end of the war, when the Japanese first began to use the Tokkotai, Skinner wrote that it "looks as if the Japs are using men rather than birds. Perhaps we can get American morale up that high, but if not, I can provide perfectly competent substitutes." A technical report produced by the American Office of Scientific Research and Development after the war concurred, devoting four pages to "organic target seeking." The report concluded, "The experience of the Division, so far as it is conclusive, would point to the general observation that an organic system of control should not be rejected simply because it is organic. . . . Such an attitude is far from scientific, and there is implicit in the success of the Japanese program with organic homing systems the suggestion that further study in this field might well be profitable."[14]

The Basij

On September 22, 1980, Iraqi military forces invaded Iran. The invasion caught the Iranian government by surprise, and its armed forces performed poorly in the war's opening stages. Only Saddam Hussein's poor leadership served to slow the Iraqi advance during the early months of the war and gave the Iranians time to regroup. By 1981 the Iran-Iraq War had developed into an existential struggle for the Islamic Republic of Iran, which had been declared in 1979 after the overthrow of Shah Mohammad Reza Pahlavi by followers of Ayatollah Ruhollah Khomeini. To counter the Iraqis' conventional military advantage, Khomeini, Iran's supreme leader, turned to the same force that had allowed him to consolidate control of the revolution—articulation of the crisis in religious terms, which mobilized the Iranian citizenry in the name of God.

Khomeini drew upon the martyrdom of Hussein at Karbala in 680—the most powerful symbol and source of ritual in the Shiite tradition—to unify the Iranian people against the Iraqi invasion. Hussein, the foundational figure of the Shiite branch of Islam, was a grandson of the Prophet Muhammad who resisted the transfer of the office of the caliph from the Prophet's immediate family. In doing so, he challenged the authority of the Umayyad caliph Yazid. Consequently, Hussein and his followers were massacred near the city of Karbala, now in Iraq. Hussein established a Shiite tradition of self-sacrifice, even unto death, rather than submission to tyranny. The martyrdom of Hussein is celebrated each year on the holy day of Ashura.[15]

Although Hussein's martyrdom established reverence for self-sacrifice in the Shiite tradition, in revolutionary Iran the propensity for self-sacrificial violence was first demonstrated by groups with a Marxist agenda. In the 1970s members of the Sazeman-e Mojahedin-e Khalq-e Iran (People's Mojahedin Organization of Iran) willingly went to their deaths to oppose the Shah, declaring publicly that "examples of heroism, self-sacrifice, and martyrdom" were necessary for the liberation of the Iranian people. Later, when the group was brutally repressed by the Khomeini government, its members responded by carrying out a wave of assassinations and on at least five occasions in 1981–1982 members of the Mojahedin killed both themselves and their victims by detonating hand grenades.[16] These attacks seem to have resulted from individual rather than organizational decision making but nevertheless demonstrated that martyrdom could be an effective weapon. The Khomeini government's subsequent decision to encourage martyrdom among its supporters therefore stemmed partially from the desire to reclaim martyrdom so that it could be used for the benefit of the Islamic republic.

Khomeini and other Iranian religious leaders immediately called the Iraqi invasion a jihad, or holy war. They emphasized to the Iranian people that the revolution had successfully returned Islamic values to Iran but had since been under attack. They described Saddam Hussein as a heretic and in their sermons regularly referred to him as Saddam-i-Yazid, a tyrant whose threat to Iran (and thus to Islam) was as great as was Yazid's to the seventh-century Shiite community.[17] During this holy war, Khomeini reserved a special place for martyrs—those who would willingly shed their own blood to defend Islam. Using the authority of his position as supreme religious leader, he called upon Iran's population to emulate the sacrifice of Hussein and drive the modern-day Yazid out of Iran.

Iran's religious leaders sacralized the war by promising their followers that dying for the cause of their faith was the noblest form of Islamic observance possible. Khomeini went so far as to say that martyrdom in the name of God was the ultimate perfection that a human could achieve and would guarantee prospective martyrs a place in paradise.[18] As the Iranian state struggled to field a competent military and organize the Revolutionary Guards, older men and especially boys too young for the military took matters into their own hands. In November 1981 thousands of these untrained, poorly armed irregulars, known as the Basij (the "mobilized"), accompanied Iranian regular forces in a defensive battle, where they were massacred by the Iraqi military.

Khomeini was quick to exploit the passion and fervor that drove these irregulars and to institutionalize the Basij as auxiliaries to the Iranian army. He reinforced the enthusiasm of the first Basij by declaring that the kind of sacrifice that Hussein had made voluntarily was now an obligation of the Iranian people. "We should sacrifice all of our loved ones for the sake of Islam," he said. "If we are killed, we shall have performed our duty."[19] In February 1984 President Ali Akbar Hashemi Rafsanjani declared that "all Iranians from twelve to seventy-two should volunteer for the Holy War."[20] The Iranian state recruited thousands of young boys, some no older than nine, for service. Unsurprisingly, many were not particularly religious and had no real sense of what martyrdom truly meant. One former child soldier who survived and was interned in an Iraqi POW camp later recalled, "We didn't understand the words 'patriotism' or 'martyrdom,' or at least I didn't. It was just an exciting game and a chance to prove to your friends that you'd grown up and were no longer a child."[21]

Wearing headbands to declare their purity and allegiance to Khomeini and keys around their necks that symbolized the key to paradise, the Basij were deployed to the front, where they were sent in waves to be slaughtered by the Iraqis. The exact number of young men sacrificed in such a manner remains unknown, but it was significant. One Iranian recruiter asserted that he had sent more than 4,000 youths to their deaths in the span of a few months. An Iraqi source testified that at least 23,000 such young men were killed in a single "human wave attack" in 1983.[22]

Although the Basij did not kill themselves, their dispatch by the Iranian government was an important step toward the development of suicide bombing in the Middle East and a clear case of a leadership group deliberately using religious symbolism to prepare its followers for systematic self-sacrifice. The Basij served strategic and tactical roles, but tactically their impact was limited; even when used offensively, their purpose was more to absorb than to inflict damage. Martyrdom would become a much more flexible and deadly tool when leaders began to use it for offensive operations, a step that represented but a single iteration in the recursive process of technological development.

This iteration involved a young boy named Mohammad Hosein Fahmideh. As one of the Basiji volunteers early in the war, Fahmideh reportedly grabbed a hand grenade, threw himself under an advancing Iraqi tank, and detonated the explosive, destroying himself and the tank. The loss of the tank and the example of Fahmideh are said to have rallied the Iranians. Upon learning of the boy's death, Khomeini encouraged others to emulate Fahmideh, saying, "Our leader is that 12 year old child who threw himself with his little heart against the enemy" and referring to him as a guide to the Iranian people.[23] Fahmideh came to be revered as one of the great Iranian martyrs and is memorialized today in Tehran's Martyr's Museum. According to the government of revolutionary Iran, "At the warfront, a miraculous event occurred: An event which must be called a legend, an event which is unbelievable. During the first days of the aggression, a thirteen year old boy, while holding some explosive ammunition, slipped under the enemy's tank and when the tank passed over him, it exploded. Although the boy himself was martyred, he caused such a fear in the enemy's heart that all the enemy tanks withdrew back to their own territory."[24] Fahmideh's death was apparently a spontaneous act. Nevertheless, its effectiveness and the aura of heroism that came to surround it suggest that this accidental, contingent act could serve as the template for a much more systematic form of violence.

THE LEBANESE CONTEXT

All of the factors that led to experimentation with human bombers in previous eras were present to an extraordinary level in Lebanon in the early 1980s. Elements of the Lebanese clerical establishment, particularly those who would come to be affiliated with Hizballah, had strong connections to Iran's leadership and shared Khomeini's militant interpretation of the faith. Lebanon had been torn by a multifront civil war for years, and its Shiite community lacked a strong force or body to represent its interests and to defend its people. The invasion of Israel in 1982 heightened this sense of crisis by introducing a force whose military capabilities far exceeded those of any of the indigenous Lebanese factions. Finally, car bombs lacking human guidance systems had already been used extensively in the Middle East as dreadful mass-casualty weapons.

The Shiite Community

Lebanon is a mosaic of different religious faiths and confessions whose borders and government owe more to the legacy of European colonization than to indigenous factors. Shiite Muslims have been one of the larger confessional groups in Lebanon since the formation of the state by the French but were marginalized by the Lebanese constitution, drafted in 1946 to create an independent Lebanon, which privileged Maronite Christians and Sunni Muslims.[25] By the 1970s differential population growth among the various Lebanese confessional groups resulted in Shiites becoming the largest single group. The Lebanese constitution, however, was not amended, so the Shiites remained marginalized politically and economically despite their number. In addition, after 1970 the Palestine Liberation Organization (PLO) became a major actor in Lebanese politics, operating as a state-within-a-state, including carrying out military operations against Israel from southern Lebanon. In 1975 this combination of factors, as well as the desire of neighboring states to advance their own agendas in Lebanon, led to the collapse of the Lebanese government and the emergence of a multifront civil war.

The most important figure in the political mobilization of Lebanese Shiites in the 1970s was the cleric Musa al-Sadr, a highly respected reformist scholar. Al-Sadr was born in the Iranian city of Qom in 1928 and arrived in Lebanon in 1959. Central to his emergence as a political leader was his recognition of the fact that Lebanon's Shiites had been encouraged by their leadership to adopt an attitude of political submissiveness. He fought this tendency by emphasizing selected elements of Shiite history and tradition to mobilize the population. In particular, he reinterpreted the pivotal figure of Hussein, as Khomeini would do several years later. The message al-Sadr hoped to convey, however, was one of political choice, not fanaticism or recklessness. He stripped Hussein's martyrdom of sorrow and reinterpreted it as a tale of courage for his followers.[26]

Al-Sadr worked at the grassroots level to mobilize Lebanese Shiites and helped create a political identity for them. He initiated a small network of schools and clinics to provide Shiites with services that the state neglected to provide. He tried to work with other groups and to utilize nonviolent methods, but was ultimately forced to accept the reality of Lebanon's civil war and acknowledge that his people needed an armed force of their own. The following year, in 1975, the movement formed a militia, which came to be known as Amal, which means "hope" and is also an acronym for Battalions of the Lebanese Resistance.[27]

During a trip to Libya in 1978, al-Sadr disappeared. Speculation abounded that he had been killed by the Libyan government, headed by Muammar al-Qaddafi, but his disappearance remains a mystery.[28] Al-Sadr's disappearance, the civil war, and the Iranian Revolution pulled at Lebanon's Shiite community, revealing deep fissures. A number of Lebanese Shiite clerics had long-standing personal and ideological connections to revolutionary Iran, but Amal's leadership was reluctant to be subordinate to Khomeini, so from 1979 to 1982 the organization had an ambivalent relationship with Iran.[29] Instead, Amal's leaders turned increasingly toward Syria. Al-Sadr had approached Syria as a last-ditch ally to shore up his precarious position between the Maronites and the PLO, the latter of which followed its own agenda in southern Lebanon regardless of the harm this brought to the Shiites (in the form of Israeli reprisals); he even used his clerical authority to legitimize Syria's minority Alawite sect, to which Syrian president Hafez al-Asad belonged, as a genuine branch of Shiite Islam.[30] Syria, seeking a means to keep the PLO in check in Lebanon, found it in Amal. In 1980 and 1981 Syria trained and armed Amal fighters. As the Amal-Syrian connection strengthened, the relationship between Amal and the Palestinians worsened to the point of hostilities.[31]

Formation of Hizballah

The situation in Lebanon turned catastrophic in summer 1982, when Israel launched a full-scale invasion into southern Lebanon with the intention of wiping out the PLO. The initial stages of the offensive were a triumph for Israel, as its armed forces destroyed the conventional weapons of the PLO, routed the Syrian air force, and within days reached the outskirts of Beirut.[32] The Israeli advance was followed by a siege of Beirut that achieved the objective of crushing the PLO's army as a fighting force, but at great human cost. The PLO had dispersed its fighters among civilian areas and buildings, and Israeli forces pursued them there, neither side taking into consideration the human devastation caused by their actions. Consequently, thousands of Lebanese noncombatants and other civilian residents were killed in the fighting.[33] By the end of the summer, southern Lebanon and East Beirut were under Israeli military occupation.

The Israeli invasion ended the caution that had led Iran to limit its role in Lebanon. The Khomeini government began to assert itself aggressively in the aftermath, encouraging and supporting a number of radical Shiite militias, each bound to a particular leader and region, to coalesce as an anti-Israeli force. This aggregation of groups would in several years evolve into Hizballah. Shaped as it was by the chaotic social environment of the early 1980s, Hizballah's early history is characterized by change, opportunism, and flexibility, and any effort to present it concisely will invariably superimpose the appearance of more order in regard to its emergence than actually existed at the time.

The formal foundation of Hizballah is usually traced to the seizure of an army barracks in Lebanon's Bekaa Valley by Islamic Amal, a Lebanese Shiite faction under the leadership of Abbas al-Musawi, and members of Iran's Revolutionary Guard, whom Khomeini had dispatched to mobilize Lebanese Shiites.[34] This relationship had begun on a theological level many years earlier, when Musawi and other clerics had studied alongside the future leaders of Iran at Shiite holy places in Iraq. The Israeli occupation provided the impetus for their relationship to turn into a political and military collaboration.

From its base in the Bekaa, Hizballah spread into Beirut and then into southern Lebanon. The organization developed a national leadership structure and formally announced its existence in an open letter in 1985. In these early years, Hizballah served as an integrating force, tying together local groups and leaders and providing an alternative for Shiites who were dissatisfied with Amal. The goals of the organization were twofold: creating a new, authentic form of Shiite identity within the context of Khomeini's Islamic revolution and combating the Israeli occupation. Suicide bombing proved to be effective for promoting both agendas.

SUICIDE BOMBINGS, 1981–1983

Shiite groups were responsible for six major suicide bombings in Lebanon between 1981 and 1983. The first bombing, in 1981 (noted at the beginning of this chapter), was likely carried out by the remnants of the Iraqi al-Dawa, which had been formed in 1958 in Iraq to serve as an Islamic alternative to the secular Baath Party.[35] Over the decades, there grew within al-Dawa a strong connection between Iraqi, Lebanese, and Iranian Shiite clerics and a corresponding opposition to Saddam Hussein's government.

In 1977 al-Dawa became more aggressive after Iraqi forces attacked pilgrims en route to Karbala; the Iranian Revolution further inspired its militancy.[36] Muhammad Bakr al-Sadr (a relative of Musa al-Sadr), at that time the most respected Shiite cleric in Iraq, was particularly moved by Khomeini's achievement and proceeded to direct Shiite opposition against Hussein's government. In March 1980 the Iraqi regime outlawed al-Dawa, and the following month the group responded by attempting to assassinate Tariq Aziz, a close aide to Hussein (and later foreign minister and deputy prime minister). On April 9 Hussein's government executed al-Sadr and his sister in retaliation.[37] Afterward, much of al-Dawa's leadership fled to Tehran, while some remained in Iraq as a clandestine force and carried out several attempts on Hussein's life in the 1980s. Remnants of al-Dawa also fled to Lebanon, where they were subsumed into Hizballah in the early 1980s. It seems likely, then, that Iran played some role, direct or indirect, in this first Lebanese suicide attack—the Iraqi government blamed Iran for the blast—and the integration of al-Dawa members into

Hizballah suggests an element of continuity between the attack at the Iraqi embassy and those that followed.

Possibility and perceived need—the key factors contributing to the emergence of suicide bombing—were both present in Lebanon in the early 1980s. The revival of the martyrdom of Hussein by Musa al-Sadr and the militarization of martyrdom under Ayatollah Khomeini created a culture of death similar to that which existed among the anarchist terrorists of Imperial Russia and the Japanese military. The individuals and groups that would become Hizballah set themselves apart from other religious denominations, and more important, from other parts of the Shiite community (such as Amal) through an uncompromising adherence to what they saw as the most authentic form of Shiite Islam.[38] Some of them would testify to the authenticity of their identity and faith through their willingness and desire to sacrifice their own lives. Jihad and martyrdom came to be affirmations of their individual and collective identities and the performance of these rituals a source of pride and even an expectation that these men had for one another. They were actively encouraged to embrace this radical position.

Upon arriving in the Bekaa Valley, members of Iran's Revolutionary Guards began teaching their Lebanese protégés that a willingness to die was a precondition for effective resistance. A notice on the door of an office used by the guards in Baalbek proclaimed them to be "lovers of martyrdom." By the end of summer 1982, the first significant Shiite resistance to the Israeli occupation had taken place south of Beirut, on the beaches of Khalde. At that time Lebanese Shiites, imitating the Iranians, wore headbands and flung themselves at the Israelis with little regard for their own survival.[39]

If Iran's encouragement of a culture of martyrdom created the possibility for suicide attacks, the Israeli invasion created the perceived need. On an ideological level, the Israeli invasion provided an enemy against which jihad and martyrdom could be executed. Furthermore, the overwhelming disparity of force between the sides—and the seeming Israeli indifference toward civilian casualties—facilitated the emergence of suicide bombing on a practical level by necessitating armed struggle and legitimizing any effective form of attack, no matter how extreme. Other than suicide bombing, there seemed to be few options that would allow small groups to project force in Lebanon, especially into fortified areas. The 1981 bombing served as a powerful demonstration of this capability, and in 1982 these factors led to the selection of vehicle-borne suicide bombers as a potential new technology for the members of Hizballah.

1982: Hizballah Strikes Back

By August 1982 the Israel Defense Forces (IDF) had achieved its main objective of routing the PLO. International mediation was required to halt the carnage and arrange for the evacuation of the PLO's armed forces from Lebanon. Under UN auspices, a multinational force (MNF) consisting of U.S., French, and Italian troops quickly deployed to Beirut to oversee the evacuation, in which between six thousand and seven thousand members of the PLO headed for exile in Tunisia. Having carried out its mission, the MNF quickly withdrew, leaving behind a power vacuum in West Beirut. In the meantime, the Lebanese parliament selected a new president, Bashir Gemayel—a Maronite Christian, the requisite confession for holding the office—but because he was the Israeli government's preferred candidate, large parts of the Lebanese population rejected him, assuming that he would create a government sympathetic to Israeli interests.[40] Gemayel was assassinated in a bombing on September 14, less than a month after his election.

In response the IDF moved into West Beirut, which it had previously refrained from occupying. During the next few days, militants from the Christian Phalange committed one of the war's most notorious atrocities with the tacit complicity of the IDF. Beginning on September 15, Phalangist militia members entered the Palestinian refugee camps of Sabra and Shatila under the pretext that they were rounding up arms caches and purging Beirut of alleged terrorists. In actuality, they carried out a systematic massacre of Palestinian and Lebanese civilians, presumably as retaliation for Gemayel's assassination. The killing lasted until September 17. Figures vary, but it is likely that least eight hundred to a thousand Palestinian civilians were murdered in three days.[41] While the IDF was not directly responsible for the massacre, Israeli soldiers were stationed outside the camps, and its leaders undoubtedly knew that a slaughter was taking place. The incident elicted international condemnation for Israel.[42]

The newly organized forces of Hizballah struck back at the Israelis on November 11, when seventeen-year-old Ahmad Qassir drove a white Mercedes filled with approximately 500 kilograms of explosives into IDF headquarters in Tyre. The explosion destroyed the building, killing seventy-five Israelis and a smaller number of Palestinian and Lebanese prisoners. So complete and unexpected was the devastation that for years Israel maintained that the explosion was the result of a natural gas leak rather than an attack. This explanation remained viable because Hizballah did not initially claim responsibility for the attack, and the identity of the assailant remained unknown. Only later did Hizballah acknowledge the attack and in 1985 reveal Qassir's identity. Apparently Qassir, who wanted to protect his family from Israeli reprisals, had requested a period of ano-nymity following the attack. After Israel redeployed its forces to a narrow zone of occupation along Lebanon's southern border Qassir's name was disclosed. His family has since remembered him as a martyr and hero.[43]

1983: Legitimation through Use

On the afternoon of April 18, 1983, a suicide bomber drove a Chevrolet pickup truck loaded with approximately four hundred pounds of explo-sives into the front of the U.S. embassy in Beirut. As in the previous two cases of vehicular suicide attacks, the results were devastating. The front of the building collapsed. Sixty-three people were killed, and more than a hundred were injured. Robert Ames, a former CIA station chief in Lebanon, had been meeting with eight other intelligence operatives in a top-floor room to discuss terrorism at the time of the blast. All nine were crushed when the building collapsed, crippling U.S. human intelligence capabilities in the region for years.

The attack on the U.S. embassy was far more sophisticated than the bombing of the IDF headquarters in Tyre the previous November; the tim-ing in particular was precisely planned. It was no mere coincidence that the CIA's top intelligence sources in the region were meeting in the building when the attack occurred; rather, it is far more likely that the bombing was planned to coincide with the meeting, suggesting that the bombers had access to extremely high-level intelligence.[44] A green Mercedes had served as a spotter vehicle, facilitating the precise timing. The responsible organi-zation also proved to be adept at covering its tracks. Forensic investigations of the explosives and the vehicles used yielded little, and the identity of the bomber remains unknown.[45] The attack was initially claimed by several groups, including the previously unknown Islamic Jihad Organization (IJO), which is now generally credited with the operation.

After the Sabra and Shatila massacres, the MNF had returned, but with an open-ended timetable. In this new context, the MNF was to be an impartial, honest broker among the various warring factions, helping to rebuild the Lebanese state. This status, however, was difficult to maintain given the desire of the different groups to manipulate it to their advantage and the tendency of some to see the MNF in the worst possible light. The lack of trust in the force as an honest broker made its members the targets of some groups.

During summer 1983, the perception intensified among many Lebanese that the United States was firmly on the side of Israel and its Lebanese Christian allies. In September, in response to a request from the Lebanese government, U.S. naval forces provided artillery support for Lebanese Christian forces fighting in the mountains outside Beirut. By firing on a coalition of Druze, Syrian, and Palestinian forces, the U.S. military reaffirmed the impression that it had taken sides in the conflict. Many of its members did not recognize this at the time, and those who warned of the danger were ignored. For example, Col. Timothy Geraghty, a Marine commander in the area, protested the partisan use of force, arguing, "This will cost us our neutrality. Do you realize if you do that, we'll get slaughtered down here?"[46] He would soon be proven correct.

At 6:45 a.m. on Sunday, October 23, a young man drove a yellow Mercedes stake bed truck through a Lebanese Army checkpoint on the highway leading to the Beirut airport, where U.S. Marines had established their base.[47] As the Marines slept, the truck smashed through a barbed-wire barrier south of the four-story operations building and proceeded northward through an open gate between two sentry posts at a speed of approximately thirty-five miles per hour. According to an eyewitness, the driver smiled as he rammed the vehicle into the operations building, where one-fourth of the more than one thousand Marines of the U.S. contingent slept. The truck smashed through the south entrance to the building, overran a guard post, and came to a halt in the building's lobby. One or two seconds later, it exploded.

The explosion demolished the first floor and tore a crater approximately 40 feet by 30 feet by 8 feet through reinforced concrete. It sheared through concrete support columns nearly five feet in diameter and lifted the building into the air, after which it completely collapsed. The shape of the building—rectangular with an open courtyard—had intensified the effects of the blast, and the Federal Bureau of Investigation (FBI) later determined that the blast had also been enhanced through the use of explosive gas and was the equivalent of approximately six tons of TNT. At the time, the FBI's forensics laboratory described the explosion as the most powerful it had seen. Two hundred forty-one U.S. service personnel, most of them Marines, were killed in the attack.

Approximately twenty seconds later, a second bomber targeted French paratroopers based five miles to the north. His vehicle made it into the interior of the nine-story headquarters of the First Parachute Chasseur Regiment, and when the explosives detonated, the blast separated the building from its foundation, lifted it into the air, and shifted the nine floors twenty feet, at which point they collapsed into rubble next to the massive crater left by the bomb. The attack killed fifty-eight elite paratroopers, France's first combat fatalities since 1962, during the Algerian war for independence. The near-simultaneity of the two blasts, coupled with the devastation and loss of life, indicated a high level of planning, intelligence, and resources. Islamic Jihad Organization claimed responsibility for both attacks.

The next major attack was directed at Israeli forces in Tyre, in November 1983. In this operation, a suicide bomber driving a truck again managed to penetrate the compound of Israel's military headquarters and detonate a half-ton of explosives. Sixty people were killed, including twenty-eight Israeli troops.[48] The following month, a large car bomb exploded at the U.S. embassy in Kuwait. The driver missed the most populated part of the complex, and only a fourth of his explosives detonated, limiting the human toll to five fatalities. This attack, and five others at approximately the same time, was credited to al-Dawa, the group that had introduced suicide bombing to the Middle East two years earlier.[49] In recent years, however, al-Dawa has attempted to distance itself from these attacks, claiming that they were the work of Iranian security agents who had seized control of the al-Dawa cell in Kuwait.[50]

The embassy bombing in Kuwait may not have been a suicide attack; an eyewitness reported that the driver had fled the vehicle and had managed to get several steps away before it exploded, suggesting remote or timed detonation.[51] For this reason, it is doubtful that this attack should be included with the other bombings of 1983, although at the very least it demonstrates the importance of having a human guidance system for vehicular bombs. In all, the four confirmed suicide attacks in 1983 devastated the forces of three states, claimed more than four hundred lives, and defied all efforts at prevention of such actions and retaliation after them.

By any criteria, the wave of suicide bombings in 1983 must be considered a success for Hizballah and its backers. In the short term, the attacks inflicted extraordinary damage on military and political targets, including those, such as the U.S. embassy, with powerful symbolic value. In the medium term, the attacks contributed to the withdrawal of Hizballah's adversaries from Lebanon within the course of two years. In the long run, the attacks drew global attention to militant Shiite groups. Of importance here, Hizballah established itself as a major player in the Lebanese conflict and differentiated itself from other forces, such as Amal, through its sheer brutality.

Spread of Suicide Bombing

The following year, 1984, was relatively quiet in comparison to 1983, with only two successful suicide attacks in Lebanon. In April Ali Safiadan, a teenager, demonstrated the operational flexibility of the vehicular-borne suicide bomb. When two Israeli armored personnel carriers passed the green Fiat in which he was sitting, he started the engine, rammed the vehicles, and detonated the bomb his vehicle was carrying. One of the Israeli vehicles was completely destroyed; twelve people died in the attack, which was credited to Hizballah. Safiadan may have had personal motivations for carrying out the attack, as his brother had been a prisoner of the IDF and had been killed in the bombing of the IDF headquarters the previous November. Unlike the smiling bomber who killed so many U.S. Marines, an eyewitness recalls that Safiadan was crying shortly before carrying out his attack.[52] The following September, another suicide bomber, utilizing a van, destroyed the new U.S. embassy in East Beirut, killing fourteen people a mere seventeen months after the first embassy bombing.[53]

In 1985 there were twenty-two suicide attacks in Lebanon, only two of which Shiite organizations carried out. Of these, one is credited to Amal, Hizballah's rival, whose leader, Nabih Berri, had publicly threatened suicide attacks against Israeli targets in September 1984.[54] Furthermore, on April 9, 1985, suicide bombing ceased to be an exclusively male phenomenon. On that day, seventeen-year-old Sanaa Muhaidily drove a white Peugeot laden with explosives into Israeli forces in southern Lebanon, killing herself and two soldiers.[55] Less than two weeks later, on April 20, Loula Abboud, a young Christian woman, participated in an attack on Israeli soldiers in the town of Aoun. Abboud and some comrades drew Israeli fire, after which Abboud continued to shoot, enabling her companions to escape. She then allowed the Israelis to close in on her for the purpose of detaining her, at which point she blew herself up, killing several soldiers in the process.

Muhaidily, a Sunni Muslim, had fought for the Syrian Social Nationalist Party (SSNP), a secular, nationalist organization. The SSNP, which has existed in varying forms since the 1930s, is dedicated to the creation of a greater Syrian state that would include much of the eastern Mediterranean. Muhaidily had volunteered to undertake an attack. She, along with several other bombers deployed by the SSNP, recorded a video prior to the operation, announcing her intentions and asking her loved ones to be happy for her. She described the attack in romantic terms, asking that it be remembered as a wedding—a beginning rather than an end—and asked that she be remembered as the "Bride of the South."[56] The idea of such a beautiful girl volunteering to die for the cause of liberating southern Lebanon from Israeli occupation was profoundly moving to her community. After her death, Muhaidily was remembered in song and poetry, and she even received praise from Syrian president Asad. She is still recognized on the SSNP's website as one of the organization's thirteen official martyrs.

Loula Abboud's death differed from those of previous suicide bombers in that it began with a military ambush. Nevertheless, her death had an element of premeditation, and she clearly used her own life in a tactical manner. Her motivation seems to have been primarily one of nationalism, like Sanaa Muhaidily's. It is noteworthy that she left her family to fight the Israelis on the day after Easter, and her family considers her to be a martyr in the Christian tradition.[57]

The Muhaidily and Abboud attacks reveal a great deal about the way in which suicide bombing was diversifying and diffusing. While both women died for secular causes, both seem to have conceived of their deaths within a romantic framework of martyrdom that gave meaning to the act of dying while killing others. They shared this framing of suicide bombing as a transcendent act with the earlier suicide attackers, but otherwise there was much to differentiate their attacks. The inclusion of women as suicide bombers was an important difference, but so too was the spread of the desire to participate in suicide bombing among adherents of faiths other than Shiite Islam. The scale of the attacks was also different. These were both smaller-scale attacks, necessitating less preparation and resources than the massive bombs of 1983. The smaller scale of the operations allowed state sponsors (Iran and Syria) to play a lesser role, supporting and encouraging the violence but not being as directly involved in preparations as they had been in the 1983 attacks.

POSSIBILITY AND NECESSITY

Shiite Islam and Martyrdom

Following the 1983 bombings, the initial response among many observers was to postulate an intrinsic connection between Shiite Islam and suicide attacks. The centrality of Hussein's martyrdom to Shiite ritual facilitated this misinterpretation. Such thinking is problematic not only because it equates the worship of hundreds of millions of people with the extreme practices of a relatively small minority, but more generally it can lead to a dangerous underestimation of the power and mutability of suicide bombing by equating it with a particular culture.

To begin with, the path from Karbala to Beirut is not as clear as it might initially appear. Throughout the twentieth century, there was little evidence of a wholesale reverence for martyrdom on the part of Shiites. Musa al-Sadr and Khomeini deliberately revived this tradition for their own political purposes.[58] Furthermore, as promoted by al-Sadr, the example of Hussein was not one of violent fanaticism, but of choice and courage. Only later did the particular historical circumstances of Lebanon's war push his followers toward the use of force. Shiites, after all, were among the *last* to use deadly force systematically in the Lebanese civil war.

That al-Sadr and Khomeini had different understandings of how the martyrdom of Hussein should be understood underscores an essential fact: the Shiite community, even the relatively small community in Lebanon, was far from homogeneous. In particular, many Shiites objected to Khomeini's doctrine of the *vilayat-i faqih*, which translates loosely as "rule of the jurisprudent."[59] This doctrine called for political and religious authority of the Shiite community to be consolidated in the hands of the most learned cleric, the jurist-theologian, who serves as supreme leader. This dispute over acceptance of a vilayat-i faqih was at the heart of the split between Amal and the clerics who formed Hizballah. The use of suicide bombers quickly became a means of competition between the two groups for credibility, signaling a deep division within the Shiite community.[60] The disagreement erupted into an Amal-Hizballah war in the late 1980s, claiming the lives of approximately three thousand Lebanese.[61] Thus at the social/cultural level, it is impossible to speak of one definitive Shiite Islam in Lebanon when the suicide bombings began.

Suicide bombing became possible when organizations began using the symbols and rituals of Shiite Islam to legitimize themselves to the broader community and to exert control over their members. The leaders of Hizballah, like Musa al-Sadr before them, used public ritual and practice to win support for their interpretation of Islam. The dedication of Hizballah's individual fighters, demonstrated by their willingness to die for the cause, provided convincing evidence that Hizballah's was indeed the most authentic form of worship.[62] Then, the legitimacy that the organization gained from social acceptance allowed it to serve more effectively as a mediator between individual followers and the divine.

For the organization, martyrdom served as a two-way conduit for social and cultural support and also as a managerial tool for influencing the behavior of individual followers. As already noted, martyrdom held different meanings for individual members, forming a vital part of individuals' identities. Naim Qassem, a founding member of Hizballah and the organization's acting deputy secretary-general since the early 1980s, sums up the situation as follows: "[T]here are two fruits to the act of *jihad*: martyrdom *and* victory. The martyr wins martyrdom, while the nation and its freedom fighters win victory."[63] All three levels of technology practice—the social/cultural level (the Shiite community), the organizational level (Hizballah and its freedom fighters), and the technical level (the martyr)—are acknowledged in Naim's succinct statement, illustrating that even from the perspective of Hizballah officials, suicide bombing is a socially sanctioned process that transforms individuals into weapons. In this Hizballah established a model for organizing and managing a brutally effective form of attack that has been copied, modified, and used time and time again since the early 1980s.

Effective Technology

The need for an effective means to counter U.S. and Israeli military superiority must also be considered as a driving factor in the introduction of suicide bombing. During the Israeli invasion of 1982, the PLO possessed vastly greater conventional arms than did Hizballah, as did the Syrian air force, which was routed by Israel that summer. Of the three, however, Hizballah proved to be much more effective at resisting against the Israelis over the long run. The PLO and the Syrians failed because they engaged the Israelis on Israeli terms—that is, in open combat, force on force, system on system. The Israeli weapon systems had been designed to locate, target, and destroy exactly the kind of weapons that the PLO and the Syrians deployed. Thus their weapons were not just ineffective, they were counterproductive, indicating to the Israelis where they were located and providing the kind of targets that Israeli weapons were designed to seek out and destroy.

Hizballah's leaders recognized that they needed light, portable, easily concealable weapon systems.[64] Suicide bombers fulfilled all of these requirements. They became a uniquely effective and portable weapon guidance and control system that offered some of the benefits of the U.S. and Israeli high-tech systems but at the same time were undetectable by these systems. Hizballah therefore proved adept in its selection of appropriate technology.

Effectiveness rather than religious obligation drove the use of suicide bombing at the organizational level. In fact, the use of suicide attackers was theologically problematic as a means of resistance since Islamic law forbids suicide. Overcoming this prohibition required clerical authority as well as some substantial after-the-fact rationalization. A central figure in the "legalization" of suicide bombing was Ayatollah Sayyid Muhammad Husayn Fadlallah, perhaps the most respected senior Shiite cleric in Lebanon in the early 1980s. Although not a member of Hizballah, after some hesitation he endorsed the group's agenda, making him a key spiritual leader, or "oracle," of the organization.[65] In a series of interviews in summer 1985, Fadlallah sanctioned suicide attacks as being consistent with Shiite practice despite the prohibition on suicide. Rather than viewing "self-martyring operations" as intrinsic to the Shiite experience, Fadlallah legitimized them on practical grounds: "The self-martyring operation is not permitted unless it can convulse the enemy. The believer cannot blow himself up unless the results will equal or exceed the [loss of the] soul of [the] believer. Self-martyring operations are not fatal accidents but legal obligations governed by rules, and the believers cannot transgress the rules of God."[66] In short, Fadlallah asserted that the legitimacy of suicide bombing derived from its effectiveness. Thus it was a tool to be used in resisting the enemy and establishing Islamic rule, not an element of Islam itself.[67]

In 2005 Hizballah deputy secretary-general Qassem reiterated this rational, utilitarian justification for suicide missions. To him, martyrdom itself is not a sufficient goal. His understanding appears to differ significantly from that of individual believers for whom martyrdom is an affirmation of identity. He wrote, "Martyrdom alone does not achieve victory or tip the existing balance, and all other possible means should be used in the conflict. However, martyr operations fill a significant gap in the imbalance of powers."[68] Qassem insists that such operations should be used sparingly and only when necessary. They are to be well planned in advance so that they have a high probability of inflicting enemy casualties and therefore justifying the loss of the martyr.

No other technology available to militant groups has been able to solve the problems of guidance and detonation (and minimal detectability) in a single package with the elegance and simplicity of the suicide attacker. The vehicular-borne bombs of the early 1980s eliminated the challenges of planting or dropping off a concealed bomb and then safely withdrawing the operatives. In addition, the inertia of the moving vehicle made stopping the attack in its final stages nearly impossible. Marine Commandant Paul X. Kelley came under criticism from Congress after the Marine barracks bombing for the level of security at the base given that suicide bombers had already been used against the U.S. embassy in April. In particular, he was criticized because Marine guards' M-16s were kept unloaded while on sentry patrol. He responded with the pragmatic observation that an M-16 cannot stop a five-ton truck moving at thirty-five miles per hour, and regardless, at that point killing the driver would be insufficient.[69]

The suicide bombers of the early 1980s succeeded because they attacked the assumptions built into their adversaries' defenses as much as they attacked the physical defenses themselves. For example, the Marines in Beirut had been concentrated in the operations building because their commanders worried that dispersing them would make them more vulnerable to the sporadic, indirect fire that the base experienced on a regular basis. Concentrating the troops in one location may have solved this problem, but it made the operations building a perfect target for an alternative form of attack. The Department of Defense report that analyzed the attack of October 23 concluded, "From a terrorist perspective, the true genius of this attack is that the objective and the means of attack were beyond the imagination of those responsible for Marine security."[70]

In addition to invalidating the defensive assumptions of the enemy and providing tactical mission capabilities, suicide bombers also expanded the mental horizon of what was possible for groups such as Hizballah. Eliminating fear of death meant that suicide attackers and their organizations could not be deterred or intimidated by the superior firepower of their adversaries, no matter how overwhelming. They thus undermined another assumption of their adversaries—that modern weapon technologies would confer a psychological as well as a physical advantage upon their users. According to Fadlallah, this transformation was a "rebellion against fear" that allowed Hizballah's members to regard with contempt the high-tech weaponry brought to bear by Israel and the United States and to dismiss American and Israeli soldiers as cowards who hid in their machines.[71]

Management: The State Role

Examining only Hizballah is insufficient for understanding the dramatic suicide attacks of the early 1980s. The roles of Syria and especially Iran must be analyzed as well. The latter was so crucial to the emergence of suicide bombing that some directly credit Iran, rather than Hizballah, for the bombing of the U.S. embassy and the French and American contingents of the MNF. Hizballah has never directly claimed credit for the attacks, and it would be uncharacteristic of it not to venerate its suicide bombers if they had carried out such missions.[72] Former government and intelligence officials in particular assert that even at the time of the attacks, there was solid intelligence connecting the blasts to the Iranian government.[73] Although the fluidity and complexity of the relationship between Iran and the various Shiite groups in Lebanon makes discerning an unambiguous chain of responsibility problematic at best, there is circumstantial evidence favoring such an interpretation.

The three attacks are readily distinguishable from the other suicide bombings that occurred from 1981 to 1985: they required extraordinary intelligence and timing; they were larger scale than the other vehicular bombings; they were all claimed by a mysterious group, Islamic Jihad Organization; and the identities of the bombers were never publicly revealed.[74] Imad Mugniyah, one of the most shadowy and notorious figures to emerge during this time and the individual most responsible for planning IJO bombings, was a member of both Hizballah and Iran's Revolutionary Guards. He later lived in Tehran and Damascus.[75]

Based on the still incomplete empirical and circumstantial evidence it seems likely that the IJO-claimed bombings of 1983 were carried out by Iran, aided by Syrian intelligence and some assistance from Hizballah, and that the Iranian government wished to convey its responsibility, albeit obliquely. Had Iran's leaders wished to distance themselves from the attacks completely, they could certainly have recruited Lebanese drivers to deliver the bombs, revealed their identities, and credited the attacks to any of the various militant Shiite groups active at the time. Such a strategy, however, would not have allowed the United States to interpret the attacks as an Iranian challenge to U.S. power in the Middle East. On the other hand, revealing too direct a connection would have risked inviting military retaliation by the United States. It is likely, then, that Iran created the IJO as a front organization to differentiate these attacks from others carried out by Hizballah more directly and make Iran's role an open secret. In this way, Iran was able to send a clear message to the United States while avoiding retaliation.

These many years later, it is still difficult to say anything definitive about the Islamic Jihad Organization's role in the bombings.[76] Whatever assumptions one makes, however, Iran played a large role. Iran organized Lebanon's most militant Shiites, introduced them to suicide bombing, and supported these operations financially and logistically. Iranian leaders provided the legitimacy that many young Lebanese clerics sought and helped create the corporate body that integrated the very different Shiite groups of southern Lebanon and the Bekaa Valley into a formidable fighting force. Regardless of whether IJO was Iranian, Lebanese, or a mix of both, the attacks claimed by it could not have taken place without Iranian complicity.

Syria's President Asad was, at the time, Iran's primary ally in the Middle East owing to mutual need rather than ideological kinship. Asad's long-term agenda was to counter Israeli power in the Middle East. Asad therefore shared political goals with Iran despite the secular nature of his dictatorship and despite an ambivalent, and sometimes antagonistic, relationship with Hizballah. It is likely that Syria provided the intelligence that permitted the bombing of the U.S. embassy in April 1983 to be so devastating to the U.S. intelligence community. Syrian leaders had probably been tipped off by their Soviet allies about the CIA meeting and had provided this information to the Iranians.[77] Syria was also important in that all the secular militant groups that copied Hizballah's use of suicide bombing in the mid-1980s were under its influence.[78]

CONCLUSION

The systematic use of suicide attackers by Shiite groups and their imitators in Lebanon in the early 1980s is significant in that it marks the organizational appropriation of the type of violence with which Russian militants had unsystematically experimented a century earlier. It is clear from the post-hoc rationalizations of clerics associated with Hizballah and related groups that suicide bombing was not inherent in the Shiite tradition, but was introduced based on a sense of need and justified in terms of effectiveness. In 1985 Israeli forces withdrew to a narrow, fortified zone of occupation in southern Lebanon, making suicide missions against them more challenging. Since suicide missions could no longer be counted on to inflict significant casualties, Hizballah shifted away from their use and concentrated instead on becoming an effective guerrilla force.[79]

Declining effectiveness is only part of the explanation for Hizballah's reluctance to continue making use of the weapon that had brought it international notoriety. Its shift toward a more conventional guerrilla strategy is also consistent with a general trend toward moderation that since the early 1990s has transformed Hizballah into a dominant actor in Lebanese politics and a reliable provider of social services to many of Lebanon's Shiites.[80] Its shift is also indicative of the challenge that subordinating individual self-sacrifice to organizational needs poses to a group that seeks the authenticity of martyrdom but does not wish to be seen as being coercive or manipulative of its followers.

Hizballah's efforts in this regard were only partially successful. Fadlallah, in particular, justified suicide attacks by arguing that the Shiite community had no choice but to resort to extraordinary means to defend itself from the weapons of the United States and Israel. He was able to clear suicide attackers of the stigma of suicide, however, only by taking the opposite position—that the attacks were *not* exceptional and that the deaths of the bombers were not different from ordinary battlefield deaths, which of course clashed with the imagery of heroism and martyrdom through which suicide bombers were commemorated.[81] Hizballah leaders, therefore, were never able to reconcile fully the altruism of self-sacrifice—the strategic dimension of martyrdom—with the organizational self-interest that drove the tactical use of suicide bombers. The group has used them only sparingly, and not at all since 1999. Nevertheless, martyrdom and the implied threat of resumed suicide attacks have continued to characterize Hizballah's rhetoric, perhaps because the organization has been prudent in the use of its "martyrs" and has not diluted their demonstrative power or their prestige within the organization's history.

3

MARTYRDOM AND CONTROL

The Reinvention of Suicide Bombing by
the Liberation Tigers of Tamil Eelam

On the evening of May 21, 1991, former Indian prime minister Rajiv Gandhi was campaigning on behalf of the Congress Party in the town of Sriperumbudour, near the city of Madras (since renamed Chennai), the capital of the Indian state of Tamil Nadu. An enthusiastic crowd had gathered to hear him speak in the shadow of a statue of his mother, Indira Gandhi, who while serving as prime minister had been assassinated by two of her Sikh bodyguards in 1984 in a revenge shooting. Rajiv Gandhi was mobbed by his supporters, many of whom hoped to honor him by placing a garland of flowers around his neck. One woman in particular struggled forward and was temporarily restrained by a police officer. Gandhi asked the officer to relax, and she allowed the young woman to approach Gandhi, ostensibly to garland him. The woman dropped the garland, however, and bent down to retrieve it. At this point she was close enough to touch Gandhi's feet. She then triggered the explosive belt she was wearing around her waist. The blast killed Gandhi and his assassin as well as nine police officers and seven civilians. In the months after the assassination, there was some confusion about who had been responsible for it, but today the attack is credited to the Liberation Tigers of Tamil Eelam (LTTE), a guerrilla organization that until its defeat in spring 2009 was the most violent and uncompromising advocate of a separate state for the Tamil people of Sri Lanka.[1]

Rajiv Gandhi's assassination represented a watershed in the history of suicide bombing for several reasons. First, Gandhi was the most significant political figure to be killed by a suicide bomber since Alexander II's death 110 years prior. He was a former prime minister, son of a prime minister, and grandson of Jawaharlal Nehru, the first prime minister of independent India. He was also the head of India's Congress Party, at the time of his death the most prominent party in the country. Second, the professionalism involved in the attack's execution was extraordinary, equaling the sophistication, if not the overall power, of the Beirut blasts of the early 1980s. Investigations revealed that Gandhi's murderer, a young woman known as Dhanu, had been part of a team of five members that had planned and trained elaborately to carry out the attack. The team had included another woman who served as a backup bomber in case Dhanu proved to be unreliable. The dedication of the members of the organization was also stunning. In the months following the attack, nine LTTE members committed suicide rather than submit to incarceration by Indian authorities in connection with the investigation. Third, one member of the team sent to kill Gandhi was a photographer tasked with documenting the attack for propaganda purposes.[2] He was killed by the blast and his camera was damaged, but the film proved salvageable. The photos provide chilling images of the last few seconds of Rajiv Gandhi's life.

During the 1990s the Liberation Tigers of Tamil Eelam came to be known as the masters of suicide bombing.[3] The LTTE made use of the truck bomb associated with the Middle East, pioneered the use of the suicide belt for more precise missions (such as assassinations), and made extensive use of boat-borne suicide bombers as "smart torpedoes" in its war against the Sri Lankan navy.[4] There is, however, considerable disagreement regarding the number of LTTE suicide bombings. The LTTE and its Black Tigers, the division from which the suicide bombers were drawn, wished to portray themselves as a military force and usually did not claim their attacks against civilian targets. They therefore denied responsibility for many of the operations attributed to them by Sri Lankan authorities.[5] In addition, the willingness of LTTE members to commit suicide to evade capture muddies the picture somewhat. In most instances, LTTE members killed themselves by swallowing cyanide, but there were some exceptions. For example, in March 2000 Sri Lankan forces surrounded four LTTE members after a failed guerrilla attack on a government motorcade. Rather than submit to capture, the four attackers committed suicide by blowing themselves up.[6] In a sense, it was a suicide bombing, but classifying it as a suicide operation, like the one that killed Rajiv Gandhi, would be inappropriate given that neither the bombers nor the organization planned for the attack to be a suicide bombing.

Although it is problematic to assess the exact number of suicide attacks carried out by the LTTE, the figure is undoubtedly high. Ami Pedahzur had identified 86 successful suicide attacks through 2004. The Worldwide Incidents Tracking System (WITS), the U.S. National Counterterrorism Center's database, recorded an additional 23 LTTE suicide attacks between 2005 and the defeat of the organization in 2009, for a total of 109 between 1987 and 2009.[7]

One of the most striking characteristics of the LTTE's use of suicide attackers is how constant it remained during the course of the nearly two decades that it utilized them. While suicide bombing in the rest of the world became subject to increasingly decentralized control, LTTE suicide bombing remained under the strict control of Vellupillai Prabhakaran, the group's leader. Prabhakaran's role in directing LTTE suicide bombing demonstrates that in technological systems, users matter. They play the obvious role of selecting and developing specific technological solutions in lieu of others, of course, but they also transform specific technologies through *how* they choose to use them. The realm of use has historically driven change and evolution in technology so that even technologies that have common origins and material components will demonstrate significant differences when employed by different cultures.[8]

Prabhakaran chose to develop and then use suicide attackers for his own reasons, some of which were consistent with suicide bombing in other contexts, the tactical effectiveness of suicide bombers, for example, accounting for some similarities. His agenda, however, was significantly different from that of Hizballah leaders and the Russian revolutionaries in that he endeavored to create a cult of personality and charismatic leadership to dominate the Tamil political scene. Suicide bombing proved to be effective for furthering this agenda as well.

BACKGROUND

"Resplendent Island"

The largest ethnic group on the island of Sri Lanka is the Sinhalese, who constituted approximately 74 percent of the population, estimated at 5.5 million, in 2006. The Sinhalese have their own language and tend to be Buddhist. The next largest group, the Tamils, who tend to be Hindu, comprises approximately 16 percent of the population. The Tamils fall into two categories. The larger of the two, Sri Lankan Tamils, 10 percent of all Sri Lankans, live primarily along the eastern and northern shores of the island. Their connection to the island dates back thousands of years. Members of the other group, the plantation Tamils (6 percent of the population), are more recent arrivals, having immigrated from India in the last two centuries to serve as agricultural laborers on plantations in the elevated middle sections of the island. The other major ethnic group, Muslims, makes up approximately 10 percent of the population.[9]

The Portuguese first colonized Sri Lanka, followed by the Dutch, and then the British. It became an independent state only in 1948. Early in the twentieth century, British colonial policy favored the Tamil minority, who held a disproportionate share of government positions. Upon independence, the Sinhalese sought to redress the situation, but what ensued was a systematic policy of reverse discrimination that eventually left large numbers of Tamils disenfranchised and disadvantaged.[10] In 1956 the Sinhalese-majority government passed an act decreeing Sinhalese to be the only recognized language on the island. After protest and dissent, the act was amended, in 1958, and Tamil was allowed to be used in the northern and eastern parts of Sri Lanka; elsewhere, however, Sinhalese remained the official language. Language thus became a means of discrimination, resulting in the systematic loss of government jobs by Tamils. A quota system instituted at the university level limited Tamil enrollment. This led to increasing unemployment among Tamils through the 1970s.[11]

On May 22, 1972, the Sri Lankan government introduced a new constitution, which established Buddhism as the state religion and Sinhalese as the only recognized state language. The country's name was changed from Ceylon, which had been its name since independence, to Sri Lanka, which is Sinhalese for "resplendent island." The constitution had relatively weak provisions for the protection of minority rights, and Tamils worried that the centrality of Buddhism in the constitution would encourage and reinforce the discrimination they were already experiencing. The constitution immediately provoked an organized Tamil reaction, with four Tamil political groups forming the Tamil United Front (TUF), a coalition that observed May 22 as a day of mourning. In autumn the TUF called for a campaign of political action against the government. On October 3 the leader of the TUF resigned from the national assembly to protest the treatment of Sri Lanka's Tamils under the constitution. In May 1973 the TUF officially decided to push for an independent Tamil state, to be known as Tamil Eelam.

The Origins of Tamil Militancy and the LTTE

Tamil youth, who watched their employment and educational opportunities dwindle, became increasingly frustrated with the inability of Tamil politicians to convince the government to address their community's issues.[12] As the decade wore on, they became more radical and created underground groups that became increasingly violent. Numerous armed gangs claiming to be politically motivated formed, but most of them quickly dissolved. Only five such organizations proved to be effective and durable enough to last for more than a couple of years.

The first paramilitary organization to emerge was the Tamil Eelam Liberation Organization (TELO) in 1974. The following year it was followed by the Eelam Revolutionary Organization of Students (EROS). One of the members of the Tamil United Front of 1972 had been a student organization called the Tamil Students League. In 1973–74 this organization became more radical and began calling itself the Tamil New Tigers. Its founder was arrested in 1975, after which the organization fell under the sway of Vellupillai Prabhakaran, who in 1976 changed the name of the organization to the Liberation Tigers of Tamil Eelam. In 1979 the People's Liberation Organization of Tamil Eelam (PLOTE and sometimes

PLOT) formed when an LTTE leader split with Prabhakaran.[13] The fifth group, the Eelam People's Revolutionary Liberation Front (EPRL), made its debut in 1980.

Of the five groups, the Tamil New Tigers/LTTE were the most militant and least ideological. From the start, the Tamil New Tigers distinguished themselves through their use of assassination; indeed, Prabhakaran rose to prominence within the group when he murdered the mayor of the city of Jaffna, Alfred Duraiappah, a Tamil, in July 1975. Tamil extremists viewed Duraiappah as a traitor because he did not support the secessionist movement. The following March, Prabhakaran led a successful bank robbery to raise funds for the group. In May 1976 he formally announced the existence of the LTTE, writing the group's constitution and designing its tiger logo. The LTTE set up a self-supporting training camp in the jungles of the north and by mid-1976 was established well enough that its members began attacking the Jaffna police network. In the first half of 1977, they killed four police officers, one of whom was a detective investigating the murder of Mayor Duraiappah.[14]

The following August deadly anti-Tamil riots broke out in the Jaffna peninsula in the north and quickly spread; hundreds of Tamils were killed or displaced. In many cases, the police and military contributed to the violence instead of acting as impartial supporters of law and order. The government, unconstrained by any effective opposition, became increasingly authoritarian, and in 1979, in response to the violence of Tamil separatists, such as the LTTE, passed the Prevention of Terrorism Act (PTA). The act, which was applied retroactively to offenses committed prior to 1979, permitted the army and police to hold prisoners incommunicado and without charge for up to eighteen months. Since there was no registry of detainees, and arrests were not subject to judicial review, the act stripped citizens of constitutional rights and weakened prohibitions against arbitrary killings and arrests. Authorities promptly abused the powers allotted by the act, conducting widespread arrests and detentions of Tamil civilians.[15] In summer 1981 violence intensified. That June, a policeman was killed in a conflict with the LTTE, and in response, civilians in complicity with the local police went on a rampage in Jaffna, looting and destroying Tamil property.[16]

Eelam War I

On the night of July 23–24, 1983, LTTE leaders dramatically escalated the scale of their violent activities by ambushing a Sri Lankan military convoy and killing thirteen soldiers.[17] Newspaper headlines and other coverage of the soldiers' funeral enraged many Sinhalese, who then launched what can only be described as a pogrom against their Tamil neighbors, killing approximately 2,000 Tamils in late July and early August. The character of the violence was particularly brutal; many of the Tamils were beaten or hacked to death, while others were burned alive in their homes or shops. More far-reaching was the refugee problem that followed the assault. More than 175,000 Tamils were displaced by the violence. In the city of Colombo alone, about 100,000 Tamils were driven from their homes. On July 25 thirty-five Tamil political detainees at Welikade prison were murdered by fellow prisoners with the complicity of prison guards.[18]

The violence against the Tamils suggested a high degree of government complicity. Seemingly disorganized mobs possessed information about the location of Tamil-owned factories, businesses, and shops. Furthermore, during the first days of the violence, the government and military made little effort to intervene, showed no sympathy for the victims of the violence, and afterward made no effort to compensate Tamil civilians for their losses or bring the perpetrators to justice. Lacking democratic options for changing the situation, Tamils began to analyze the conflict in racial and existential terms. Thus summer 1983 can rightly be considered the point at which Sri Lanka descended into civil war, a period which the LTTE referred to as Eelam War I.

In August 1983 the government passed the Sixth Amendment to the constitution, requiring parliamentarians to swear allegiance to Sri Lanka and to condemn any form of separatism. This led the TUF to boycott parliament and therefore closed off political reconciliation, contributing to the appeal of the radicals.[19] In Tamil regions, men between the ages of fifteen and thirty were subject to mass arrests, which often resulted not only in torture but in large-scale disappearances, as extrajudicial killings on the part of the authorities became commonplace. The LTTE and other militant groups then began to massacre Sinhalese civilians as retribution. Attributing specific atrocities to any one of the many militant Tamil groups is problematic, but the LTTE was likely responsible for civilian massacres in November 1984 and May 1985 in which 70 and 150 persons died, respectively.[20]

In 1985 Prabhakaran reluctantly joined with leaders of other Tamil resistance groups and participated in talks with the Sri Lankan government in Thinpu, Bhutan.[21] The talks quickly broke down, and in the aftermath the LTTE pursued its own version of Eelam more brutally than ever, targeting political and military rivals in the Tamil community and at the same time escalating its attacks against the Sri Lankan state. On April 17, 1987, LTTE militants stopped three buses, singled out Sinhalese riders, and murdered all 127 of them. Four days later, they detonated a massive bomb in Colombo that killed 113 people.[22] By this point, the LTTE was considered the most dangerous group in the Tamil insurgency.

Predatory Rationalization

The LTTE's growth came at the expense of its rivals, in a literal sense. It was initially a minor player in the very crowded field of Tamil militancy. The LTTE had begun Eelam War I as one of dozens of militant groups. Rohan Gunaratna counted thirty-six of them in the early 1980s. The LTTE's small size, some twenty-five to fifty members, combined with the youth of its leadership (Prabhakaran had not even turned thirty when Eelam War I began) led security officials to refer to the group condescendingly as "the boys."[23] Prabhakaran recognized that to make his personal vision of Tamil Eelam a reality, the LTTE had to compete not only with the Sri Lankan state but also with other Tamil militants. In late 1985 Prabhakaran decided to eliminate LTTE's major Tamil rivals. This approach allowed the LTTE to expand its geographical base and to distinguish itself through sheer brutality and determination.

In April 1986 the LTTE attacked the Tamil Eelam Liberation Organization, killing hundreds of its members, including its leader, Sri Sabaratnam. In December it killed more than one hundred members of the Eelam People's Revolutionary Liberation Front. In September 1987 a third wave of LTTE bloodshed eliminated more than seventy members of rival groups, including PLOT. The strategy, which one author refers to as predatory rationalization, did indeed simplify the Tamil political scene, leaving the LTTE as the most dominant organization.[24] It was a rational strategy insofar as it secured the political marketplace for the LTTE, but it also had a devastating impact on the Tamil community by weakening its independence movement as a whole.

Tamil groups were not the only to suffer at the hands of the LTTE. As early as 1983 the LTTE was using violence against the Tamil community more generally to intimidate moderates and prevent them from pursuing less radical means of resistance. It executed such "traitors" and then displayed their bodies publicly, often with signs declaring that this was the punishment awaiting all traitors. As the LTTE gained control of territory in the north in the later 1980s, it infiltrated every layer of local governance and carried out the type of routine political killings characteristic of the most brutal police states.[25] When a group of academics from Jaffna University published a critique of the LTTE, one of them, Rajani Thirinigama, was assassinated; the others fled to Colombo.[26] By 2000 Tamils in LTTE-controlled areas were sufficiently intimidated that the organization no longer needed to use violence to impose its will. As one respondent to an academic study explained, "People know what the LTTE is capable of. Violence is not necessary."[27]

Discipline and Cyanide

The willingness of the LTTE to use such violence against members of its own ethnic community demonstrates an extraordinary degree of ruthlessness and discipline, characteristics that can be traced to Vellupillai Prabhakaran. Born in 1954, Prabhakaran was the son of a tax official. He was extremely young when he entered the militant movement, and left his family to flee a police crackdown in 1972, at the age of eighteen. From that point until his death in 2009, Prabhakaran lived essentially on the run. He had no formal military or academic training. Most of his knowledge—from Tamil history and culture to practical issues of weapon use and leadership—he taught himself.[28]

Prabhakaran credited his success to self-discipline. He suffered innumerable hardships along with his followers and always adhered to a strict moral and ethical code within the context of the movement. He did not smoke or drink, and he prohibited his followers from indulging in them as well, going so far as to write moral guidelines into the organization's 1976 constitution. Prabhakaran's moral strictness struck even some of his most ardent supporters as being excessive.[29] There was, however, a purpose to this thoroughgoing effort to control the behavior of his followers.

The LTTE had been a small outfit in its infancy, so the need to overtake other militants and to deal with the threat of police informers meant that any factionalism or dissent within the group would pose significant long-term risks. Prabhakaran therefore eliminated potential dissent by placing himself at the heart of the group and at the center of the Tamil national movement. He required members to pledge allegiance to him personally and subjected them to the harshest of disciplinary measures. LTTE members who committed serious transgressions of the group's rules were executed. This combination of fear and respect drove the group's core toward an unwavering commitment to Prabhakaran.

The most dramatic and visible symbol of dedication was introduced to the group in 1984 in the form of a small glass vial of potassium cyanide, which LTTE cadres received when they formally joined the group and swore allegiance to Prabhakaran. The use of cyanide was inspired by Sivakumaran, one of the heroes of Prabhakaran's youth. Sivakumaran, a member of the Tamil Student Federation, had swallowed cyanide rather than submit to arrest in the early 1970s.[30] There seems to be no earlier evidence of such a form of self-sacrifice in Tamil lore and history. The acceptance of the cyanide vial on the part of a prospective LTTE member quickly became a mark of distinction because it proclaimed the recruit's willingness to die rather than betray the organization or its leader. The first cyanide "martyr" acknowledged by the LTTE took his own life in May 1984.[31]

From its introduction, the distribution of cyanide to new LTTE members served several practical purposes. The pledge to commit suicide rather than submit to torture and interrogation by Sri Lankan authorities helped to decrease the likelihood that members might compromise the organization; it therefore contributed to group security over the long run. As a physical reminder of death, the presence of the vial of cyanide suspended around the neck helped recruits overcome their fear of death, thus contributing to their bravery in battle. By July 1988 a Sri Lankan newspaper reported that two hundred Tamils had already achieved "martyrdom" by taking cyanide.[32]

Indian Intervention

Much of the population of the Indian state of Tamil Nadu, located eighteen miles across the Palk Strait from Sri Lanka, is ethnically similar to the Sri Lankan Tamils, and so Tamil Nadu became a source of regular support and encouragement for the Tamil independence movement in Sri Lanka. The size of Tamil Nadu's population also made it a vital pillar of support for India's Congress Party, and in the early 1980s Prime Minister Indira Gandhi began to support the Tamil independence movement covertly. After the anti-Tamil violence in 1983, this support became more overt, with hundreds of Tamil guerrillas from various groups training in India every year.[33]

As internecine violence weakened the Tamil secessionist movement in 1987, the Sri Lankan armed forces launched Operation Liberation, a campaign to reassert governmental control in Tamil lands. Despite a number of deficiencies, the Sri Lankan army was clearly superior to the poorly coordinated forces of the rebels; it encountered little resistance during the operation, which lasted from May 26 to June 10. Rajiv Gandhi, who had succeeded his mother as Indian prime minister, reacted angrily toward what he described as brutality in the suppression of the Tamil independence movement. On June 4, before the end of Operation Liberation, the Indian air force dropped supplies to the Tamils in a violation of Sri Lankan sovereignty and airspace.[34] Shortly afterward India sent ships loaded with humanitarian supplies to relieve the Tamil population.

The initiation of Indian intervention ended Operation Liberation. By the end of July, Gandhi's government had produced an accord to reconcile the warring factions and had assumed responsibility for enforcing it, a position that would appease Indian supporters of the Tamil movement and also give India a measure of control over the Sri Lankan Tamils. The Indian Peacekeeping Force (IPKF) became responsible, among other things, for disarming Tamil militant groups, especially the LTTE, which had always been far more independent of India than the others. Large numbers of Tamil civilians were favorably disposed toward the IPKF, hoping that it would put an end to the conflict. On the other hand, many Sinhalese were appalled by India's military intervention in their internal affairs.[35]

Prabhakaran, unwilling to concede political power over the Tamil community to anyone, viewed the occupation warily from the beginning. He made an initial show of supporting the occupation and handing over arms, even going so far as to claim that the LTTE could resort to nonviolent tactics if necessary; it soon became clear, however, that the LTTE was withholding the bulk of its arsenal.[36] Indian leaders were wary of the LTTE and pressured it more aggressively than they did any of the other Tamil groups, going so far as to fly Prabhakaran and several other LTTE leaders to India to try to persuade them to accept the accord. After returning to Sri Lanka in early August, Prabhakaran denounced the agreement. In protest, the LTTE's Amirthalingam Thileepan began a fast unto death, refusing food and water beginning in mid-September. He died on September 26, 1987, making him the first Tamil martyr in the struggle against India.[37]

The following month, seventeen LTTE members captured by India were scheduled for deportation and questioning. Prabhakaran apparently had cyanide smuggled in to the prisoners, and all seventeen attempted to commit suicide. Twelve died immediately, three others succumbed soon thereafter, and two survived because of medical intervention.[38] This mass suicide triggered full-scale warfare between the LTTE and the IPKF, which held advantages in equipment and numbers of troops but was utterly unprepared to fight the kind of guerrilla war at which the LTTE was beginning to excel.

The ongoing conflict between the LTTE and the IPKF took the lives of more than a thousand Indian soldiers and was thus deeply unpopular in India. At the same time, it fueled Sinhalese anger toward the occupation and the curtailment of Sri Lankan sovereignty that it represented. The leaders who had negotiated the accord, Rajiv Gandhi and Sri Lankan president J. R. Jayewaredene, had both left office by 1989. Their successors were not politically invested in the accord, and the new Sri Lankan president, Ranasinghe Premadasa, demanded the evacuation of the IPKF. In 1989 the LTTE and the Sri Lankan government negotiated a cease-fire, removing justification for the Indian presence. In 1989 the IPKF began a phased withdrawal that was completed in early 1990.[39]

THE DEVELOPMENT OF SUICIDE BOMBING BY THE LTTE

Captain Miller

The LTTE's first suicide attack occurred in July 1987. During the course of Operation Liberation, Sri Lankan forces had taken control of a school building near the town of Nelliady, in Tamil territory, and had made it into a temporary military base. On July 5 the Tigers launched a mission to retake it. The building was heavily reinforced and protected by barbed-wire barriers, making the operation a challenge. One Tiger, twenty-one-year-old Vallipuram Vasanthan—a local man more commonly remembered by the name Captain Miller (sometimes spelled Millar)—volunteered for the mission, agreeing to drive a vehicular bomb into the heart of the defenses.[40] Miller's comrades packed a truck with explosives and then attached the young man to the controls of the vehicle, tying his hands to the steering wheel and one of his feet to the accelerator. They used sticks to wedge his body into the driver's seat so that he could not move even if he wanted to or even if killed. According to one account, Prabhakaran was present during the preparation and gave the signal for the attack to proceed. Other LTTE members then started the truck and moved away.

Miller was quite possibly dead shortly after the truck cleared the first set of barricades and the defenders opened fire; it did not, however, matter. The truck continued forward, rammed the main building, and exploded. Miller's companions quickly followed up his attack with a conventional military assault, and the outpost was taken. Casualty figures vary, but twenty to forty Sri Lankan defenders were killed, and at least twenty more were injured in the blast and ensuing attack.[41] LTTE members videotaped the incident for recruitment and propaganda purposes.

Miller posthumously received a promotion to the rank of captain and is remembered as one of the most respected and revered martyrs in LTTE lore. His face became the insignia for the Black Tigers, a new LTTE division from whose ranks the suicide bombers of the 1990s and 2000s would be drawn. In addition, July 5 became a holiday, Black Tigers Day, celebrated every year to commemorate Miller's sacrifice. On the fifteenth anniversary of the attack, the LTTE unveiled a statue of Captain Miller, flashing a victory sign with his right hand, near the site of the crumbling, but still standing, school building.[42]

Eelam War II and Beyond

Shortly after the Indian withdrawal, the rapprochement between the Sri Lankan government and the LTTE ended, with the LTTE resuming attacks against Sri Lankan forces in June 1990. This marked the beginning of what the LTTE called Eelam War II. The early stages of this renewed conflict were reminiscent of previous LTTE campaigns, with ambushes and assassinations of Sri Lankan and rival Tamil figures prominent among the operations.

The group began its systematic use of suicide bombers almost immediately upon launching Eelam War II, with an attack on a naval vessel on July 10. Some doubt remains as to whether the mission was a deliberate suicide attack. In November 1990 the LTTE used a suicide truck bomber to spearhead an assault on a Sri Lankan military facility. By the end of the year, the Black Tigers had been recognized as a new and dangerous force. Six months later, LTTE suicide bombers would assassinate Rajiv Gandhi.

In 1992 the LTTE used an individual suicide bomber to assassinate Vice Adm. Clancy Fernando of the Sri Lankan navy.[43] In May 1993 the LTTE dispatched a suicide bomber to carry out another bold mission—President Premadasa's murder, which would put the group in the exclusive company of the People's Will as being the only two organizations to have assassinated a sitting head of government in a suicide attack. The mission demonstrated the LTTE's patience and the dedication of its individual members. It took approximately two years for the assigned bomber to infiltrate the president's circle, which he accomplished by befriending a Tamil member of his personal staff. Despite the would-be bomber's two years of relative autonomy, he showed no hesitation when called upon to take his own life. Twenty-three other people died in the attack.[44]

Suicide bombers came to be a regular component of Eelam War II and the next phases of the conflict, Eelam War III and Eelam War IV. Suicide attackers were often used for individual assassinations, such as those discussed above, but they were also deployed in conjunction with conventional military operations. Although the LTTE did not claim mass-casualty suicide attacks against civilians, these too became a regular part of the fighting. After a brief cease-fire in 1995, the Sri Lankan army went on the offensive, capturing the city of Jaffna by the end of the year. On January 31, 1996, the LTTE responded with its most destructive suicide attack to date, when an LTTE member drove a truck packed with explosives into the central bank building in Colombo, killing ninety people and injuring more than a thousand.[45] On December 18, 1999, an LTTE suicide attacker attempted to assassinate Sri Lankan president Chandrika Kumaratunga as she campaigned for reelection. Kumaratunga survived, but was severely injured and permanently lost sight in one eye; twenty-one people died in the attack.[46] In a stunning assault on October 15, 2006, an LTTE suicide bomber drove a truck bomb into a convoy of Sri Lankan military buses, killing himself along with 103 military personnel and injuring another 150. Thirteen buses were damaged or destroyed, and the body of the driver was found 160 feet away from the scene of the explosion.[47] The attack ended another cease-fire, in effect since 2004, and ushered in the final phase of the conflict, which ended with the LTTE's defeat in 2009.

The LTTE also used suicide attackers in its ongoing campaign against Tamil rivals. On May 29, 1999, one of its suicide attackers killed the leader of a rival Tamil group cooperating with the Sri Lankan military.[48] On July 29 an LTTE operative assassinated Neelan Tiruchelvam, a moderate Tamil politician and vice president of the Tamil United Liberation Front (TULF). The bomber, on foot, approached within a few feet of Tiruchelvam's car, which was stopped in heavy traffic in Colombo, and detonated himself. Tiruchelvam's driver and the security officer in the car with him survived the attack.[49]

Management: Training the Tigers

The exact date at which the Black Tigers came into being as an organized unit is unclear. Since Captain Miller's face became the insignia for the group, and he is considered to be the first Black Tiger, his death was obviously a foundational event. Observers had begun to write about the Black Tigers by 1988–89, but it was not until the assassination of Rajiv Gandhi, in 1991, that Prabhakaran discussed the group publicly.[50]

The size of the Black Tigers was a closely guarded secret, but it is clear that membership was a mark of distinction. Within the LTTE, cadres competed with one another for the honor of membership in the elite unit, and their training was intense.[51] The extensive preparation of the Black Tigers stands in marked contrast to the workings of many other organizations that utilize suicide attackers; typically, they see their prospective bombers as being expendable and therefore invest minimal resources in their training.

The LTTE also made extensive use of female suicide attackers, sometimes called the Black Tigresses and sometimes the Freedom Birds, beginning in the early 1990s. The initial women's unit was formed in the 1980s. Women had become a significant percentage of the overall strength of the LTTE long before they were used for suicide missions. While there is debate over the percentage of women within the LTTE at large, and specifically within the elite corps, the number was undoubtedly significant. Female attackers contributed to the capabilities of the LTTE as well as to its overall legitimacy by suggesting that the group was more open to gender equality than was Tamil society writ large.[52]

The reliability demonstrated by Black Tigers was the product of an extensive program of training and indoctrination that led to active competition among members for positions of prestige within the organization. By all accounts, life for LTTE cadres was intense and harsh. They endured great physical hardship, with few if any material comforts to offset the severity of their training. In such an environment, honor and prestige were among the few desirable commodities. Within the LTTE this mindset became so powerful that Black Tigers confessed that they feared failing Prabhakaran and dishonoring themselves more than they feared dying. To cement their commitment to their missions, prospective bombers met with Prabhakaran and posed for a photo with him shortly before departing.[53] This element of ritual was comparable to the production of videotaped testimonials by Lebanese suicide attackers and can be thought of as a form of public contract obligating the individual to follow through with the attack.

Perceived Need and Possibility: Building the Faith

One reason that suicide attackers were introduced effectively into the Tamil struggle was the reality that the LTTE faced significant disadvantages in confronting the Sri Lankan army. Although the disparity in arms was not as great as the disparity between Israeli forces and the Shiites in 1980s Lebanon, the Sri Lankan army in the 1990s possessed significant advantages over the LTTE in terms of armor and airpower. Most important, the behavior of the Sri Lankan forces allowed the Tamil minority to perceive the conflict in existential rather than political terms. Even Tamil opponents of the LTTE described the violence of the 1980s in terms of genocide and holocaust.[54] It was therefore relatively easy for Prabhakaran to frame the conflict in these terms, claiming in his 1995 Great Heroes' Day speech, "This war is not, as the government claims, against the LTTE. This war is against the Tamil people, against the Tamil Nation. The objective of this war is to destroy the Tamil Nation. This racist war of Sinhala chauvinism has a long history."[55] While exaggerated, the actual policy of the Sri Lankan government provided sufficient credibility to Prabhakaran's rhetoric that it resonated with much of the Tamil population. The extremity of the situation thus legitimized the extremity of the LTTE's response.

The veneration of Captain Miller and his Black Tiger successors within the LTTE was but one facet of a much larger, systematic effort on the part of Prabhakaran to intensify group discipline and dedication to prepare the group for the pursuit of Tamil Eelam following the withdrawal of the IPKF. Central to this transformation was Prabhakaran's success in fashioning the LTTE and the idea of Tamil Eelam as a secular faith.[56] As Peter Schalk notes, the LTTE became "a political movement with religious aspirations," sacralized by the blood sacrifice of its members. Prabhakaran took the willingness of his followers to die, even to kill themselves, and turned it into social capital that held the organization together. The LTTE created holidays and rituals within the subculture of the organization based on the veneration of martyrs. This work was the responsibility of the Office of Great Heroes in Jaffna, a division established exclusively for the manufacture of symbolism and ritual.[57]

The LTTE calendar was divided into five intervals punctuated by holidays created to commemorate the LTTE dead. The primary LTTE holiday, Great Heroes' Day, was established on November 27, 1989, in memory of the movement's first official martyr, a young fighter named Lt. Shankar. Over the years this celebration became longer and more elaborate, until by the end of the 1990s it had become a week-long festival of events culminating at 6 p.m. on the evening of November 27 with LTTE family members gathering around cemeteries and war memorials while ceremonial bells toll throughout LTTE-controlled territory.[58] July 5, the date of Miller's attack, became another holiday, and the deaths of LTTE hunger strikers were commemorated as well.

In English language translations of Prabhakaran's speeches and other LTTE official propaganda, the term "martyr" was consistently used when referencing LTTE dead. Native English speakers sympathetic to the movement also preferred this word. According to Schalk's analysis, the word "tiyakam," which the LTTE chose for its suicide attackers, is more subtle, reflecting the characteristics of classical martyrdom as well as the practical implications of tactical martyrdom.[59] "Tiyakam" means abandonment of life, in this case, the voluntary abandonment of life. Those who make this sacrifice are referred to as "tiyaki." LTTE culture emphasized that the tiyaki die representational deaths for the people of Tamil Eelam, but there is another dimension to tiyakam. Schalk argues that it is a specific *kind* of death—the abandonment of life in the act of taking life, that is, dying while killing.

Even before the end of the Indian occupation, the LTTE occupied much of the Jaffna peninsula. Its control of the territory allowed the LTTE to build the physical infrastructure of martyrdom, immortality, and transcendence in the form of its own cemeteries and shrines. In doing so, the LTTE created a secular form of resurrection by substituting ritualized burial of dead martyrs for the more traditional Hindu custom of cremation. The Office of Great Heroes proclaimed that the bodies of martyrs were not corpses, but seeds to be planted in anticipation of the establishment of Eelam. The LTTE then turned the graves into shrines for its secular martyrs, establishing the dead as having an ongoing presence among the living. LTTE martyrs were thus offered symbolic immortality in the form of ritualized remembrance, but some took this symbolic immortality literally, believing that the cause was the path to immortality. In 1995 the LTTE took the process of burying martyrs away from family members and made it an organizational function, mandating that LTTE dead be interred in the LTTE's cemeteries and that memorial services be performed by the LTTE irrespective of the families' wishes. LTTE ritual thus supplanted tradition and custom in the treatment and remembrance of the dead.[60]

Prabhakaran drew attention to the transcendence of the LTTE's dead during his Great Heroes' Day speeches. In 1993 he declared, "From the tombs of the dead martyrs who lie in rest in the womb of our soil rises the cry for freedom. This cry for freedom is the articulation of the will and determination of more than 6000 martyrs which underlie the motive force behind our struggle." In 1997, when he condemned the destruction of LTTE cemeteries after the reconquest of Jaffna city by Sri Lankan forces, Prabhakaran charged, "The enemy forces committed the unpardonable crime of desecration, disrupting the spiritual tranquility of our martyrs. Their war cemeteries underwent wanton destruction, their tomb-stones up-rooted and flattened and their memorials erased without a trace. I call this act of desecration of the graves of martyrs whom the Tamils venerate as their national heroes as wicked, immoral, and uncivilized. . . . This is a grave act of terrorism which has left an indelible stain in the soul of the Tamil nation."[61]

Prabhakaran took pains to emphasize that the LTTE was not a religion, so as not to offend the sensibilities of the different religious traditions represented through its membership and also to serve as a contrast to the Buddhist chauvinism of the Sri Lankan forces.[62] He was careful to portray the LTTE in the terms of the moderate socialism typical of revolutionary movements in the 1970s, arguing that Tamil Eelam would be a politically neutral state that would provide social justice for all. The vaguely leftist, secular ideology of the LTTE convinced some analysts that the LTTE's use of suicide bombers was different from their use by religious groups, like Hizballah.[63] The underlying assumption in this case is that the secular and the sacred are somehow mutually incompatible with one another.

Such an assumption is based on a very narrow understanding of nationalism, faith, and the transcendent. Nationalism emerged first as a religious collective identity that differentiated the national monarchies of England, Spain, and France well before the secular nationalism of the post-Enlightenment era.[64] As the nineteenth century passed, more and more states consciously used nationalism as a form of faith tradition to bind their members together irrespective of social class and set them apart from national rivals.[65] Dale van Kley has described this phenomenon as a kind of "conservation of the sacred." By this he meant that as

Western Europe entered a more secular era, sacred values did not disappear but instead were transferred to secular belief systems and symbols.[66] Revolutionary social movements in the nineteenth century copied this characteristic, with both nationalist and Marxist movements cloaking themselves in the sacred garb of "faith." James Billington, in his comprehensive analysis of revolutionary faith, observes that the most dedicated revolutionaries tended to emerge in opposition to religiously justified autocracies and became holy warriors in their own right in what he calls "that rarest of all forms of true believer, the militant atheist."[67]

The LTTE fit into this tradition of militant atheism emerging in opposition to—and substituting for—traditional religion, just as the Russian revolutionaries had a century earlier.[68] Martyrdom for LTTE members thus held many of the same rewards as it did for members of other faith traditions. They could anticipate respect and meaning in this life, remembrance in its aftermath, and some form of immortality. Their rewards were therefore not entirely posthumous. In this respect Prabhakaran's project of the later 1980s was a success if judged on its own terms. The LTTE succeeded in mixing a level of enchantment with its rational methods, which allowed the group to instrumentalize martyrdom and make it part of an otherwise rational campaign to establish a modern state. As more and more suicide attackers joined Miller in the LTTE's pantheon of heroes, the phenomenon became self-reinforcing, with suicide bombing as well as cyanide serving to legitimize the cause and reinforce the discipline of the group. What is most extraordinary about the assassination of Rajiv Gandhi, after all, is not that one young woman killed herself in order to kill Gandhi, but that nine other people willingly killed themselves to avoid capture after the assassination.

THE UNIQUENESS OF LTTE SUICIDE BOMBING

The Tamil Kaliayev: Reassessing Miller's Attack

It was several years after Miller's attack that the LTTE began using suicide bombing systematically. Given the apparent success of the first LTTE human bomb, this puzzled analysts.[69] In *Dying to Win*, Robert Pape explains this pause by arguing that the decision to utilize suicide bombing is a rational choice made by groups whose territory had been occupied by another, religiously different group. Based on this assumption, Pape concludes that the LTTE chose not to utilize suicide attacks against the IPKF because from a Tamil perspective, the Indian occupation was of a different character than that of the ongoing Sri Lankan occupation of Tamil Eelam. Pape asserts that because the Indian army was religiously similar—being largely Hindu—it did not pose the type of existential threat that the Buddhist Sri Lankan forces posed and thus provoked no suicide bombing.[70]

Pape's explanation, however, is inconsistent with one of the most significant characteristics of LTTE violence—the extent to which it was also directed against a religiously and ethnically *similar* community, that is, the Tamil community. This tendency extended to suicide attackers, which the LTTE used against Tamil rivals on at least three occasions, one being the high-profile assassination of Neelan Tiruchelvam. In another attack, on July 7, 2004, a female LTTE suicide attacker attempted to kill a rival Tamil politician. When she was stopped by the authorities, she detonated herself, killing four police officers, but failed to kill her target.[71] When the LTTE used a suicide bomber to assassinate Rajiv Gandhi, the Indian state of Tamil Nadu had been at that time a source of support for the Tamil separatist movement. Gandhi's murder led to such a backlash among LTTE supporters that some analysts theorized that the attack could not have been carried out by the LTTE.[72] If one steps back and looks at Rajiv Gandhi from Prabhakaran's perspective—that is, as a potential rival for the allegiance of the Tamil community—the assassination is entirely logical.

All of these attacks are consistent with the history of the LTTE and its treatment of "traitors" and potential rivals, whether in the form of killing collaborators, the wholesale slaughter of rival leaders and groups, or the murderous enforcement of discipline within the organization itself. There is nothing to suggest that the Sinhalese were singled out for particularly brutal attention in the form of suicide attacks and much evidence to the contrary. As Rohan Gunaratna, an authority on the LTTE, observed, "Internecine warfare for supremacy by the LTTE [was] characteristic of the personality of the LTTE leader. Prabhakaran eliminated his fellow Tamil opponents more ruthlessly than his ethnic enemy."[73]

The lack of LTTE suicide missions between June 1987 and June 1990 is not so puzzling if one understands suicide bombing as a technological process that takes time to build and learn to use rather than a behavior or a tactic. The latter implies that suicide bombing is relatively constant over time—one attack is very much like another—which is how Captain Miller's attack tends to be treated. Miller's attack, however, was not the same as the assassination of Rajiv Gandhi. The Black Tigers were established after Miller's death, so it makes no sense to view his mission as the first Black Tiger suicide operation. Instead, given the absence of an institutionalized mechanism for producing suicide bombers, Miller's attack was largely improvised.

Miller's mission has much more in common with Ivan Kaliayev's assassination of Grand Duke Sergei Alexandrovich eighty-two years earlier. Both attacks were contingent and opportunistic, executed with minimal advance planning and preparation. Miller and Kaliayev came from secretive, intensely militant groups with cultures that prized the willingness of individuals to sacrifice their lives for the revolutionary cause, so both went willingly to their deaths. That neither organization deployed additional suicide attackers in the immediate aftermath of their initial successes suggests another similarity: the lack of a dedicated organizational component for preparing and exploiting suicide attacks on a regular basis.

As of 1987–88 many of the mechanisms the LTTE later used to ensure the reliability of its bombers and to capitalize on their attacks were not yet in place. Much of the symbolism and ritual was a work in progress; the shrines and cemeteries had not yet been built, competition for positions of honor within the newly created Black Tigers was just beginning, and the dedicated training programs did not yet exist. Instead, since Prabhakaran already held sway over his members, and a willingness to die certainly existed, the LTTE had the necessary components for carrying out what was essentially a suicide bombing "trial run," but it lacked the capacity, and perhaps even the motivation, to deploy such attackers regularly. From this perspective, there is no interruption of LTTE suicide bombing to be explained away, but instead the Indian occupation served as a time in which the LTTE, as a consequence of the intensification of its ideology, developed the capability of deploying attackers like Miller more regularly and reliably, and most important, under Prabhakaran's unquestioned control.

The political environment surrounding Miller's attack generally does not receive the attention it warrants. Miller's mission, in July
1987, was not undertaken in the midst of an ongoing campaign against
Sri Lanka. Operation Liberation had ended in June with the advent of
direct Indian intervention in Sri Lankan affairs. The Indian government
imposed a cease-fire, and on June 25 Indian ships docked at Jaffna so that
Indian aid could be distributed. Many Tamils hailed the Indians as sav-
iors, an especially galling turn of events for Prabhakaran. Faced with the
prospect of the Indian government winning the competition for the allegiance of the Tamil people, Prabhakaran desperately needed some way of
changing the political dynamic.

Miller's attack was meant to make a statement, but in this regard
the success of the mission was mixed. It was certainly an effective tactical
strike against a military target, but the scope paled in comparison to the
LTTE conventional attacks staged the preceding April, in which 127 and
113 people were killed.[74] In the years following, the LTTE and its supporters tended to exaggerate the strategic impact of Miller's attack, ignoring
the fact that the Sri Lankan army had already halted its offensive and
that Miller's bombing was an isolated attack during a cease-fire that did
nothing to change the behavior of the Indian and Sri Lankan governments.[75] Miller's attack was therefore enough of a success to warrant further exploration as one facet of the LTTE's increasing power during the
Indian occupation and afterward, but perhaps not so successful that the
LTTE's reluctance to follow it up immediately with further attacks should
appear puzzling.

The lengthy pause between Miller's attack and the resumption of
suicide bombing by the LTTE therefore suggests a case of independent
reinvention of the technology. Prabhakaran was probably influenced by
Hizballah's suicide attacks, but the Lebanese group's contribution to the
development of LTTE suicide bombing did not extend beyond an inspirational role.[76] There seems to have been no opportunity for the kind
of systematic collaboration and exchange of ideas between the LTTE
and Hizballah that typically characterizes the diffusion of innovations
and might have allowed the LTTE to develop a mature suicide bombing
capability more quickly.[77] In the 1970s and early 1980s a small number of Tamil fighters trained in Lebanon in camps run by the Palestine

Liberation Organization, and some may even have fought against the Israelis. This direct contact ended with the expulsion of PLO fighters to Tunisia in 1982, and so far there appears to be no evidence that a similar relationship developed with Hizballah in subsequent years.[78]

Use and Control

The LTTE shared considerable similarities with other groups that deployed suicide attacks and appreciable differences as well. The similarities consisted of the development of a radical, sacred ideology that facilitated the use of, and social acceptance of, self-sacrificial violence to create the possibility of suicide missions. Another similarity was the perception of an existential crisis on the part of the community that created the need for such attacks. The differences between LTTE suicide bombing and other cases are most obvious in the extensive training of the Black Tigers, which in turn was a consequence of the use of suicide bombing by the LTTE leadership. Therefore, analyzing LTTE suicide bombing without attempting to understand how it contributed to Prabhakaran's quest for unquestioned control will always lead to an incomplete picture.

Since every deployed Black Tiger suicide attacker represented the ultimate dedication to the movement and to Prabhakaran, each one reinforced Prabhakaran's authority within the LTTE and within the Tamil nationalist movement more generally. From this internal perspective, suicide bombing was an intensification of the trend toward unwavering commitment and discipline within the group that began with the group's constitution and was reinforced through the cult of cyanide. LTTE suicide bombing was therefore unique in that it reinforced the political power of a single individual, Prabhakaran, rather than a political or religious cause.

There were, however, two sides to this image of perceived power. In 1990 Tamil critics of the LTTE wrote, "The long shadow of the gun has not only been a source of power and glory, but also of fear and terror as well."[79] Projecting an image of unparalleled discipline and ferocity for Tamils, the Sri Lankan state, and the international community was vital for Prabhakaran, because the reputation it produced obscured very real weaknesses and fissures that called into question the LTTE's sole claim to power. The LTTE did not enjoy the unquestioned support of all the

Tamil people, as Prabhakaran liked to believe. It commanded the support of many and intimidated the rest into silence and acquiescence.[80]

The LTTE fighters, respected internationally, displayed another fissure. The dedicated cadre of thousands of fighters whose loyalty to Prabhakaran was outwardly unquestioned was supplemented considerably by involuntary child soldiers. In the 1990s 40 to 60 percent of LTTE soldiers killed in combat were under age eighteen. The LTTE's propaganda and the brutish behavior of the Sri Lankan forces explain the motivation of some young Tamils to join the LTTE, but coercion played a significant role as well. For a time, the LTTE mandated that every Tamil family send at least one child to join the organization. Once inducted, these child soldiers had no contact with their families and were subjected to exceptionally brutal training and discipline.[81] Within the LTTE's cadre of fighters, there was less uniformity than the image of the dedicated suicidal Black Tiger would suggest. Essentially, the disciplined true believers that made up much of the LTTE held captive a significant percentage of the rest of the organization and forced them to fight against their will.

Faced with these contradictions, the most pressing of Prabhakaran's needs was the ability to control the image of the LTTE as perceived within the Tamil, Sri Lankan, and international communities. The commitment of his bombers served this agenda extremely effectively, suggesting uniformity within the LTTE that exceeded the reality. This allowed Prabhakaran to manipulate the expectations of these different audiences, making the LTTE appear more powerful than it truly was, and by extension making Prabhakaran seem to be more powerful than he was.[82]

CONCLUSION: "THE ULTIMATE COMMITMENT TO THE MOVEMENT"

Viewing suicide bombing as a technology allows one to contextualize the phenomenon more effectively within Prabhakaran's control agenda and provides a plausible explanation for the two puzzling differences that set LTTE suicide bombing apart from suicide bombing elsewhere in the world during the 1990s and early 2000s: The first is the lack of suicide missions during the Indian occupation, and the second is the centralized control and extensive training of LTTE suicide attackers.

As noted, suicide bombing is a technology that requires careful cultural construction and management to make it sustainable. This process of construction may well explain the lengthy pause between Miller's attack and the suicide missions that accompanied Eelam War II. Undoubtedly Prabhakaran could inspire or compel individuals to kill themselves in 1987, but suicide bombing requires more than this. The deaths of the attackers must have an attractive, transcendent quality to appeal to others in order for the phenomenon to feed back into itself and become self-sustaining. It took some time for such a sacred culture to take root and complement Prabhakaran's previously established authority, but once it did, the combination of sacred cause, unquestioned leadership, and military necessity combined to form one of the most effective suicide-bombing complexes ever seen.

Prabhakaran's desire to extend his personal power over the entire movement explains the differences that set LTTE suicide bombing apart from other cases. Control within the LTTE was never shared and authority was not delegated. Unlike the faith traditions in Imperial Russia and war-torn Lebanon, the faith of the LTTE was manifested in a living person, who could control how the tools of the faith would be used. No other individual, not even Ayatollah Khomeini, had this type of unquestioned control over the symbols of revolutionary faith. Accordingly, suicide bombing within the LTTE was unique, remaining part of Prabhakaran's personal control agenda throughout the struggle, never escaping his meticulous oversight or assuming a life of its own as in other contexts.

EPILOGUE

In May 2009 the twenty-six-year struggle of the LTTE to create an independent homeland ended when the LTTE was militarily defeated by the Sri Lankan armed forces and Vellupillai Prabhakaran was killed. Because of the viciousness of the fighting on both sides, tens of thousands of civilians lost their lives as well.[83] In the final months of the struggle, Prabhakaran had continued to dispatch suicide bombers, using them on at least three occasions, but to no avail. Months after the end of the fighting, tens of thousands of Tamil refugees were still living in refugee camps. The tone of the Sri Lankan state tended to be one of triumphalism rather than reconciliation, raising the question of whether the basic problems that had fueled the Tamil insurgency had been (or would be) addressed.

As of two years after Prabhakaran's death, there had been no further suicide attacks by former Black Tigers, not even to avenge his death. Ironically, this situation may well indicate that Prabhakaran was too successful in centralizing power and personifying the cause for his followers. He left no successor—he probably did not trust anyone enough to confer such a status on anyone—so the movement collapsed with his death. Lacking leader and thus cause, the pressures that had driven members of the Black Tigers to commit suicide for two decades vanished, and so the use of the Black Tigers seems to have ended with the death of their user.

Part II
DIFFUSION

4

TRIAL RUNS

The Provisional IRA and
the Workers' Party of Kurdistan

On October 24, 1990, gunmen from the Provisional Irish Republican Army (IRA) entered the Londonderry home of Patsy Gillespie, a fifty-five-year-old Catholic father of three who worked as a cook's assistant at a nearby British Army canteen.[1] As a civilian worker for the British Army, he was seen as a collaborator by the IRA and therefore a valid target in the organization's war against the British.[2] The gunmen took Gillespie's family hostage in order to force him to drive a truck provided by the IRA to a nearby army checkpoint. It was the second such time that Gillespie had been commandeered in such a manner. The IRA members told Gillespie's wife to expect him back from the mission within a half hour. They were lying. The IRA had no intention of allowing Gillespie to survive this particular mission. In fact, the mission depended on his death. The vehicle Gillespie was forced to drive was laden with a thousand-pound bomb and was being followed by an IRA vehicle. When British Army personnel stopped Gillespie's vehicle at the checkpoint, an IRA member detonated the bomb by remote control, killing Gillespie and five soldiers.

The IRA attempted two other "human bomb" attacks of this nature on the same day. John McEvoy, a sixty-five-year-old man dying of cancer, was compelled to drive a bomb-laden truck to a target near the city of Newry in order to protect the eight members of his family that had been taken hostage by the IRA. McEvoy managed to escape from the vehicle and shout a warning, but the blast still killed one British soldier and injured ten others along with some police officers.[3] The third bomb was delivered by Gerry Kelly to an army base in the city of Omagh. Kelly had been tied to the vehicle and told that he would have plenty of time—fifty minutes—to free himself before the bomb went off. Instead, the bomb partially detonated as soon as Kelly was clear; the army defused the remainder of the bomb.[4]

The bombings of October 24 were meant to be a dramatic, three-pronged attack at the heart of British defenses by hitting previously inaccessible targets and delivering a sizable body count. For the IRA's public image, however, the attacks were a catastrophe. The following day, Londonderry MP John Hume, leader of the Catholic Social Democratic Labor Party, condemned the group in a radio interview: "The anger at this particular atrocity is far deeper than anything I have seen in this city since 1972. The one word that is on everybody's lips is the word 'coward.' Let me repeat it. I hope you are listening, you cowards, using a human being in the way that you did."[5]

By the early 1990s suicide bombing had been invented, reinvented, and legitimized through its successful use in two different contexts. From that point on, the story of suicide bombing is one of the diffusion of a particular innovation rather than its reinvention. Despite the examples set by Hizballah and the LTTE, the diffusion of suicide bombing has been a curiously slow process, suggesting that although suicide bombing can spread readily from culture to culture, there are also constraints that serve to slow its diffusion or even prevent it.

Two other groups—the Provisional IRA and the Workers' Party of Kurdistan (Partia Karkaren Kurdistan, PKK)—attempted to deploy human bombers in the 1990s, but they were unable to use them effectively over a lengthy period of time. The IRA exhibited many of the requisite attributes necessary for suicide bombing—most notably a perceived need for effective control technologies and an organizational reverence for self-sacrifice—but the threat posed by the British military was not sufficiently extreme to motivate republicans in Northern Ireland to support such a radical form of resistance. In addition, the IRA's reverence for its martyrs never came to resemble the cultures of martyrdom that had emerged in Russia, Lebanon, and Sri Lanka, making suicide missions inconsistent with IRA cultural norms. The leader of the Workers' Party of Kurdistan, Abdullah Ocalan, proved to be a poor user of suicide bombing. His methods of recruitment did not reinforce a preexisting willingness toward self-sacrifice, forcing him instead to resort to violent coercion in order to deploy suicide attackers. Because of this, the use of suicide bombers did not enhance group solidarity or strengthen the connections between the PKK and its reference community.

THE SPREAD OF INNOVATIONS

Hybridization and Reinvention

Some analysts have explained the spread of suicide bombing by referring exclusively to rational factors: Suicide bombing is effective, the argument goes, so many groups are anxious to try it.[6] Utility is indeed an important factor that seems to drive organizational decision making, but other cultural and psychological factors matter as well, which is why suicide bombing, like all technologies, does not automatically flow from one society to the next. There is always friction as the original culture and that of the adopter collide. In cases where the technology is transferred successfully, this friction transforms the initial technology into something slightly different, which explains the lack of uniformity in the ways that different groups have manufactured and used their suicide bombers.

The successful transfer of technology or innovation always requires local modification when the product of one culture is adapted to the norms and constraints of another. Such changes are sometimes understood as "resistance" to the new technology, but this term is misleading in that it connotes deliberate opposition instead of a process of learning and choosing. This "resistance," while it does serve to winnow out inappropriate technologies, is fundamentally a learning process, a "positive opportunity for de-centralized innovation and learning by self-reflexive actors."[7] The diffusion of technological innovation is therefore a process of the ongoing reinvention of a basic technology by its users; every successful case of transfer results in a new technology that is a hybrid of imported and indigenous characteristics.

Diffusion of Innovations

The diffusion of technological innovations is governed by many factors. Everett M. Rogers developed a model for it in his classic text *Diffusion of Innovations*. He cites five particular attributes of innovations that contribute to their spread:

- the *relative advantage* offered by the innovation
- the *compatibility* of the innovation with a group's ideas, beliefs, and needs
- the *complexity* of the innovation
- the *trialability* of the innovation, that is, the extent to which a technology can be explored prior to a large-scale commitment of resources
- the *observability* of the innovation, which measures the degree to which the advantages of the technology are observable by others.[8]

Suicide bombing can satisfy all five of these attributes, with three of Rogers' five factors being consistently applicable to it. Observability, the ease by which the results of the innovation can be seen and understood by others, is one attribute that contributes to the diffusion of suicide bombing. It is positively related to adoption of a new technology, and this is very much the case in suicide bombing, whose value stems largely from its public, spectacular nature.[9] Complexity, which Rogers defines as "the degree to which an innovation is perceived as relatively difficult to understand and use," is another applicable factor.[10] Complexity is a matter of perception. Rogers suggests, "The complexity of an innovation, as perceived by members of a social system, is negatively related to its rate of adoption." In contrast to a weapon systems developed by state powers, suicide bombing does not require complicated and expensive hardware, making it appropriate for use by small, covert groups lacking in material resources and infrastructure. Suicide bombing is consequently a technology that may be experimented with fairly easily. Rogers calls this characteristic "trialability," and finds that it is positively related to the rate of adoption of an innovation, especially among early users. As the case of Captain Miller of the LTTE demonstrates (see Chapter 3), suicide bombing is easy to utilize on a trial basis. Trial runs of a technology can reveal the utility (or lack thereof) of the technology for solving a set of problems and also allow for limited reinvention, in which the basic innovation is customized to the user's needs.

Relative Advantage and Compatibility

Based on these three criteria, suicide bombing is a technology that has the potential to diffuse readily among militant groups, subject of course to Rogers' other two criteria—relative advantage and compatibility. These two factors vary significantly when assessed among different groups and can affect the willingness of organizations to decide whether to attempt suicide bombing. At the same time, they can indicate whether suicide bombing will become a culturally acceptable form of weapon technology.

Relative advantage is to the adoption of an innovation by a new culture what perceived need is to the process of innovation itself—that is, the extent to which an idea or tool solves a specific problem relative to other solutions. Rogers defines relative advantage as "the degree to which an innovation is perceived as being better than the idea it supersedes."[11] There are numerous ways in which an innovation can be "better": through lower costs, economic or otherwise, greater effectiveness, or greater reliability, to name a few. Whatever the particular advantage, the perception that an innovation is inherently better than its predecessors is one of the strongest indicators that a new technology will be adopted. This contributes to the perception that technology transfer is primarily about effectiveness.[12]

Compatibility, in turn, is to diffusion what possibility is to innovation—that is, the extent to which a technology is consistent with a particular set of cultural or social norms. Of these norms, Rogers suggests that the most important are compatibility with values and beliefs, compatibility with previously introduced ideas, and compatibility with a group's perceived needs.[13] Members of extremist groups, the most frequent users of suicide bombing since the early 1980s, have chosen to fight and perhaps to die for a cause, which means that suicide bombing is potentially compatible with overall group norms. Suicide bombing can be consistent with previously introduced ideas, for example, martyrdom, which is a universal phenomenon in the world of armed struggle. Suicide bombing is also compatible with the perceived needs of a variety of organizations because they seek reliable control.

Of course, compatibility with the values, beliefs, and needs of some organizations does not imply compatibility with the values, beliefs, and needs of all organizations. The individual willingness for self-sacrifice varies tremendously between groups and also within groups. When individual members of militant groups demonstrate publicly a willingness to sacrifice their lives, they claim an elevated moral position for themselves and legitimize their sponsoring organizations in the eyes of their supporters, creating a positive feedback between individual suicide attackers and society. If willing volunteers are not available, the group either cannot proceed or must use more coercive and less inspiring means of recruiting its attackers; this, however, might break down the relationships between the individual, cultural, and organizational levels of the suicide-bombing complex. Organizations have considerable latitude in how they manipulate these relationships, but they cannot make something from nothing and are therefore constrained by what their members and societies are willing to accept.

Since these factors vary greatly, there have naturally been instances in which suicide bombing did not offer enough of a relative advantage to a group or was incompatible with cultural and social norms, resulting in limited or ineffective use. As a consequence of this, in the 1990s the number of interested users exceeded the number of capable users. The latter have dominated analytical interest for obvious reasons, but the less-proficient users warrant analysis as well, because their challenges in developing an effective suicide bombing capability shed light on the limitations of suicide bombing, which, after all, has remained a rare form of attack relative to gunfire, rockets, mortars, and improvised explosive devices (IEDs).

NON-DIFFUSION: THE LACK OF SUICIDE BOMBING IN NORTHERN IRELAND

The October 24 proxy bomb attacks highlight one of the more curious aspects of suicide bombing in the late 1980s and early 1990s—its conspicuous absence from the conflict in Northern Ireland. On the surface, all of the necessary preconditions seem to have been present. Northern Ireland was viewed by the IRA and its leaders to be under a colonial occupation by a religiously different adversary. A veneration of self-sacrifice within the republican tradition dated to at least the late 1700s and had been manifested in 1981 in the fasting deaths of Bobby Sands and nine other republican prisoners. In addition, the IRA was constantly searching for more accurate and reliable weapons that would allow it to strike difficult-to-access military targets while limiting counter-productive civilian casualties. This need drove them to innovate constantly in the realm of control technologies, which was costly and sometimes deadly for the organization. Thus the lack of suicide bombing in such an environment, when its utility was being demonstrated in Lebanon and then later in Sri Lanka, is noteworthy.

Background

The Troubles—as the conflict pitting Irish republicans against Northern Irish authorities and the British government was known—emerged in Northern Ireland in the late 1960s, when the Catholic civil rights movement encountered opposition and adversity, leading to wide-scale civil disturbances, arson, and murder. During the chaotic months of late summer and autumn 1969, the IRA was irrelevant, having dwindled in the north to just a few poorly armed members. In August British soldiers were deployed in Northern Ireland to restore order, but soon inadvertently alienated much of the Catholic population. This created the opportunity for a resurgent IRA—renamed the Provisional IRA after a split within the organization in December 1969—to step forward as the defender of Northern Ireland's Catholics.[14] To replace the established authorities as the defender of order, the IRA needed to act with restraint and control.[15] For much of the 1970s, however, the chaotic and multifaceted nature of the conflict ensured that deadly violence, indiscriminate and often unrestrained, was the norm. After a leadership change during 1976–77, the IRA reorganized and adopted restraint against civilian targets in a clearly articulated military strategy presented in the Green Book, its new training manual that articulated a five-part guerrilla strategy.

Bombs played a significant role in the first three parts of the strategy.[16] The first part involved a war of attrition against enemy personnel, including British military and Northern Irish police forces, with the stated goal of causing as many casualties and deaths as possible. The second part required a bombing campaign in waging economic warfare against the United Kingdom by making financial interests in Northern Ireland unprofitable and discouraging further investment. The third part was to make the six counties of Northern Ireland "ungovernable except by colonial military rule." The fourth provision called for national and international publicity and propaganda campaigns to gain support for the IRA's position. The only way to reconcile the first three parts with the fourth was through the controlled use of force.[17]

Such control was not always successful. The nature of the IRA, despite its conventional military language and disciplined imagery, precluded complete control of the periphery by the core. IRA operatives from rural areas often found themselves at odds with the urban leadership of Belfast and preferred armed struggle to politics, which they considered to be a betrayal of the republican cause.[18] Because the middle and lower ranks of the organization had a fair degree of flexibility in target selection, violence initiated by them could and did take the form of revenge killings and sectarian violence. Centrally directed, high-profile operations on the other hand were supposed to conform to the ideal of controlled force. When they did not, the reason was often technical failure, which drove the IRA to innovate constantly in the means by which it could control its bombs.

Deadly Innovation: The IRA and Control Technologies

From the beginning of the Troubles, the use of various kinds of emplaced explosives against police and British soldiers became an essential and effective element of the IRA's campaign. The first mines, even then referred to as IEDs, were relatively primitive and were often wired to a detonator controlled by an IRA member.[19] These bombs required a great deal of preparation, especially in the concealment of the command wires and in perfecting the timing of the detonation. The triggerman was at risk unless concealed in an area safe from the blast and positioned in a place where he could escape quickly. In areas where the IRA enjoyed a permissive operational environment it was able to use such bombs effectively, but on the whole the obstacles to the successful use of "trap bombs" were many.[20]

To minimize these complications and to ensure the safety of its volunteers, the IRA tried to separate its bombers from their weapons while still allowing for ongoing feedback from the mission environment. Creating a space between the bomber and the weapon, however, came with a price that put the missions at risk of failure. Automatic detonation via timers permitted no feedback, was inflexible, and allowed the possibility of deactivation of the weapon prior to triggering. Remote manual detonation, first by command wire and eventually by radio control, was potentially more flexible, but its drawbacks included the possibility of mechanical failure and intervention or jamming by the authorities.[21]

The possibility of intervention escalated an ongoing arms race between the IRA and British authorities.[22] The fuses, simple timers, and trigger wires used in the early stages of the Troubles were soon replaced with radio-controlled devices, sometimes derived from model aircraft kits. The authorities could jam these devices relatively easily, forcing the IRA to innovate to bypass the army's countermeasures. The authorities then devised new methods for jamming, which led the IRA to use portable radar guns—originally designed to catch speeding motorists—to detonate bombs.

Still, in spite of such innovation and flexibility, the IRA's experience with bombs was a decidedly mixed affair, with successes counterbalanced by numerous failures. The more complex the bomb, the more likely it was to fail. According to Eamon Collins, an IRA member from the town of Newry, in the early 1980s as much as 50 percent of the organization's bombings failed to detonate as planned.[23] Even more problematic was the danger involved in experimentation with such technologies as detonators and anti-tampering devices. Lt. Gen. George Styles, responsible for British explosive ordnance disposal efforts early on in the Troubles, took solace in the fact that the job of the IRA bomb makers was at least as dangerous as, if not more so than, that of the British soldiers responsible for disarming the bombs. "Yet, the heartening fact for people like me," he wrote in his memoir, "is that the more difficult the bomb-maker tries to make his bomb, the more liable he is to blow himself up. In fact he usually does."[24] The numbers bear him out. Bombing accidents killed approximately 120 IRA volunteers during the Troubles. In comparison, British authorities and police killed perhaps 300 volunteers.[25]

"Maximum Ruthlessness": The IRA, the Police, and the British Army

The IRA's experimentation with control technologies was driven partially by the need for restraint in the use of force, but this restraint did not extend to operations against the police or the British military, which the IRA attacked with ferocity. The "Green Book" states clearly that the IRA's struggle with the British military should consist of a "war of attrition against enemy personnel which is aimed at causing as many deaths and casualties as possible so as to create a demand from their people at home for their withdrawal."[26] Consequently, throughout the Troubles, "Military targets were executed with maximum ruthlessness, to take maximum life."[27]

The attack that the IRA considered to be its finest military operation of the Troubles illustrates this commitment to maximum ruthlessness. On August 27, 1979, the group set up a complex ambush utilizing two emplaced bombs near Narrow Waters castle on the border with the Republic of Ireland. The first bomb, hidden along the road, was detonated by radio remote control as a patrol of British paratroopers passed by, killing six and injuring several others. IRA snipers just over the border in Ireland then opened fire, forcing the troops to fall back to the castle gatehouse, an obvious defensive location. Anticipating this maneuver, the IRA had hidden a larger bomb in the gatehouse. They armed this second bomb by using a radio remote control to activate a commercial timer that in turn detonated the bomb after a half-hour delay. The second blast caught the soldiers by surprise and was by far the more lethal of the two. The ambush killed eighteen elite paratroopers.[28] Early on the morning of August 21, 1988, an IRA roadside bomb killed eight British soldiers near the town of Armagh, and on September 21, 1989, an IRA bomb planted in the Royal Marine's College, in Deal, Kent, killed eleven guardsmen and injured twenty-one others.[29]

Sacred Cause

The IRA's willingness to kill was complemented by a sacred cause that its members believed was worth dying for.[30] For many members of the IRA, whatever their religious feelings, Irish nationhood was a transcendent, moral, historically necessary cause. It had been bound in sacred ritual and imagery since the beginning of Irish national consciousness. It is no exaggeration to say that self-sacrifice launched the IRA's form of nationalism. In 1798 Theobold Wolfe Tone, leader of the United Irishmen and one of the founding fathers of republican nationalism, was captured by the British while attempting to lead a French attack to free Ireland from England. Tone slashed his own throat while in prison and suffered terribly for several days before finally succumbing and becoming republican nationalism's first martyr.[31] After Tone's death, republican nationalism was influenced by the emotion and passion of nineteenth-century German Romanticism, which reinforced the Catholicism central to the self-identification of many Irish nationalists, leading them to glorify Tone and others as martyrs.

In the early twentieth century, the sacralization of republican nationalism reached its high point in the orations of Patrick Pearse, an Irish author and political activist who would become one of the leaders of the Easter Rebellion of 1916. In a 1913 speech commemorating Tone's death, Pearse told his audience, "We have come to the holiest place in Ireland; holier to us even than the place where Patrick sleeps in Down." The following year while commemorating Robert Emmet, an Irish nationalist executed by the British in 1803, Pearse made the connection between sacred cause and self-sacrifice explicit: "There are in every generation those who shrink from the ultimate sacrifice, but there are in every generation those who make it with joy and laughter, and these are the salt of generations, the heroes who stand midway between God and men."[32] Pearse and other nationalist leaders who staged the Easter Rebellion against the British did so knowing full well that it would not succeed in practical terms, but believing that the example of men willing to fight and die for Ireland was necessary for the movement. Their selection of Easter Monday as the day to launch the rebellion was of course deliberate. According to Pearse, it would establish a "theology of insurrection." In a letter to his mother, Pearse even compared himself to Jesus Christ.[33]

During the Troubles, the republican nationalism of the IRA replaced Catholicism with secular nationalism of a vaguely socialist type, but the sacredness of these earlier sacrifices and of the cause overall remained. Catholicism per se was not at the heart of radical republican nationalism; rather nationalism appropriated many of the symbols and rituals of Catholicism for a movement driven by people whose commitment to

Catholic Christianity varied broadly in contrast to their staunch dedication to Irish nationhood. This is not to downplay the significance of republican nationalism or the power of self-sacrifice at the heart of so much of its ritual, but to argue that for the IRA, as with the Russian Party of Socialist Revolutionaries and the LTTE, a secular phenomenon became an unquestioned article of faith justifying and on rare occasions necessitating self-sacrifice on the part of its true believers.[34]

The IRA and Suicide Bombing: Deliberate Restraint?

The introduction of suicide bombers into Northern Ireland would have been consistent with a sacred ideology worth dying for and would have had the potential to allow the IRA to strike its enemies with maximum ruthlessness while minimizing unintended civilian casualties. Thus the lack of suicide attacks is puzzling. To date the explanation offered by scholars has been one of voluntary restraint by the IRA; that is, the lack of suicide attacks must have resulted from a conscious decision not to use them for fear of the negative effect that indiscriminate civilian casualties might have on the republican cause.[35]

This explanation is flawed because it depends on a direct correlation between suicide attacks and indiscriminate civilian casualties that does not exist. Suicide bombing is not inherently indiscriminate. Rather, it is the exact opposite—precise and controllable. When suicide bombers cause indiscriminate civilian casualties, it is because their users *want* to cause indiscriminate civilian casualties. Suicide bombing can also be used to minimize casualties, which is one reason why Russian terrorists, such as Kaliayev, risked killing themselves while carrying out their bombings. Therefore, if the IRA wished to limit counterproductive civilian casualties, its leaders would only have needed to deploy suicide attackers against military targets—as it did with its proxy bombers—rather than exclude their use altogether. In fact, rather than demonstrating restraint, the whole purpose of using proxy bombers was to signal an escalation to British authorities. According to one IRA member involved in the attacks, the IRA hoped to "shake the Brits out of their complacency" by utilizing this new form of attack.[36]

Instead of restraint, a more convincing explanation for why suicide bombing failed to spread to the IRA is that the conditions in Northern

Ireland during the Troubles were not conducive to the production of willing suicide attackers. Republican paramilitaries never developed a culture of martyrdom, so individual suicide, even in the course of an attack, was incompatible with overall group norms. In terms of necessity, British restraint in the use of force meant that the threat posed to the Catholic community by the British Army was not nearly as extreme as in the other cases examined here, making the need for an extreme form of resistance less compelling. The cost of suicide attacks, in terms of the value of volunteers' lives, and the less pressing need for such attacks on the part of community need meant that suicide operations came at a price that IRA volunteers and their supporters in the nationalist community were unwilling to pay.

COMPATIBILITY

The Hunger Strikes and the Republican Tradition of Self-Sacrifice

The IRA's attitude toward life within the organization differed markedly from the one held regarding the British and members of the police force of Northern Ireland. Despite the sheer ruthlessness that the IRA often displayed toward them, never did a subculture of volunteers enthusiastically seeking to end their own lives emerge during the Troubles. On the contrary, the safety of IRA volunteers was always a top priority for the organization. Eamon Collins, who became an informer and left the group after being arrested in the 1980s, wrote that the group had two golden rules about operations, the first of which was "regardless of whether an objective had been achieved successfully, if a volunteer were captured or killed in the process, then the operation was a failure." According to Sean O'Callaghan, another disillusioned former member, "As far as everybody was concerned a successful operation was one where damage was inflicted and everybody escaped unscathed."[37] The obvious exceptions to this overall outlook were of course the deaths of ten republican prisoners during the 1981 hunger strike. Upon closer examination, however, the deaths of these ten men were the exceptions that proved the rule: The men came to be revered, even venerated decades after their deaths because their behavior was so contrary to the culture of the IRA.

The hunger strikes carried out by republican prisoners in 1980 and 1981 were the consequence of an unanticipated yet ruthlessly steady confrontation between the prisoners and authorities that had begun in the late 1970s. In the early 1970s paramilitary prisoners had been granted special category status. Unlike other prisoners, they were housed in compounds resembling POW camps. They wore normal clothing and could associate freely with one another. Paramilitary prisoners from all groups considered special category status to be de facto political prisoner status.[38]

Beginning in 1976 the British changed strategies and began to de-escalate and criminalize the conflict. This shift entailed revoking special category status and transferring paramilitary prisoners to recently constructed prisons, where they would be housed in individual cells and required to wear uniforms like regular criminals.[39] For republican prisoners, this was not a possibility. To them, acquiescing to the change of status would have meant accepting that the entire tradition of Irish republicanism was a criminal phenomenon. The British failed to recognize the extent to which the criminalization strategy attacked the sacredness of Irish republicanism and were therefore unprepared for the prisoners' response.[40] The first prisoner confronted with the change, Kieran Nugent, refused to wear his prison uniform, telling prison officials that the only way to keep it on him would be to nail it to his back. Word of his defiance quickly spread, and republican prisoners collectively began to refuse to wear their uniforms, wrapping themselves instead in their blankets. Within months, hundreds of prisoners were protesting in such a manner.[41]

The conflict between prisoners and their warders steadily escalated.[42] Prisoners who were "on the blanket" were refused towels to wrap themselves in to walk to the shower facilities, so they refused to wash, turning the blanket protest into a dirty protest. The prisoners eventually refused to clean out their chamber pots or their food trays, which guards sometimes dumped on the floor anyway. The result was that the cells of "blanketmen" became caked in rotting, uneaten food, urine, and feces. In warm weather, maggots hatched in the filth and crawled through the cells and through the hair of the protesters.[43] The prisoners drafted a set of five demands and presented them to the British, but they lacked any means to force a favorable settlement. By 1979, with years of misery behind them and no end in sight, the prisoners were beginning to feel trapped.

Many went off the blanket, threatening to undermine the entire protest. In April of that year, recalled prisoner Leo Green, "We were in a corner and were increasingly aware of it."[44]

The only option the prisoners felt they had left was to escalate the conflict even further by going on a hunger strike. The first hunger strike began in October 1980, when seven prisoners—one from each of the six counties in Northern Ireland and one representing Belfast— simultaneously refused food.[45] By December, the health of several strikers had deteriorated significantly. When the British appeared willing to grant concessions on the five demands, Brendan Hughes, the leader of the strike, called it off rather than allow Sean McKenna, who had slipped into a coma, to die. The British never followed through on the anticipated concessions, so the strike ended in failure.[46]

In March 1981 a new group of prisoners, led by Bobby Sands, decided to carry out a second hunger strike. They did so against the wishes of senior IRA and Sinn Fein leaders who feared that a second failed strike would only harm the image of the republican cause.[47] To increase pressure on the government, the prisoners decided to stagger the strike, with one new prisoner refusing food each week so that there would be constant pressure and less chance of the strike collapsing. Of course this strategy also put extraordinary pressure on the prisoners themselves, for if the first man were to see the strike through to the end, the succeeding strikers would not be able to back down without feeling the shame and humiliation that came with betraying a dead comrade who had himself already made the ultimate sacrifice for the movement.[48] Sands refused food on March 1, 1981, and died sixty-six days later. The British government refused to capitulate to the prisoners' demands, so the strike continued.

Within two weeks of Sands' funeral, three more hunger strikers— Frank Hughes, Raymond McCreesh, and Patsy O'Hara—also died, for a total of four deaths within seventeen days. It was six more weeks before a fifth hunger striker, Joe McDonnell, died, on July 8. This time lag occurred because the strike had originally been confined to the first four men. Only later, as it became clear that their deaths would not force the British to budge, did the IRA leadership decide to select replacement strikers and to continue the hunger strike.

The strike continued over the summer and into early autumn. The deaths of the first hunger strikers made compromise on the part of the remaining strikers all but impossible. By the end of the summer, hunger striker Liam McCloskey recognized this, remembering, "We were caught in our own trap where there were ten men dead and we felt we had to keep going and look for a way out of it."[49] By September family members began to intervene by authorizing medical treatment of hunger strikers who had lost consciousness. The strike was called off in October. Ten prisoners—seven from the IRA and three from the Irish National Liberation Army—had fasted to death.

Technically the strike failed. The British government never formally gave in to the strikers, although in the aftermath of the strike it did meet many of the five demands in practice. On a political level, however, the strike had a profound effect. During Sands' fast, the local MP for his district, Frank McGuire, had died. Sinn Fein ran Sands as their candidate in the election to replace him, and Sands narrowly won, capturing more than 30,000 votes.[50] Although Sands never took his seat in Parliament, the election opened up the possibility of complementing the armed struggle with an electoral strategy, which would eventually supersede the armed struggle, allowing Sinn Fein to eclipse the IRA.[51]

Furthermore, the strike rehabilitated the republican cause on a moral level. Thuggish and sectarian behavior on the part of IRA members had been bolstering the British criminalization strategy, convincing many that the IRA was little more than an organized crime racket. Criminals, however, did not voluntarily starve themselves to death for an abstract political principle. Despite Prime Minister Margaret Thatcher's ongoing effort to portray the hunger strikers as criminals, the men's resolve stunned people around the world, lending moral legitimacy to their newly discovered political track. So important were the strikers for reviving the IRA's cause, and so extraordinary was their suffering for a movement that tended to avoid self-sacrifice, that years later the men were still regarded with reverence among former republican prisoners. Anthony McIntyre, a former "blanketman," wrote nearly three decades later, "The hunger strike was the most intense moment in the history of the Provisional IRA. It has assumed the status of sacred. Those of us involved in the blanket protest still shake with emotion when the memory of the ten men visits our consciousness."[52]

"Becoming Suicide"

As negotiations with the British over special-category status collapsed in early July 1981, the resolve of the prisoners and of the IRA leadership only hardened. Brendan "Bik" McFarlane, the prisoner representing the hunger strikers to the Army Council, originally believed that the first four prisoners to go on strike would be sufficient to make their political point. In a communication to the IRA leadership, he wrote, "If public pressure failed to move the government by the time the first four had died, the republican movement would have effectively shot its bolt. And after four, with the authorities still adamant, more deaths would start to look like suicide, which would be damaging for the movement." In a message dated June 28, he wrote to Gerry Adams, who would later become president of Sinn Fein, "If we continue with the hunger strike we will be faced with a situation whereby Joe [McDonnell] will die, followed by others and after X amount of deaths public opinion will hammer us into the ground, forcing us to end the hunger strike with nothing to show but deaths that could have been avoided and a shattering defeat in the bargain."[53] By July his attitude had changed considerably, and he wrote to Adams, "I believe it would be wrong to capitulate. We took a decision and committed ourselves to hunger strike action. . . . It's rough, brutal, and ruthless, and a lot of other things as well, but we are fighting a war and must accept that front line troops are more susceptible to casualties than anyone."[54]

Despite the resolve of the strikers, McFarlane's concern that public opinion would "hammer" the strike into the ground was becoming a reality by the end of the summer. Families of the hunger strikers in particular mistrusted the IRA, and some believed that the organization was pressuring the men to continue the strike. Joe McDonnell's family had concerns that the external leadership of the IRA was using the prisoners, and Geraldine Scheiss, girlfriend of hunger striker Kieran Doherty, came to believe that the behavior of the prisoners made it seem, she said, "almost as if they had been programmed."[55]

Father Denis Faul, a Catholic priest who was sympathetic toward the prisoners but at the same time opposed IRA violence, also noticed the shift that took place in the strike as it dragged on over the summer. Faul initially declined to condemn the hunger strikers as committing suicide, but as more and more republican prisoners died, he said "the motivation doesn't seem to me to be about drawing the attention of the British public to the situation by fasting. It seems to me to be about drawing attention to death and big funerals. This thing is no longer a valid public political protest. It's becoming suicide."[56] Faul was instrumental in convincing the families of some of the hunger strikers to authorize medical intervention in the event of unconsciousness and therefore helped undermine the solidarity that drove the strike. For this reason, he was vilified by many within the IRA as a traitor and became the scapegoat for the failure of the strike.

From the perspective of this analysis, Faul's comment suggests that the hunger strike was coming to be seen more like tactical martyrdom—the organizational use of individual self-sacrifice for specific short-term goals—than martyrdom as understood within the context of the Catholic faith and tradition. Martyrdom has been viewed as the definitive act of witness because the martyr's willingness to suffer death rather than concede the truth of his or her position demonstrates certainty beyond a doubt. Authenticity and thus the public, symbolic power of martyrdom derives from this certainty and passes from the martyr to the cause for which the martyr died. The martyr's certainty is in turn only possible through self-realization and the freedom to pursue it.[57] The families and Father Faul therefore became a significant threat as they called into question the very legitimacy of the strike. If the men were not acting freely but instead were being compelled, like frontline troops in times of war, then the strike was less about the authenticity of individual commitment and more about an organization using the devotion of its members for its own purposes, a situation far less acceptable to the hunger strikers' families and the broader Catholic community. To further complicate matters, Protestant clergy in Northern Ireland universally condemned the hunger strikes, going so far as to charge the Catholic Church with hypocrisy for its refusal to recognize the deaths of the prisoners as suicides.[58]

The misgivings of the families, Father Faul's criticism, and the lack of uniformity among Christian clergy regarding the "martyrdom" of the hunger strikers thus called into question whether the last six hunger strikers truly sacrificed themselves or were sacrificed by others. This distinction is not trivial. In the hunger strikes and in suicide bombing, public perception of the intention and freedom of possible suicides plays a significant role in determining acceptance of their deaths.

The hunger strikes proved to be a complicated experience with self-sacrifice for the IRA leadership. The organization's leaders recognized that the willingness to die for the cause was contrary to republican paramilitary culture, a norm that could be set aside only in the most extreme instances. They also understood that the length of the strike and the number of men who died nearly became counterproductive in terms of public perception, providing critics with grounds to allege that it had degenerated from political protest into organizationally driven mass suicide.

Finally, the hunger strikes provided the IRA leadership an opportunity to witness the diminishing power of repetitive self-sacrifice to mobilize supporters outside the republican community. Bobby Sands' funeral was an international event. In Northern Ireland, perhaps 100,000 people lined the route between St. Luke's Church, near Sands' home, to Milltown cemetery, where he was buried.[59] There was markedly less attention for Joe McDonnell's funeral. After Mickey Devine, the last hunger striker to perish, died on August 20, few outside of family and the republican paramilitary community paid close attention.[60] Based on this experience, to the leaders of the IRA the prospect of recruiting willing bombers, using them repeatedly over time, and expecting the Catholic community to support such behavior probably seemed implausible. They therefore devised an alternative, but failed to anticipate the public revulsion at such callous use of human life.

RELATIVE ADVANTAGE

British Restraint

The high cost of blood within the IRA is only half of the equation explaining the lack of suicide bombing in Northern Ireland. The other half is the perceived need on the part of the nationalist community to support the use of extreme forms of resistance against the British military. This was by design and was the result of Britain's patient and often underappreciated efforts to de-escalate the conflict from the mid-1970s onward.

The use of British force was instrumental in escalating the Troubles in the early 1970s, particularly the 1972 shooting of twenty-seven unarmed Catholic civilians, thirteen of whom died, on Bloody Sunday in Derry. The British strategy of de-escalation and criminalization therefore entailed a much greater level of restraint in the use of force. After beginning this process in 1975, the British never again used tracked vehicles or heavy armor in the conflict. They never again fired on crowds or carried out collective punishments, such as curfews, and never made use of helicopter gunships or fixed-wing aircraft to attack ground targets. For the most part, the British Army and state endeavored to appear as though they were remaining within the confines of the law, even though certain members did not always do so in practice.[61]

The British were careful not to introduce the most devastating tools of modern warfare into the conflict, and in doing so denied the IRA a powerful rhetorical tool that would have allowed them to escalate the conflict from their side.[62] In other conflicts, the availability of overwhelming force to one side created a sense of desperation that opponents seized on to justify the use of suicide bombing to their communities and to pressure members to become bombers. In the case of the IRA, however, the sense of desperation was not strong enough to create the motivation for anyone to become a suicide attacker.

British restraint also had an effect at the community level. In the cases examined thus far in this volume—the Kamikaze, Hizballah, and the LTTE—the civilian population suffered terribly at the hands of their adversaries. Indiscriminate brutality toward civilian populations provided leaders, such as Prabhakaran, the opportunity to depict their struggles in existential terms and was essential in creating the synergy between organizations, societies, and individuals that allowed suicide bombing to be adopted in Japan, Lebanon, and Sri Lanka.

In Northern Ireland, British soldiers harassed, intimidated, and humiliated Catholic civilians with regularity, but the situation never escalated into a war between the British government and its Catholic citizens in Northern Ireland. In 1988 Gen. Patrick "Paddy" Waters, incoming head of British forces in Northern Ireland, told the historian Martin van Crevald that his mission was not to smash the IRA but to ensure that as few people as possible died on both sides of the conflict. This required patience and the willingness of British soldiers to make themselves vulnerable to an "army" that was far less powerful than they were. During the Troubles, from 1969 to 1998, the IRA killed approximately one thousand British soldiers, police, and other authority figures. On the other hand, the authorities, including the army, killed approximately three hundred IRA members. The ratio was therefore more than three to one, IRA deaths to military and police deaths. This stands in stark contrast to every other known case of counterinsurgency, in which the forces of "order" have always killed far more people than they had lost.[63] The IRA could therefore condemn the British presence in terms of colonial occupation, but it could not describe it as genocide or an existential war. Under these conditions, the "need" for suicide bombers was simply not compelling, and the use of proxy bombers was therefore doubly counterproductive. It suggested hypocrisy on the part of a group willing to fight for a cause, but not to die for it, and demonstrated an excess that the political and military situation simply did not warrant.[64]

LIMITED DIFFUSION: THE WORKERS' PARTY OF KURDISTAN (PKK)

Background

The PKK is one of several parties claiming to represent the approximately 16 million people of Kurdish ethnicity spread throughout Turkey, Syria, Iran, and Iraq. In all these states, the Kurds have been a minority, a status that left them open to abuse, the most extreme example being the attempted genocide by the Iraqi government of Saddam Hussein in the late 1980s.[65] Many Kurds believe that the establishment of a Kurdish state is therefore the only answer to resolving their concerns and history of discrimination, abuse, and attempted genocide.

The Workers' Party of Kurdistan, formed in 1978, is among the most resilient and brutal of the groups who have fought for Kurdish nationhood. After years of preparation, the PKK launched its armed struggle against the Turkish state in 1984.[66] By 1999, when the group's captured founder and leader Abdullah Ocalan stood trial in Turkey, the struggle launched by the PKK had claimed more than 30,000 lives, many of them civilians murdered as a result of the indifference and cruelty of the PKK and the Turkish government.

The charismatic leadership of Ocalan is a distinctive feature of the PKK. In many ways Ocalan played a role similar to that of Prabhakaran's in the LTTE. Ocalan is a university dropout with no tribal or familial distinctions. In their place, he substituted leftist rhetoric of a Leninist nature, calling for a secretive, professional revolutionary movement and the creation of a one-party state.[67] Ocalan assumed the role of leader, tolerating no alternatives and no dissent, thus using ideology to substitute for more traditional forms of cultural capital. The centrality of Ocalan as leader and ideologue created an organization that one analyst called a "political cult."[68] Once having joined, members are expected to remain in the organization for life. New members must swear allegiance to Ocalan, and only by extension to the PKK and the idea of Kurdish statehood.

Ocalan, like Prabhakaran, always viewed alternative Kurdish nationalist movements as threats to his own. The PKK therefore dealt violently with other Kurdish groups and was responsible for inflicting an extraordinary amount of harm on members of the Kurdish community while in theory fighting for their statehood.[69] In addition, beginning in 1985 it was PKK policy to hunt down and kill former members who criticized the group. During the later 1980s, fear of spies, informers, and rival claims to leadership led to murderous internal purges of the PKK, weakening it internally and eroding morale.[70] The PKK did, however, have an internal history of self-sacrifice as political protest. In 1982 a PKK prisoner named Mazlum Dogan hung himself in protest of Turkish prison conditions. The following May, four other prisoners burned themselves to death in protest, and by the summer several had started a hunger strike that resulted in the deaths of four by September.[71]

Given the similarities between the PKK and the LTTE, it is hardly surprising that Ocalan attempted to avail himself of the new weapon that by the mid-1990s was being used so effectively by Prabhakaran. The PKK's experimentation with suicide bombing took the form of two waves of attacks, the first consisting of three operations in 1996 and the second consisting of ten attacks during 1998–99. Authorities managed to prevent several others. The first three were the most effective, resulting in nine, five, and four fatalities, respectively, as well as numerous injured.[72] After these attacks, the group refrained from using suicide bombers for almost two years. Then, when Ocalan called on his followers to resume suicide bombing, they proved to be relatively ineffective, with eleven bombers killing only six people.

The Importance of Use

Ocalan chose to begin suicide attacks during a period of weakness in the PKK's history. By 1995 the group had been devastated by the Turkish government's measures against it and by infighting with other Kurdish groups. The public sensation caused by LTTE and (after 1994) Palestinian suicide bombings probably suggested to Ocalan that the use of such attacks would provide the PKK its best chance to reverse its fortunes. Ocalan may also have hoped to use suicide bombings to provoke additional repression by the Turkish government, as its heavy-handed counterterrorism had generated sympathy for the PKK in the past.[73] Whatever Ocalan's actual internal calculus, from a perspective outside the group, the motivation for the use of suicide bombers seems to have been desperation. According to the most thorough study of the PKK, "Certainly, the turn to suicide bombing underscored something Ocalan refused to publicly admit: that the rebels had lost the initiative and without some radical, tactical, and strategic change, had no way to regain it."[74]

The brutality of the Turkish state in suppressing the Kurdish nationalist movement thus suggested the need for suicide bombing to Ocalan and also pushed certain PKK members toward the self-sacrificial mindset conducive to suicide bombing. Need and possibility were present, at least to an extent, allowing the group to begin using suicide attackers, but Ocalan's poor use of it was most likely the factor that prevented suicide bombing from becoming sustainable within the organization.

The greatest propensity for self-sacrifice had been among male prisoners, a situation that is not surprising given the brutality and despair of prison life. Ocalan, however, chose instead to use female members of the group for the first few attacks. There seems to have been agreement among the upper echelon of the PKK leadership for the need for suicide attackers, but the recruitment of young women was not on a voluntary basis.[75] For example, the PKK's second suicide attack, which took place on October 25, 1996, was carried out by a woman named Leyla Kaplan, but she was not the first candidate to be considered for the mission. The first woman chosen for the attack refused the mission. She was immediately executed in front of Kaplan.[76]

The decision to force women to become suicide attackers limited the power of suicide bombing to serve as a means of individual empowerment and group solidarity. For women, membership in the PKK had been potentially liberating in that it allowed them to break away from the confines of a rigidly paternalistic and traditional Kurdish culture and fight for a cause under conditions of relative equality.[77] Killing themselves on behalf of the PKK may have been a much less attractive proposition, however, especially given the attitude of some male members, who viewed women as a burden and suggested that the suicide missions would be a good way to use them effectively while simultaneously decreasing their numbers.[78] In addition, the attacks were not accompanied by the type of publicity that had become characteristic of suicide bombing by the LTTE and Hizballah.[79] Without group identity or the promise of secular or religious immortality, there was simply no way for prospective bombers to be assured that their deaths would be remembered and honored, and therefore no way for them to know with conviction that the sacrifice would be worthwhile. The PKK's use of suicide bombing in the mid-1990s was therefore a trial run that produced ambiguous results. Its cost in terms of morale seems to have been high, and its payoff in terms of coercive power somewhat limited.

The resulting balance was insufficient for encouraging regular use of suicide bombers, but not great enough to completely delegitimize the technology, so two years later Ocalan could again call upon PKK members to carry out suicide attacks. As before, the decision appears to have been based on desperation. In early 1999 Ocalan was captured by the Turkish government and was sentenced to death on June 29. Although he appeared to be conciliatory and cooperative with the authorities during his captivity, he called on his followers to carry out attacks, including suicide missions, to pressure the authorities. His followers responded with a wave of poorly coordinated violence, including several attempted suicide missions. This second wave of attacks lacked centralized direction

TABLE 4.1 **Suicide Bombings by the Workers' Party of Kurdistan, 1996–1999**

	LOCATION	FATALITIES	INJURED
FIRST WAVE			
June 30, 1996	Tunceli	9	30
October 25, 1996	Adana	5	12
October 29, 1996	Sivas	4	1
TOTAL		**18**	**43**
SECOND WAVE			
November 17, 1998	Yuksekova	0	6
December 1, 1998	Lice	0	14
December 24, 1998	Van	1	22
March 2, 1999	Van Province	1	3
March 4, 1999	Batman	0	4
March 27, 1999	Istanbul	0	10
April 5, 1999	Bingol	0	0
July 5, 1999	Adana	0	17
July 7, 1999	Iluh	0	0
August 28, 1999	Tunceli	0	0
TOTAL		**2**	**76**

Source: Ami Pedahzur, *Suicide Terrorism* (Cambridge, U.K., and Malden, Mass.: Polity Press, 2005), 243–44.

and without competent organizational mediation was far less lethal than even the PKK's first wave of attacks (see Table 4.1).[80]

By this point, the civil war launched by the PKK had claimed tens of thousands of lives, and in comparison the actual effects of PKK suicide bombing were meager indeed. After being sentenced to death, Ocalan called on his followers to end their struggle, perhaps in an effort to win clemency. The Turkish government had been under pressure from leaders in the European Union to spare Ocalan's life, so when Turkey abolished the death penalty for civilians in 2002, Ocalan's sentence was commuted to life in prison.[81]

CONCLUSION: MANAGING EXPECTATIONS

The diffusion of an innovation such as suicide bombing from an established user to a new cultural context is governed by numerous factors, the most important of which are the extent to which the innovation is compatible with the culture of the new society and the degree to which the innovation is perceived to be better for solving a given problem relative to other solutions. These two factors are integral at all three levels of the suicide-bombing complex: in the minds of prospective bombers, in the decision making of their sponsoring organizations, and in the support (or lack thereof) of their reference community (i.e., culture). When people at all three levels are of like mind regarding the ability of suicide bombing to solve their problems and are accepting of the price in human life, suicide bombing becomes sustainable. All levels, however, need not share the same position on the desirability of suicide bombing as a potential form of attack. When elaborate cultures of martyrdom, such as the one that characterized the LTTE, are absent, or when the military situation does not justify the militancy of suicide bombing, there is less pressure compelling societies to support suicide bombing and less motivation on the part of individuals to become suicide attackers. In such instances, the challenge for the sponsoring organization, should its leaders still desire to deploy suicide attackers, is to manipulate the expectations of individuals and communities in an effort to bring them into alignment with the organization's decision making. As this chapter illustrates, they are not always successful. The IRA's leaders wanted to use the power of suicide bombers to shock the British, but they knew that few of their ranks would be anxious to volunteer for such missions. They had already learned via hunger strikes that there would be little support in the nationalist community for "martyrs" who might have been pressured to carry out a suicide mission. Abdullah Ocalan forced his variant of suicide bombing upon an unenthusiastic subset of his followers and thereby could not reinforce group coherence or connect the group to the broader Kurdish nationalist community.

These two trial runs suggest a self-limiting factor that is potentially inherent to suicide attacks. Suicide bombing is by definition an organizational phenomenon. The legitimacy that makes the self-sacrifice of the individual admirable and acceptable to the community derives paradoxically from the individual's stated commitment to comrades, cause, and society, a decision that must be made free of organizational coercion. Leaders who seek to deploy suicide attackers must therefore minimize the rather significant role that they play in selecting and preparing suicide attackers to prevent themselves from being seen as cynical manipulators of human lives. Their task is made easier when a culture that devalues individual lives relative to the good of the community is firmly entrenched or when extreme need makes suicide bombing appear as a necessary force equalizer. Among Palestinian Islamists in the 1990s, the first factor was present, making the sustained use of suicide bombing possible. By the new millennium, the second factor, military need, was present as well, leading to an exponential increase in the number of suicide attacks carried out against Israeli targets.

5

MANAGING MARTYRDOM, PART I

Palestinian Suicide Bombing in the 1990s

In 1992 members of Hamas, then a relatively new Islamist organization with its stronghold in the Gaza Strip, attempted what at that time was an ambitious form of attack against Israel.[1] Several members of the organization had booby-trapped a car with explosives in a suburb of Tel Aviv with the hope of inflicting a large number of civilian casualties. Security forces, however, found the car and were able to disarm the explosives.

After this failure, members of the group apparently decided to follow the example of Hizballah and integrate a human with a bomb to ensure a more reliable detonation.[2] In April 1993 Yahya Ayyash, a Hamas explosives expert who came to be known as "The Engineer," rigged a Volkswagen with an improvised hodge-podge of explosives taken from other weapons. A young man named Saher Taman al-Nabulsi drove the car to the target, a highway rest stop near Mehola Junction. Saher had been involved in the failed attack of the previous year and was wanted by Israel for the murder of two Israelis. He apparently decided to become Hamas' first human bomb rather than continue to face arrest or death at the hands of Israeli authorities. He drove the rigged vehicle between two buses with Israel Defense Force (IDF) personnel inside and detonated the explosives. In some ways the results were amateurish. The blast was relatively weak and was deflected upward by the two buses; twenty soldiers and one civilian were injured, and the only fatalities were Saher and a Palestinian who worked at the rest stop.[3] The militants learned from the attack, however, and future suicide missions would prove to be far more deadly.

The improvised manner in which suicide bombing became part of the Israeli-Palestinian struggle more than a decade after being developed in Lebanon is consistent with the broader model of technological diffusion discussed in preceding chapters. As the above example shows, unsophisticated trial runs can be relatively easy to stage. Hamas' early use of suicide bombing was haphazard and ineffective. In the mid-1990s, trial and error, as well as the direct transfer of know-how from Hizballah, allowed Palestinian Islamists to master suicide bombing and to use it in a manner similar to that of the Tamil Tigers: the controlled, calculated use of suicide attacks to inflict harm, intimidate adversaries, and to send a message about the sponsoring groups' identity and intentions.

BACKGROUND

The Intifada and the Palestinian Authority

The Israeli invasion of Lebanon in 1982, while inadvertently contributing to the rise of Hizballah, succeeded in its intended purpose of destroying the Palestine Liberation Organization (PLO) as a conventional military organization and driving it from southern Lebanon. The upper ranks of the PLO eventually settled in Tunisia, leaving behind a movement and a people without an effective organizational means for pursuing Palestinian statehood. While the PLO leadership occasionally staged irritating raids against Israel, for the most part it was isolated from the reality of Palestinian life under Israeli occupation and developed a reputation for materialism and corruption.[4]

In the occupied territories of the 1980s a deceptive calm masked tension building under the surface. This tension exploded into a systematic campaign of civil disobedience, strikes, and demonstrations throughout the occupied territories beginning in December 1987.[5] The spark of the uprising, the accidental deaths of several Palestinians caused by a careless Israeli truck driver, was less important than the root cause of the rebellion—a deep sense of frustration and humiliation felt by Palestinians. The uprising, or intifada, came to serve two purposes.[6] First, in the words of the Palestinian scholar Sari Nusseibeh, the intifada "exorcised demons of humiliation, inferiority, and self-contempt" from nearly two million Palestinians living under Israeli occupation. Second, it allowed a young, indigenous Palestinian leadership the opportunity to mobilize this discontent and direct it toward a more coherent end—Palestinian statehood.

Local leaders from the factions of the PLO formed the National Unified Command, which wrote and distributed leaflets instructing Palestinians on ways to resist the occupation, limited the armed conflict (for instance, by calling for an end to the use of Molotov cocktails), coordinated general strikes and other protests and activities in the occupied territories, and of great significance, maintained pressure on the Israeli government for several years. This ongoing pressure eventually made resolution of the Palestinian situation an important domestic issue in Israeli politics and engaged the United States as a potential broker in any peace process.

The intifada took the PLO leadership in Tunis by surprise, but as the uprising continued it became clear that recognized leadership would be necessary to turn the pressure of the intifada into concrete political gains. From exile in Tunisia, PLO chairman Yasser Arafat seized the opportunity, and over the next several years the PLO, representing the interests of Palestinians in the occupied territories, recognized Israel and renounced terrorism, helping to initiate a formal dialogue with Israel, beginning with the Madrid conference in October 1991. After some false starts, the two parties made significant progress in Oslo, Sweden, during secret negotiations that were publicly affirmed when Arafat and Israeli prime minister Yitzhak Rabin shook hands on the White House lawn in September 1993. The two agreed to a Declaration of Principles stating that much of the Gaza Strip and parts of the West Bank would be transferred to Palestinian administration, giving more than one million Palestinians a measure of control over their daily affairs. The following year, through an agreement signed in Cairo, the Palestinian Authority (PA) was created to serve as the administrative instrument for Palestinian self-governance. Arafat assumed leadership of the Palestinian Authority, adding the title president of the Palestinian Authority to his positions as chairman of the PLO and leader of Fatah, the dominant faction in the PLO.[7]

The peace process, however, was flawed from the beginning, and in retrospect it is clear that the partial successes of the early years stemmed entirely from deferment of fundamental issues to a later date. The Oslo-Cairo process dealt with Palestinian self-governance, but did not address the long-term issue of a Palestinian state. The administrative and legal status of Jerusalem remained unresolved as did the Right of Return of Palestinian refugees (and their descendents), allowing them to go back to their pre-1948 homes, now in Israel.[8] Successive Israeli governments accelerated construction of settlements in the West Bank during the 1990s, throwing into question the credibility of Israel's stated intentions to exchange land for peace. Furthermore, Arafat's willingness to make the compromises necessary for a lasting peace also remained an open question.[9] Finally, Arafat and his Fatah associates returned to a different and much more divided Palestinian community than the one they had left a decade earlier. Years of occupation and the ineffectiveness of the PLO had led to the emergence of an Islamist movement for Palestinian liberation whose leaders were not beholden to the PLO and its program of secular nationalism and who were much less prone to compromise.

The Islamist Alternatives: Hamas and Palestinian Islamic Jihad

Hamas and Palestinian Islamic Jihad took shape in the late 1980s, but they were the product of decades of opposition to the perceived encroachment of Western politics and values into the Middle East. After World War I, when Western powers partitioned the lands formerly controlled by the Ottoman Empire, many Arabs living there sought an alternative to Western culture and governance. By the late 1920s, some of them appeared to have found it in the form of political Islam. In 1928 in Egypt, Hassan al-Banna founded the Society of the Muslim Brothers, also known as the Muslim Brotherhood. Banna was concerned about the retreat of Islamic civilization and cautioned his followers that nominal political independence was worthless without intellectual, social, and cultural independence.[10]

A Palestinian branch of the Muslim Brotherhood was established immediately after World War II and participated in a limited fashion in the 1948 war against Israel. After the war, Gaza was administered by Egypt. Egyptian governments had over the years suppressed the Brotherhood and extended this treatment to Gaza, a policy that encouraged underground militancy. The group could operate somewhat more freely (and was consequently less militant) in the West Bank, which at the time was administered by Jordan. When Israelis captured Gaza and the West Bank (including East Jerusalem) during the 1967 war, the local branches of the Muslim Brotherhood reacted by intensifying their activities and creating an infrastructure of social support services. In 1978 the Muslim Brotherhood founded the Islamic University, which has been the principal stronghold of it and its successor organizations in Gaza ever since.[11]

In the occupied territories, Palestinians became increasingly frustrated by the PLO's lack of success in ending the occupation. Islamic groups aggregated around mosques and universities and developed a vague organizational framework, but they did not challenge the occupation openly. Their relationship with the PLO, Fatah in particular, was often adversarial. The desire to avoid a split within Palestinian society encouraged coexistence, but major ideological differences led to skirmishes between supporters of Fatah and of the Islamic groups in the 1980s.[12]

The intifada provided the impetus for the Gaza branch of the Muslim Brotherhood to transform itself into Hamas, formally the Islamic Resistance Organization, for which "Hamas" is an acronym and in Arabic means "zeal" or "enthusiasm." In the days following the outbreak of the intifada, several leaders of the Muslim Brotherhood in Gaza, including Sheikh Ahmed Yassin, acknowledged as the founder of Hamas, met to discuss the situation. Understanding that the intifada's grassroots opposition to Israeli occupation was something fundamentally new, they decided to play a much more active role in the resistance.[13] Members of Hamas did not participate in the National Unified Command of the intifada, however, but kept their independence, drawing upon the movement's history as an educational and social phenomenon to present Hamas as an Islamic alternative for leadership toward Palestinian statehood.[14]

Yassin and the others articulated the goals of Hamas in its charter, released in 1988. In the document, the leadership of Hamas declares that the land of Palestine and the Islamic faith are inseparable and that to cede one inch of Palestine, which for them stretches from the Mediterranean Sea to the Jordan River, is not permissible (see especially articles 11 and 12).[15] Although Hamas began as a relatively nonviolent movement— in the 1970s and early 1980s the Israeli government had been supportive of the Islamists as an alternative to the PLO and did not designate Hamas as a terrorist organization until eighteen months after its official founding—the group's charter clearly defines Hamas as a military organization that rejects peaceful resolution of the Palestinian issue. The charter also recognizes the PLO as a "father, brother, relative, and a friend," but then goes on to differentiate Hamas from the PLO based on the latter's secular nature: "Therefore, in spite of our appreciation for the PLO and its possible transformation in the future, and despite the fact that we do not denigrate its role in the Arab-Israeli conflict, we cannot substitute it for the Islamic nature of Palestine by adopting secular thought. For the Islamic nature of Palestine is part of our religion, and anyone who neglects his religion is bound to lose."

In its early years, Hamas as an organization had to reconcile a number of mutually opposing tendencies. Its leaders had to distinguish themselves from groups such as Fatah, but not to the point of Palestinian civil war. Much of Hamas' legitimacy stemmed from its credibility as a resistance group, but pushing an uncompromising Islamic war for the liberation of all Palestine too strongly would have threatened its most important source of appeal to the Palestinians—its growing network of charitable and social institutions. Thus Hamas' reputation as a scrupulous and fair social welfare organization put limits on its militancy. Consequently, the uncompromising nature of the charter was offset somewhat in practice by a degree of pragmatism and flexibility on the part of Hamas.[16]

Even more ideological and less prone to pragmatic accommodation than Hamas was Palestinian Islamic Jihad (PIJ), which also grew from the Gaza branch of the Muslim Brotherhood. The founders of PIJ were inspired by the Islamic revolution led by Ayatollah Khomeini in Iran. The primary ideological difference between Hamas and PIJ was that the former existed as a specifically Palestinian movement while the latter began as a catalyst for Islamic revolution throughout the Arab world. Personal agendas and animosities among rival leaders served to put distance between the two groups as well. PIJ, as a smaller group with fewer resources and obligations than Hamas, has not demonstrated any of the tendencies toward accommodation that Hamas has shown.[17]

THE BEGINNING OF PALESTINIAN SUICIDE BOMBING

Escalation of Militancy: External Factors

The Dome of the Rock, a shrine built to commemorate the site from which Muhammad ascended to heaven, and the nearby al-Aqsa mosque stand in the heart of the Old City of Jerusalem. These two holy sites constitute the centerpieces of a thirty-five-acre complex of buildings and gardens called the Haram al-Sharif (Noble Sanctuary) by Muslims. The Haram al-Sharif is believed by many in the Jewish and Christian communities to have been built upon the remains of the Temple of Solomon, destroyed and then rebuilt more than two millennia ago, and is thus the holiest site for Jews. The faithful believe that it is the point from which the world unfolded during the creation and is the place where God created Adam.[18] Faithful Jews refer to the site as the Temple Mount.

In August 1990 the leader of a conservative Jewish group called the Temple Mount Faithful announced a plan to lay a foundation stone for the Third Jewish Temple on the Mount, which would have symbolized the recapture of the site for the Jewish community. Leaders of Hamas interpreted the announcement as a threat and called for demonstrations. As the day of the ceremony approached, scuffles between Palestinians and Jews became a regular occurrence. On the morning of October 8, large crowds gathered, and some of the Palestinians began pelting Israeli police and Jewish worshippers with stones and bottles. The police responded with gunfire, killing twenty-one Palestinians and wounding nearly a hundred. Thirty-four Israelis, including police, were injured.[19]

The Hamas leadership responded by calling for its own jihad against the Israelis and began organizing a military wing, the Izz al-Din al-Qassam Brigades.[20] This new wing took its name from Sheikh Izz al-Din al-Qassam, a Palestinian from Haifa who had led an insurrection in Mandate Palestine, assassinating British officials and Jewish civilians in the early 1930s before being killed by the British.[21] The emergence of the al-Qassam Brigades corresponded with an increase in lethal knife attacks on Israelis. Within two months, eight Israelis were murdered in such a fashion.[22] The stabbings continued for the next two years and increasingly were carried out by members of Hamas. This "War of the Knives" lasted until December 1992, ending when Hamas members killed six Israeli soldiers in two separate attacks and kidnapped a seventh, Sgt. Maj. Nissim Toledano, to use as a bargaining chip. After negotiations between the Israeli government and Hamas broke down, Toledano was murdered and his body found in a ditch on December 15.[23]

Israeli prime minister Rabin then arrested more than a thousand members of Hamas and Palestinian Islamic Jihad and attempted to deport 415 of them to Lebanon. The Lebanese government refused to accept them, so they began 1993 in makeshift camps in Israeli-occupied southern Lebanon, near the Israeli border. Hizballah, however, accommodated the militants during their exile. During this time, Hizballah undoubtedly instructed these Palestinians in the strategies and tactics of resistance, including providing advice on how to organize and carry out suicide attacks.

Escalation of Militancy: Internal Factors

The deadly attacks of late 1992 were unusual in comparison to the overall level of Palestinian violence against Israelis during the intifada. In the early stages of the uprising, the leadership of the Unified Command had deliberately tried to keep Palestinian actions non-lethal, advocating and instructing on acts of civil disobedience in its leaflets. The Palestinians had access to a small number of guns, but purposely did not use them in their confrontations with Israeli forces. Regardless, Palestinian youths throwing stones and being shot at by Israeli soldiers created a public image of the intifada as one of Palestinian violence, though their collective actions generally involved non-lethal, civil disobedience. Restrictions on the use of deadly violence did not, however, extend to affairs within the Palestinian community. As events unfolded, another dimension of conflict emerged—that of intra-Palestinian strife and competition in which violence would become far more deadly than Palestinian violence directed against Israel.

The struggle within the Palestinian community resulted in part from the withdrawal of Israeli security forces from many parts of the occupied territories in late 1987 and early 1988. In the freer and more lawless environment, paramilitaries from the various Palestinian factions competed with one another to establish order and primacy. It was especially important for Hamas, as a relatively new organization that had not formally taken part in the leadership of the intifada, to distinguish itself. Even before they began to target Israelis, members of Hamas had been killing and intimidating Palestinians to carve out a secure operational space and establish their credentials as a legitimate Islamic police force. For Hamas leaders, "purifying" the Palestinian community in such a manner was essential. During the 1980s, collaboration with Israeli security forces had become widespread, with thousands of Palestinians informing on their neighbors. As early as 1982–83, the Organization of Jihad and Da'wa had been created as a new body within the Gaza Muslim Brotherhood to root out, arrest, interrogate (sometimes brutally), and kill suspected collaborators. The members and cells of this body would several years later form the nucleus of the al-Qassam Brigades. [24]

During the intifada, Islamic morality became one of the first areas into which Hamas extended its self-appointed right to judge and punish. Hamas leaders believed that an abandonment of Islamic morals had weakened the Palestinian community, so they sought to impose and enforce conservative Islamic social values on it. To this end, Hamas members carried out numerous "honor killings"—executions of Palestinian women judged to have transgressed standards of moral conduct through their behavior. According to B'Tselem, the Israeli Information Center for Human Rights in the Occupied Territories, more than a hundred women were executed for moral crimes during the period of the intifada. Many of these executions were carried out by Hamas, some by the al-Qassam Brigades. [25]

All the paramilitaries targeted suspected informers within their midst, but Hamas was particularly thorough and brutal. They staged dozens of public show trials in which suspected informers (as well as those accused of common criminal offenses) were tried and sometimes publicly executed. The number of collaborator killings among all Palestinian groups in Gaza increased from 1 in 1987 to 199 in 1992. B'Tselem credits Hamas with 150 such executions during the course of the entire intifada, from 1987 to 1993. [26]

Today, many observers assume that Hamas' legitimacy in the eyes of its followers stems from its uncompromising stance toward Israel, but Hamas first took a hard line with its own community. Initially its legitimacy stemmed from its members' ability to protect their community by purging it of internal enemies. [27] The violence directed against Israelis was the consequence of a more confident and established Hamas turning its militant groups toward external rather than internal threats.

The Cairo-Oslo process polarized Palestinian paramilitaries. Fatah and its affiliates joined the peace process and eventually became a legitimate security force through the PLO's role in the creation of the Palestinian Authority with a mandate to police the community. It could therefore continue to use violence, but now it was legally sanctioned. Hamas and Palestinian Islamic Jihad, unable to legitimize themselves through politics, continued on the path that had brought them through the intifada—using violence to establish their credibility and to undermine their adversaries. The legitimacy granted to Fatah by the Cairo-Oslo process meant that Hamas and PIJ needed to escalate their campaigns to continue distinguishing themselves through force. In this light, intra-Palestinian violence during and following the intifada, the first lethal attacks directed against Israelis, and eventually the use of suicide attackers can all be seen as part of a continuum of escalation, as these groups sought more powerful weapons to make the kinds of political statements that they could not make in any other way without sacrificing their principles and identities.

THE CONTROLLED USE OF SUICIDE BOMBING, 1993–1998

On September 13, 1993, when Yasser Arafat and Yitzhak Rabin signed the Declaration of Principles, they validated a peace process begun in secret meetings in Oslo the previous year and marked the formal conclusion of the intifada. Hamas saw the Declaration of Principles as an existential threat because it committed the PLO to a political program that it could not accept.[28] An implication of the Declaration of Principles and the creation of the Palestinian Authority was that Fatah would be responsible for combating terrorism and helping to secure Israel. This aspect of the arrangement effectively guaranteed armed conflict among Palestinian factions.

Hamas and Palestinian Islamic Jihad responded to the signing of the Declaration of Principles with an escalation of violence that for the first time included the repeated use of suicide attackers. On the eve of the signing, Hamas guerrillas ambushed and killed three Israeli reservists, and a Palestinian carrying Hamas leaflets stabbed a bus driver to death before being fatally shot himself. In what may well have been another failed suicide attack, a Palestinian driver was killed when his vehicle collided with an Israeli bus. The car had been booby trapped with containers of gasoline and propane, suggesting that it was meant to explode upon collision.[29] The bomb did not detonate, so only two people on the bus were injured. The following month, another Hamas member, twenty-year-old Kamal Bani Odeh, rammed an Israeli commuter bus and detonated his vehicle, killing himself and injuring thirty passengers. As had been the case in previous attacks, the lack of Israeli fatalities can be attributed to the poor technical preparation of the attack. Odeh's vehicular bomb consisted of gasoline, hand grenades, and nails meant to serve as shrapnel, all of which destroyed the car and charred the side of the bus, but did not produce the powerful blast necessary to cause additional fatalities.[30] In all, there were seven attempted suicide bombings in the fall and early winter of 1993, five attributed to Hamas and two to Islamic Jihad; none of them caused fatalities apart from the bombers themselves.[31] These failures reflect the haphazard, improvised way in which suicide bombing was imported into the Palestinian context.

One consequence of the peace process was that many of the Hamas and Palestinian Islamic Jihad members who had been deported to Lebanon in late 1992 were allowed to return to the occupied territories in late 1993 and early 1994. They arrived prepared to use the practical knowledge that they had gained from Hizballah during their Lebanese exile.[32] Hamas leaders immediately began to plan much more dramatic attacks to capitalize on these new capabilities, but they still had to tread carefully, because a majority of Palestinians at the time were supportive of the peace process. Hamas therefore needed a pretext for its attacks that would allow its leaders to claim that they were acting in self-defense in order to sell the attacks to the Palestinian people, minimize the possibility of a Fatah backlash, and justify the attacks under Islamic law.[33]

On February 25, 1994, Baruch Goldstein, a Jewish settler in the West Bank, opened fire with an assault rifle at Friday morning prayers in the Ibrahimi mosque near the Tomb of the Patriarchs, in Hebron. He managed to kill twenty-nine worshippers before a crowd beat him to death.[34] The attack provided Hamas with the pretext it needed. After the customary forty-day period of mourning, on April 6, a young man drove his car to a bus stop in Afula, in northern Israel, and detonated the car and himself, destroying a bus and killing eight Israelis in the process. Forty-four people suffered injuries. Hamas claimed that the attack had been in retaliation for the Goldstein massacre and promised four more attacks. The following week, a second suicide bomber attacked a commuter bus, this time in Hadera, killing five Israelis and injuring thirty.[35]

Arafat did not know how to respond. He declined initially to condemn the first attack, lest he appear subservient to Israel and contribute to the appeal of Hamas. Two days after the bombing, the PLO issued a statement expressing its regrets over the loss of Israeli life. American leaders condemned Arafat for such a tepid response, and the Israeli opposition called for an end to peace talks. The Hamas attacks of April 1994 were therefore successful on a number of levels. They confirmed Hamas as an uncompromising advocate of Palestinian statehood, resonated with many Palestinians still horrified by the Goldstein massacre, and weakened Arafat and the peace process.

Six months later, both Hamas and PIJ resumed suicide attacks. On October 19 Hamas carried out its deadliest bombing to date, in the heart of Tel Aviv. Instead of using a car bomb, the bomber, twenty-seven-year-old Saleh Abdel Rahim al-Souwi, boarded a bus while carrying a large bag that contained twenty to forty pounds of explosives. The explosion killed twenty people in addition to al-Souwi; forty-eight others were wounded.[36] Over the next ten months, four more suicide attacks credited to Hamas would kill eighteen Israelis. Three attacks credited to PIJ would result in thirty-two Israeli deaths.[37]

The attacks put pressure on Arafat to reign in the militants, plus he undoubtedly understood the attacks as a challenge to his authority. By mid-November, Palestinian Authority police banned street demonstrations and arrested hundreds of Hamas and PIJ members.[38] The attempted repression culminated with Black Friday, November 18, when PA police fired on Islamist activists who were organizing a protest after Friday prayers at Gaza's Filastin mosque. The gunfire turned the protest into a riot in which at least fifteen people were killed, two hundred injured, and hundreds more arrested.[39] Undeterred, Hamas struck back. On January 22 two Hamas suicide bombers killed nineteen Israelis and injured more than sixty others.[40]

The suicide attacks, however, were unpopular with many Palestinians, who were still optimistic about the peace process. In addition, despite their actions, Hamas' leaders also did not want to disrupt Israeli redeployments from Palestinian territory or to sabotage upcoming Palestinian elections, both of which were popular.[41] Each attack usually resulted in Israel temporarily closing its borders to Palestinian workers, thus generating resentment toward Hamas. Recognizing the need to work with the PA, Hamas leaders agreed to a truce in which they promised not to carry out attacks from areas controlled by the authority. With the exception of one unsuccessful attack credited to PIJ, no suicide bombings occurred from August 1995 until February 1996.

In October 1995 Israeli agents assassinated Fathi al-Shiqaqi, one of the founders of Palestinian Islamic Jihad, in Malta.[42] On January 6 of the following year, Israeli forces killed Yahya Ayyash, the Hamas bomb maker called "The Engineer," hiding a small bomb in his cell phone and detonating it when he answered a call.[43] Ayyash was Hamas' best explosives expert and played a leading role in planning and executing the suicide attacks of 1994 as well as other Hamas missions. He was therefore immensely popular as a symbolic figure of resistance to Israel. Even Arafat paid tribute to the bomber after his death, calling him "the struggler, the martyr, Yahya Ayyash."[44] After a forty-day period of mourning, Hamas once again resumed suicide attacks against Israeli targets and in two attacks on February 25 killed twenty-five people and wounded seventy-seven.[45] Two more deadly attacks, one each by Hamas and PIJ, took place in early March. These killed nineteen and twenty people, respectively, bringing the total of Israeli fatalities in the aftermath of Ayyash's assassination to more than sixty people in little more than a week.

The resurgence of suicide attacks in 1996 has received attention because it came shortly before an Israeli general election in May and therefore undoubtedly played a role in the narrow victory of the more conservative candidate, Benjamin Netanyahu, over Rabin's successor, Shimon Peres. Since Netanyahu and his Likud Party had pledged to reject the peace process, this chain of events suggested to some that Hamas and PIJ deliberately used their suicide bombers to influence the electoral outcome and therefore derail the peace process.[46] There is certainly a superficial correlation between these events, but upon closer examination, such an interpretation raises more questions than answers. Among the most important, if the intent of the Islamists was only to disrupt the elections or to undermine the Labor Party of Shimon Peres, why were no attacks launched closer to the election date?

The attacks of February and March undoubtedly poisoned Israeli-Palestinian relations and undermined confidence in the Labor Party and the peace process, but this was true of all Palestinian suicide attacks in the 1990s. The immediate motivation for the timing of these attacks seems genuinely to have been revenge for the assassination of Ayyash. The bombings were initiated by local al-Qassam Brigades leaders, who undoubtedly sought to avenge Ayyash's killing. A Hamas spokesman said of the attacks, "Israel assassinated Yehia Ayyash, the leader of our military wing and should be accountable for this. We retaliated by carrying out suicide missions. For us, Labour and Likud are the same. They're two faces of the same coin."[47] That these attacks ended up having a particularly disruptive impact on the peace process as a consequence of the Likud victory was probably a welcome development from the perspective of Hamas hard-liners, but it was not the sole motivating factor.

Post-1996 there were eight more suicide attacks in the 1990s: five in 1997 and three in 1998.[48] The first wave of suicide attacks ended in 1998. The election of Labor Party candidate Ehud Barak as prime minister of Israel followed in 1999, along with resumption of the peace process at the highest levels. At the time, 70 percent of Palestinians still had faith in the peace process, and fewer than 20 percent supported suicide attacks.[49] More important, support for Hamas had dropped to 12 percent among Palestinians. PIJ could claim the support of only 2 percent.[50] Arafat and Israeli intelligence had decimated Hamas' al-Qassam Brigades and succeeded in cutting off much of Hamas' funding, which consequently limited its charitable work, further eroding its support. There were no attacks in 1999 and none in 2000 until after the outbreak of the second intifada (see Chapter 6).

THE SUCCESSFUL DIFFUSION OF SUICIDE BOMBING

Hizballah as Change Agent

As Table 5.1 shows, after some initial, ineffective experimentation, suicide bombing quickly became the spectacular weapon that Palestinian militants sought to mobilize their communities and to inflict grievous harm on Israelis. In this instance of successful technological diffusion, to cultural compatibility one must add an additional factor, what Everett Rogers calls a change agent, which also played a significant role. A change agent is an individual or organization that helps influence the innovation decisions of others in a direction consistent with the goals of the agent.[51] In the Palestinians' case, Hizballah played the role of change agent when it hosted members of Hamas and Islamic Jihad in 1993 in southern Lebanon. Assisting Palestinian militants in their struggle against the Israeli government promised to benefit Hizballah's own guerrilla war against Israel in southern Lebanon, so this transfer of knowledge was not particularly altruistic. Rather, it was done with the interests of Hizballah firmly in mind, making the organization a classic change agent as understood in terms of technological diffusion.

One can infer, based on changes in Palestinian suicide bombing, how the Lebanese instructors influenced their Palestinian protégés. The physical devices associated with suicide bombing seem to have been the least important. The Palestinians were already imitating Hizballah-style vehicular attacks using improvised explosives, but they clearly lacked the sophistication that characterized the bombings in Lebanon. The Palestinian militants learned by doing, however, and one can discern a steadily improving competence in their vehicular bombs from 1992 to 1994. Ayyash, in particular, embodied this culture of learning by doing, steadily improving his own capabilities and training numerous other Hamas explosives experts, until his death in 1996. On the whole, the technical elements of Hamas' attacks show steady evolution and improvement through 1993–94 rather than a dramatic change that would point to imported knowledge.

Hizballah's greatest gifts to the Palestinian militants were instruction in the management techniques for manufacturing the human guidance systems for its weapons and practical advice on the strategic and

TABLE 5.1 **Suicide Bombings by Hamas and Palestinian Islamic Jihad (PIJ), 1993–1998**

	GROUP	BOMBERS	FATALITIES	INJURED
April 16, 1993	Hamas	1	2	5
September 12, 1993	PIJ	1	0	0
September 14, 1993	Hamas	1	0	0
September 26, 1993	Hamas	1	0	0
October 4, 1993	Hamas	1	0	0
October 4, 1993	PIJ	1	0	30
November 2, 1993	Hamas	1	0	0
December 12, 1993	PIJ	1	0	1
April 6, 1994	Hamas	1	8	51
April 13, 1994	Hamas	1	5	30
October 19, 1994	Hamas	1	22	46
November 11, 1994	PIJ	1	3	6
December 25, 1994	Hamas	1	0	13
January 22, 1995	PIJ	2	18	69
April 9, 1995	PIJ	1	8	30
April 9, 1995	Hamas	1	1	3
June 25, 1995	Hamas	1	0	3
July 24, 1995	Hamas	1	6	31
August 21, 1995	Hamas	1	4	100
November 2, 1995	PIJ	2	0	8
February 25, 1996	Hamas	1	26	80
February 25, 1996	Hamas	1	1	0
March 3, 1996	Hamas	1	19	6
March 4, 1996	PIJ	1	20	75
March 21, 1997	Hamas	1	3	48
April 1, 1997	PIJ	1	0	7
April 1, 1997	PIJ	2	0	0
July 30, 1997	Hamas	2	16	178
September 4, 1997	Hamas	3	8	200
July 19, 1998	Hamas	1	0	1
October 29, 1998	Hamas	1	1	8
November 6, 1998	PIJ	2	0	20
TOTAL		**39**	**171**	**1,049**

Sources: Mohammed M. Hafez, *Manufacturing Human Bombs: The Making of Palestinian Suicide Bombers* (Washington, D.C.: United States Institute of Peace Press, 2006), app. I, p. 79; Ami Pedahzur, *Suicide Terrorism* (Cambridge, U.K., and Malden, Mass.: Polity Press, 2005), 242–53; data confirmed with START Center's Global Terrorism Database.

symbolic exploitation of suicide bombers. Specifically, Hizballah members seem to have impressed upon the Palestinians the importance of video-taped testimonies for ensuring the reliability of their recruits prior to the mission and for exploiting the media value of the attacks after the fact. Hamas began using testimonies of this nature in October 1994.[52] That Hamas and PIJ had learned from Hizballah how to improve their suicide bombing added to the intimidating character of the attacks. Palestinian militants did not hesitate to exploit this connection, announcing in Gaza mosques after the bombing of October 20, 1994, that the attack was carried out using knowledge and techniques learned from Hizballah.[53]

Compatibility: A Culture of Martyrdom

Apart from Hizballah's advice on management and symbolic exploitation of suicide attacks, the emergence of a culture of martyrdom in the 1990s is the most important factor explaining why suicide bombing came to be supported by a sizeable percentage of the Palestinian community. This subculture that increasingly glorified violent death relative to life was the product of years of cultural management on the part of Islamist groups and their supporters. It took a preexisting reverence for self-sacrifice on behalf of others and turned it into something similar to the culture of death that surrounded the Tamil Tigers' suicide bombers.

Prior to the 1990s, martyrdom was a commonly used term among Palestinians but it tended to refer to anyone who had died fighting the Israelis regardless of whether or not he or she had intended to sacrifice his or her life.[54] During the 1990s, the Islamist groups deliberately sought to transform this generalized perception of martyrdom and break down the barriers between life and self-sacrifice as part of a campaign of popularizing their interpretation of Islamic values throughout the West Bank and Gaza.[55] Observers during the 1990s noted the change. Imagery of militancy and self-sacrifice—in the form of television programs and graffiti and songs and rhymes taught to children—became part of the cultural backdrop.[56] Like Hizballah and the Tamil Tigers, the Palestinian Islamists turned the dead into celebrities and used them to inspire their followers to behave in similar fashion. Palestinian martyrs were glorified not only in song and memory but also through rituals and holidays established entirely for this purpose.[57]

As a consequence, self-sacrifice became an expectation shared by militants and a growing percentage of supporters in the broader community. This culture of martyrdom was encoded and transmitted to the next generation in the forms mentioned above and also more systematically through education and schooling.[58] In a poll conducted by the Islamic University in Gaza in 2001, 73 percent of children aged nine through sixteen said they hoped to become martyrs.[59] The acceptance of this subculture made the task of aligning the expectations of individuals and communities with the agenda of militant groups easier for Palestinian Islamists than it had been for the IRA or PKK. As long as there was no pressing military need for suicide attacks, however, and as long as the peace process presented an alternative to violent conflict, the culture of martyrdom was restricted to a minority of Palestinians. Suicide bombing was even temporarily abandoned in the late 1990s.

Militancy and Identity

The willingness to die, and to kill oneself, was a characteristic that members of the terrorist brigade of the Party of Socialist Revolutionaries in Russia used to set themselves apart from (and above, in a moral sense) their peers, not just their adversaries. Love of martyrdom similarly distinguished and elevated members of Hizballah above rival Shiite militants, for example, Amal. Membership in the Black Tigers was a mark of honor and distinction for members of the LTTE. In the occupied territories, the same process was already at work in 1991 when a section of the al-Qassam Brigades began calling itself the Martyr's Brigade, creating a new and prestigious role for its members and presenting itself as a model for Palestinian youth to follow.[60]

In later years, competition among militant Palestinian groups would help fuel the escalation of suicide bombing in a process that Mia Bloom calls outbidding, meaning that militant groups escalate violence as a way to "outbid," or outdo, one another in order to differentiate themselves in the political marketplace. Her analysis is most relevant to suicide bombing in the second intifada, but it sheds insight on the earlier phase of suicide bombing as well. Even before the dramatic escalation of suicide attacks in the 2000s, Bloom notes, disillusionment with the peace process and dissatisfaction with the corruption of the Palestinian Authority under

Arafat had "provided radical groups with an opportunity to increase their share of the political market by engaging in violence." As shown above, deadly intergroup rivalry and competition among Palestinians predates the use of suicide attackers by years.[61]

Some have criticized Bloom's analysis as being inconsistent with other instances of suicide bombing, particularly the LTTE's use of suicide attackers, which began after the LTTE had eliminated its rivals and established a near monopoly on the Tamil independence movement. This objection, however, is more the consequence of mistaking cause and effect during the process of militant escalation than it is a valid critique of the phenomenon. Escalation of violence does not cause suicide bombing; rather, some groups choose to escalate violence as a way to establish their own identities, internally and externally. Violence is therefore the effect, while affirmation of group identity is the ultimate cause. As perhaps the most extreme form of group-mediated violence, suicide bombing affords the most militant groups the opportunity to affirm (or to confirm) their radical identities. Groups that have already differentiated themselves through competition and outbidding are more likely to be able to use suicide bombing because it is compatible with established organizational norms. It follows that the cultures of martyrdom examined to this point were not established with the specific long-term goal of making suicide bombing possible, but instead were established to create group identities, bind members together, and collectively to make their radicalism and enthusiasm available to their leaders for organizational use. Suicide bombing is but one such use made possible by these cultural antecedents.

Understanding the importance of radicalism and competition for identity formation also offers a plausible explanation for why suicide bombing has tended to be taken up by relatively young groups.[62] New groups, spun off from previously existing organizations, must create new identities for themselves in the political marketplace of their communities and a new internal culture to provide group coherence and camaraderie. Extremism can be an effective way to do this. Hizballah differentiated itself from Amal through its dedication to an uncompromising vision of Islam characterized by reverence for individual self-sacrifice. The LTTE, originally one new group among many, also distinguished itself through its extremism, and in time its extremism would make Prabhakaran's use of suicide bombers possible. For Hamas and Islamic Jihad, suicide bombers became symbols representing the convictions and values of their members. The bombers then played a significant role in establishing the political identities of Hamas and Islamic Jihad, differentiating the two groups from Fatah, and served as one means by which the two sought to compete with one another for a share of the Palestinian political marketplace.

CONCLUSION: THE PALESTINIAN HYBRID

Palestinian militants decided to use suicide bombing on a regular basis in late 1993 to undermine the peace process and differentiate themselves from their rivals. They developed the capability to use suicide attackers through a process of trial and error, in which members of Hamas and Palestinian Islamic Jihad integrated their practical knowledge with the managerial techniques already developed by Hizballah. Suicide bombing became sustainable when a significant percentage of Palestinian society came to accept it as a legitimate means of resistance and political mobilization.

Palestinian suicide bombing did not simply spring into existence as a well-organized activity. Instead, leaders deliberately shifted cultural and organizational parameters to facilitate the emergence of a culture of martyrdom, which in turn facilitated the introduction of suicide bombing. Palestinian suicide bombing then was a mix of indigenous know-how, generated through trial and error, and imported knowledge facilitated by a willing and experienced change agent. It was a hybrid that resembled Hizballah's suicide bombing in some respects and in others demonstrated considerable originality (for example, in the use small, human-portable bombs).

One characteristic of this first wave of suicide attacks is worth noting. During the 1990s, as Hamas and Islamic Jihad bomb makers developed their technical competency, the nature of suicide missions began to change. The first attacks were with vehicle-born weapons, but by late 1994 suicide attackers had begun to resort to human-borne weapons, such as belts. This shift to smaller, simpler bomb designs helped make suicide bombing even more transmissible, potentially allowing smaller groups with fewer material resources and logistical capabilities to carry out suicide attacks. This trend, accompanied by an intensifying culture of martyrdom and, after 2000, a more pressing military need, facilitated the use of suicide bombing by small, relatively autonomous local groups and set the stage for the dramatic escalation of Palestinian suicide bombing in the new millennium.

6

MANAGING MARTYRDOM, PART II

Palestinian Suicide Bombing in the Second Intifada and After, 2000–2010

On the evening of March 27, 2002, nearly 250 Israelis gathered to celebrate the Feast of Passover in the dining room of the Park Hotel in Netanya, north of Tel Aviv. A young Palestinian man named Abdel Azziz Basset Odeh entered the hotel lobby and loitered for a while. When one of the hotel guests noticed his suspicious behavior and shouted a warning, Odeh quickly entered the dining room and detonated the explosives strapped to his body. Nineteen people were killed immediately; within days the death toll would climb to 29 dead and 154 injured. The devastation to the hotel was so extensive that authorities initially worried that the building might collapse.[1]

The attack had been designed to inflict maximum loss of life. Odeh's bomb consisted of approximately forty pounds of explosives and shrapnel and was so large and difficult to conceal that one account reports that he was disguised as a pregnant woman. Killing so many Israeli civilians, many of them elderly, on a holy day was meant to be a provocation toward the Israeli government, but the message the attackers hoped to send was even broader. At the time of the attack, Arab leaders were meeting in Beirut to discuss a peace plan drafted by Saudi Arabia. Gen. Anthony C. Zinni, the U.S. mediator sent to negotiate a cease-fire between the Israelis and Palestinians, was in the area as well. Hamas representatives made it clear that the brutality of the attack had been strategic, intended to enrage the Israelis to such an extent that neither a cease-fire nor a lasting peace would be possible. Hamas spokesman Mahmoud al-Zahar declared, "The Palestinian people do not want to see Zinni succeed in his assignment to the region. The bombing tonight came as a reaction to what is happening in Beirut. We want to remind the Arabs and the Muslims what resisting the occupation means."[2]

The Park Hotel bombing had much in common with previous use of suicide attackers by Hamas and Islamic Jihad. It was planned well in advance and designed to achieve several objectives simultaneously. Suicide bombing by Palestinians was in a state of flux, however, and by the end of the year, three significant differences emerged that would distinguish the suicide bombing of the second intifada from the suicide attacks of the 1990s. First, the most obvious difference was the exponential increase in the number of attempted and successful attacks. Second, the technology had spread to groups, including Fatah and the Popular Front for the Liberation of Palestine, that had not previously utilized it, and became a means by which the various factions competed with one another for the allegiance of the Palestinian people. There was thus more of a bottom-up dynamic, with local leaders using their bombers opportunistically rather than directing them with the level of forethought that characterized the attacks of the 1990s. Third, women were used as suicide attackers, first on an improvisational basis and later with more regularity.

COLLAPSE OF THE PEACE PROCESS

Although there had been optimism among many Palestinians regarding the peace process in 1999 and the Islamist parties were apparently in retreat, underneath the surface there was less reason for hope. It was clear from both the Israeli and Palestinian perspectives that the Cairo-Oslo process, which had postponed resolution of the toughest issues dividing the two parties, had been taken as far as it could go. Therefore, upon assuming office in mid-1999 as Israeli prime minister, Ehud Barak indicated that he wished to pursue a final, comprehensive peace agreement and was generally regarded as being willing to take the necessary steps in order to reach one.[3] Two major factors (among others) stood to undermine the process. The most important, by far, was the ongoing construction of Israeli settlements in the West Bank. The number of settlers in the West Bank (including East Jerusalem) and Gaza had nearly tripled between 1990 and 2000. The building of settlements had not been explicitly forbidden in the Cairo-Oslo process agreements, so many Palestinians came to believe that the entire peace process was actually meant to distract and forestall Palestinian political initiatives while Israelis continued to colonize the occupied territories at will.[4]

The other factor was PA president Yasser Arafat, who governed the Palestinian territories like a private fiefdom and presided over the Palestinian Authority like an autocrat, dispensing offices to his subjects based on personal loyalty rather than professional competence. Although Arafat was hard working and ascetic, his cronies did not share these traits, so the Palestinian Authority became mired in corruption.[5] The PA also became an extension and tool of Fatah, as Arafat used the PA's law enforcement capabilities to weaken his opponents and to strengthen his own faction.[6] Lacking the ability to deal with the important, big-picture issues—settlements, refugees, and borders—and no interest in governing effectively at the local level, the Palestinian Authority became representative, in the eyes of many Palestinians, of the shortcomings of the peace process as a whole.

With these factors looming in the background, the administration of Bill Clinton brokered meetings between Barak and Arafat in the United States over the summer of 2000. At the time, however, neither Barak nor Arafat had the political capital to make the compromises necessary for a final peace. Barak had just narrowly survived a vote of no confidence in the Knesset before departing for talks at Camp David, demonstrating that despite whatever popular support for the peace process might have existed, the political reality was that Barak was increasingly isolated. Arafat, for his part, believed that he was being pushed too far on the issues of Jerusalem and especially refugees.[7] After the summit collapsed, over the next several months U.S. mediators attempted to broker a loose framework for peace, the terms of which Arafat felt he could not accept and thus ultimately rejected in January 2001. By that point, violence had completely replaced the peace process as the defining characteristic of the Israeli-Palestinian relationship.

THE SECOND INTIFADA BEGINS

When campaigning for election as prime minister, Ehud Barak had promised that within a year he would withdraw Israeli forces from the occupation zone in southern Lebanon because being there no longer served a strategic purpose. Hizballah's media-savvy leaders took credit for the eventual withdrawal, in May 2000, claiming that its guerrilla campaign had driven out the Israeli occupier. Palestinian militants agreed with this assessment and by summer 2000 had begun to consider whether a Hizballah-style guerrilla campaign might be an effective way to attack Israel.[8]

With the peace process effectively stalled in mid-2000, all that was necessary to reignite hostilities was a spark, which occurred in September in the form of a visit to the Haram al-Sharif, the Islamic holy site in Jerusalem's Old City, by Ariel Sharon, one of Israel's most polarizing politicians. The Palestinian Authority had approved the visit of a Likud Party delegation headed by Sharon, but the excursion was unusual in that it violated modern Jewish custom, which prohibits worshippers from ascending and praying on the Temple Mount.[9] Furthermore, Sharon, a conservative hard-liner and supporter of the settler movement, had purchased an apartment in East Jerusalem and was preparing to challenge Ehud Barak in elections to be held in early 2001. Thus his decision to visit the Haram al-Sharif was interpreted by many to be a provocative political move, intended symbolically to lay Israeli claim to the heart of East Jerusalem.[10]

Some Palestinian leaders proclaimed on television that Sharon's visit would desecrate the Haram al-Sharif and called on Palestinians to defend the area. On Thursday, September 28, when Sharon climbed up to the Temple Mount, surrounded by hundreds of police, a skirmish broke out between the security forces and Palestinians.[11] The following day, after Friday prayers, hundreds of Palestinians exited the al-Aqsa mosque and threw stones down onto the plaza adjoining the Western Wall and pelted police with rocks. Israeli soldiers responded with live ammunition, killing eight Palestinians. The next day, footage was broadcast around the world reportedly showing Muhammad al-Dura, a boy huddling with his father against a wall for protection, being shot and killed in an exchange of fire between Israeli and Palestinian forces. He was immediately portrayed as the first martyr of the second, or al-Aqsa, intifada.[12]

While the uprising of late 2000 was cast in the same terminology as the intifada that erupted in 1987, it rapidly became far more lethal, as Palestinian leaders, including Arafat, encouraged their followers to use deadly violence. As events unfolded, it became clear that the inspiration and model for this uprising was Hizballah's guerrilla war against Israel, not the civil disobedience of the first intifada. Thus stone throwing and civil disobedience were accompanied by small-arms and mortar fire and the use of Molotov cocktails. Israel responded, in turn, much more lethally than it had in 1987. After six days of confrontations, sixty Palestinians were dead. By October 10, ninety Palestinians had been killed and more than two thousand injured, as opposed to a handful of Israeli fatalities, mainly among the Israel Defense Forces (IDF).[13]

Arafat's role in the second intifada was particularly controversial. Some believe that he deliberately instigated the violence to pressure Israel.[14] This interpretation, however, appears to credit Arafat with having more control over the various factions than he actually possessed. Nonetheless, Palestinian Authority leaders, Arafat first among them, could have done more to restrain the violence and consequently must share blame for its escalation.[15] It is likely that Arafat believed that more violence might help his position. If this was, indeed, the case, he was terribly mistaken. He was unable to control the fighting, which became decentralized, with local commanders and fighters taking the initiative, driving and escalating the violence from the grass roots. Furthermore, when Israel responded by retaking territory in the West Bank—in the process destroying infrastructure, raiding PA offices, and carving up the area with new barriers, Israeli-only roads, and checkpoints—the PA's ability to deliver services collapsed. At this point, Hamas stepped up its role of tending to the needs of the Palestinian people.[16] It used this situation to its advantage to make steady political gains at the expense of Fatah.

SUICIDE BOMBING IN THE SECOND INTIFADA

Escalation

Suicide attackers were not used in the early weeks of the second intifada, suggesting that Palestinian fighters initially had in mind a guerrilla war against the Israeli military more so than terrorist attacks against Israeli civilians. Hizballah, after all, had used suicide attackers only sparingly in its guerrilla war against Israel. The first suicide bombing of the second intifada was carried out by Palestinian Islamic Jihad (PIJ) on October 26, when twenty-four-year-old Nabil Arair attacked an IDF post in Gaza, killing himself and injuring one Israeli soldier. It was the first suicide attack in nearly two years. Over the next several months, PIJ and Hamas attempted several more attacks, some of which inflicted numerous injuries, but which failed to cause any Israeli fatalities. Eventually, on March 4, 2001, a Hamas bomber killed three people, and from that point on suicide attacks became the most reliable means available to Palestinian militants for killing Israeli soldiers and civilians alike. Suicide bombings—which had dropped to zero in 1999 and only three to five attempted attacks in 2000—climbed steadily throughout 2001. By year's end, Hamas and PIJ had conducted approximately thirty attacks.[17]

The turn toward suicide bombings made operational sense from a Palestinian viewpoint because other forms of armed resistance were not having much of an effect on Israeli armed forces or society. That is to say, after six months, the Palestinians found themselves fighting a very unsuccessful guerrilla war. Gal Luft, a former lieutenant colonel in the Israel Defense Forces, observed the following:

> From the Palestinian perspective . . . the results of the guerilla campaign in the first year were poor, especially considering the duration of the fighting and the volume of fire. Palestinian forces launched more than 1,500 shooting attacks on Israeli vehicles in the territories but killed 75 people. They attacked IDF outposts more than 6,000 times but killed only 20 soldiers. They fired more than 300 antitank grenades at Israeli targets but failed to kill anyone. To demoralize the settlers, the Palestinians launched more than 500 mortar and rocket attacks at Jewish communities in the territories and, at times, inside Israel, but the artillery proved to be primitive and inaccurate, and only one Israeli was killed.[18]

Given this situation, Luft understood the switch toward suicide attackers to be a switch to a much deadlier and more effective strategy. During 2001 this strategy evolved in such a way that more conventional resistance groups, including Fatah and its armed branch, the Tanzim, would continue the guerrilla campaign while the Islamist groups steadily supplemented the guerrilla war with a wave of terror attacks targeting Israel's civilian population.

In 2002, as groups that had never previously attempted suicide attacks began using them, the total exceeded fifty, which represented more than all the successful and attempted suicide attacks from 1993 to 2000. These attacks, many carried out without warning in densely populated civilian areas, resulted in hundreds of Israeli dead and wounded of all ages and walks of life. In one of the most devastating cases, an attacker wearing an explosive vest detonated himself outside a Tel Aviv discotheque on a Friday evening, June 1, 2001. He killed twenty-one people, primarily teenagers and young adults, many of them recent émigrés to Israel from Russia and other post-Soviet states.[19] More than one hundred people were injured.

The number of successful suicide attacks in the second intifada peaked in 2002 and then declined rapidly as the uprising wound to an end in 2005 with a cease-fire between Israeli and Palestinian forces in the aftermath of Arafat's death, in late 2004. After the intifada, three attacks succeeded in early 2006, only one in 2007, one in 2008, none in 2009, and one in 2010. Overall, suicide attacks comprised less than one-half of 1 percent of all Palestinian attacks from 2000 through 2006, but they caused 50 percent of civilian fatalities.[20] The escalation of suicide bombing in the second intifada and its subsequent cessation occurred as illustrated in Figure 6.1, which also includes numbers from the first wave of suicide bombing in the 1990s to provide perspective.

DIFFUSION AND DE-CENTRALIZATION OF PALESTINIAN SUICIDE BOMBING

Between March 1999 and December 2000 Palestinians' approval of suicide bombings soared from 26 percent to 66 percent while the number opposed declined from 66 percent to 22 percent.[21] Furthermore, the bombers, immortalized in videos broadcast by Hizballah's al-Manar television, became celebrities, seemingly the only heroes young Palestinians could claim as their own. Lacking confidence in the political process and politicians, and mired in economic misery, violence and displays of determination became important sources of honor for many Palestinians,

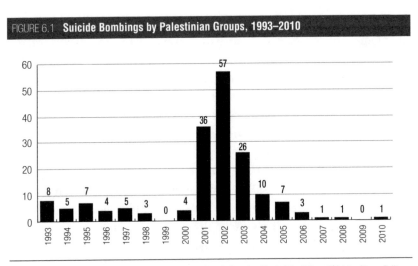

FIGURE 6.1 **Suicide Bombings by Palestinian Groups, 1993–2010**

Sources: Data for 1993 through 2004 are from Ami Pedahzur, *Suicide Terrorism* (Cambridge, U.K., and Malden, Mass.: Polity Press, 2005), app., 242–53, and Mohammed M. Hafez, *Manufacturing Human Bombs: The Making of Palestinian Suicide Bombers* (Washington, D.C.: United States Institute of Peace Press, 2006), app. I, 79. For 2005 through 2010 sources and details, see Table 6.1.

which served to elevate the social status of the suicide bomber.[22] In this environment, groups that were not utilizing suicide attackers, such as Fatah, risked losing political credibility. Thus in early 2002 the al-Aqsa Martyr's Brigades, a new organization within Fatah, took credit for their first suicide attack.

Formed in late 2000, the al-Aqsa Martyr's Brigades were a loosely structured outfit, having been organized by lower-ranking local cadres who retained operational autonomy to such an extent that they have been described as "a cluster of loosely connected gangs."[23] The brigades could respond directly to popular pressure to strike at Israel, and did so in the name of Fatah, while their autonomy allowed Arafat a degree of deniability. Arafat even occasionally made half-hearted attempts to shut down the groups. The Marxist-oriented Popular Front for the Liberation of Palestine conducted three suicide attacks during 2003–2004 that were likely motivated by a desire to avenge the group's leader, Abu Ali Mustafa, who had been killed by Israeli forces in 2001.[24]

The killings and assassinations of senior Palestinian leaders by Israeli forces caused authority and initiative to be handed down to younger, less-established leaders, who often chose targets based on their availability and the possibility of striking them effectively, not on whether the attacks would result in political gains that could be consolidated. This created a bottom-up dynamic in which centralized control was ceded to local commanders. The result, as some militant leaders later admitted, was that from 2002 onward a coherent strategy for suicide bombing no longer existed. Instead it resembled "organized anarchy."[25]

The Shahida

On the morning of January 27, 2002, Wafa Idris, a twenty-six-year-old Palestinian woman and member of Fatah, traveled from her home in Ramallah to Jerusalem, passing without incident through an Israeli checkpoint. She loitered for a brief time in a shoe store, appearing to a sales clerk to be nervous and preoccupied. In her knapsack she was carrying a bomb to give to her brother Khalil, also a Fatah member who was then to carry out a suicide mission on behalf of the al-Aqsa Martyr's Brigades. Idris had been chosen to carry the explosive under the assumption that as a woman, she would arouse less suspicion traveling into Jerusalem. Having spent time in the store, Idris hurried toward the exit while attempting to remove some cosmetics from her knapsack. Her bag became stuck in the door, and as she struggled to free it, the bomb detonated prematurely, killing Idris and an eighty-one-year-old Israeli man. Dozens of people were hurt.[26]

That same day Arafat had addressed a huge crowd of Palestinian women from his compound in Ramallah, declaring them to be his "Army of Roses" that would crush Israeli tanks and lead the way to Jerusalem.[27] When Wafa Idris became the first such *shahida* (female martyr), her act had an electrifying effect on the Palestinian people. Soon, dozens of other women were asking for a chance to emulate her by martyring themselves.[28] The leaders of Fatah initially did not know how to respond to the incident because they believed that women should have a supporting rather than a leading role in military operations. It soon became clear to them, however, that shahidas could potentially be very effective weapons since social customs and dress codes made Muslim women more difficult for Israeli guards to search. Furthermore, the Israeli press took an almost lurid interest in female suicide bombers, giving the attacks even greater propaganda value.[29]

Fatah leaders decided to declare Wafa Idris the first martyr from the al-Aqsa Martyr's Brigades, making political capital out of what was likely an accident. Not to be outdone, the Islamists responded in kind, deploying their first female suicide bomber in early 2003. Religious officials formulated Islamic justifications for female suicide attacks where none had previously existed, just as they had developed justifications for male suicide attackers after the fact.[30] For example, Hamas leader Sheikh Yassin was initially critical of the phenomenon but changed his position when Hamas began to utilize female suicide bombers in early 2003, arguing that jihad was an imperative for all Muslims, men and women, and that all would be rewarded in the afterlife.[31] According to the journalist Barbara Victor, Yassin was unwilling to show her the Quranic passages detailing the rewards that female suicide attackers would receive in paradise. Instead he replied, "It is my job and the job of other sheikhs and Imams to interpret the Koran. . . . The people have our trust. Women along with all Muslims have the right and the duty to participate in suicide bombings to destroy the enemy and bring an Islamic state to all of Palestine."[32] By 2006 sixty-seven Palestinian women had either carried out suicide attacks or had attempted to do so.[33]

Leaders of Fatah and Hamas and other organizations created a dignified image of female suicide bombers, holding them up as women anxious to take part in the armed struggle with the full support of Palestinian society. The media were sometimes complicit in this process by portraying female suicide bombers as representing a move toward equality in a patriarchal society.[34] Empirical research, however, reveals a different picture. Often the motivations for female suicide attackers were different from those of male bombers, with personal crises typically serving as the catalyst driving young women to volunteer to carry out attacks.[35] Once having volunteered, peer pressure and other forms of coercion were used to force women to carry out their missions, regardless of whether it was ultimately what they truly wished. Furthermore, the psychological process in which bombers were recruited and deployed was especially cynical and hypocritical in the case of female bombers. Women continued to play no role at all in the upper ranks of the groups that used them and were not treated with a sense of camaraderie on the part of their handlers. While they were celebrated publicly, they remained unequal to male bombers throughout the process.[36]

THE DYNAMICS OF SUICIDE BOMBING IN THE SECOND INTIFADA

Explaining the Escalation: Relative Advantage and Compatibility Revisited

Because of preexisting trends and the first wave of suicide attacks in the 1990s, a culture of martyrdom already existed in Palestinian society at the start of the second intifada. This devaluing of life relative to death made intentional death in the course of militant attacks socially and culturally acceptable. Also, during the second intifada, there was a strong perceived need on the part of Palestinian organizations for a weapon providing some type of relative advantage for striking at Israel. The use of violence by Israel contributed significantly to this process.

There were thousands of automatic rifles at the disposal of the Palestinians in late 2000—in part because of the creation of the PA security forces—but Israeli forces were difficult to reach. Fortified borders and outposts separating them from the Palestinian population had been created during the 1990s as the Palestinian Authority took administrative control over territory from which Israeli forces had withdrawn or redeployed. IDF soldiers were therefore in a much better defensive position when violence erupted in September 2000 than they had been in the 1990s, which accounts for the poor performance of Palestinian conventional attacks and helps explain the decision to escalate the struggle by using suicide bombers.[37]

For the most part, Israeli forces responded in kind, with small-arms fire the norm during 2000 and 2001. Nevertheless, two weeks after fighting began in late September 2000, ninety Palestinians had been killed and two thousand injured, while the IDF had suffered only a few casualties. By November 319 Palestinians had been killed by Israeli forces, more than half of them while participating in civilian demonstrations. Autopsies showed that most had been shot in the head or neck, indicating that Israeli troops, even when attempting to quell protests, were not shooting just to intimidate or disperse crowds, but to kill. Shlomo Ben-Ami, a member of Ehud Barak's cabinet at the time, found the IDF response to be completely disproportionate to the provocation.[38] Thus, while the Israeli military did indeed demonstrate a level of restraint relative to its overwhelming capabilities, from a Palestinian perspective Israel was killing and injuring large numbers of Palestinians and suffering few casualties in return. Such an external factor goes a long way toward explaining why suicide bombing came to be used in the second intifada, but this external factor alone is insufficient for explaining the growth and diffusion of suicide bombing during the course of the fighting. For that, internal factors must be considered as well.

When the peace process ground to a halt and Palestinian militants perceived a need for suicide attackers, glorification of the bomber served to stoke the internal dynamics of escalation. Sari Nusseibeh witnessed this process, writing, "For me, the clearest signal that the Palestinians were at their wits' end was the way the [Israeli] invasion intensified the cult of the suicide bomber."[39] This internal process was exactly the opposite of that in the late 1990s, when the Islamists toned down their rhetoric and temporarily abandoned suicide attacks in imitation of more socially acceptable parties, such as Fatah. In the second intifada the process was reversed, with Fatah emulating the Islamists, who in turn felt compelled to be more violent to set themselves apart. Thus a positive feedback loop contributed to the dramatic escalation in attacks.[40] In short, the spread and intensification of Palestinian suicide bombing resulted from the external factor of Israeli brutality interacting with the internal factor of a deliberately created culture of violence that fueled Palestinian suicide attacks.

Explaining the Decline

The exponential increase in suicide bombing from 2000 through 2002 was matched by an equally dramatic decline after 2003. As with the increase, the decline was the result of at least two factors, which collectively lowered the effectiveness and therefore the advantage offered by suicide bombing and opened up alternatives to it as a means of political mobilization.

The response of the Israeli government was largely responsible for reducing the effectiveness of suicide attacks. In the aftermath of the Passover bombing, the government launched Operation Defensive

Shield, reoccupying territory in the West Bank and Gaza Strip that had been placed under the administrative (and sometimes security) control of the Palestinian Authority. At the same time, the government began construction on a massive barrier separating Israel and Israeli settlement blocs in the West Bank from Palestinian areas.[41] Palestinians entering Israel and East Jerusalem were subjected to lengthy waits and searches, and Israeli security personnel became adept at behavioral recognition techniques that allowed them to better spot incoming attackers. By June 2002 the Israelis were detecting more than 50 percent of would-be attackers, and according to Ariel Merari's data, the following year they stopped 184 out of a total of 210 attempted suicide attacks.[42]

The effectiveness of these security measures may well have had a deterrent effect among potential bombers as it became far more likely that they would face an indeterminate period in an Israeli jail instead of achieving the coveted status of martyr. At the very least, it became more difficult for Palestinian organizations to dispatch their bombers to targets in Israel. After peaking in 2003, the total number of attempted (as opposed to successful attacks) declined steadily, with the exception of a spike in attempted attacks in 2006 (see Table 6.1). The greater costs in preparation and planning and the higher probability of failure served to erode the relative advantage that suicide bombers had provided in the first years of the second intifada.[43]

While the Israelis' measures reduced the advantages suicide bombing offered the Islamists, changes in the political arena played a role as well, by opening up the possibility of political participation for Hamas and transforming the character of the organization's rivalry with Fatah. After Arafat's death in late 2004, Fatah's new leader, Mahmoud Abbas, agreed to a cease-fire in early February 2005.[44] For the most part Fatah adhered to this truce when it came to the use of suicide bombers and regularly condemned Islamist suicide attacks in 2005 and 2006. When members of the al-Aqsa Martyr's Brigades carried out a suicide attack in March 2006, it was in response to Hamas' victory in legislative elections held in January and should be understood as an effort by Fatah to regain militant credibility after it had lost its leadership role in the Palestinian Authority.[45] Leaders of Palestinian Islamic Jihad chose not to participate in the elections, and their organization continued to play

TABLE 6.1 **Suicide Bombings by Palestinian Groups, 2005–2010**

	GROUP	LOCATION	DEAD	INJURED
January 18, 2005	Hamas	Gaza	1	7
February 26, 2005	Islamic Jihad	Tel Aviv	6	30
July 12, 2005	Islamic Jihad	Netanya	5	88
August 28, 2005	Islamic Jihad	Beersheba	0	52
October 26, 2005	Islamic Jihad	Hadera	6	24
December 5, 2005	Islamic Jihad	Netanya	5	50
December 29, 2005	Islamic Jihad	Tulkarm	3	8
January 19, 2006	Islamic Jihad	Tel Aviv	0	20
March 30, 2006	Fatah	Kedumim	4	0
April 17, 2006	Islamic Jihad	Tel Aviv	9	60
January 30, 2007	Fatah and Islamic Jihad	Eilat	3	0
February 5, 2008	Hamas	Dimona	1	11
March 4, 2010	Jalil al-Ahrar	Haifa	1	12

Sources: Worldwide Incidents Tracking System, National Counterterrorism Center, wits.nctc.gov (accessed on April 7, 2010); Greg Myre, "Suicide Bomber Kills an Israeli Security Officer in Gaza," *New York Times,* January 19, 2005; Greg Myre, "Islamic Jihad Says It Was Behind Tel Aviv Bombing," *New York Times,* February 27, 2005; Steven Erlanger and Greg Myre, "Suicide Bomber and Two Women Die in Attack in Israeli Town," *New York Times,* July 13, 2005; Steven Erlanger, "Israel Suffers First Suicide Attack since Gaza Pullout," *New York Times,* August 28, 2005; Greg Myre and Dina Kraft, "Suicide Bombing Kills at Least 5, Israeli Police Say," *New York Times,* October 26, 2005; Greg Myre, "Palestinian Bomber Kills Himself and 5 Others Near Israel Mall," *New York Times,* December 6, 2005; Steven Erlanger, "3 Killed by Suicide Bomber at Checkpoint in West Bank," *New York Times,* December 30, 2005; Dina Kraft and Greg Myre, "Palestinian Suicide Bomber Wounds 20 in Tel Aviv," *New York Times,* January 20, 2006; Myre, "Bomber Kills 3 Israelis as Hamas Takes Power"; Greg Myre and Dina Kraft, "Suicide Bombing in Israel Kills 9; Hamas Approves," *New York Times,* April 18, 2006; Greg Myre, "Suicide Attack Is First in Israel in 9 Months," *New York Times,* January 30, 2007; Isabel Kershner, "Hamas Claims Responsibility for Blast," *New York Times,* February 6, 2008.

the role of spoiler, claiming most of the relatively few successful suicide attacks after 2004. In 2010 there was one successful suicide attack, which was credited to Jalil al-Ahrar (Galilee Freedom Battalions), a new fringe group composed of Israeli Arabs and sometimes referred to as the "Imad Mugniyah group," after the Lebanese-born militant responsible for planning the Islamic Jihad Organization bombings in Lebanon in 1983.

Hamas responded in two ways to the changing environment during 2004–2006. First, it kept up pressure on Israel, but increasingly resorted to unguided rocket attacks from Gaza into Israel rather than suicide bombings. Rockets were less accurate and far less deadly, rarely resulting in a fatality. However, they could be fired on a regular basis and in large numbers, thus causing fear and anxiety among Israelis within striking distance. More important, since rockets are an indirect-fire weapon that goes over defenses rather than through them, the rocket campaign could not be stopped by the same measures that were making suicide bombing less effective. This is another instance where a new perceived need led to the use of a different technology.[46]

Second, in the PA elections in 2006 Hamas' candidates challenged Fatah's on the grounds of corruption and the provision of social services. Hamas' victory was a surprise to most. The elections were deemed free and fair by international observers and earned Hamas the right to form the PA government. The U.S. and Israeli governments, however, refused to work with a Palestinian government that included Hamas, which in their eyes was only a terrorist organization. Hamas continued to launch rocket attacks on Israeli towns; meanwhile, efforts between Hamas and Fatah to form a Palestinian national unity government proved to be short-lived. The underlying tensions between Hamas and Fatah erupted into civil war in June 2007. Hamas routed Fatah and PA forces in Gaza and took control of the territory, resulting in a de facto division of the Palestinian territories, with Fatah governing the West Bank and Hamas ruling in Gaza, its traditional base.[47]

The character of the intra-Palestinian violence in 2007 was different from that in the 1990s. Hamas had previously avoided open conflict with the Palestinian Authority and instead differentiated itself from Fatah by taking a more extreme position on Israel. In 2007 the rivalry between the two was much more direct, expressed through political competition for the allegiance of the Palestinian people and military competition for resources and territory. The competitive dynamic that had earlier fueled extreme violence against Israel in the form of suicide attackers came instead to be directed toward the Palestinian community itself, in the form of intense fighting between the two factions. The necessity of having community support for the use of suicide attackers almost certainly precluded their use in this fratricidal struggle.

The Israeli government instituted an economic blockade against the Gaza Strip in the aftermath of the Hamas takeover, justifying it as a response to the ongoing rocket attacks that Hamas continued to carry out in 2007 and 2008. The blockade soon came to have a crippling effect on Palestinian daily life. In mid-2008 Hamas and Israel reached a six-month cease-fire agreement that allowed for a partial restoration of deliver-ies of food and other necessary supplies. When the cease-fire expired in December, Hamas militants again escalated their rocket attacks. At the end of the month, Israel responded with Operation Cast Lead, an inva-sion of Gaza that lasted through much of the following January. Despite Israeli efforts to limit the damage, the civilian population suffered more than one thousand deaths and four thousand injuries.[48]

In October 2008, during the cease-fire that predated Operation Cast Lead, members of Palestinian Islamic Jihad granted an interview to a BBC reporter and revealed to him that they were training female suicide bombers while waiting for the end of the cease-fire to use them against Israel.[49] Shortly thereafter, during the fighting in early 2009, members of Hamas claimed via the Internet that they were in the process of train-ing a cadre of suicide bombers, referred to as "Ghosts," and alleged that "tens" of these bombers had already infiltrated Israel and were awaiting orders to retaliate for IDF operations in Gaza. Despite these claims, there were no Palestinian suicide attacks against Israel in 2009.[50] Hamas even refrained from rocket attacks throughout 2009, leading Israeli defense minister Ehud Barak to assert that Operation Cast Lead had succeeded in deterring Hamas from attacks on Israel.[51] Others have suggested, how-ever, that Hamas was not deterred, but instead simply showed signs of responsibility by restraining its militancy in accordance with the wishes of its constituency, which had largely lost hope in violent solutions.[52] It would be premature to say that suicide bombing has ended in the Israeli-Palestinian struggle. Rather, the current situation is one in which suicide bombing offers few political or military advantages.

MANAGING MARTYRDOM

Technology Practice and Suicide Bombing

Ariel Merari's empirical research on suicide bombing, spanning more than two decades, reveals the phenomenon to be an extremely complex process that cannot easily be reduced to a single-variable explanation. Instead, he argues that a full explanation of suicide bombing must address three interactive components: the community, the organization, and the psychology of the individual.[53] In 2006 Max Taylor and John Horgan proposed a similar model for understanding terrorism more generally that was based on the understanding that terrorism is an ongoing process, rather than a fixed state, that emerges from interactions between at least three groups of variables—what they call "setting events," personal psychological factors, and the social/organizational context.[54] In both models seemingly fixed qualities matter less than do interactions, because interactions are what change behavior and ultimately decide whether terrorism (or suicide bombing) becomes established as a response to a perceived grievance. Both of these models bear a striking resemblance to the model of technology practice originally presented in the introduction and then modified to incorporate suicide bombing (see Figure I.4, on page 17). This model is reprinted here as Figure 6.2.

As noted in the introduction, it is typical in technologically advanced societies for people to understand technology in a restricted sense, focusing purely on the technical element—the knowledge, tools, skills, and so on that affect the world and solve problems found in their societies. In a similar vein, many analyses of suicide bombing have focused on a restricted understanding of the phenomenon—the psychology of the individual bomber—as opposed to the organizational and cultural phenomenon of suicide bombing. Now that a great deal of empirical detail is

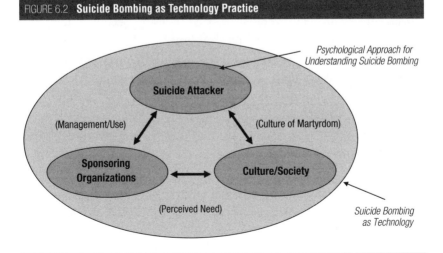

FIGURE 6.2 Suicide Bombing as Technology Practice

Source: Adapted from Arnold Pacey, *The Culture of Technology* (Cambridge, Mass.: MIT Press, 1983), 6.

available on suicide bombing by Palestinians, theirs makes an ideal case for illustrating suicide bombing as a form of technology. Such an understanding must begin at the organizational level.

The Organizational Level

Mohammed Hafez asserts that organizations "are the essential nexus between societal conflicts and individual suicide bombers. Without organizations, aggrieved individuals cannot act out their violence in a sustained manner."[55] His insight into suicide bombing by Palestinians represents a truism of technology—the centrality of organizations and management for determining issues of production, consumption, and use.

In the case of suicide bombing, organizations have sought to make self-sacrifice a regular occurrence by controlling and narrowing the range of actions available to certain individuals. They have then marketed these tactical martyrs to their community as an advantageous form of weaponry. In short, they have sought to control directly management and perceived need, two of the three relationships that characterize the overall process of suicide bombing. At the same time, they have demonstrated that they can have an influential, albeit indirect role in the third relationship, the creation and maintenance of the culture of martyrdom that facilitates community acceptance of the death of the suicide bomber.

The production of suicide attackers and subsequent execution of suicide attacks involve several specialized skill sets, such as intelligence gathering, weapon production, and recruitment and training, necessitating the involvement of several specialized groups to carry out a mission. Intelligence gathering and manufacturing of bombs are skills that are more generally used within militant groups, leaving recruitment and training as the area of "specialization" for the production of human bombers.

The organizational element of Palestinian suicide bombing proved to be surprisingly consistent across the ideological spectrum in the early 2000s. Merari found no "Hamas style" or "Fatah style," but instead identified minor differences that varied at least as much within the organizations as between them. There was a clear division of labor between leadership and the pool of candidates from which prospective bombers were selected. Leaders did not participate in suicide attacks, and some admitted that they would not allow members of their families to become suicide attackers. Some even had difficulty understanding why the people they recruited and trained were willing to blow themselves up. This arrangement was logical in that leaders of militant groups often have valuable experience and specialized skills that are difficult to replace, whereas the loss of the relatively inexperienced individuals often used as bombers is much easier for a given organization to endure. Merari also found that the significant organizational gap between managers and bombers correlated with strong differences in personality types between the two, as managers and other leadership figures were much more confident and sure of themselves than were the would-be bombers he was able to interview.[56]

Management: Controlling Individual Recruits

Recruitment was facilitated by the many different personal motivations that compelled individuals to first explore the prospect of becoming a suicide bomber. General research on the motivations of Palestinian suicide attackers, coupled with more specialized research revealing differing motivations between male and female suicide bombers, demonstrates that there was a broad spectrum of individual motivations for suicide bombing, ranging from the selfless or altruistic to the more personal, private, and selfish.[57] Some individuals were driven by a sense of powerlessness, frustration, humiliation, or despair. Others seem to have been driven by a desire to demonstrate their commitment to their faith and to the organization to which they belonged. Others had more personal motives, such as avenging the death, injury, or humiliation of a loved one. Some were driven by economic concerns, knowing that their deaths as suicide attackers would bring financial benefits to their surviving family members.[58]

Underlying this broad range of motivations was a relatively consistent set of personality characteristics among suicide attackers and would-be suicide attackers. Merari found many suicide bombers to be socially marginal with a keen sense of social failure, which in turn likely made them susceptible to the lure of becoming a suicide attacker.[59] For such people, suicide bombing offered a socially respectable means to resolve their particular personal crises and alleviate feelings of marginality and failure.[60] These benefits, like the benefits for the Black Tigers, were not posthumous, although posthumous rewards were undoubtedly an important factor for religiously motivated recruits. The decision to become a bomber also brought with it a sense of control and empowerment and was therefore a form of transformation, not only from the perspective of the organization but also from the perspective of the recruit. Many young people in particular could not resist the possibility of being transformed from a weak individual into the most powerful weapon Palestinian groups had to offer. Indeed, many young people in their testimonies spoke of their decision in terms of transformation or "becoming."[61] The benefits that collectively accrued to the bombers and to their loved ones in this life and the hereafter made deciding to become a suicide attacker a potentially attractive option, even for those who otherwise might not have considered taking their own lives.

Training and indoctrination followed recruitment. The length of the training process varied significantly, depending on the particular time and group, but regardless of duration focused less on practical military training and more on the use of ceremonies and rituals to establish control over the behavior of the individual, thus binding him or her to the organization and mission. In some cases, the preparation consisted of trials to test the commitment of the recruit, for example, mock burials or dress rehearsals of the pending attack.[62] In other cases, care was taken to deflect the attention of the bomber from the finality of the act. In these instances, the commitment was ritualized as a form of marriage, a rite of passage that signified a beginning rather than an end.[63] From an organizational perspective, the specific preparation was less important than the overall objective, which was to bind the recruit to the organization, community, and therefore to his or her own commitment through a dramatic public ritual.

An important element of the ritual process was production of a last testament from the bomber, sometimes written but often in the form of a videotaped testimony. These recorded commitments served a number of purposes. They were powerful propaganda tools directed at the organization's adversaries for purposes of intimidation and at their own communities for purposes of inspiration and recruitment.[64] From an organizational perspective, the tapes proved that their bombers went to their deaths willingly and had not been coerced or deceived.[65] This is important for establishing the legitimacy of the group. If young people are willing to kill themselves for it, goes the logic, the group and its cause must obviously be worth the sacrifice. On the other hand, if the group has to manipulate or trick people to get them to carry out attacks, as the Provisional IRA did with its coerced human bombs, the group's leaders must be hypocrites and cowards.

The tapes also served the organizations' needs in another, very practical respect—as a control mechanism over the potential bomber.[66] Making the tape public established the candidate's commitment to the cause and to the group. It, in theory, intensified the prospective bombers' sense of belonging and camaraderie, which in turn were powerful motivating factors.[67] After that point, any effort by the bomber to back out of the mission would be seen not only as an act of individual cowardice but also as a shameful betrayal of his or her comrades. The commitment represented on the videotape was understood to be so binding that from that point onward, potential bombers were referred to as living martyrs.[68] The tapes were therefore one of the most important steps in compressing the behavior of potential bombers, closing off potential alternatives or "escape routes" until death or humiliation remained the only choices.[69] It is clear from the testimonies of some bombers who were intercepted before completing their missions that the use of such videotaped testimonials had indeed been intended to coerce and intimidate those who otherwise would not choose to kill themselves.[70]

The celebration of martyrdom that the making and viewing of these tapes promotes may exploit general psychological trends that predispose individuals for suicide by making them more familiar and comfortable with the prospect of ending their own lives.[71] Psychologist Thomas Joiner has explored individual suicide at length, beginning with the premise that violent self-injury is extremely difficult for nearly all people. His clinical work on suicides and attempted suicides suggests that this resistance to self-injury is difficult to overcome, leading him to conclude that those who are most likely to succeed in suicide are those who have diminished their own fear through repeated self-injury. What Joiner calls mental practice—rehearsing acts of self-violence in the mind as a means of overcoming the natural inhibitions toward self-injury and death—is a variation on repeated physical self-injury. Analyzing more than three thousand patients deemed to be at risk for suicide, Joiner asserts, "Through mental rehearsal of violent death by suicide, these patients have acquired more of the ability to enact lethal self-injury."[72]

Joiner's work complements earlier research on individual suicide that indicates that suicide is largely a learned phenomenon. Understanding suicide in such a manner sheds light on it as a social phenomenon, particularly suicide "contagions," which are episodes in which highly publicized or extensively reported suicides seem to encourage additional individuals to take their own lives. David P. Phillips, who in the early 1970s was among the first to study this phenomenon systematically, dubs this the "Werther Effect," in reference to Goethe's *Sorrows of Young Werther*. After the book's publication, Goethe apparently became concerned that he had inadvertently inspired young German men who had read the book to take their own lives in imitation of the story's hero.[73] Although the Werther Effect was not reliably documented in Goethe's time, Phillips believes there were several cases of the phenomenon in twentieth-century America.

Some recent research examines the factors that influence the social impact of individual suicides. In one well-known case, sensational media reporting on individuals who had killed themselves by throwing their bodies in front of trains in Vienna's subway network led to enough copycat deaths that the researchers established guidelines for media reporting to tone down the events and make them seem less attractive to potential imitators. After the new guidelines went into effect, subway suicides in the city declined appreciably, though they did not disappear.[74] Based on cases such as these, the researcher Graham Martin wrote that as of the late 1990s, "We must now accept that reports that are 'front page', repeated and/or multi-channel, have suicide prominent in the report or in the title, glorify suicide in some way, are accompanied by photographs, discuss in detail the method of suicide and, in particular, concern celebrities, will influence others to suicide."[75] All of the elements of this description—particularly glorification and celebrity—apply to the use of suicide bombers' video testaments, footage of attacks, and commemoration in music videos to promote suicide bombing in Palestinian circles.

In his pioneering study, Phillips endeavored to reconcile his finding that suicide has a social aspect to it with Durkheim's pioneering work that argued that individual suicides were the result of social alienation (or what he called anomie, in contrast to his conception of altruistic suicide, as discussed in Chapter 1). Phillips suggested that alienation was indeed at the heart of individual suicide, but that alienated individuals had two mechanisms by which to deal with their issues. The first, of course, was suicide. The second was to overcome isolation by affiliation with a social group or movement. The two were simply different answers to the same problem, and in the rare cases of suicide contagion, both were simultaneously present. Suicide was still a way out, but by imitating others, suicidal individuals were in fact seeking belonging and affiliation.[76] For Palestinian suicide attackers (as well as others), the potential of becoming a suicide bomber offered them a two-pronged solution to their alienation—through affiliation with a respected social movement and suicide.

The findings on suicide indicate that training methods emphasizing mental rehearsal of the act of suicide and the public glorification of suicidal violence, regardless of its regional and cultural manifestations, confer significant power on militant organizations that use such attacks. These organizations not only recruit individuals and encourage them to commit suicide, but also make them more capable of taking their own lives than they might otherwise be. The organizations endeavor essentially to create suicide contagions similar to the spontaneous suicide contagions documented by researchers.

Marketing: Controlling the Community

For suicide bombing to be effective as a coercive strategy directed against an adversary, the bombers must be understood by that adversary as being representative of the mindset of their community. If the entire group is thought to be willing to fight to the death, the phenomenon becomes intimidating; alternatively, if the bombers are seen as being aberrant or pathological, the effect is greatly diminished. From an organizational perspective, this situation encourages the mobilization of strong public support for the use of suicide bombers. Furthermore, effective control and management of prospective recruits require the complicity of families and communities, which in turn requires organizations to make efforts to market suicide attacks as a necessary and admirable means of resistance in order to make the suicide of young people socially acceptable. For this part of the suicide-bombing process, the acceptance of families is paramount, for if a family accepts (and better yet welcomes) the decision of a son or daughter to become a suicide attacker, then the biggest hurdle standing in the way of overall community acceptance is cleared.

For Palestinians, external factors, in the form of Israeli violence, went a long way toward convincing the community that the use of suicide attackers was justified. As seen in other instances of suicide bombing, a sense of existential crisis can be used to justify the most extreme forms of resistance, and certainly the Palestinians' case is not an exception. Palestinian militant groups justified the use of suicide attackers in terms of necessity. For example, one member of Hamas' external leadership declared, "This weapon [the suicide bomber] is our winning card, which turned weakness and feebleness into strength, and created parity never before witnessed in the history of struggle with the Zionist enemy. It also gave our people the ability to respond, deter, and inflict harm on the enemy; it no longer bears the brunt of punishment alone."[77]

Of course, it was one thing to establish the general need for suicide attackers, but quite another to convince a family that taking its child's life is necessary. To justify individual acts of suicide bombing, organizations make use of the videotaped testimonials to convince a family that the decision was made by the individual and that the group was simply facilitating the desire of the individual to strike back on behalf of the community. Militant groups also exploit the complex and sometimes contradictory emotional state of parents grieving for a lost child. Most parents are emotionally shattered by their child's death, especially death by suicide. The depth of the loss in turn leads to a search for meaning, which often leads to rationalization of the child's death, to give it purpose, and thus to temper the sense of loss. In the case of suicide bombers, parents often demonstrate two very different emotional states: pride in the deed but at the same time grief at the death of their child.[78] Militant groups work to publicize the former and minimize the latter.

Members of Hamas sometimes visited the family members of their suicide attackers to ensure that they did not soil the heroic image of the shahid by expressing their grief inappropriately. This is another aspect of managing suicide attacks that they may well have learned from Hizballah, whose leaders carefully controlled media access to families of suicide attackers.[79] Palestinian journalist Zaki Chehab relates an instance of this type of image management. In the immediate aftermath of the death of a Hamas suicide bomber named Ismail, Chehab visited the young man's family. Both father and mother were weeping. Two muscular young men from Hamas arrived and went to work on the father, using a number of strategies to assuage his grief. They encouraged him to be proud and assured him that the first people to follow a martyr to heaven were his parents. They asked him, "Would you rather your son had died in a car accident or from drowning or as a drunk than dying as a hero for killing Israeli soldiers?" After fifteen minutes, the father's grief had been converted into pride and gratitude. Chehab notes,

> This poignant scene provided an insight into the personal and organizational side of Hamas. The two men were Ismail's comrades in Al Qassam. They knew in advance that he was embarking on his mission, and kept complete secrecy until the news broke of what they considered was his success. They had come not only to comfort the family, but also to perform a typical Hamas public relations mission. It is imperative for the family of a Hamas fighter to be seen in front of the world as proud of their beloved son rather than bitter or tragic and they should extol Hamas' belief in the battle and the glorious afterlife their son is destined to experience.[80]

The claims made by militant groups to reassure their communities—including that their suicide attackers were acting in accordance with their families' wishes—should therefore be treated skeptically.[81]

Authenticity and the Culture of Martyrdom

In Palestinian circles, *istishhadia,* or martyrdom, is differentiated from individual suicide, which is forbidden by Islamic law. Suicide, which is premised on self-interest—what Durkheim called egoistic suicide—is a sin. Martyrdom, done on behalf of others—what Durkheim called altruistic suicide—is a noble deed because it is oriented toward others. According to one Hamas thinker, "[O]nly a fine line separates suicide from sacrifice. Which is determined by the intention of the actor."[82] Because this line is so fine, from the perspective of the individual, acts of suicidal violence are most likely to be perceived as authentic martyrdom when they receive organizational confirmation; the bomber must state his or her intentions and work through a group in order to prove that the act is public and social rather than individual and selfish. This situation confers an extraordinary power on sponsors of suicide attacks.

Such organizational power is challenging to maintain, however, because the public recognition of authentic martyrdom ordinarily requires that the individual be acting freely and without organizational influence or coercion. Organizations are thus faced with the challenge of trying to perform two very different tasks at the same time—providing direction and control through the group to the individual attacker *and* guaranteeing the certainty of the individual's freedom to the community. In the case of the Tamil Tigers, this challenge was not so pronounced given Prabhakaran's power over his recruits and contempt for dissent at any level. For groups without such power, the task is more difficult; recall the challenges that the Provisional IRA had in maintaining the legitimacy of the hunger strike over the summer of 1981.

Palestinian groups, particularly the Islamists, solved this paradox by minimizing detection of the coercive elements of bomber management and promoting a full-fledged culture of martyrdom that made suicide bombing redemptive at the individual and community levels and therefore acceptable to both. This culture of martyrdom is the third relationship of the suicide bombing complex and the most challenging for groups to manipulate because they can influence it only indirectly.

Videotaped testimonials of suicide attackers served this purpose by making it appear as though martyrdom was being chosen freely by young Palestinian men and women. Leaders of their sponsoring organizations understood that it was imperative for their role in writing and producing the testimonials to remain hidden. Even when evidence existed that the leadership had written particular testimonials, they nonetheless attributed them to the bombers to make the act seem more authentic. It was essential for the leadership to appear as mediators or brokers, rather than drivers, in the process, lest they be seen as cynically manipulating the lives of their followers.[83]

Mohammed Hafez has shown that Palestinian Islamist organizations went to great lengths to recast cultural symbols and traditions to make suicidal violence meaningful rather than nihilistic. This was a deliberate process of construction, using culture to constrain the possibilities of individuals and shape the relationship between these individuals and their communities. Hafez wrote, "Religion, culture, and identity serve as 'tool kits' from which organizers of collective action strategically select narratives, traditions, symbols, rituals, or repertoires of action to imbue risky action with morality." He documented five strategies through which this was achieved.[84] In this manner, the act of suicide was reinterpreted as an opportunity and a challenge that had the potential to redeem both the individual and the community. Securing community support via this relationship was vital for making suicide bombing a reliable rather than a sporadic form of attack; many failed attackers have indicated that they would not have considered carrying out a suicide mission if they had believed it was against the wishes of the Palestinian community. Merari goes so far as to say that it was community support that normalized the very idea of suicide missions and that without such backing suicide attacks "would probably have seemed bizarre to the suicides themselves."[85]

CONCLUSION

Suicide bombing by Palestinians is the best documented example of such attacks as a constructed process directed toward the production of a particular weapon system. Like most manufacturing processes, it was characterized by organizational differentiation, the acquisition and maintenance of task-specific skill sets, and a clear division of labor. The managers within the system sought to extend their control over the production process, the psychological training of individual recruits, and the prospective market. They exercised this control directly when possible, and indirectly when necessary, by influencing the culture of martyrdom that linked bombers and community. All the various facets of Palestinian suicide bombing—the psychology of the bombers, the videotapes, the seemingly proud families, and the cultural reverence for martyrdom—were therefore related, and more important, deliberate.

Because the makers and marketers of Palestinian suicide bombers were so concerned about maintaining a positive public image of their role in the process, their attacks also reflected a more general trend in suicide bombing—the challenge of reconciling the tactical utility of suicide bombers at the group level with the need to maintain the authenticity of martyrdom at the individual and community levels. Instances of intense external pressure, such as existed in 2001 and 2002, tended to compress the two levels of tactical martyrdom by making it acceptable in lieu of other means of resistance. When external pressures eased, as they did in late 2004 and afterward, however, issues of legitimacy trumped those of practicality. This made suicide bombing difficult to sustain, and it was discontinued (at least for the time being). The lesson for militants was that for groups whose control over their members and communities is limited or contested, reconciling the tactical and strategic utilities of martyrdom is the most challenging managerial task in the overall process of suicide bombing.

Part III
COMMODIFICATION

7

GLOBALIZED MARTYRDOM

The Jihadi Movement and Suicide Bombing after 9/11

On August 19, 2003, an orange flatbed truck driven by a suicide bomber pulled up to the new security wall defending the United Nations' central administration building in Baghdad. The bomber detonated the truck's payload, approximately one ton of explosives, devastating the building, killing seventeen people immediately, and injuring more than one hundred. Eventually twenty-two people would die of injuries sustained in the blast. Among the dead was the UN coordinator for Iraq, Sergio Vieira de Mello. The positioning of the truck suggested that the blast had been directed at his office. Within months, the number of UN personnel in Iraq dropped from 650 to approximately 40, leaving American administrators and their allies the challenge of rebuilding the country essentially on their own, after the U.S.-led invasion to overthrow the Baathist regime earlier in the year.[1]

uicide bombing, in the form that came to plague Iraq and much of the rest of the world in the new millennium, differed significantly from previous iterations of the technology. In the previous instances of suicide bombing, militant groups manipulated their histories, faiths, and symbols to build the cults of martyrdom that would allow them to produce suicide attackers on a regular basis. Despite similarities between the groups, the process was always local. In contrast, for the past fifteen years this process has been carried out on a global scale, as descendents of the various resistance groups that fought the Soviet Union in Afghanistan sought to continue their war by promoting a radical religious agenda around the globe. They developed an elaborate culture of martyrdom without national roots, instead creating one based on defending the Muslim *umma* (community) and the broad expanse of territory where Islam predominates. The 9/11 al Qaeda attacks lent legitimacy to this movement and placed suicide bombing firmly at its center, establishing al Qaeda in particular as a global brand and suicide bombers as its trademark.

SETTING THE STAGE

Global Jihadism

Understanding violent Islamist extremism is a challenging endeavor. Even knowledgeable analysts are split over basic issues, such as what to call the phenomenon. I refer to it as the "global jihadi movement." There are two parts to this designation that warrant explanation. First, "global jihadi" designates a member of an extremely small minority of Sunni Muslims that uses violence to promote a religious agenda dedicated to combating the influence of Western political and economic structures in the Muslim world. The neologism "jihadism" is preferred here rather than the more common "Islamism," which denotes an ideology in which Islam plays a political role and is therefore a much broader term than is jihadism. Jihadism, and the individuals who pursue it, jihadis, have deviated so significantly from political Islam as most commonly practiced that it is appropriate to consider them as different phenomena.[2]

Second, examining global jihadism as a movement rather than as an organization helps convey the complexity of a phenomenon that cannot be understood in terms of normal organizational models. Global jihadism is composed of loosely coupled, amorphous social groups, tightly coupled, rigidly ordered paramilitary organizations, and everything in between.[3] In terms of ideology and practice, it is individualistic nearly to the point of anarchy, further complicating analysis in terms of fixed organizational patterns. Seeing jihadism as a movement allows one to understand it as a conglomerate of individuals and organizations characterized by fluid relationships and structures.[4] Within this movement, suicide bombers have become the technology of choice, not only because of their effectiveness, but also because they reinforce individual and group identities.

The ideology of the global jihadi movement originated in the 1950s and 1960s with the ideas of radical members of the Muslim Brotherhood, particularly Sayyid Qutb. In 1952 Gamal Abdel Nasser rose to power through a military coup in Egypt. He soon embarked upon an ambitious project of secular, pan-Arab leadership. Nasser sought initially to co-opt Egypt's Islamists and use them for his own ends, but when this failed, the Muslim Brotherhood and his government became bitter enemies. In early 1954 the government arrested more than 450 of the Brotherhood's members. Qutb, a respected scholar and author who had only recently joined the Muslim Brotherhood, was one of those imprisoned. Radicalized by the abuse that he and his comrades suffered during nine years in jail, Qutb articulated his rage in his well-known tract *Milestones*. He presented a vision of the Islamic world challenged by external enemies and internal threats, including the ignorance of God demonstrated by Nasser's secular dictatorship. He called on devout Muslims to defend their faith, even if it meant open defiance of the state.[5] As the Muslim Brotherhood accommodated itself to Nasser's successor, Anwar Sadat, its leaders rejected violence and the most radical of Qutb's beliefs in the 1970s. Violent jihadism—such as that carried out by al-Jihad, the Egyptian group that assassinated Sadat in 1981—was the product of splinter groups that rejected the more moderate approach adopted by the Muslim Brotherhood.[6]

Radical Islamists inspired by Qutb to carry out revolutionary violence against repressive regimes usually did so on a local level. The 1979 Soviet invasion of Afghanistan, however, had the powerful transformative effect on political Islam of providing an external focal point against which grievances from within the entire Islamist community were directed. The Soviet invasion was perceived by many in the Arab world as an attack on Islam, a view encouraged in particular by the government of Saudi Arabia. Saudi state-run media presented the invasion as a threat to the entire Muslim community regardless of nationality, inadvertently laying the groundwork for a broader form of pan-Islamist ideology. Pan-Islamism came to emphasize an uncompromising fight against external (non-Islamic) enemies and for internal unity within the Islamic community.

Abdullah Azzam, a founding member of Hamas and one of the founders of al Qaeda, was among the first to envision and begin working toward the transformation of pan-Islamism into a globalized struggle, or jihad, as the path the Islamic community should take.[7] Azzam stressed that it was the duty of individual Muslims everywhere to take up jihad and was explicit in insisting that martyrdom was part of this duty, mentioning it repeatedly before his death in 1989.[8] The most significant manifestation of this first wave of global jihadism was the influx in the 1980s of thousands of young Muslim men from dozens of countries into Afghanistan to answer Azzam's call.[9]

After the Soviet withdrawal from Afghanistan, completed in early 1989, a minority within the pan-Islamist community underwent further radicalization. Believing they had beaten a superpower, they imagined themselves as a global vanguard defending the Islamic world from the political and economic challenges of modernization and globalization.[10] This worldview led these militants to perceive the United States as their primary adversary, but true to their global perspective they also launched jihads in Bosnia, Kashmir, and Chechnya before the end of the decade.

The Office of Services (Maktab e-Khamidat), founded by Abdullah Azzam and Osama bin Laden, was the primary network for soliciting funds for and recruiting volunteers to the Afghan jihad in the 1980s prior to its becoming the organizational core of al Qaeda in August 1988.[11] On August 23, 1996, in Afghanistan, bin Laden issued his Declaration of Jihad Against the Americans Occupying the Land of the Two Holy Sanctuaries. In it, he repeated Azzam's theme that the lands of Islam were under threat and added the presence of U.S. military forces in Saudi Arabia to the roll call of affronts against Islam. He emphasized that jihad was an individual duty required of all Muslims, regardless of nationality. In a taunt aimed at William Cohen, the U.S. secretary of defense, bin Laden alluded to self-sacrifice being a defining characteristic of the struggle. "I'm telling you, William," bin Laden wrote, "these young men love death as much as you love life. They have inherited honor, pride, bravery, generosity, sincerity, courage, and a spirit of sacrifice."[12]

To reach a broad audience, the form of Islam preached by bin Laden jettisoned much of the faith's cultural context and turned struggles rooted in practical grievances against specific governments into a generalized struggle against modernity. This radical Islam, described by Olivier Roy as neo-fundamentalism, is characterized, as are other fundamentalist movements, by efforts to define the faith as abstract, free of individual cultures—that is, a "pure" faith existing beyond time and space. The proponents of this form of Islam view religious practices with local peculiarities or characteristics as polluting their idealized form of Islam.[13] In theory, this globalized Islam functions above and beyond local cultures and is therefore capable of mobilizing recruits on a global scale based on universal grievances.[14]

Jihadism and Martyrdom

Martyrdom was at the heart of this neo-fundamentalist Islamic ideology. During the campaign against the Soviet Union, the Arab jihadis recruited by Osama bin Laden demonstrated a veneration for self-sacrifice in combat that surprised their Afghan hosts. State-run media outlets in Saudi Arabia provided extensive coverage of the fighting, emphasizing miracles and martyrdom.[15] When these fighters left Afghanistan, their identities became even more wrapped up in a shared willingness to sacrifice their lives for Islam. This emphasis on martyrdom came to distinguish this group of men from those in such organizations as the Muslim Brotherhood, and in their eyes elevated their moral stature above all others as well. A shared willingness to die for Islam allowed alienated individuals to feel as though they were part of a collective whole. This mutual purpose facilitated bonds of camaraderie, which helped draw young men to the movement. The prospect of a glorious death also promised individual self-fulfillment to prospective members of the jihadi community.

Many of the young men attracted by the jihadi mindset suffered from the dilemma of being "torn between a profound sense of personal and social belonging to the Muslim world and an awareness of the backward aspects of Muslim societies and the inferior political status of Islam." This dissonance fueled the acute sense of anxiety instilled in these men by rampant globalization and political impositions of the Western world; it also led them to search for a way out. Religiously sanctioned jihad emphasizing altruistic self-sacrifice became their escape route.[16] As a result, suicide attacks came to dominate al Qaeda and the global jihadi movement to a much greater extent than has been the case with other groups. Other militant groups *have* cults of martyrdom as "subsets" of their primary identities, whereas al Qaeda and its affiliates *are* a cult of martyrdom, stripped of the local history and social relationships that connect such groups as Hizballah, the Tamil Tigers, and Hamas to their constituencies.

It is suspected that in the early 1990s bin Laden and other al Qaeda members met with elements of Hizballah, including Imad Mugniyah, and received practical instruction on the use of suicide bombing.[17] They were probably motivated by the use of suicide bombing by Palestinian Islamists as well. In November 1995 radical Islamists utilizing a truck bomb attacked a U.S.-run training center for the Saudi National Guard in Riyadh. Seven people, including five Americans, were killed in the blast. Although the blast was not a suicide attack, it marked a dramatic escalation of tension between the Saudi state and its Islamist critics. The attack was inspired by Osama bin Laden, then exiled in Sudan, but was not organized or directed by him or his immediate network.[18] Two days later, Egyptian Islamic Jihad, headed by Ayman al-Zawahiri and not yet a formal element of al Qaeda, carried out a suicide truck bombing against the Egyptian embassy in Pakistan, killing sixteen people.[19] Three years later, in 1998, bin Laden's al Qaeda organization demonstrated its suicide-bombing capabilities in simultaneous attacks against U.S. embassies in Kenya and Tanzania. The attacks, and the U.S. response— a counterproductive cruise missile strike directed against militant training camps in Afghanistan—solidified bin Laden's alliance with the Taliban, ensuring that they would not hand him over to the West and elevating his prestige above the numerous other militants in the area.

The suicide operation against the USS *Cole* two years later, in 2000, confirmed bin Laden's symbolic leadership of the jihadi movement, which the 9/11 attacks then revealed to the world. Bin Laden later told a colleague that the 9/11 attacks were speeches in the form of action. Lawrence Wright has described bin Laden's self-declared war on the United States as a "dazzling advertisement" for bin Laden and his cause.[20] The scale of the 9/11 attacks was meant to impart an "attractive" quality to young militants seeking empowerment. From that point on, prospective jihadis who joined the movement and desired to become suicide attackers would be associating themselves with that spectacle, making their decision one of empowerment. The 9/11 attacks thus legitimized the jihadi movement more generally and suicide bombing more specifically.

Suicide Bombing in Chechnya

Violence and repression by state governments have contributed to the spread of suicide bombing by creating the perceived need for extreme forms of resistance and increasing the odds that the suicidal ideology of the jihadis will resonate with a broader audience. Harsh state repression, as seen in the case of the Palestinians, can contribute to narratives of brutality and injustice that help break down individual mental barriers toward murder and even suicide. Albert Bandura, in his analysis of the mental mechanisms that enable killing, notes, "The task of making violence morally defensible is facilitated when nonviolent options are judged to have been ineffective and utilitarian justifications portray the suffering caused by violent counterattacks as greatly outweighed by the human suffering inflicted by the foe."[21] The transformation of the conflict in Chechnya in the 1990s illustrates how the use of force helped align a local conflict with the global militant Islamist strategy, altering its ideological character and in doing so facilitating the introduction of suicide bombing.

The conflict between the Chechen people and the Russian state is centuries old. At heart, it is a nationalist conflict, with the Chechens seeking territorial independence. The cultural differences between the Chechens, who speak a central Asian language and tend to practice Islam, and the Slavic, Orthodox Christian Russians have hampered acceptance of a Soviet identity in Chechnya and the integration of Chechnya into Russia. Instead, a separate sense of Chechen nationhood remains, with Islam serving to differentiate it and legitimize resistance to Russian conquest. During World War II, Stalin believed that separatist sentiment might lead the Chechens to side with Nazi Germany and destabilize the Soviet Union from within. To prevent this imagined betrayal, Stalin deported the entire Chechen population, as well as the nearby Crimean Tatars, to the deserts of Kazakhstan. Thousands died amidst the tumult of the move and the bleak conditions of their temporary residences. Only in 1957 were they allowed to return to their homes.[22]

When the Soviet Union collapsed in 1991, Chechen nationalists renewed the push for independence. In response, Russian president Boris

Yeltsin declared war on the breakaway province in 1994, and over the next two years Russian forces fought the separatists to a standstill, after which Chechnya entered a lawless period in which kidnapping and gangsterism dominated. During this time, Islamist fighters, many of whom had trained in Afghan camps as part of the global jihadi movement, began arriving in the area to make the conflict ideologically their own.[23]

For the Islamists, the conflict was not one of Chechen nationalism versus Russian imperialism, but Islam against the West. In their minds, Chechnya was another theater of the conflict that had taken place in Afghanistan the preceding decade and required jihad. The Islamists had training, weapons, and funding and were quickly able to integrate into the warring criminal factions that characterized the Chechen political landscape. The Islamists launched an invasion of neighboring Dagestan in 1999 that served to intensify the ongoing antagonism with Russia. When newly elected president Vladimir Putin renewed the war in 2000 in response to a number of terrorist attacks in Russia that he blamed on Chechens, he used the full power of the Russian military to devastate Chechnya.

The Russians conducted a massive bombing campaign focused particularly on Grozny, the capital, but other towns and villages were affected as well. Some were literally wiped off the map. By 2005 between 40,000 and 100,000 of Chechnya's prewar population of approximately 1,000,000 had been killed in the various phases of the fighting. More than one-third had become refugees.[24] In addition to state-ordered violence, Chechen citizens were subject to abuse by Russian soldiers, including beatings, murders, abductions, and rapes. Malnutrition and disease became the norm for Chechen children. After years of living under these conditions, many young Chechens had all but given up on life, leading the journalist Anna Politkovskaya to describe war-torn Chechnya as "a small corner of Hell."[25] The Russian state thus created the need among Chechens for an extreme form of resistance. The jihadis who entered Chechnya brought with them the ideology and organizational experience to make such resistance possible.

Dzokhar Dudaev, who had led and radicalized the Chechen nationalist movement in the 1990s, warned the Russians in November 1994 that the Chechens would have no choice but to form suicide battalions because "we do not have armaments, military vehicles, military equipment, a military-industrial complex. We were left naked, and therefore we have been forced to establish suicide battalions."[26] Clearly a desperate, self-sacrificing mindset had already taken hold among elements of the Chechen resistance before the Islamists co-opted the struggle. By framing the conflict as part of a larger global conflict to defend Islam, the Islamists were able to bring religious meaning to a struggle that for many had become meaningless. Using well-established techniques for mobilizing suicide attackers, they easily found susceptible recruits among Chechnya's brutalized population and were thus able to turn trauma and grief into tools for manufacturing bombers.[27]

In mid-2000 Chechen groups began conducting suicide attacks, including numerous operations by female suicide bombers. In fact, the first Chechen suicide attack was carried out by two women, Khava Barayeva and Luisa Magomodova, who on June 7, 2000, drove an explosive-laden truck into the headquarters of a Russian Special Forces unit, killing two and injuring five. In summer 2002 jihadis took over the Chechen resistance at the highest level by creating a new governing body called the Madzhlisul Shura and declaring the source of all decisions to be the Quran and the Sunna. Under its leadership, Chechen suicide bombing came to be characterized by high-profile, mass-casualty missions.[28]

Between 2000 and late 2005, twenty-eight acts of suicidal terrorism, most of them bombings, were attributed to Chechen groups. Two attacks—the 2002 siege of the Dubrovka Theater in Moscow and the Beslan school takeover in 2004—were dramatic hostage-taking operations in which Chechen operatives with explosives strapped to their bodies made it clear that they were prepared to die during the course of the mission. By the end of 2005, 939 people had been killed and 2,913 injured in the violence. Of the 112 perpetrators of these attacks, 48 (or 43 percent) had been women.[29] In one of the most daring operations, female suicide bombers simultaneously brought down two Russian airliners on August 24, 2004, killing ninety people.[30] A group called the Islambouli Brigades of al Qaeda claimed responsibility in a web posting.[31] Although the authenticity of this claim is impossible to verify, it suggests the desire of al Qaeda leaders to link themselves to suicide attacks in Chechnya.

In July 2006 Shamil Basaev, military commander of the Chechen resistance since the 2002 jihadi takeover, was killed in an explosion, the cause of which is still disputed, weakening the resistance as a whole. Its remaining members drew upon small militant groups in Chechnya and the surrounding republics to carry on the struggle, which had the effect of further radicalization. On October 31, 2007, Dokka Umarov, who had been involved in the struggle since 1994, proclaimed that the resistance had been replaced by a new Islamic state, which he declared to be the "Caucasus Emirate," with himself at the head.[32]

The new, self-proclaimed emirate laid claim to all Muslim populations in the Russian Caucasus. Umarov made use of militants throughout the region to escalate the violence, beginning in 2008. The Islamists resumed suicide attacks, launching four in 2008 and fifteen in 2009. Most of them were in Chechnya, but several took place in neighboring areas. On the whole, militant violence led to the deaths of 586 people in 2008 and more than 900 in 2009.[33] The violence did little to mobilize the support of the population, however, and on the whole the Caucasus Emirate enjoyed little backing.

Suicide bombing also failed to generate popular support within Chechnya. Observers saw no graffiti or posters celebrating suicide attackers; rather, suicide attacks, especially those by women, seem often to have been greeted with disbelief.[34] Instead of creating a positive culture of martyrdom that connected individuals and the population to their groups, the militants depended on a combination of fatalism among locals stemming from Russian brutality and the fanaticism of Islamists who sought to recast the nationalist struggle according to their worldview. Chechnya is therefore a striking example of how a globalized jihadi ideology managed to exacerbate and escalate a local conflict in an attempt to turn it into a global jihad, complete with suicide attackers, even when local participants in the conflict tended not to believe in the same radical version of Islam as they did.

Jihadi Suicide Attacks after 9/11

After the September 11 attacks, the next high-profile suicide attack directed against Western targets took place on October 12, 2002, at two nightclubs on the Indonesian island of Bali, killing 202 people, including 88 Australian tourists. The attacks were the work of a radical splinter of Jemaat Islamiya (JI), an independent jihadi organization with strong local ties that had existed since 1996. JI had previously demonstrated its competence in bomb manufacturing in a wave of attacks across Indonesia on Christmas Eve 2000 that killed nineteen people and injured one hundred twenty. Their decision to use suicide attackers in the 2002 operation was undoubtedly influenced by the 9/11 bombings, but from an operational perspective, it seems any role played by al Qaeda's leadership was extremely limited.[35]

JI remained active throughout the decade, combining conventional attacks with at least two more attention-grabbing suicide bombings. On October 1, 2005, a JI operative carried out another attack in Bali, killing 26 people and injuring 129. On July 17, 2009, multiple suicide attacks directed against hotels in Jakarta resulted in the deaths of seven people and injuries to fifty-three more.[36] The group's connections to the local population eroded over this period, however, since most were unwilling to sanction the indiscriminate murder of civilians. Successful counterterrorism operations isolated and weakened the organization as well. By the 2009 attacks, JI's operational core consisted of small groups of alienated individuals with preexisting social ties whose actions did not represent the wishes of the Indonesian people.[37]

In 2003 a wave of deadly suicide blasts hit Turkey. On November 15 two suicide truck bombs killed twenty-seven people outside two synagogues in Istanbul. Five days later, two more bombers targeted a bank and the British consulate, killing thirty people and wounding four hundred. The planning for these attacks dated to at least 2000. The mission leader, a Turk named Habib Aktas, had met with Osama bin Laden and received approximately $10,000 from al Qaeda to finance multiple suicide operations. The Turkish cell received general direction from al Qaeda, along with the cash, but determined for itself how best to carry out the missions with little involvement from al Qaeda central regarding the planning and execution.[38]

Over the next several years, local cells assumed greater responsibility for the planning and execution of suicide bombings. This pattern had begun to emerge months before the Istanbul blasts in the form of a devastating multiple-bomber operation against targets in Morocco. On May 16, 2003, fourteen bombers staged simultaneous attacks against several targets in Casablanca. Two bombers aborted their mission and were apprehended by the authorities, but the remaining twelve killed thirty-three civilians in addition to themselves in five attacks. Despite the high number of fatalities, in a number of ways the attack was fairly amateurish in its execution. The weapons used—homemade explosives carried in backpacks—were relatively crude. Furthermore, the targets were poorly chosen. By including a Jewish community center and a Jewish cemetery among the targets, the planners clearly intended to send a message across the Arab world that they thought would resonate because of anger toward Israel. The bombers did not, however, manage to kill any Jews. Twenty-eight of the thirty-three dead were Muslims.[39]

The attackers were men of low income and poor education who had been recruited from a Casablanca slum, which is also where much of the planning for the mission took place. Socioeconomic factors therefore go a long way in explaining the willingness of these men to be led toward carrying out what they were told would be a redemptive act.[40] The leadership that manipulated these men consisted of local religious authorities angry at the Moroccan government for its efforts to modernize the state.[41] In 2007 another wave of attacks began in Morocco when three bombers blew themselves up in Casablanca after a confrontation with police on April 10. A few days later, on April 14, two suicide bombers attacked American targets, including the U.S. consulate in Casablanca. (In March a militant had blown himself up, probably accidentally, in a cybercafe, but did not kill anyone else.)[42]

Moroccan radicals were a significant contingent of the foreign fighters who traveled to Iraq to become suicide bombers after the U.S.-led invasion.[43] The Moroccan attacks of 2003 and 2007 bore hallmarks of al Qaeda operations, in particular staging simultaneous attacks using several bombers. The execution of the attacks, however, was far less professional than al Qaeda's, and after initial investigations, authorities suggested that the operations—along with the simultaneous bombings of four commuter trains in Madrid in 2004 that killed nearly two hundred people—were entirely local affairs.[44] It now seems, however, that established members of al Qaeda played some role in guiding the attacks, perhaps by providing the technical knowledge necessary for the manufacture of the homemade explosives used in the attacks.[45]

The men who carried out these attacks were recruited locally and had never attended terrorist training camps or participated in violent jihad abroad. In many ways, they were completely apolitical and seem to have been attracted to the idea of martyrdom as a way to transform their identities and escape personal situations that had become intolerable. An analysis of the Madrid bombers suggests that the men involved had only superficially integrated into the surrounding culture; several had criminal backgrounds. Association with one another in a jihadi cell provided them an oasis of communal identity through which to combat the troubling social and economic trends they saw taking place around them.[46]

Al Qaeda in the Arabian Peninsula

In the immediate aftermath of the destruction of al Qaeda's central command in Afghanistan in late 2001, suicide attacks by al Qaeda and its affiliates became sporadic and geographically dispersed. A few years later, in 2003, a sustained campaign of militancy in which suicide bombings played a prominent role took shape in Saudi Arabia. A well-established Sunni movement had been critical of the Saudi government throughout the 1980s and 1990s, but the kingdom had been relatively free of militant attacks since the siege of the Grand Mosque, in Mecca, in 1979. After that event, the Saudi government had pursued a successful mix of policies that included cracking down on known radicals, encouraging potential militants to go to Afghanistan to fight, and enforcing the public elements of religious observance. As a consequence, the only major militant attack carried out by Sunni extremists on Saudi soil in the 1990s was the previously mentioned bombing of a U.S. training center in Riyadh in November 1995. (The bombing of the Khobar Towers housing complex that killed nineteen U.S. servicemen in 1996 was carried out by the Hizballah al-Hijaz and was not a suicide mission.)[47]

In 2002, in the aftermath of the dispersal of al Qaeda's centralized command, veterans of its Afghan network began to return to Saudi Arabia, where, as ordered by bin Laden, they were to carry out attacks. They received additional ideological legitimacy and self-justification from conservative clerics displeased by the Saudi state's deviations from the traditional practice of Islam. These returning fighters were undoubtedly further antagonized by Israel's violent suppression of the second intifada, which had begun in late 2001, and by the U.S.-led invasion of Iraq in March 2003. In mid-2003 a preemptive effort on the part of the Saudi security forces to crack down on the militants provoked a dramatic escalation of hostilities by the newly formed al Qaeda on the Arabian Peninsula.[48]

On May 6, 2003, Saudi police raided a suspected al Qaeda safe house in Riyadh, resulting in a gun battle with militants.[49] The police failed to arrest the suspected members of al Qaeda they had been targeting, and six days later the militants struck with a bold operation. On May 12 nine suicide attackers driving three bomb-laden trucks targeted a residential complex near Riyadh that housed American and other foreign workers. The attacks killed twenty-five people and wounded dozens of others. Saudi officials definitively linked several of the dead bombers to the al Qaeda cell they had been investigating.[50] For the next eighteen months, ongoing battles between security forces and al Qaeda on the Arabian Peninsula were pitched enough to lead observers to question the stability of the Saudi government. In a particularly audacious attack, on April 21, 2004, a massive car bomb devastated a police office in downtown Riyadh, killing four people. In the days preceding the operation, gun battles with militants had resulted in the deaths of six police officers. Officials estimated that they arrested between four hundred and five hundred militants.[51] These figures are probably not indicative of the true scale of the challenge by the militants because of the Saudi state's penchant for secrecy and its desire to downplay threats to its stability and legitimacy.[52]

The attacks of al Qaeda on the Arabian Peninsula were organized and executed locally, but the influence of bin Laden and the al Qaeda hierarchy regrouping in Pakistan was undeniable. Most of the fighters were citizens of Saudi Arabia, had experience fighting on behalf of al Qaeda elsewhere, and still considered themselves to be part of bin Laden's movement.[53] For purposes of ideology and inspiration, the group can be considered a branch of al Qaeda central.

By late 2004 Saudi security forces had successfully quelled the budding insurgency through an energetic and large-scale police effort and an innovative prisoner reeducation and rehabilitation program. In the latter, implemented in 2004, respected clerics who had grown disillusioned with the destructive nihilism of bin Laden's movement used formal instruction in Islamic history, practice, and jurisprudence to de-radicalize terrorist sympathizers.[54] In addition, the militants had been unable to win the support of religious officials or fellow Saudi citizens. Instead, Saudis viewed them as misguided at best, terrorists at worst. Either way, their actions created an environment hostile to them in the kingdom.[55] The decline in violence in Saudi Arabia can also be attributed to the draw of the growing insurgency in neighboring Iraq, as hundreds of young Saudis decided to fight and die there rather than in the streets of their homeland.

A number of the militants who eluded capture crossed into neighboring Yemen, where they allied themselves with Yemeni militants, including al Qaeda in Yemen. In 2009 al Qaeda in the Arabian Peninsula (AQAP) announced that it had reestablished itself in Yemen.[56] The group attracted international attention in late 2009 when it claimed responsibility for Umar Farouk Abdulmutallab's unsuccessful attempt to destroy an American passenger jet as it flew into Detroit on Christmas by detonating explosives he had concealed in his undergarments. Abdulmutallab claimed that he had been trained and equipped in Yemen.[57]

SUICIDE BOMBING IN IRAQ

On August 19, 2009, exactly six years after the suicide attack directed against UN headquarters in Baghdad, two suicide blasts in the Iraqi capital killed nearly one hundred people and injured more than six hundred. Only weeks earlier, the United States had formally handed control for internal security to the government of Iraq.[58] Between the 2003 blast and the one in 2009, Iraq experienced at least 1,286 suicide bombings, more such attacks than any other country, resulting in 12,144 deaths and nearly 29,000 people injured. According to the National Counterterrorism Center's database, in June 2005 in Iraq there had been fifty-one suicide attacks; in comparison, in every *year* of the intifada, except for one, there were fewer than fifty-one attacks.[59] The casualty figures were 277 dead and 751 injured.

Prior to the U.S.-led invasion, there had been no suicide attacks in Iraq, and despite speculation that suicide attackers would be used to defend the Iraqi state, few took place in the early stages of the invasion. From March through September 2003, suicide attacks averaged one to three per month, but increased in the last quarter of the year, with nine attacks in December alone, bringing the total for 2003 to thirty-three.[60] The number of attacks doubled in 2004 and then increased five-fold the following year, for a total of 348 suicide attacks in 2005. The number of operations declined in 2006 (but remained high), spiked in 2007, and then declined significantly in 2008, 2009, and 2010 (see Figure 7.1).

Practice led militant groups to become more creative and sophisticated in their use of human bombers. Many of the most brutal suicide attacks of the entire occupation occurred in 2007. Sectarian hatred— stemming from a deliberate effort by Sunni militants to draw Iraq's majority Shiite population into a civil war the previous year—contributed to the savagery. On March 6, 2007, two suicide bombers simultaneously targeted a Shiite religious procession, killing at least 106 people.[61] By June there had already been more than a dozen suicide attacks, averaging 50 deaths each.[62] Later that summer, a truck bombing in Amerli, in northern Iraq, killed at least 150 people, and on August 14, a series of suicide truck bombings in a rural area near the Syrian border killed as many as 500 people and injured perhaps 1,500.[63]

As of December 31, 2010, there had been 1,396 suicide attacks in Iraq, causing 13,601 deaths, for an average of 9.7 fatalities per attack.

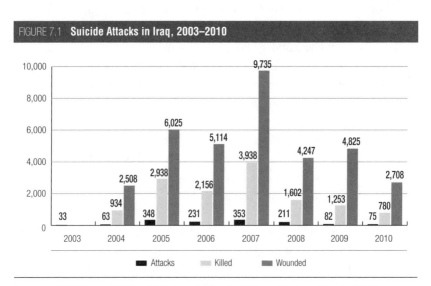

FIGURE 7.1   **Suicide Attacks in Iraq, 2003–2010**

Sources: For 2003, Mohammed M. Hafez, *Suicide Bombers in Iraq: The Strategy and Ideology of Martyrdom* (Washington, D.C.: United States Institute of Peace Press, 2007), 94; for 2004 through 2010, Worldwide Incidents Tracking System, National Counterterrorism Center, wits.nctc.gov (accessed November 12, 2009; April 1, 2010; and April 1, 2011).

According to Mohammed Hafez, Iraqi security forces were the most common targets, suffering 44 percent of total suicide attacks between 2003 and August 2006. Civilian targets accounted for 23 percent of attacks, while coalition forces were targeted only 15 percent of the time. Government and political party figures, tourists, and international organizations were also targeted with regularity.[64]

Building the Complex

Militants were able to establish and then escalate suicide bombing rapidly in Iraq because all of the elements necessary for a sustainable suicide-bombing complex emerged quickly in the breakdown of order following the overthrow of Saddam Hussein's government. Within a year, there had evolved an angry, alienated population fragmented into antagonistic communities traumatized by violence and desperate for means of defense. The organizational element was present outside Iraq's borders and was able to move in at once, bringing with it an ideology, a culture of martyrdom, and experience in training and managing suicide attackers. Young Iraqi males were vulnerable to the lure of martyrdom, and hundreds of foreign fighters entered the country already having been indoctrinated, ensuring that militant groups in Iraq would have a reliable supply of recruits once they set up shop.

A suicide attack requires a human guidance system as well as a warhead, so it is important to note that prospective militants in Iraq had a wealth of conventional explosives at their disposal that they could use for the latter. In particular, the misguided American preoccupation with Iraqi "WMDs" prohibited troops from detonating bunkers containing artillery shells and ammunition for fear of dispersing chemical or biological agents that might be nearby. U.S. forces lacked sufficient numbers to guard the many sites where such weapons were stored, and many tons of this material soon made their way to the insurgency.[65]

The failure of the United States and its coalition partners to have devised an appropriate plan for administering Iraq to maintain peace and order quickly proved to be catastrophic. The Iraqi state had always been an artificial construct, owing more to British colonial ambitions after World War I than to any underlying logic taking into consideration social or ethnic realities. After the overthrown of Hussein's government, Iraqi society was no longer held together by force, and thus fragmented along ethnic, tribal, and religious lines.[66] Tensions quickly rose between Iraq's Sunni and Shiite populations while the Kurdish minority set about consolidating power in the region where it had been able to establish autonomy years prior.[67] The decisions to dissolve the Iraqi army and to purge members of the Baath Party from government left tens of thousands of men outside the political and economic life of the country and with little reason to support the occupation or the newly created government. Many of these men remained armed, with government-issued guns, and had formal military training. The use of force by the U.S. military contributed to this alienation, and by 2004 an indigenous insurgency had emerged, composed of former Baathists and nationalists who opposed the occupation and the subsequent political empowerment of Iraq's Shiite and Kurdish communities at the expense of the Sunnis.[68] In polls conducted during 2004–2005, support for attacks on American forces was as high as 85 percent in some Sunni areas.[69]

The global jihadis from outside Iraq, ready to exploit the situation, quickly began to integrate into local Iraqi forces, creating a second insurgency dedicated to creating a Sunni-led Islamic state in Iraq. Once these experienced militants had arrived, stoked the fears of the Sunni population, and availed themselves of the permissive environment afforded by the lack of troops and the abundance of weapons and alienated young men, Iraq had all the ingredients necessary for producing suicide attackers.

The fundamental difference between the suicide-bombing complex as it emerged in Iraq and the other instances of localized suicide bombing examined here was the presence of imported organizational elements that trained and marketed suicide attackers to the local audiences that the jihadis were supposedly defending. In other instances of suicide bombing, a shared ideology in the form of common, realizable political goals connected the three facets of the suicide-bombing complex. In Iraq, these connections were much weaker. Many Iraqis were secular in their overall outlook, making ideological reconciliation with the global jihadis and their movement impossible.[70] Many Iraqis who collaborated with the foreign fighters did so out of a sense of desperation borne of a need to protect their communities.

Thus much of the insurgency, and especially the intensive use of suicide attackers imported from other areas, was a problem of the United States' own making. According to David Kilcullen, many of the insurgents who fought the U.S. and Iraqi security forces were what he calls "accidental guerrillas."[71] Global jihadis moved into an area to exploit a local conflict and join it to their transnational agenda. Through high-visibility attacks, such as suicide bombings, the jihadis provoked a violent reaction from the United States. U.S. forces were unable to differentiate between the local and the global and attacked both, unintentionally creating solidarity between the foreign fighters and their local hosts.

Weapons and Cultures

Martyrdom was Hizballah's defining weapon in its war against the mechanized forces of its adversaries in its formative years. Not only was this weapon effective, but from the group's perspective it embodied the values for which the organization claimed to be fighting—faith and the willingness to sacrifice for the community. Suicide bombing continues to play a similar cultural role for the jihadi movement, providing it with an effective counterpart to the electronic firepower of its foes and allowing the movement to affirm individual and group identities.

The use of modern tools of war, particularly airpower, against such groups reinforced the cultural dimensions of the struggle and lent legitimacy to the anti-modern narrative that bin Laden was selling and others continue to peddle. From the perspective of states, the use of airpower represents technological sophistication and a desire to prevent indiscriminate casualties. It is also used as a means of communication and intimidation to convince adversaries of the futility of ongoing resistance.[72] From the receiving end, however, airpower appears neither advanced nor humane, but brutal—because it is used against foes who have no symmetrical means of response—and hypocritical because even precision weapons cannot help but cause unintended civilian casualties, giving the appearance that they are used exclusively to shield their users from risk regardless of the cost to noncombatants. From a historical perspective of those on the receiving end, the use of a weapon that is extremely effective and exposes its users to minimal risk has rarely been viewed with awe, but more typically as being unfair precisely because of its efficiency or the overwhelming advantage it offers one side.[73]

The use of force, particularly airpower, in the Iraqi theater (and elsewhere) contributed to the production of accidental guerillas in two ways. First, on a practical level, it created fear and anxiety in those communities it was supposed to protect and therefore caused their leaders to seek help from elsewhere. Second, on a more abstract level, it undermined faith in the value systems of the countries employing it, particularly these countries' respect for human life. This in turn lent credibility, at least temporarily, to the alternative agenda of the jihadi movement, facilitating jihadis' integration with people who wanted security and stability rather than jihad.

The situation in Iraq worsened throughout 2005 and 2006, as the jihadis escalated sectarian tensions leading to a civil war between Iraq's Sunnis and Shiites. As early as August 2003, global jihadis had begun using suicide attackers to murder Shiite public figures, attempting to provoke a violent response from the Shiite community and the occupation forces.[74] Their effort was largely successful, and by 2006 the Iraqi government of Nuri al-Maliki had chosen sides in the struggle, acting as a sectarian (Shiite) combatant instead of an honest broker.[75] The imported insurgents, however, had started a civil war that they were not capable of winning, and mass executions of Sunnis by Shiite death squads and widespread ethnic cleansing became commonplace.[76] This sectarian bloodshed in turn set the stage for the rejection of the foreign fighters by their Iraqi hosts, an event that was encouraged by U.S. forces and, once it occurred, contributed to a reduction in overall attacks and suicide bombings, in particular in 2008 and 2009. The escalation of suicide missions by foreign fighters and their eventual isolation from their hosts is best illustrated via the experience of al Qaeda's Iraqi franchise from 2003 through 2010.

Use and Misuse: The Rise and Fall of al Qaeda in Iraq

From 2003 until 2006, al Qaeda's presence in Iraq was dominated by Abu Musab al-Zarqawi. Zarqawi, a Jordanian, had traveled to Afghanistan in 1989 to take part in the fight against the Soviets. Upon his return to Jordan in 1992, he became involved with Islamist groups challenging the state and was imprisoned in 1994. He was released as part of a general amnesty in 1999 and returned to Afghanistan, swearing allegiance to Osama bin Laden in 2001. After the U.S. invasion of Afghanistan in late 2001, Zarqawi fled via Iran to Iraq, where he hid in the autonomous Kurdish region until after the U.S.-led invasion in 2003.[77] By early 2004 Zarqawi had become the leader of a coalition of jihadi movements called Tawid wal Jihad (Unity and Struggle) and began to wage war against the American occupiers.

On October 17, 2004, Zarqawi formally pledged allegiance to Osama bin Laden for a second time and in doing so transformed his coalition into al Qaeda's Iraq-based franchise. This oath of allegiance demonstrated the symbolic importance of bin Laden: By officially sanctioning the Zarqawi coalition, he reinforced al Qaeda's commitment to Iraq and legitimized Zarqawi's group globally. The relationship had something to offer bin Laden as well; by allowing him to "share" in the carnage that Zarqawi unleashed in Iraq, it looked as though al Qaeda central was actually doing something for the global jihad.[78] During the first two years of the U.S. occupation, Zarqawi's network was responsible for 14 percent of attacks on coalition forces but 42 percent of suicide bombings. Another estimate has the Zarqawi network being responsible for 30 percent of all the suicide bombings in the first three years of the occupation.[79]

The formal connection to al Qaeda allowed Zarqawi's Iraq group to make use of a globally recognized name and well-established recruitment network to attract hundreds of fighters from throughout the Islamic world to escalate the conflict in Iraq. In the first years of the occupation, foreign fighters constituted a significant percentage of suicide attackers, but the exact extent of their role was at the time unclear. In 2007, however, the U.S. Army seized hundreds of documents in the town of Sinjar, near the Syrian border, that exposed the workings of part of the recruitment network. The documents included records on nearly seven hundred foreign fighters recruited to Iraq. Although the records do not offer a complete picture of the insurgency or use of foreign fighters, they are nonetheless extensive enough to be revealing of the entire movement.[80]

Of the foreign fighters gleaned from the documents, the greatest number, 244 (41 percent), were from Saudi Arabia, with Libya second, with 112 fighters (18.2 percent). For the most part, they were young and were not veterans of previous conflicts. Rather, they seem to have been recruited and radicalized far from arenas of conflict. Most of the fighters designated a desired "work" category, with more than half (217 of 389, or 56.3 percent) selecting suicide attacker or seeker of martyrdom. According to the U.S. National Counterterrorism Center's database, there were 394 suicide attacks in Iraq from August 2006 to August 2007, inflicting more than 16,000 casualties. Foreign fighters coming through Sinjar may have represented as much as 75 percent of these attackers.[81]

Zarqawi's reliance on al Qaeda's global network gave him the freedom to indulge himself in the Iraqi environment because he was not constrained by the need to justify his group's attacks to the local populace, and its approval was not necessary to sustain the flow of recruits. The resulting dynamic therefore differed from other instances of suicide bombing examined: Instead of unifying the Iraqi population and militant organizations in a common cause, Zarqawi's brutality widened the rift between the two. Foreign fighters on the whole tended to look down on the Iraqis because they were not ideologically committed. Zarqawi himself expressed contempt for the Iraqi population: "The Iraqi brothers still prefer safety and returning to the arms of their wives, where nothing frightens them," he wrote, frustrated with those who could not see that "safety and victory are incompatible." He continued, "People cannot awaken from their stupor unless talk of martyrdom and martyrs fills their days and nights."[82]

Zarqawi's cavalier attitude came to undermine al Qaeda's efforts to promote itself as a legitimate defender of Iraq's Sunni community. As early as July 2005, bin Laden's deputy, Ayman al-Zawahiri, had written a letter to Zarqawi in which he urged him to be mindful of the legitimacy of the struggle on a global level and therefore to limit violence toward civilians.[83] Zarqawi responded with a lecture in autumn 2005 entitled "It Is Allah Whom Ye Should More Justly Fear," in which he criticized jihadi scholars who tried to advise fighters while living in areas of relative security.[84]

In November 2005 Zarqawi claimed credit for several suicide attacks in Amman, Jordan, that killed dozens of Muslims. One of the attacks had targeted a wedding party. Tens of thousands of Jordanians responded by taking to the streets and calling for Zarqawi to "Burn in Hell."[85] As the image of the global jihad deteriorated internationally, the connection to the Iraqi population began to break down as well. In early 2006 al Qaeda replaced Zarqawi with an Iraqi and changed the name of their Iraqi franchise to the Mujahidin Shura Council in an effort to distance it from the Amman bombings and to make it seem more like a legitimate local movement.[86] After Zarqawi was killed by a U.S. air strike in summer 2006, the name of the organization changed again, becoming the Islamic State of Iraq in October, officially putting an end to the al Qaeda brand name in Iraq.[87]

By 2007 global jihadis in Iraq had so thoroughly alienated their hosts that the Iraqis began to turn on them. U.S. forces recognized the split and were able to systematically begin using it in 2007 for their own purposes, paying tribal leaders to resist the jihadis and in doing so serve as auxiliary "peacekeeping" forces.[88] Collectively known as the Awakening, with the tribal groups referred to as the Sons of Iraq, these movements contributed significantly to the decrease in bloodshed in Iraq after 2007.

The decline of al Qaeda's Iraq franchise was not caused by the use of suicide bombers. Rather, Zarqawi was indifferent to how suicide attackers were deployed, and their poor use reflected the larger failings of the group that undermined its legitimacy and helped exacerbate its rift with local forces. In his letter to Zarqawi in 2005, Zawahiri cautioned that "we are in a battle, and that more than half of this battle is taking place in the battlefield of the media. And that we are in a media battle in a race for the hearts and minds of our Umma." He repeatedly urged Zarqawi to consider the importance of maintaining a connection to the Iraqi people.[89] Zarqawi, motivated more by his own sense of divine mission, did the opposite, in the process undermining al Qaeda's political project. In addition to Zarqawi's indifference in how suicide attackers were used, by 2007–2008 Iraqi groups had begun to use coerced or involuntary bombers as well, undermining the very legitimacy of suicide missions. Such "remote-control martyrs" included mentally disabled women used as involuntary proxy bombers.[90]

Epilogue

The decline of al Qaeda's original Iraqi franchise did not mark the end of the organization or of suicide bombing in Iraq. In late 2009 terrorism experts cautioned that elements of the Baath Party had reconciled with the remnants of al Qaeda's Iraq franchise.[91] The newly reorganized al

Qaeda operation was thought to be responsible for some dramatic suicide attacks that damaged the credibility of the Iraqi government, led by
Maliki. These included the two blasts in August 2009, discussed at the
beginning of this section, in which nearly 100 people died. On October
26, 2009, two nearly simultaneous suicide truck bombs devastated the
Iraqi Ministry of Justice and provincial council complexes, killing 155
people and injuring 500. It was the deadliest attack in Iraq in more than
two years.[92] Al Qaeda in Iraq claimed credit for all of these missions.[93] On
December 8 five suicide bomb attacks significantly damaged a number of
government agencies, including the Ministry of Labor and Social Affairs
and the Ministry of Finance. Iraqi government officials put the death toll
at 77, but foreign journalists estimated it at approximately 127, with 400
injured.[94]

All three attacks targeted symbolic institutions, directly challenging
the legitimacy of the Maliki government and its ability to keep order.
They also demonstrated a high level of technical capability and preparation as they were all large, simultaneous vehicular bombings. The
October bombers had to pass through checkpoints to get to their targets, suggesting collusion or incompetence on the part of the security
forces.[95] Nevertheless, the attackers have derived no political benefit from
their use of force. Regular suicide attacks continued throughout 2010, but
the militants never came close to disrupting national elections, held in
March, suggesting that even a reformed al Qaeda that makes better use
of suicide attackers will be more a persistent and bloody nuisance than an
existential threat to the Iraqi state.

CONCLUSION: THE LATE MAJORITY

The previous chapters borrow heavily from Everett Rogers' *Diffusion
of Innovations* to provide an explanatory mechanism for the spread of
suicide bombing. According to this model, innovations spread relatively
slowly at first. After the innovation diffuses to a small number of early
adopters, it begins to spread more rapidly as its overall utility and its
applicability in different contexts become established. Use begets use, and
eventually a large class of relatively late adopters, which Rogers calls the
late majority, pick up the innovation in imitation of earlier groups as

much as in response to their own needs. Ultimately, previously reluctant laggards begin to make use of the innovation, also motivated by a need to imitate and appropriate a generally accepted innovation as much as by any "objective" necessity of their own. This overall pattern of diffusion takes the form of a bell-shaped curve (see Figure 7.2).

The overall pattern as well as the characteristics attributed to each sector of innovators conform to the global spread of suicide bombing in a general sense. In this case, Hizballah and its Iranian sponsors were the innovators; other Lebanese groups, such as Amal and the Syrian Social Nationalist Party, that copied Hizballah's use of suicide attackers, were the early adopters. The Tamil Tigers, Hamas, Palestinian Islamic Jihad, and to a lesser extent the Workers' Party of Kurdistan and the Provisional Irish Republican Army comprised the early majority.

Much of this chapter has concerned itself with the two categories on the right side of the bell curve. The late majority consists of al Qaeda central, Chechen rebels, and al Qaeda's Saudi and Iraqi branches. Palestinian latecomers, for instance, Fatah, also fall into this category. The most significant laggards—those who began to use suicide bombing only recently—are analyzed in the following chapter. As characterized by Rogers, those belonging to the late majority tend to be skeptical and do not embrace an innovation until numerous peers have done so, which seems to be the case here. In comparison with the Tamil Tigers and

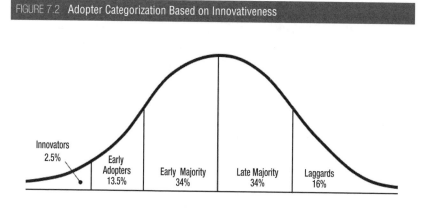

FIGURE 7.2   Adopter Categorization Based on Innovativeness

Innovators 2.5%
Early Adopters 13.5%
Early Majority 34%
Late Majority 34%
Laggards 16%

Source: Everett M. Rogers, *Diffusion of Innovations,* 5th ed. (New York: Free Press, 2003), 281.

Hamas, global jihadis were relative latecomers to suicide bombing. Once they began to use suicide attackers, however, the jihadis became enthusiastic change agents, doing their best to export the technology around the world.

Throughout the 2000s members of the global jihadi movement, inspired by the al Qaeda core, have traveled to different regions and taken suicide bombing with them. Al Qaeda shrewdly marketed the suicide bomber not only as an alternative, but as an equalizer, as a force that inverts the military superiority of state governments by expanding the possibilities of the individual through self-sacrifice. Demonstrations play an important role in diffusion by proving that a technology can work in a given environment.[96] Proving the utility of suicide bombing is clearly why in many of these cases imported global jihadis carried out initial attacks, knowing that the power of the demonstrations would go a long way toward determining whether a skeptical public might be convinced to embrace suicide bombing.[97]

Al Qaeda therefore encouraged the use of suicide bombing by sometimes skeptical clients in order to serve the movement's global agenda instead of the local needs of the clients themselves. This effort has yielded mixed results. In the new millennium, the pattern appears to be one of suicide bombing developing relatively slowly, then expanding rapidly—fed by the integration of the enthusiastic global movement with radical locals—after which it declines as the global movement finds that violence alone is insufficient for mobilizing an appreciable percentage of the local population. The suicide bombing of the new millennium may well prove to be less sustainable over time than was the suicide bombing of the 1990s because of the rapid, indiscriminate use of the weapon in areas not predisposed to it.

THE BUSINESS OF MARTYRDOM

It would therefore be appropriate to view global jihadism as a tremendously successful entrepreneurial initiative. From a corporate branding perspective, or the business of helping a corporation to create an enduring emotional tie between itself and its consumers, al-Qaida provided a perfect vehicle to "sell" global jihadism.[1]

— Jarret M. Brachman, *Global Jihadism*

On March 3, 2008, a suicide bomber detonated himself on a U.S. military base in Kabul, Afghanistan. The attack received relatively little media coverage at the time, probably because in neighboring Pakistan a wave of suicide bombings had claimed the lives of more than a hundred people over the previous three days.[2] The attack finally received attention weeks later, when militants released a DVD of it, in which the face of Maulavi Jalaluddin Haqqani is juxtaposed to the huge explosion caused by the bomber. Haqqani had been a leader of the Afghan resistance against the Soviet Union in the 1980s and later became one of the most important commanders of a resurgent element of militant groups often referred to collectively as the Neo-Taliban. These groups operate out of Afghanistan as well as the Federally Administered Tribal Areas (FATA) of neighboring Pakistan's North-West Frontier Province (renamed Khyber Pakhtunkhwa in April 2010).[3]

Haqqani's forces became one of the most significant elements of the Neo-Taliban starting around 2006.[4] His group is believed to have been responsible for an operation against the Indian embassy in Kabul on July 8, 2008, that is one of the most dramatic by the Neo-Taliban insurgency. The attack killed 54 people and injured nearly 140, most of them simply waiting outside the embassy gates to obtain visas. U.S. and Afghan officials credited the attack to Haqqani, with some insisting that it was carried out with the assistance of Pakistan's Inter-Services Intelligence Agency (ISI), whose presumed agenda included destabilizing the Afghan government as well as striking at India, Pakistan's long-term adversary.[5]

The embassy bombing received greater attention than the base attack because of the number of fatalities it inflicted and the volatile history of relations between India and Pakistan. The first attack, however, is more revealing of the ways in which suicide bombing had changed and continued to change after the 9/11 attacks. This operation illustrates the spread of suicide bombing into Pakistan and Afghanistan, where suicide attacks were generally unheard of prior to 2001. In addition, the marketing of the attack reveals the Neo-Taliban's connection to the global jihadi movement—and indeed the rest of the world—through technology.[6] The identity of the March 3 bomber points to the effectiveness of the movement's appeal. Unlike the embassy bomber, a Pakistani citizen, the March 3 attacker was a German citizen of Turkish ethnicity named Muhammad Beg. Apparently, Beg voluntarily traveled from Turkey to Pakistan to join the Haqqani network and then became a human bomb.[7]

The first groups that trained and deployed suicide attackers used their bombers for tactical as well as strategic purposes, but the globalized martyrdom of al Qaeda has lost much of its strategic value and instead now tends to serve a shorter-term, demonstrative purpose—recruiting alienated young Muslim men to the movement by selling them a form of identity myth that makes sense of their frustrations and anxieties. While the global reach of electronic communications has allowed the movement to effectively mobilize the small percentage of the Muslim world predisposed to al Qaeda's message, the global jihadi movement has remained marginal because it offers nothing of substance to the majority of the world's Muslims.

FRANCHISES AND LIKE-MINDED MOVEMENTS IN SOUTHWEST ASIA

The Neo-Taliban and Suicide Bombing in Afghanistan

On September 9, 2001, two al Qaeda operatives posing as journalists were granted an interview with Ahmed Shah Massoud, leader of the Northern Alliance, at that time the primary opposition to the Taliban in Afghanistan. They hid a bomb in one of their camera cases which they then detonated during the course of their "interview," killing themselves and injuring Massoud, who died the following day.[8] This was possibly the first suicide attack to take place in Afghanistan.[9] Throughout the many years of the Soviet occupation and subsequent Afghan civil war, with their attendant violence and atrocities, suicide bombing never established a foothold in this part of the world. Only after 2004 did suicide bombing become a common occurrence, imported, and in some cases imposed on the local population, by remnants of al Qaeda and its allies in the global jihadi movement.

In the first years after the 9/11 attacks, the war in Afghanistan appeared to be a decisive victory for the United States and its allies. When Hamid Karzai, then seen as a hard-working politician with a domestic constituency and international support, won the presidency of Afghanistan in 2004, his election was held up as an indicator of progress in the building of an Afghan state. Lacking a firm commitment to security and reconstruction, however, the new Afghan government proved itself to be largely ineffective. The warlords of the 1990s reemerged, funded by explosive growth in the opium trade. Drug money left the warlords wealthier than the government, and Karzai was extremely ineffective in his dealings with them.[10]

Meanwhile, the people of Afghanistan found themselves trapped between two very different adversaries fighting with different types of precision weapons, which caused significant civilian casualties in spite of (or in some cases because of) the intelligence used to guide the weapon interactively to its destination. The NATO powers lacked the numbers of troops necessary to police the entire country effectively, so prior to 2009 their forces combated the insurgency of the Neo-Taliban using airpower; few alternatives existed. From January to August 2008, NATO forces conducted 2,400 air strikes in Afghanistan.[11] The use of even the most accurate precision-guided munitions carries with it the risk of causing unintended civilian casualties, so when the number of air strikes is high, civilian deaths become a certainty.[12] As in Iraq, the use of airpower by U.S. and allied forces in Afghanistan was sometimes counterproductive in that it inadvertently solidified alliances between the local population and militant groups despite underlying ideological differences.[13]

This combination of factors created a climate conducive to the resurgence of the Taliban. Although typically called the New Taliban, Neo-Taliban, or just Taliban, the opposition to the Afghan government and its foreign allies is less an organized movement than a broad, diverse range of groups with different ideologies and agendas across the spectrum. The outfits operating in the south of Afghanistan and into Baluchistan tend to consist of remnants of the original Taliban. Their orientation is local, and they are nominally governed by a twenty-three-member *shura* council headed by former Taliban leader Mullah Mohammad Omar in Quetta, in Pakistan's Baluchistan province.[14]

To the north and east, in the tribal regions of Pakistan's Khyber Pakhtunkhwa, the picture is more complex. Here remnants of the insurgency against the Soviet Union have reestablished themselves, sometimes with the complicity of Pakistan's ISI.[15] Members of the Taliban and al Qaeda were welcomed by tribal groups in Khyber Pakhtunkhwa as they fled Afghanistan during 2001–2002. Al Qaeda reconstituted and continues to play a role in the local insurgency in addition to encouraging and supporting terrorist attacks around the world.[16] Militants known collectively as the Tehrik-e Taliban Pakistan (TTP), or Pakistani Taliban, from the tribal regions, have launched their own insurgency against the Pakistani state. They are more closely affiliated with al Qaeda than with other militant groups in the area.[17]

The original Taliban was militantly anti-technology—they smashed TVs and outlawed photography—but elements of the Neo-Taliban have published online journals, shot, edited, and marketed DVDs, and used the Internet for publicity and recruitment.[18] Many of the most technology-savvy elements of the Neo-Taliban are the ones most closely connected to al Qaeda and its global agenda. This use of technology to fuse the local Afghan insurgency with al Qaeda's global agenda allowed for the importation of suicide bombing into Afghanistan and then into Pakistan.

Even after the spectacle of 9/11 and the rapid destruction of the Taliban government, Afghan militants did not immediately turn to suicide attacks. Only in 2005 did suicide bombings become a staple of the Neo-Taliban insurgency. Brian Glyn Williams suggests two reasons for the delay. First, suicide attacks were fundamentally alien to the culture of the Pashtun people, who make up much of the Neo-Taliban, and second, suicide bombing was not seen as being powerful enough to redress the imbalance of forces between the Neo-Taliban and its adversaries.[19] Thus relative advantage and cultural compatibility were both lacking.

Remnants of al Qaeda, which included holdovers from the pre-9/11 area and veterans of other theaters, particularly Iraq after 2003, worked diligently to create a climate into which they could import their preferred type of weapon. By late 2003 they could point to successful attacks in Iraq, such as the bombing of the UN building in August 2003, as evidence that suicide attacks were the only way to combat the Afghan government and its American sponsors effectively. They made dramatic use of the video propaganda produced by Abu Musab al-Zarqawi in Iraq, dubbing videos of bombings, suicide attacker testimonies, and executions into Pashtu. By 2004 a local al Qaeda operative had begun producing Afghan-specific videos with titles such as "Pyre for the Americans in Afghanistan." The first few sporadic attacks in 2003 and 2004 were carried out by Arabs already indoctrinated in the culture of martyrdom and served as trial runs to demonstrate the effectiveness of suicide attacks to the skeptical Pashtuns.[20]

This marketing campaign paid off within two years. Mullah Omar, who had previously condemned suicide attacks, reversed his position and laid the groundwork for the ideological acceptance of suicide bombing in Taliban culture. With suicide attacks no longer taboo, Neo-Taliban fighters began to embrace them, calling suicide bombers "Mullah Omar's Missiles" and "our atomic bombs."[21] Mullah Dadullah became the local Taliban commander most enthusiastic about the use of suicide bombers. In early 2004 Dadullah reportedly sent a team to train with Zarqawi, an old acquaintance from the latter's Afghan years, and the next year Zarqawi sent a three-man delegation to Dadullah to present further video material justifying suicide attacks. With this direct transfer of know-how, Dadullah was able to begin training suicide bombers systematically in his stronghold in Pakistan.[22]

There was significant resistance to this new form of weapon, and many Pashtuns seem to have been reluctant to become suicide attackers. For the most part, as was the case in Chechnya, bombers were not recognized as heroes by the local populace, and public support for suicide attacks remained low.[23] One peculiarity is the relative ineffectiveness of Neo-Taliban suicide bombers who collectively killed far fewer people per attack than suicide bombers in other areas of conflict. This can be partially attributed to target selection by the Neo-Taliban attackers. For the most part, at least through 2007, they tended to focus on military and political targets, which were well defended, rather than mass-casualty attacks against civilians, as was common among Iraqi suicide bombers.[24] In all, there had been 518 suicide attacks in Afghanistan as of December 31, 2010, killing 2,232 people at an average of 4.3 fatalities per attack, less than half the average number of fatalities per attack in Iraq (see Figure 8.1).

The poor operational record of Neo-Taliban suicide attackers also reflects the low quality of recruits and the training they received. Because

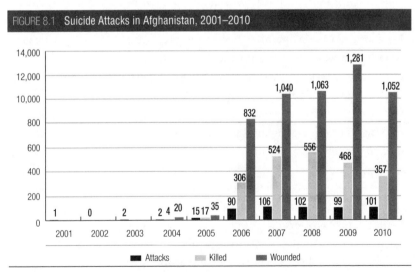

FIGURE 8.1   Suicide Attacks in Afghanistan, 2001–2010

Sources: For 2001 through 2003, United Nations Assistance Mission to Afghanistan, "Suicide Attacks in Afghanistan, 2001–2007," New York, September 2007, 42; for 2004 through 2010, Worldwide Incidents Tracking System, National Counterterrorism Center, wits.nctc.gov (accessed November 12, 2009; April 1, 2010; and April 1, 2011).

of the unwillingness of many Pashtuns to embrace suicide bombing, the pool of recruits from which Neo-Taliban leaders can choose has been limited. A significant percentage of Neo-Taliban suicide attackers have had physical or mental disabilities and have likely been coerced or misled in some way. Many abandoned their attacks at the last minute, demonstrating a lack of ideological commitment. Some were detonated by remote control.[25]

The movement also relied on children, even twelve years old or younger, to carry out its suicide attacks.[26] The advantages for the use of young people are straightforward. The constant violence that Afghanistan has endured has left thousands of children orphaned.[27] Since they have no families to be consoled, it is easier for militant groups to use them in a more overtly coercive manner—without the corresponding social backlash—than has normally been the case in suicide bombing. The disadvantages, of course, are diminishing returns at the tactical and strategic levels. The poor training and abilities of such bombers lead to marginal operational capabilities, and their lack of social standing makes it difficult for the Neo-Taliban to use their bombers to generate legitimacy in the long run.

Suicide Bombing in Pakistan

The introduction of suicide bombing to Pakistan quickly followed its appearance in the Afghan theater. One suicide attack took place in 2005, followed by five in 2006 and then by at least forty-one in 2007, including the assassination of former prime minister Benazir Bhutto on December 27, 2007. The following year, there were fifty-eight suicide attacks, including the devastating strike on the Marriott Hotel in Islamabad on September 20 that killed sixty people and injured more than two hundred. Such was the physical and symbolic devastation of this attack that within Pakistan the media referred to the blast as "Pakistan's 9/11."[28]

The original Taliban had served several Pakistani national security goals by providing strategic depth against India and serving as a training ground for producing militants that could be sent to pin down Indian forces in the disputed parts of Jammu and Kashmir. When al Qaeda drew the U.S. military into southwest Asia, it ruined years of planning by the ISI and left the organization scrambling to pursue a consistent policy. It now seems that in the immediate aftermath of the 9/11 attacks, the ISI played a double game, supporting U.S. goals by rounding up al Qaeda suspects but at the same time hedging its bets by sheltering Taliban leaders.[29]

This policy was only partially successful, as within the Neo-Taliban movement attitudes toward Pakistan and the ISI range from cordial to adversarial. Allied factions, such as the Haqqani network, operate openly in Pakistan with the de facto blessing of the army.[30] Hostile factions, including the remnants of al Qaeda and its most closely allied factions, have been at war with the Pakistani government as much as they have been with the governments of Afghanistan and the United States. In 2004 the Pakistani army invaded the tribal region of South Waziristan in an effort to impose control and in doing so alienated many local tribal leaders, some of whom then formed the Tehrik-e Taliban Pakistan, which became openly hostile to the Pakistani military and state.[31]

In July 2007 the government of Pakistan stormed the Lal Masjid, a bastion of Islamist criticism of the Pakistani government, after a tense standoff with militants. By the end of the siege, approximately one hundred people had been killed.[32] The attack on the mosque triggered a breakdown of a tenuous cease-fire between Neo-Taliban factions and the Pakistani government, after which the militants responded with ferocity. Of the forty-two suicide attacks that took place in Pakistan in 2007, thirty-six occurred after clashes erupted at the mosque on July 3. Overall, Neo-Taliban forces and their al Qaeda allies killed 250 members of security forces in the months immediately after the siege.[33] In October 2009, as the Pakistani army renewed its offensive against Taliban factions, they responded with an especially brutal campaign of suicide attacks, many of which targeted civilians. At least five suicide bombings took place that month, the last of which was a particularly deadly attack in a bazaar that killed at least 120 people, most of them women and children.[34]

In all, there had been 239 suicide attacks in Pakistan as of December 31, 2010, killing 3,759 people and injuring nearly 10,000 (see Figure 8.2). Many of these attacks were claimed by the Tehrik-e-Taliban Pakistan. The number of fatalities per attack, approximately 15.7, is testimony to the high lethality of suicide bombing in Pakistan due to the militants' willingness to hit vulnerable civilian targets. As was the case with Afghan suicide bombers, many Pakistani suicide attackers were young boys who

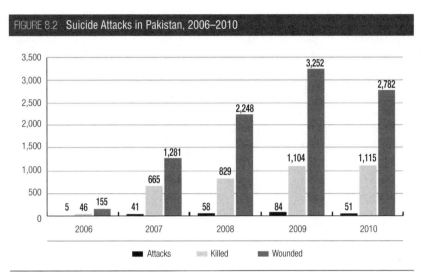

FIGURE 8.2   Suicide Attacks in Pakistan, 2006–2010

Source: Worldwide Incidents Tracking System, National Counterterrorism Center, wits.nctc.gov (accessed November 24, 2009; April 1, 2010; and April 1, 2011).

had been orphaned or had physical or mental disabilities that made them particularly susceptible to indoctrination and coercion by militant leaders. One Taliban leader asserted, "Children are tools to achieve God's will."[35]

AFRICAN FRANCHISES

The Algerian Franchise: Al Qaeda in the Islamic Maghreb

On December 11, 2007, Rabah Bechla, a sixty-three-year-old grandfather of seven, rammed a white van laden with explosives into the United Nations' offices in Algiers and detonated it, destroying much of the building. Algerian officials put the death toll from the attack at forty-one, but emergency personnel on the scene said that it was much higher, perhaps as many as sixty. At approximately the same time, another suicide attacker, a thirty-year-old man named Larbi Charef, targeted Algeria's constitutional council. A passing bus full of students absorbed much of the blast, which killed and wounded many of them. The two attacks were brutal and stunning, all the more so because a grandfather of seven hardly fit the profile of the typical suicide attacker, prompting a local journalist to comment, "If a grandfather can blow himself up, anyone can."[36]

The Algerian civil war of the 1990s resulted in the deaths of per-haps 100,000 people.[37] During the conflict, the most radical members of the various armed resistance groups were Algerians who had returned from fighting the Soviets in Afghanistan. They were a relatively small percentage of the overall opposition, but because of their experience and determination, they became a decisive element, pushing it toward a radi-cal rejection of democracy in favor of the violent establishment of a con-servative form of a religiously governed state.[38] During this time they maintained contact with Osama bin Laden and the al Qaeda network through personal connections forged during their time in Afghanistan. By the later 1990s, this faction of the resistance called itself the Salafi Group for Preaching and Combat (Groupe Salafiste pour la Predication et le Combat, GSPC).[39] The violence of the group, which included massacres of civilians, led to its isolation as the government of Algeria ended the civil war by co-opting moderate factions through a program of amnesty and reconciliation.

In 2004, needing money, recruits, and legitimacy, the GSPC reached out to al Qaeda through Zarqawi's Iraqi franchise. By 2006 it had become part of the al Qaeda network, renaming itself al Qaeda in the Islamic Maghreb (AQIM), and began to reinvent itself as a part of the global struggle for Islam.[40] The al Qaeda brand brought with it respect and legit-imacy among militant circles, allowing the group to retain local mem-bers who otherwise would have traveled to Iraq to wage jihad; this in turn allowed the group to attack the Algerian government much more systematically. The organization even began to run training camps for militants from neighboring Morocco and Tunisia.

The use of suicide attackers in Algeria demonstrated the GSPC's transformation into an al Qaeda franchise. As early as 2004 Algerian recruits in Iraq had begun making martyrdom videos prior to suicide attacks against U.S. targets and by 2005 had become a significant percent-age of the foreign fighters wreaking havoc in Iraq.[41] The introduction of suicide bombing into Algeria therefore did not necessitate any new orga-nizational developments, cultural conditioning, or training, but instead a diversion of recruits and resources from one theater to another. The first suicide attack to occur in Algeria took place on April 11, 2007, killing thirty-three people.[42] An attack on August 19, 2008, killed forty-three people at a police college, forty-one of whom were civilians according to authorities.[43]

As was the case with Zarqawi's attacks in Iraq, the suicide missions carried out by al Qaeda's Algerian franchise were not welcomed by the Algerian people, including local Islamic scholars, who criticized them. That they continued to be conducted suggests that the Algerian people were not the audience at which the attacks were aimed. Rather, high-visibility operations were carried out to get publicity for the global movement when its fortunes were waning as a consequence of its decline in Iraq.[44] Its isolation from the local context has prevented AQIM from building a self-reinforcing relationship with the local populace. The group carried out fewer attacks in 2008 than in 2007, but the number of suicide missions it conducted increased. In contrast, the group was responsible for only one suicide attack in 2009 and one in 2010.[45]

Somalia: Al-Shabab

Somalia is one of the countries recently afflicted by suicide bombing. Years without effective centralized government have left the country vulnerable to foreign invasion, poor, devastated, and ravaged by criminal gangs and warlords. Nevertheless, through all the years of lawlessness and corruption, there were no suicide attacks until 2006. That September, suicide bombers attempted unsuccessfully to kill the interim president. The following November, three suicide bombers killed two police officers.[46] These attacks were initially blamed on al Qaeda, which has long had a presence in East Africa, but by 2008 were attributed to a new, indigenous group, Harakat al-Shabab al-Mujahideen (Movement of Warrior-Youth), or simply al-Shabab (which means "youth"). As of late 2010 al-Shabab occupied a middle ground between its emergence as a local group and its ambitions to join the global jihadi movement. Although it publicly and repeatedly pledged allegiance to Osama bin Laden's movement, bin Laden never formally recognized the group as an al Qaeda affiliate.[47]

In October 2008 five bombers simultaneously attacked Somali government and UN sites in northern Somalia, killing twenty-one people. The following February suicide bombers killed eleven African Union peacekeepers in Mogadishu. In May a bomb being prepared for a suicide attack detonated prematurely, killing several members of al-Shabab. The next month a suicide attack carried out by three men in a Toyota truck killed twenty people, among them the minister of security, Col. Umar Hashi Adan. On September 17, 2009, two suicide bombers again attacked peacekeeping forces of the African Union, killing seventeen. Al-Shabab claimed all these attacks.[48] An operation in Mogadishu on December 3 killed nineteen people, of whom three were government ministers. On July 11, 2010, the group signaled an intensification of its campaign by carrying out simultaneous suicide bombings in Kampala, the capital of Uganda, killing seventy-six people.[49]

Of the many recent suicide bombings, the assault of October 2008 has generated the most significant concern among security analysts, primarily because of the identity of one of the suicide attackers. Twenty-six-year-old Shirwa Ahmed was born in Somalia but had lived most of his life in Minnesota and was the first American citizen to carry out a suicide attack. Ahmed was one of a small number of Somali Americans from Minnesota who had journeyed to Somalia to fight on behalf of al-Shabab. These men were undoubtedly influenced by al-Shabab's propaganda videos, which are available online.[50] Much of their radicalization, however, seems to have stemmed not from jihadi propaganda, but from their inability to assimilate fully into American society. Ahmed and his fellow travelers came from a socially isolated minority in which broken families were common and discrimination of varying sorts a regular occurrence. Lacking a sense of familial or national belonging, many of these young men sought refuge in Somali American gangs. By that point, much of the process of radicalization had already been completed, and it was up to al-Shabab to give shape to the somewhat incoherent frustrations of these men by indoctrinating them into the world of jihad and martyrdom. As of October 2009, a total of six Somali Americans had died fighting for al-Shabab.[51]

COMMUNICATION AND CONTROL

The July 7 Bombers

Although suicide bombing on the global level intensified in the years after the 9/11 attacks, the reach of the radicals seemed to be limited, with no major operations in Europe or the United States for several years. On July 7, 2005, however, the jihadi movement seemingly demonstrated a long geographical reach when three suicide attackers blew themselves up on different trains in the London subway system; a fourth bomber, who was delayed by a glitch in his bomb, chose to detonate himself and his weapon on a bus since the subway had been closed in the aftermath of the first three attacks.[52] The weapons, as in previous instances of locally initiated terrorist attacks, were relatively unsophisticated homemade explosives carried in backpacks. The attacks killed fifty-two people and became a major news story on both sides of the Atlantic because of the closeness of the United States and the United Kingdom, the shared language, and the nationality of the attackers, all four of whom were British citizens.

Three of the bombers were of Pakistani descent, and the fourth was a naturalized immigrant from Jamaica. The United Kingdom has a large community of Pakistani immigrants and their second and third generation descendents. Many émigrés have sought to preserve their cultural traditions and sense of communal identity, sometimes leaving their children conflicted in terms of their individual identities because they cannot identify fully with either the land of their birth or the land of their parents' identity.[53] Over the years, some radical young Muslims, many from the Pakistani community, have taken advantage of permissive British policies regarding freedom of speech and expression to agitate openly against the state.[54] By the start of the new millennium, British counterterrorism officials were regularly investigating plots initiated by radicals residing in the United Kingdom. In 2004 months of investigation led to Operation Crevice, during which seven hundred police officers raided nearly two dozen locations and broke up an al-Qaeda-directed terrorist cell.[55]

Operation Crevice missed the 7/7 plotters because they had only minimal connections to known jihadi figures. Despite suspicions that the attack must have been planned and directed by someone with more experience in such matters and with closer connections to the global jihadi leadership than the bombers had, no such mastermind or fifth bomber appears to have been involved. Instead, the London bombers "were essentially an autonomous clique whose motivations, cohesiveness, and ideological grooming occurred in the absence of any organized network or formal entry into the jihad."[56] More striking perhaps is that in this cell there was apparently little division of labor or differentiation of roles. The four members helped to radicalize each other in a process of mutual feedback. All four seem to have participated in target selection and contributed to building the bombs.

The attackers did, however, receive technical assistance from al Qaeda's established leadership. In late 2004 two of the London bombers traveled to Pakistan and received training in the production and use of homemade explosives as well as ideological encouragement. From that point on, the cell remained in contact with radicals in Pakistan and in the United Kingdom.[57] Attacks carried out without such technical assistance—such as attempted copycat bombings in London on July 21, 2005, and suicide bombings in Glasgow in July 2007—have been far more amateurish. Individual initiative on the part of the London bombers and direction from established jihadis were necessary components of the July 7 bombings.

Leadership and Control in Terror Networks

Reconciling the roles of individual and organizational control within small jihadi groups, particularly those using suicide attacks, has proven to be problematic to this point. Bruce Hoffman notes, for example, that outside technical advice is necessary to provide inexperienced groups with the skills necessary to carry out even relatively simple attacks, such as the July 7 bombings. Centralized leadership is required for inspiring prospective groups and members, organizing their behavior, and especially for managing the publicity generated by their attacks. For instance, Siddique Khan and Shahzad Tanweer, the two July 7 bombers who traveled to Pakistan, recorded martyrdom videos that were subsequently used by the al Qaeda leadership to claim responsibility for the attack. Al Qaeda's media branch edited Tanweer's video so that his testimonial was framed by messages from Ayman al-Zawahiri and released that version on the first anniversary of the attack.[58] Whatever the actual motivations of the London bombers in life, their deaths were used by al Qaeda's martyrologists as evidence of the organization's ongoing relevance and power. Hoffman thus emphasizes the importance of organizational leadership, and of the established al Qaeda leadership in particular, for the global jihadi movement.

In contrast, Marc Sageman argues that the seemingly coherent behavior of the global jihadi movement results from the interactions of social networks formed by peer groups of like-minded, alienated young men. His analysis, based on extensive fieldwork and interviews with jihadis and would-be jihadis, suggests that local, personal motivations are much more significant in global jihadism than are centralized organizational control and ideology. Social and political conditions marginalize individuals, who then form close groups, or cliques, based on kinship and friendship. Membership in these small, insular groups intensifies and politicizes preexisting grievances, making the group more susceptible to the jihadi message. These small groups and the loose networks that they form initiate attacks opportunistically within the overall ideological framework of global jihadism and therefore serve to advance the jihadi agenda in the absence of centralized leadership.[59]

These two approaches to the role of organizational leadership are seemingly quite different from one another and have been at the heart of an unusually sharp public debate between Hoffman and Sageman. The two positions, however, are not as far apart as they might seem; they can both be readily accommodated within this book's analytical framework. As already shown, motivations vary at different levels of the suicide-bombing complex. It is not surprising that jihadi suicide bombers demonstrate intensely personal motivations and that they might differ from the ideological agendas of the leaders that inspire them. Hoffman and Sageman tend to frame their analyses in terms of leadership, so what they are examining are ultimately patterns of organizational control. From this perspective, both their leadership models have something to offer, for the form of control that characterizes the jihadi movement—and ultimately makes its manufacture of suicide bombers possible—is an interesting mixture, in which bottom-up control is tempered with top-down direction accounting for the loose but coherent nature of jihadism.

Endogenous and Exogenous Control

One of the most important changes in suicide bombing in recent years has been the replacement of centralized organizational control—such as that which characterized Hizballah's early attacks, the trial runs of the IRA and the PKK, and the LTTE's suicide-bombing complex—with much more fluid, decentralized control, such as that characteristic of the suicide bombing of the second intifada and of the global jihadi movement.[60]

Control in this context does not imply brainwashing or domination; rather, excessive direction on the part of the sponsoring organization would rob bombers of the ability to think and decide, which is part of what makes them so dangerous. Centralized control is also inconsistent with the empirical evidence regarding self-motivated would-be martyrs who have flocked to al Qaeda's various franchises seeking the opportunity to kill themselves. Understanding how groups weak in formal organizational structures exert such seemingly extraordinary control over some of their followers is essential in explaining the spread and diversification of suicide bombing.

Control can be spread out along a spectrum of possibilities, ranging from domination to suggestion. The endpoints of the spectrum represent two different approaches to the problem of control, which consist of intelligent and unintelligent control, as characterized by Lao Tzu, the founder of Taoism. Lao Tzu believed that intelligent control meant convincing someone to want to do what you want them to do, that is, persuasion rather than domination. Such control is intelligent because from the perspective of the individual controlled, it appears to be freedom. Unintelligent control, on the other hand, consists of forcing an individual to perform a task against his or her will, usually under threat of punishment. Unintelligent control is therefore perceived as external domination and thus is often resented.[61]

What Lao Tzu called unintelligent control is more formally referred to as exogenous control, which is "a condition imposed from without and involves a specific, centralized control structure, as well as distinct roles for the controller and controlled, and information flows vertically." Since exogenous control demands a centralized structure, it is best suited to traditional bureaucratic organizations with hierarchical structures. In contrast, intelligent control is known as endogenous control. Endogenous control is characterized by negotiation and a lack of formal organizational roles or hierarchies (that is, controller and controlled feel themselves to be fundamentally the same). It is spread among individuals instead of being concentrated in any one center.[62] Endogenous control, with its distributed control process, works best in an egalitarian, networked environment with reciprocal flows of information. In the context of suicide bombing, endogenous control makes use of deeply felt bonds to friends and family to convince the individual to sacrifice his or her life for the benefit of the group. It is the difference between having volunteers for suicide missions and having to force individuals to undertake suicide missions against their will. Only organizations with exceptional power and discipline can maintain the latter for an extended period of time.

The government of Imperial Japan during World War II was strong enough to rely heavily on "unintelligent" control. The men who became Kamikaze pilots had very little power or authority relative to the state. They knew that they were going to their deaths and had tactical control over their own missions, but they did not have the power to reject the role handed to them by the government. They were compelled to obey, or at least to demonstrate the outward signs of obedience, even if internally they rationalized their own deaths in a completely different manner. The Tamil Tigers provide another example of an organization that deployed suicide attackers using primarily exogenous control mechanisms. The leadership of the LTTE, Vellupillai Prabhakaran in particular, maintained centralized control over the entire process, from recruitment, to training, to mission operations, and memorializing the dead after the fact. Although individual Black Tigers were fully complicit in this process, their enthusiasm and obedience did nothing to change the fact that their lives were Prabhakaran's to use as he saw fit.

In the model of technology practice, a mutual relationship exists in which the technical element and the organizational element influence each other. Since suicide bombing utilizes human beings as part of its technical element, this relationship has been explored here in terms of management. The managerial relationship between organizations and their human bombers has been represented graphically by a two-way arrow to indicate that communications between the two are mutual, but there are many ways for this relationship to express itself.

Describing an organization as utilizing exogenous control does not necessarily mean that the arrow must point in only one direction, from the organization to the individual. Such extreme forms of coercive control have been used in the manufacture of suicide bombers, but they have been extraordinarily inefficient because the responsible organization is seen as being manipulative and therefore cannot make use of the legitimizing power that comes from having followers willing to die for the cause. The Provisional IRA's proxy bombers and the various cases in which individuals have been unwittingly used as remote-control martyrs fall into this category. In the opposite category, pure endogenous control, all decision making is by the individual. Classical martyrdom falls into this category because the decision to die is motivated by an authentic commitment to a cause or group but is far too unpredictable to be used at the tactical level. Individual suicide falls outside this spectrum since it is perceived to be selfish and does not contribute to organizational power on either the tactical or the strategic levels.

The most effective users of suicide attackers combine elements of endogenous and exogenous control, but often one pathway or the other dominates. In the case of practical exogenous control, like that which characterized Imperial Japan and the Tamil Tigers, the path from organization to individual dominates, with the organization taking the initiative and setting requirements and leaving the individual a narrow range of action within which to fulfill his or her obligations. In a more endogenous structure, such as global jihadism, the individual has freedom to initiate action, and the power of the organization to coerce or intimidate its followers is reduced. These structures can be understood schematically as illustrated in Figure 8.3.

Patterns of control have their limits. Groups in the middle of the spectrum, like Hamas and Hizballah, which balance endogenous and exogenous control, have found their ability to make and use suicide attackers to be severely constrained by what their communities are and are not willing to condone.

Practical exogenous control structures depend upon power expressed through clearly defined channels making them vulnerable to disruption. After the surrender of Imperial Japan, there were no more Kamikaze attacks against U.S. forces (and the occupation as a whole was surprisingly nonviolent in contrast to the brutality of the fighting in the Pacific).[63] Similarly, for two years after the defeat of the LTTE and the death of Vellupillai Prabhakaran, there were no suicide attacks by former members of the Tamil Tigers. In both cases, the ability to make and use suicide attackers ended when the group's leadership was defeated.

Practical endogenous control structures, in contrast, are resistant to such "decapitation," so the jihadi movement continues to survive despite

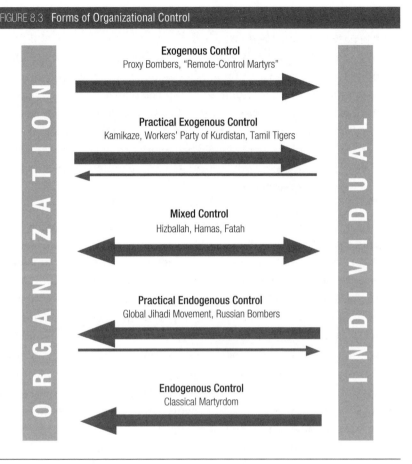

FIGURE 8.3   Forms of Organizational Control

Exogenous Control
Proxy Bombers, "Remote-Control Martyrs"

Practical Exogenous Control
Kamikaze, Workers' Party of Kurdistan, Tamil Tigers

Mixed Control
Hizballah, Hamas, Fatah

Practical Endogenous Control
Global Jihadi Movement, Russian Bombers

Endogenous Control
Classical Martyrdom

ORGANIZATION

INDIVIDUAL

Source: Jeffrey W. Lewis, 2011.

the loss of much of its leadership. Because the movement depends upon trust and ideological homogeneity among members, however, it cannot mobilize entire societies and become a mass movement. Organizations lacking formal structures depend on a high degree of trust among members, which in turn pushes these organizations toward being relatively small in size and uniform in mindset and ideology.[64] Leaders need then only provide symbols, narratives, and rituals consistent with the expectations of their followers in order to achieve the power to influence, but not to command, the behavior of their followers.[65]

Emergence

The precise mechanisms by which endogenous forms of control function have been understood only for a few decades. In the 1970s and 1980s, computer modeling of naturally occurring chemical and biological systems demonstrated that organized group behavior need not be centrally controlled but instead can emerge collectively from the behavior of a system's individual constituents.[66] That is to say, relatively simple rules can produce complex, goal-oriented behavior even when the path toward a given goal is not explicitly articulated in the rules themselves. Each autonomous actor within the system adheres to the same set of rules, and from these interactions a collective pattern of behavior emerges giving the system as a whole coherence that is not readily discernable at the level of the individual actors.[67]

It is now clear that this dynamic applies to human organizations. Loosely organized networks can produce coherent group behavior even in the absence of any bureaucratic or hierarchical control structure.[68] Individual motivations and small-group dynamics create a potential set of actors, and ideological leadership provides a set of cues to direct their behavior. This is why the models of organizational leadership suggested by Hoffman and Sageman can, indeed do, coexist comfortably with one another; the global jihadi leadership provides the rules for behavior of the movement, but within the framework established by these rules individual jihadis have considerable autonomy.

Bin Laden and Zawahiri encouraged such a leadership model to promote terrorism from the grass roots up throughout the Western world. Zawahiri, in *Knights under the Prophet's Banner*, emphasizes that responsibility falls on the shoulders of individual Muslims, who are obligated to carry on jihad even in the absence of direct orders from the global leadership. The role of the leadership is to inspire young men by making them aware of their obligations to the faith and setting an example for them to follow.[69] In December 2002 Zawahiri distributed a pamphlet, "Loyalty and Separation," in the Arabic-language daily *al-Quds al-Arabi* (London), in which he wrote, "*Young Muslims need not wait for anyone's permission*, because jihad against the Americans, the Jews, and their allies, hypocrites and apostates, is now an individual duty, as we have demonstrated."[70]

Perhaps more influential in the development of al Qaeda's global strategy has been Abu Musab al-Suri, who articulated a plan for directing a diffuse, goal-oriented global movement in *The Global Islamic Resistance Call*, a 1,600-page document published online in 2005.[71] For Suri, the global Islamic resistance is an idea or a system rather than an organization. The purpose of this system is to transform disaffected individuals into a coherent force by providing inspiration and direction in order to align individual goals with those of the group. Suri appears to have a strong understanding of what makes endogenous control work, for his book sees the global jihad as a communicative instead of an organizational phenomenon. According to Suri, "There are no organizational bonds of any kind between the members of the Global Islamic Resistance Units, except the bonds of a *'program of beliefs, a system of action, a common name, and a common goal.'*"[72]

THE BUSINESS OF MARTYRDOM: MAKING AND MARKETING SUICIDE ATTACKERS

New Electronic Media, Mutual Communication, and Feedback

The global program imagined by Suri has become a possibility due to the dramatic changes in electronic communication over the past two decades. Terrorism has always been a form of communication dependent upon media attention. Traditionally the mainstream media—first the mass print media of the late 1800s and then the electronic mass media of the post–World War II years—played the biggest role in communicating violent extremists' messages to the masses. Even in instances in which extremist groups did not attempt to claim or manage the consequences of their acts, the media communicated them powerfully.[73] The recent expansion of satellite television into areas previously dominated by state-run media, particularly countries in the Arab world, has meant that more and more people are involved in the public sphere, which has given them access to the messages of extremists (as well as others).[74]

Nevertheless, television and the print media, staples of the "old media," were always inherently limited in how they could directly benefit radical groups. Managers at the stations, not the radicals, choose what to air, and viewers received this information only passively, limiting their involvement. The migration of communication to the Internet has helped extremist groups overcome these limitations, because the web allows virtually anyone to become a "broadcaster" by posting video clips and enables secure, two-way communication even at great distances.

In recent years, the scope of Internet use by extremists has become staggering. Gabriel Weimann tracked no fewer than 4,300 websites serving listed terrorist groups between 1998 and 2005.[75] The most important element of the Internet, as opposed to other forms of electronic communication, is its capacity for two-way exchanges. Participation by individuals in online chat groups, for example, is an active process that links individuals to a larger group of like-minded colleagues irrespective of distance.[76] Experienced militants are able to communicate directly with potential recruits and to use video propaganda to push them toward action. Even before 9/11, there was a global pool of potential recruits in the form of young Muslim men who felt alienated from their cultures and societies in largely Muslim states as well as in Europe and elsewhere. These men formed isolated subcultures or islands of identity, with a few being able or willing to take the dramatic step of traveling to a place like Afghanistan to forge formal links with the global jihadi leadership. The Internet has proven to be ideal for bringing together the pieces of this fragmented global community, and one result is the cyber-mobilization of dissatisfied young men, many of whom were already on the margins of society, around the world.[77]

The majority of young men who become attracted to jihadism as an online social movement will never become suicide attackers or do anything that directly supports the movement's global military campaign. Jarret Brachman calls this group of interested but non-committed men "jihobbyists." They are enthusiasts of the global jihadi movement, but their interest will never get to the point of formally joining the movement. Instead they support jihad from the comfort of their homes by hosting websites, editing videos, or compiling audio files of speeches by well-known al Qaeda members.[78] Only a few of these jihobbyists will go to the next level and actually take part in the social activities with other members, a step away from cheerleading and toward action that Brachman calls preparatory jihad. In general, the large number of jihobbyists makes the movement a genuine social phenomenon for disaffected young men around the world.

The cyber-mobilization of potential jihadis demonstrates the power of the Internet simultaneously to unify and fragment human communities, for the creation of this virtual community has come at the expense of real human communities. Critics of the Internet have long recognized that the sheer diversity of people and information available online sometimes leads not to mutual understanding or broader awareness of cultural differences, but instead to fragmentation into relatively homogeneous subcommunities since individuals are able to seek those of a like mind online and avoid those with whom they disagree. In the mid-1990s Stephen Talbott observed, "In any event, one of the Net's attractions is avowedly its natural susceptibility to being shivered into innumerable, separate, relatively homogeneous groups. The fact that you can find a forum for virtually any topic you might be interested in, however obscure, implies fragmentation as its reverse side."[79]

The Internet has the capacity to exacerbate general tendencies that characterize human social networks. Since social networks provide a sense of belonging and approval, people tend to form social relationships with those of like mind and to distance themselves from those who think differently. Social networks are therefore the consequence of a process of self-selection and are inherently self-intensifying by their nature. As the authors of a recent study on social networks note, "When people with ideological or class-based interests are not surrounded by like-minded individuals in their physical neighborhoods, they tend to withdraw and form relationships outside those environments."[80] The Internet of course intensifies this process by breaking down physical distances and allowing for the creation of communities of geographically dispersed individuals.

Because the Internet facilitates disengagement from person-to-person interactions in favor of a virtual community of like-minded colleagues, it can facilitate detachment from reality. Potential jihadis are especially susceptible to this lure because they have already, by their own inclination, entered into the imagined world of religious fundamentalism and have likely detached themselves from real social relationships.[81] Unlike other online communities, however, potential jihadis have the opportunity to make bloody fantasies a reality through participation in jihad. The possibility of turning the online world into a reality—into a human community defined by the values of struggle and self-sacrifice in which the social outcast has the ability to become the most revered figure, the martyr—has proven to be an irresistible lure to some.[82]

The power to use the Internet for facilitating extremist violence should not be overstated. In the world of terrorism, distance-learning is no substitute for contact, training, and apprenticeship, so the Internet will be a dangerous tool for jihadis only so long as it facilitates real world interactions between new recruits and experienced fighters. The technical capabilities of online terrorists will always be rudimentary since most are by definition new to militancy and must seek knowledge regarding weapons manufacture and use. The Internet has become the de facto source of information for beginning jihadis, and here its impact has also been mixed. Much of the self-published online material regarding weapons manufacture is inaccurate.[83] Mastering even relatively simple technologies, such as bomb making, are best achieved via hands-on experience. The failures of poorly trained and inexperienced potential terrorists, for example, the "shoe bomber" Richard Reid and the two men who attempted to bomb Glasgow airport in 2007, testify to the technical challenges of even "simple" suicide bombing plots and lend credence to Michael Kenney's observation that "militants ultimately learn terrorism by doing terrorism."[84]

Marketing Martyrdom to a Global Audience

Analysts have long recognized that such radical groups as al Qaeda are capable of effectively blending aspects of religious war and modern global business. This fusion, after all, was the reason Peter Bergen called his pioneering study of al Qaeda *Holy War Inc.* Christoph Reuter has rightly noted that suicide bombing itself is just such a strange hybrid, a mix of old and new: "Notwithstanding the pretense of traditional religion in which their actions are typically cloaked, suicide bombers are quintessentially modern, in that they have left behind the traditional interpretations of religion in order to exploit only selected aspects of religion. They are a mixture of the Battle of Karbala and cable television—old myths and new media."[85] In recent years, as al Qaeda has become a social movement as opposed to a bureaucratic organization, scholars have begun to use a new business model, that of international brand marketing, to provide an analytical framework.[86]

Marketing has always been a control system for businesses, allowing them to create demand for products in order to manage markets and make them more predictable.[87] This management takes the form of the systematic manipulation of anxieties in the target audience in order to encourage members of the audience to see a particular product as the answer to deep-seated needs. Brands and trademarks are important tools in this process of manipulation. Market saturation leads to the emergence of brands as a way of differentiating products in a crowded marketplace and allows for an ongoing measure of control by creating a relationship of trust between consumer and brand name that transcends the mere utilitarian purpose the product was meant to serve.[88]

Global marketing in recent years has taken this basic idea—developing an emotional connection between consumer and brand name—to extremes, and certain brands have become icons in global spaces, addressing anxieties and desires in their target audiences far beyond the effective range of the product or service. Such "iconic" brands perform these emotional tasks because the brand has become more a symbol of a particular lifestyle or identity than an actual good or product. Douglas Holt has shown that modern global brands are marketed as stories or identity myths so that they resonate with the insecurities of their consumers. He wrote, "Brands become iconic when they perform identity myths: simple fictions that address cultural anxieties from afar, from imaginary worlds rather than from the worlds that consumers regularly encounter in their everyday lives. The aspirations expressed in these myths are an imaginative, rather than literal, expression of the audience's aspired identity."[89] For consumers, Holt concludes that "The greatest opportunity for brands today is to deliver not entertainment, but rather myths that their customers can use to manage the exigencies of a world that increasingly threatens their identities."[90]

From such a perspective al Qaeda has indeed become the most recognizable brand in the business of jihadi resistance. The service it provides is martyrdom; the product emerging from the interaction of firm and customer is today's globalized martyr. Recall that the difference between suicide and martyrdom is distinguishable only by the intent of the individual. Confirmation of individual intent only becomes generally accepted within the community when it is affirmed organizationally, so al Qaeda truly does perform a service when it claims martyrs and validates their sacrifices. These martyrs in turn confirm the legitimacy of the brand, making the process a self-perpetuating, closed loop. Take, for example, the case of a man who took part in the May 12, 2003, attacks in Riyadh.

Khalid al-Juhani was a veteran of the global jihadi movement, having joined it as a fighter in Bosnia in 1992. He became an al Qaeda member and recorded a martyrdom video in Afghanistan in 2001, a full two years before the attack in which he would take his own life.[91] This lengthy time lag between taping and the operation suggests a shift in purpose for the video testaments within the global jihadi movement. It was still a contract, publicly stating the intentions of the individual and binding him to the movement, but it had also become something more. Unlike many other martyrdom videos connected to local suicide bombing in the 1990s, this one was not recorded immediately before a specific attack for the purpose of ensuring the reliability of the recruit. Rather, it was an affirmation of identity on the part of Khalid, that is, a statement of his desire to sacrifice his life for the movement. The exact time and place of his attack, and death, did apparently not matter to him or to the organization. Instead, the significance for the individual derived from the confirmation of identity through his assertion of group affiliation; in turn, the organization stood to have its legitimacy enhanced by having yet another young man pledge his loyalty, unto death, to the movement.

In 1957 Vance Packard published a critical analysis of the American advertising industry's efforts to utilize insights from the social and behavioral sciences to control the minds of consumers, or in his words, to "engineer" their consent. In particular, he identified eight "hidden needs"—anxieties that were particularly susceptible to outside manipulation—that markers targeted. The identity myths of iconic brands are successful because they satisfy several of these needs simultaneously. In analyzing al Qaeda as an iconic brand that perpetuates itself via myth, one would find that its identity myth satisfies six of Packard's eight hidden needs by selling emotional security, reassurance of worth, ego-gratification, a sense of power, a sense of roots, and most tellingly, selling a sense of immortality.[92]

The Martyr as Commodity

There is a paradox at the heart of the global jihadi use of suicide attackers. The movement as a whole is opposed to the modern, secular world and seeks to combat modernity by placing faith and community foremost. The jihadis are doing so, however, by using the technologies and organizational structures of the modern world.[93] Use of electronic communications technologies, business strategies, and of course weapons can be excused on the basis of pragmatism; effectiveness dictates using the tools of modernity to undo modernity. Development and use of the suicide attacker, a weapon not regularly used by states since 1945, cannot be explained away so easily.

Suicide bombers are at the heart of the public image of the global jihadi movement because they are understood to embody the essence of the conflict. Assaf Moghadam suggests, "Jihad and martyrdom are . . . presented as the very antithesis of everything that the West stands for."[94] Jihadi suicide bombers, however, are as modern a weapon as one can imagine. Although their ostensible purpose is defending faith and community, they are strikingly individualistic; one recent analysis describes the movement as a whole as being characterized by "individualism bordering on anarchism."[95] Jihadi leaders encourage this individualism by undermining traditional religious authorities, established political parties, and even family relationships. In doing so, they seek to break the bonds that connect potential followers to their communities and might stand in the way of their participation in jihad. Instead of serving their communities, potential jihadis are encouraged to abandon them in order to receive individual rewards in heaven.[96]

Jihadi leaders endeavor to fragment communities by isolating individuals, instilling in them a deep sense of anxiety, and then marketing an alternative form of identity in order to alleviate this anxiety. Of note, members of the senior leadership of the jihadi movement have to this point shown little willingness to become martyrs themselves. This suggests that they understand suicide attackers as tools to be used rather than heroes that they would emulate themselves.

In the indiscriminate suicide bombing unleashed by the global jihadi movement, people have become material, social ties have been devalued, and sacred relationships have become transactions, a situation that critics of modern technology from Marx to Heidegger would have recognized and condemned. Thus the jihadi appropriation of modern technology extends beyond the use of the tools of the modern world to combat modernity; the jihadi mindset has become a caricature of the modern world as well. This paradox, perhaps more than any other factor, explains the limited appeal of the global jihadi movement even after thousands of "inspirational" suicide attacks.

CONCLUSION: BECOMING SUICIDE

After more than a decade of suicide missions, the elusive goal of suicide bombing's most enthusiastic users—restoration of Islamic governance in the form of a new caliphate unifying the world's Muslims—is no closer. Instead of marking progress toward the goal, the attacks that the movement has mustered have tended to serve shorter-term goals, such as publicizing the movement, allowing it to lay claim to defending the Islamic community, and attracting new recruits.

This emphasis on short-term rather than long-term goals has alienated the jihadis from nearly all sources of social support. In terms of the model of technology practice developed earlier in this work, the technical

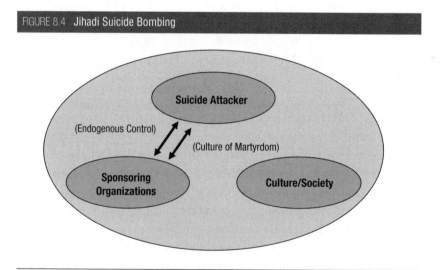

FIGURE 8.4   Jihadi Suicide Bombing

Source: Adapted from Arnold Pacey, *The Culture of Technology* (Cambridge, Mass.: MIT Press, 1983), 6.

and organizational elements of technology practice have been decoupled from the social/cultural element. Communities see little need for suicide attackers, and consequently most societies have ceased to share the jihadis' acceptance of a culture of martyrdom. Therefore, instead of a triangle of mutually reinforcing relationships, the model of suicide bombing that best illustrates the decentralized suicide bombing of "self-starters" and other loosely affiliated jihadi groups is one of a bilateral relationship that still produces feedback and radicalization, but does so in relative social isolation. There remains an endogenous managerial relationship between organizations and bombers and a shared reverence for martyrdom that makes the creation of suicide bombers possible, but without the link to a broader constituency, there is little popular demand for jihadi suicide attacks (see Figure 8.4).

This situation is analogous to that of Imperial Russia, except that whereas the Russian anarchists lacked the organizational infrastructure necessary to sustain a campaign of suicide bombing, the global jihadis lack the social connections necessary to consolidate their attacks politically. Their use and overuse of suicide bombing has become an incomplete, ineffective form of technology practice, more like sequential mass suicide than the use of self-sacrifice for an achievable political goal. The result has been the broad but shallow globalized suicide bombing of the first decade of the new millennium.

CONCLUSION

Authentic Martyrdom

I do not avoid sacrifice. I do not refuse the sacrifice of myself.
However, I cannot tolerate the reduction of the self to nothingness
in the process. I cannot approve it. Martyrdom or sacrifice must be done
at the height of self-realization. Sacrifice at the end of self-annihilation,
the dissolving of the self to nothingness, has no meaning whatsoever.[1]

—Hayashi Tadao, Kamikaze pilot, d. July 28, 1945, at age twenty-four

Those who suffer from a power complex find the mechanization
of man a simple way to realize their ambitions. I say, that this easy path
to power is in fact . . . a rejection of everything that I consider to be
of moral worth in the human race.[2]

—Norbert Wiener, founder of science of cybernetics, 1950

The annual number of suicide bombings peaked in 2007 at 520. After that, they decreased, to 405 in 2008, 299 in 2009, and 262 in 2010 (see Figure C.1).[3] Although this decline is a welcome trend, one should take into consideration that the number of attacks in 2010 exceeded the total number of attacks for every year prior to 2005. Thus, while suicide bombings have decreased significantly in a relative sense, in an absolute sense the numbers of attacks, fatalities, and injuries remained high in 2010.

The tactical effectiveness of suicide bombing continues to vary significantly depending on the quality and experience of the support networks behind individual bombers. For example, on December 11, 2010,

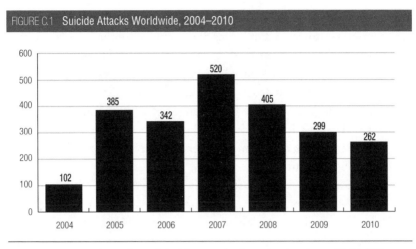

FIGURE C.1   Suicide Attacks Worldwide, 2004–2010

Source: Worldwide Incidents Tracking System, National Counterterrorism Center, wits.nctc.gov (accessed April 1, 2011).

Taimour Abdalwahhab al-Abdaly, a twenty-eight-year-old man of Iraqi descent, attempted a suicide attack in Stockholm, but managed to take only his own life. He seems to have originally become radicalized online. He then traveled to Iraq, where he became radicalized even more and received some training in explosives manufacture. He almost certainly received assistance in Stockholm from a couple of accomplices but was not part of a well-established organization, which contributed to the amateurish quality of his bomb and attack.[4] Abdaly's mission highlights two of the overall trends that have characterized the suicide bombing of global jihadis in recent years. First, electronic communication continues to give the movement a long reach by introducing like-minded individuals in geographically dispersed areas to jihad and the possibility of pursuing it. Second, effective attacks require organizations with specialized training and experience because suicide bombing is not easy to carry out.

When a well-run support network exists, suicide attacks continue to be devastating. As of early 2011, indiscriminate mass-fatality attacks against civilians were still a regular occurrence. At the same time, analysis of specific attacks revealed that suicide bombing is most dangerous when militants use it precisely rather than indiscriminately, as shown by an attack on a CIA base near Khost, Afghanistan, on December 30,

2009. On that day, Humam Khalil abu Mulai al-Balawi, a physician born in the Jordanian town of Zarqa, was able to infiltrate the base and access a meeting of CIA intelligence officers from the area. When he detonated his explosives, he killed not only himself but eight experienced agents—five from the CIA, two from the private security firm Xe (formerly Blackwater), and one from the Jordanian army who also happened to be a cousin of Jordan's King Abdullah. The attack devastated U.S. human intelligence efforts to an extent not seen since the 1983 bombing of the U.S. embassy in Beirut.[5]

Al-Balawi's attack demonstrates the effectiveness of a truly intelligent bomb—effectiveness that largely had been lacking among Afghanistan's suicide attackers. He was apparently a double agent, originally a jihobbyist who in the online world went by the name of Abu Dujanna al-Khurasani.[6] The CIA recruited him to provide information on the whereabouts of key figures, such as Ayman al-Zawahiri. Over a period of several months, he appears to have produced enough information to build trust and a rapport with his handlers so that when he requested a meeting, he was not physically searched, which allowed him to access so many intelligence agents while wearing a suicide belt.

AUTHENTICITY, MARTYRDOM, AND SUICIDE BOMBING

The transformation of martyrdom from an unpredictable event into a systematic organizational control mechanism was the primary innovation making suicide bombing possible. It has also been the most challenging element of suicide bombing to manage in practice. One of the most apparent trends emerging from a close examination of suicide bombing as a historical phenomenon is the tension between its strategic value, a consequence of its association with classical martyrdom, and its tactical utility, a consequence of the use of human beings as guidance systems by other humans. Authenticity is the key to the successful management of this tension.

The case of the hunger strike by Irish republican prisoners in 1981 demonstrates the importance of freedom and self-realization on the part of the individual for self-sacrifice to be understood as being authentic by a community. Even though it cannot be known definitively, the public perception of this internal dimension of martyrdom ultimately matters. When leadership loses the position of moral certainty, the use of suicidal volunteers for any purpose can backfire.

The Jihadi "Double Bind"

Leaders of the global jihadi movement have sought to convince Muslims around the world that their suicide attackers are indeed martyrs making the ultimate sacrifice for the faith and its followers. They have been unsuccessful in achieving this aim, largely because their ideology places them in a difficult position, or as Vahid Brown describes it, a "double bind." The group asks its followers to abandon specific local grievances for the purpose of pursuing global jihad. It legitimizes this reorientation by developing a radically new religious framework that differs not only from that of mainstream political Islam, but also from jihad as understood by Islamists for decades. The group and its leaders, however, lack the religious credentials necessary to convince all but a minority of radicals that this reorientation of strategy and redefinition of jihad is in fact legitimate. Consequently the movement has failed on both levels: it remains an outsider in significant local conflicts, such as the Israeli-Palestinian struggle, and it cannot compete with other violent Islamists in terms of religious credibility.[7]

The jihadi double bind prevents the movement from convincing local communities and their leaders that jihadi suicide bombers are in fact dying on behalf of their communities. It also prevents the movement from justifying the attacks in terms of Islam more generally. In such an instance, the organizational element, in this case the jihadi leaders, cannot disguise the fact that it is driving the violence, not the community's needs. Instead, most audiences globally seem to understand that jihadi suicide bombers are driven by individual motivations and their organizational culture. Their violence is therefore perceived as being self-motivated and their deaths sequential acts of suicide rather than legitimate acts of martyrdom.

Marginality and Lethality

The globalization of suicide bombing in the early 2000s, and its subsequent identification with the global jihadi movement, ironically may have begun to de-legitimize suicide bombing as a form of Islamic resistance in the eyes of local groups, for a striking characteristic of suicide bombing by the late 2000s was the almost complete absence of the type of localized suicide bombing carried out by groups like Hizballah, Hamas, and the Tamil Tigers in the 1980s and 1990s. The LTTE, as noted earlier, conducted several attacks in the years before its defeat in 2009, but other groups with a strong local presence—that is, Hamas and Hizballah— chose not to deploy suicide attackers during this time despite full-scale warfare with Israel.

Chapter 6 reveals how the Israeli response to Palestinian suicide bombing and the changed political relationship between Hamas and Fatah led to the virtual cessation of suicide bombing after 2005. There is a third, cultural factor that also warrants mention: the negative influence of the global jihadis and their particular culture of martyrdom on the Palestinian scene. With the exception of a few small groups, global jihadism has not put down roots in the Palestinian territories. Hamas leaders have contributed to this situation by suppressing jihadi supporters when they have emerged, but also significant is the lack of appeal that the jihadi program holds for most Palestinians. Jihadi leaders, including Zawahiri, have condemned Hamas for being insufficiently Islamic, for participating in secular elections, and for failing to implement Islamic law in the territory it controls. The jihadis have demonstrated no appreciation for the reality of the Palestinian political situation and instead encourage an abstract and absolute form of political Islam that most Palestinians reject. Therefore, even if Hamas' leaders were inclined to associate with the jihadis, such a connection might discredit them in the eyes of their Palestinian followers.[8]

It is possible that overuse and commodification of jihadi suicide bombers on the global level created a degree of popular disdain for the jihadis' campaign that may have devalued the symbolic power of Palestinian suicide bombers specifically and suicide bombing more generally. For example, in 2009 the Egyptian-born Islamist Abu Walid al-Masri, who had fought against the Soviets in Afghanistan and befriended Osama bin Laden, condemned al Qaeda's ideology, singling out suicide bombing for particular attention. He argued that al Qaeda's reliance on suicide attackers sent the wrong message—that is, that al Qaeda had a surplus of fighters and was trying to get rid of them instead of valuing them. He suggested that al Qaeda had so befouled the image of holy war that the wisest move for the Taliban would be to dissociate itself completely from the al Qaeda core.[9]

Hizballah has not claimed any suicide attackers since 1999 despite a major war with Israel in 2006. There is, however, evidence that the group used at least one suicide bomber in a spectacular operation during this period, but has been unwilling to claim the attack. On February 14, 2005, former Lebanese prime minister Rafik Hariri was assassinated by a massive bomb while traveling in an armored motorcade in Beirut. Physical evidence and eyewitness testimony both suggest that a suicide bomber in a white van was responsible for the blast. Hariri was traveling in a convoy of five vehicles that included trained guards and utilized sophisticated electronic countermeasures to foil roadside bombs specifically. A suicide bomber was probably the only practical way of reaching him, proving again that a well-trained and supported suicide bomber is among the most effective weapons in the world today. Hariri was the most important politician in Lebanon, making his death the most politically significant suicide attack there since the major bombings of 1983.

Suspicion immediately fell upon Hizballah. In summer 2011 the United Nations Special Tribunal for Lebanon, the body charged with investigating the assassination, officially indicted four members of Hizballah, charging them with involvement in Hariri's death. Hizballah had opposed the tribunal and continues to deny any connection to the assassination.[10]

If the UN tribunal is correct, Hizballah has good reason to deny responsibility for using one of its "self-martyrs" against one of the most popular politicians in Lebanon. Since the group's founding, Hizballah's martyrs—with suicide bombers the most revered among them—have continued to dominate its public discourse and to legitimize it as a resistance organization.[11] The organization, however, can derive legitimacy from its martyrs only if they are seen as heroic by the community and only if Hizballah is seen as respecting its martyrs to the extent that it is a worthy custodian of their legacy. The heroism of its martyrs stems from the public perception that they are acting freely and that their sacrifice is authentic and necessary. Hizballah's use of tactical martyrs in the form of suicide attackers is therefore made possible by—but also severely constrained by—the centrality of authentic martyrdom within the Shiite tradition the group represents. In other instances of suicide bombing, when the organization intervened too directly—or pushed the use of self-sacrifice beyond its followers' willingness to tolerate it—the illusion of freedom became difficult to sustain. Hizballah's leaders seem to have no desire to test the patience of their followers in this respect, opting for the ongoing celebration of a relatively few suicide attackers rather than diluting their value by throwing more suicide attackers at Israel (or by admitting to their use in Lebanese political feuds).

For Hizballah, the public ritual surrounding its suicide attackers continues to provide symbolic and strategic value while the organization's much greater political and military capabilities have reduced the need for the tactical advantages provided by suicide attackers. The global jihadi movement, on the other hand, has no connection to local populations and is therefore not subject to the limitations that maintaining local legitimacy places on the use of suicide attackers. The reliance of its leaders on suicide attackers should therefore be interpreted as an indication of their political weakness. Indeed, Mohammed Hafez observed regarding jihadi suicide attackers in Iraq, "Their marginality is at the root of their lethality."[12]

Suicide bombing therefore seems to be a technology with a very limited window of opportunity within which it can provide both tactical and strategic benefits. Groups lacking in (or competing for) power and legitimacy can use suicide bombing as an effective way toward both ends temporarily, provided a sense of community need exists and a willingness to die among certain members creates the possibility of systematic self-sacrifice. With the passage of time, however, the symbolic and demonstrative aspects of suicide bombing diminish as it becomes commonplace rather than rare. At this point, groups must decide whether to halt such operations. Like the jihadis (or the Tamil Tigers), they could continue to deploy suicide attackers as long as they have members willing to kill themselves. In this case, the group will continue benefiting from the tactical capabilities of human control systems. Such use of suicide bombing, however, will almost certainly come to be perceived by the broader community for what it really is—the human use of human self-sacrifice devoid of freedom and authenticity—and accordingly will fail to yield strategic benefits.

IMPLICATIONS OF SUICIDE BOMBING AS TECHNOLOGY

Sophistication and Effectiveness

> [We] would be nowhere without Radio Shack.
> —*Provisional IRA bomb maker*[13]

Readily available, over-the-counter technology lies at the heart of the most lethal and effective weapons deployed by militant groups. U.S. forces in Iraq learned the extent to which commercially available electronics had benefited their adversaries in 2006 when they confiscated several specially modified suicide vests. In addition to the necessary explosives, the vests also included web cams for transmitting video footage of the operation to the bombers' handlers in real time. The vests were also equipped with a remote detonation capability, giving the support team the ability to detonate the bomber when and where they saw fit, or perhaps in case the bomber were to have second thoughts.[14] Collectively, this hybrid of innovations—explosives, consumer electronics, and the culture of martyrdom—offered militants, at minimal expense, similar capabilities to those provided by unmanned drones for their American adversaries. Both weapon systems provide controllers with the ability to survey potential targets from a distance, to determine in real time the best place and time to attack, and then to destroy the selected target, all at no risk to themselves.

Suicide bombing provides a weapon that is uniquely suited to the needs and capabilities of terrorist groups, providing them with the best of both worlds: the precision and sophistication of the most complex technologies as well as relative simplicity and reliability. Adding to the effectiveness of suicide bombing is that the organizations employing it do not need to build manufacturing infrastructures from the ground up, but instead can utilize cultural and social factors to realign existing technological systems to their own ends. Their effectiveness in doing so suggests that the high-technology endeavors of the developed world have actually eroded, rather than enhanced, the capabilities of states relative to nonstate actors.[15]

The tactical effectiveness of suicide bombing is further explained by the fact that militant groups utilizing this weapon have emphasized their strengths by creating an alternative to the weapons of their adversaries instead of trying to appropriate their enemies' weapon technologies directly. In 1982 the quick destruction by Israel of the PLO's conventional forces and of the Syrian air force convinced Hizballah's founders of the need to pursue alternatives that would not be as easily targeted and overwhelmed by Israel's weapon systems. They chose therefore to emphasize portable, reliable, easily concealable weapons to complement their guerrilla tactics, and as a result were far more effective militarily in dealing with Israel than the PLO and Syrians had been. U.S. forces in Iraq and Afghanistan ran into similar difficulties. The sophisticated weapon platforms used in these theaters were originally designed to engage other high-tech weapons, such as aircraft and tanks, while the actual weapons deployed by insurgents were more difficult for electronic firepower systems to recognize and engage effectively. Historian Martin van Crevald observed this trend many years ago, writing "[M]any modern weapons tend to act as parasols. Whereas their own electronically supported firepower is wasted in antiguerilla operations, they allow guerilla warfare and terrorism to take place below the sophistication threshold that they themselves represent."[16]

This high "sophistication threshold" comes at a monetary cost that limits the number of weapons that can be deployed and reliably maintained. After an exhaustive statistical analysis of U.S. military programs in the 1970s, Franklin C. Spinney found that ever-increasing defense budgets were not leading to higher levels of military readiness but instead were contributing to a self-perpetuating cycle of ever-increasing complexity in weapon systems that outpaced improvements in operational effectiveness. The data, he found, suggested "a general relationship between increasing complexity and decreasing material readiness."[17] These lessons challenge the assumption that when it comes to international security, newer, more technologically advanced, and (inevitably) more expensive weapon systems are inherently better.

Such a narrow understanding of technology has been a major factor encouraging the U.S. military to underestimate the capabilities of nonstate adversaries. For example, the most effective weapons deployed against coalition forces in Iraq and Afghanistan have been relatively simple emplaced bombs, now generally called improvised explosive devices (IEDs). Such weapons were originally developed by the People's Will in the 1880s and have been a staple of guerrilla forces ever since. Nevertheless, coalition forces were unprepared to deal with these low-tech weapons, and some leaders seem to have been taken by surprise when technologically "inferior" forces were able to inflict significant harm on their better-armed and better-equipped adversaries.[18] A U.S. Air Force general interviewed by Peter Singer expressed frustration at this state of affairs, saying, "We have made huge leaps in technology, but we're still getting guys killed by idiotic technology—a 155mm shell with a wire strung out."

Of course there is nothing at all idiotic about IEDs or suicide bombers, and the effectiveness of these weapons suggests that any technological system—high-tech, low-tech, and anything in between—must be thoroughly integrated into the various layers of the human context with which it must interact in order to be effective. What has traditionally been regarded as low-tech can sometimes be more effective because it interfaces more seamlessly with the human elements of the system and allows for creativity in use. More complex technologies, on the other hand, can be expensive, be narrow in application, require higher levels of training and education, and be much more demanding in terms of maintenance, making them brittle and prone to failure.

Tactical Effectiveness versus Strategic Value

In addition to revealing the potential limitations of "high" technology, another lesson one can draw from suicide bombing is a consequence of the complexity of technology practice and the corresponding difficulties that accompany the transfer or use of technologies across cultural boundaries. All three vertices of the technology practice triangle are necessary for technology to function as a sustainable social phenomenon; the ease with which a technological system can diffuse, however, varies significantly from vertex to vertex. The technical element does flow across cultural boundaries rather easily. After all, physical devices, be they precision-guided munitions, suicide bombers, or cell phones, function in exactly the same manner around the world. It is therefore extremely tempting to think that the other levels of technology practice will move just as easily, but the diffusion of technology, as shown here, is rarely straightforward. The organizational processes by which devices are produced, manufactured, and managed are much "stickier"; that is, they tend to adhere to the culture or society that originally developed them, making them context dependent.[19] The cultural values that determine whether or not a given technology will be perceived as necessary or even desirable are even stickier, often necessitating a reconfiguration of the first two elements of a particular system and resulting in a different iteration of the technology as it is accommodated in a new environment.

When the technical element of a given technological system is introduced into a new context, it is inevitably interpreted and understood according to the values and norms of the receiving culture. This can lead to incompatibility and dissonance between devices and cultures and, in turn, sometimes explains why the diffusion of technologies can be so problematic and why seemingly effective military technologies often fail to produce political victories. Such interpretations also explain why cultures on the receiving end of airpower, however judiciously used, might see it as inhumane and also why few outside of the jihadi subculture see the use of suicide bombers as noble or admirable.

Because such physical devices as weapons function across borders, they can be attractive as a first means of settling disputes. Each successful use at the tactical level might appear to validate the system that produced the weapon, so it is easy to perceive each tactical use as a step toward strategic or political victory. Because two cultures are involved, however, evaluating the technology according to its users' set of values will always be insufficient. If the targeted culture cannot come to accept the values that produced a particular weapon system, that culture will not acquiesce to the society that produced the weapon. In such a case, no number of small tactical steps will ever lead to victory, and short of escalating the conflict to the point of extermination, such use of technology will never provide political and social stability.[20]

Levels of Intervention

In recent years, the governments of Israel and Sri Lanka have put an end to the use of suicide bombing by their respective foes by intensifying their occupations of contested land and reasserting control over territories where their foes previously had greater freedom of action. The

Israeli government dealt with Palestinian suicide bombers by reestablishing authority over parts of the West Bank, building a barrier between Israeli and Palestinian populations, and using trained personnel to spot and intercept prospective bombers. These measures allowed the Israeli government to raise the cost of suicide missions by ensuring that most of them would fail and reinforcing Palestinians' growing skepticism toward suicide attacks. The Sri Lankan military conquered Tamil territory, defeated the LTTE, and killed Prabhakaran, destroying the organizational element of Tamil suicide bombing.

These successes, even if only temporary, are consistent with the model of suicide bombing as a technological system presented in this work and suggest that there are many avenues by which suicide bombing can be counteracted, corresponding to the vertices and relationships of the technology practice triangle. Disrupting one or more vertices disrupts the intensifying relationships between them and de-escalates the entire process. The Israeli government dealt with Palestinian suicide bombing at the technical vertex by making the weapon less effective and therefore less attractive as a means of combating its occupation. The Sri Lankan state dealt with the LTTE at the organizational vertex of its suicide-bombing complex. The steps taken by U.S. forces in Iraq during 2006–2007 suggest a way of approaching suicide bombing at the cultural-social vertex. By engaging rather than confronting local Iraqi groups, U.S. troops were able to exploit fundamental ideological differences between these organizations and the jihadis. Working with local groups reduced the perceived need for an extreme form of resistance, such as suicide bombing, that also contributed to discrediting the jihadi narrative and the cultural allure of the suicide bomber.

Despite the success of this change in the U.S. approach toward the militants, very real problems in Iraqi security ensured that suicide bombers would continue to be effective at the technical level in terms of inflicting harm. The jihadi groups most responsible for suicide bombing were not eliminated, so the organizational factor persisted. Thus two of the three vertices of the Iraqi suicide-bombing complex remained after the U.S. surge. Although suicide bombing declined appreciably, it remained a significant problem. Similarly, in the Palestinian territories the culture of martyrdom, while perhaps diminished, has not been completely elimi-

nated nor have the militant organizations that previously deployed suicide attackers. Since these elements remain, there is still a possibility that
Palestinian groups might resort to the regular use of suicide bombing
should they perceive a need.

The case of the Tamil Tigers is unique because of Prabhakaran's role
in LTTE suicide bombing. Not only did his death bring about the end of
the LTTE, the organizational vertex of this particular suicide-bombing
complex, it also ended the elaborate culture of martyrdom that transformed individuals into suicide bombers because the LTTE's Black Tigers
pledged their allegiance to Prabhakaran personally. In short, two elements of the suicide-bombing complex were completely eliminated in Sri
Lanka, explaining the lack of suicide attacks since Prabhakaran's death.
While the causes of Tamil militancy have by no means been addressed,
and the possibility remains that a violent secessionist campaign on the
part of the Tamil people may resume at some point, there is no reason
to believe that suicide bombing will play the integral role in such a campaign as it did in the LTTE's failed crusade.

That suicide bombing is susceptible to intervention in many different areas is a logical consequence of the nature of technological systems.
Such systems diffuse with difficulty, or sometimes not at all, because
numerous factors must fall into place simultaneously for them to function effectively in a new context. In other words, for suicide bombing, as
for all other forms of technology, there are more ways to fail than there
are to succeed. Countering suicide bombing therefore requires recognition of the multiple ways in which the failure of suicide bombing can
be encouraged as well as prudence in action so as not to inadvertently
facilitate its acceptance by creating a perceived need for suicide bombers
or legitimizing their users.

Early on the morning of May 2, 2011, a U.S. Navy Special Forces team
killed Osama bin Laden during a raid on his compound in the city of
Abottabad, Pakistan. Information gathered from his computers suggests
that bin Laden played a more significant role in directing al Qaeda's operations than had been thought. Nevertheless, his death had little immediate operational impact on the jihadi movement. It certainly did not bring

an end to jihadi suicide attacks as Prabhakaran's death had ended LTTE suicide bombings. Instead, the weekend after bin Laden's death there were several suicide attacks against coalition forces in Afghanistan, and the following week a brutal pair of blasts in Pakistan killed eighty people. The blasts were claimed by the Tehrik-e-Taliban Pakistan, whose leaders declared that the bombings were revenge for bin Laden's death.[21]

The use of suicide attackers in these revenge operations suggests strongly that in the short term bin Laden's death put enormous pressure to act on the movement's remaining leaders. Given the declining fortunes of global jihadism more generally, and specific challenges facing its individual franchises, remaining jihadis could ill afford to let such an event go unchallenged. As Bruce Hoffman noted, "For al-Qa'ida, now is the time to 'put up or shut up' as the remaining leadership will surely attempt to prove that the movement retains its vitality despite the death of its founder and leader."[22] Overall, however, the movement did far more shutting up than putting up. Its leaders remained out of the spotlight, undoubtedly fearful that information obtained from bin Laden's computer files could put them at greater risk of being targeted. More than a month after bin Laden's death, al Qaeda still had not named a formal successor. Five weeks after bin Laden's death, Ayman al-Zawahiri finally released a video eulogizing the late leader and vowing another catastrophic attack against the United States, but many questioned the ability of the movement to make good on such a promise.[23] Shortly afterward, Zawahiri emerged as the recognized leader of al Qaeda.

Over the short term, bin Laden's death focused a movement that had become increasingly fragmented, but it also raised questions regarding the ability of even a re-focused jihadi movement to carry out high-profile operations. Over the long term, bin Laden's death may well deprive the movement of legitimacy and coherence, particularly if it proves unable to match Zawahiri's words with deeds.

The way in which bin Laden was killed—by a team of highly skilled people—is particularly significant. Throughout the 1990s, bin Laden self-consciously built up an image of himself and his movement as morally superior Davids battling the technological Goliath that is the United States. Suicide bombers were essential to this narrative, as they were supposed to embody the movement's reliance on people and of faith over machines. Had bin Laden been killed by a drone strike, the event would have played perfectly into the story he had been constructing. Instead, people played a central role in the raid that killed him, and it was the training and quality of the people—supplemented but not replaced by technology—that allowed the mission to succeed. The fact that the number of unintended casualties was kept to a minimum also mattered, as it demonstrated a respect for the lives of the United States' adversaries that had often been lacking in military missions.

That bin Laden died in a struggle with his enemies will undoubtedly contribute to his status as a martyr within the movement.[24] Martyrdom, however, is such a flexible construction that no matter how he passed away, there would have been a crew of martyrologists ready to frame his death in a manner appropriate for their own agendas. What is more significant is that his death was understood by much of the world, and the Islamic world in particular, as appropriate and just. The martyrologists of al Qaeda will construct a heroic posthumous version of bin Laden's death, but the true test will be whether this image will be accepted by anyone outside the jihadi movement.

Bin Laden's symbolic power stemmed not only from his involvement in the 9/11 attacks but also from the aura of invincibility that seemed to surround him as he eluded U.S. forces for nearly a decade. The shattering of this aura diminishes the al Qaeda brand. Political developments in the Middle East in early 2011, particularly the toppling of Hosni Mubarak's government in Egypt by peaceful protestors, compounds al Qaeda's situation. The unfolding of events in Egypt and Tunisia challenges the validity of the al Qaeda narrative, as Zawahiri, in particular, has justified his group's use of violence by claiming that dictators like Mubarak could only be toppled through force. With a diminished brand name and nonviolent alternatives competing with the jihadis' methods in the market of disaffected Muslims, it appears that whatever boost the movement received from the death of bin Laden could be short lived. This situation is of course fluid and could easily be reversed. Should the jihadis find it within their capabilities to respond dramatically to bin Laden's death, and should political gains in Egypt and elsewhere prove to be temporary, then the suicide manufacturers in the jihadi movement might yet have enough material to keep themselves in business for years to come.

NOTES

INTRODUCTION: THE HUMAN USE OF HUMAN BEINGS

1. *Guided Missiles and Techniques,* Summary Technical Report of Division 5, National Defense Research Committee, vol. 1 (Washington, D.C., 1946), 198.

2. Quoted in Hala Jaber, *Hezbollah: Born with a Vengeance* (New York: Columbia University Press, 1997), 92–93.

3. Timothy Naftali, *Blind Spot: The Secret History of American Counterterrorism* (New York: Basic Books, 2005), 18–25.

4. Michael Russell Rip and James M. Hasik, *The Precision Revolution: GPS and the Future of Aerial Warfare* (Annapolis: Naval Institute Press, 2002), 424–27.

5. Data for 2004 and 2005 are from the Worldwide Incidents Tracking System, National Counterterrorism Center, wits.nctc.gov (accessed December 2, 2010); Robin Wright, "Since 2001, a Dramatic Increase in Suicide Bombings," *Washington Post,* April 18, 2008, A18. Acquiring consistent quantitative data on suicide attacks worldwide is problematic because many researchers have compiled their own databases, which vary depending on the criteria used to define suicide attacks. This study relies on quantitative data compiled by several researchers. When possible, their figures have been compared and reconciled before discussion of them; these sources are clearly referenced in the text. Data for 2004 onward are according to the U.S. National Counterterrorism Center's Worldwide Incidents Tracking System (WITS). For specifics on how WITS data are generated, see John Wigle, "Introducing the Worldwide Incident Tracking System (WITS)," *Perspectives on Terrorism* 4, no. 1 (March 2010): 3–23.

6. Bruce Hoffman and Gordon H. McCormick, "Terrorism, Signaling, and Suicide Attack," *Studies in Conflict and Terrorism* 27, no. 4 (2004): 255.

7. Robert J. Brym and Bader Araj, "Suicide Bombing as Strategy and Interaction," *Social Forces* 84, no. 4 (June 2006): 1,973; Mohammed M. Hafez, "Rationality, Culture, and Structure in the Making of Suicide Bombers: A Preliminary Theoretical Synthesis and Illustrative Case Study," *Studies in Conflict and Terrorism* 29, no. 2 (2006): 166–70.

8. Bruce Hoffman, "The Logic of Suicide Terrorism," in *Homeland Security and Terrorism: Readings and Interpretations,* ed. Russell D. Howard, James J. F. Forest, and Joanne C. Moore (New York: McGraw Hill, 2006), 59–70; Mohammed M. Hafez, "Dying To Be Martyrs: The Symbolic Dimensions of Suicide Terrorism," in *Root Causes of Suicide Terrorism: The Globalization of Martyrdom,* ed. Ami Pedahzur (New York: Routledge, 2006), 56.

9. Mia Bloom, *Dying to Kill: The Allure of Suicide Terrorism* (New York: Columbia University Press, 2005), 83; Ami Pedahzur, *Suicide Terrorism* (Cambridge, U.K., and Malden, Mass.: Polity Press, 2005), 8–11.

10. Ariel Merari, *Driven to Death: Psychological and Social Aspects of Suicide Terrorism* (New York: Oxford University Press, 2010), 261–77.

11. Martin Kramer, "Suicide Terrorism: Origins and Response. Martin Kramer on Robert Pape's Thesis," www.geocities.com/martinkramerorg/PapeKramer .htm.

12. *The 9/11 Commission Report: Final Report of the National Commission on Terrorist Attacks Upon the United States,* authorized ed. (New York: W. W. Norton and Company, 2004), 272.

13. Ibid., 339–48.

14. Naftali, *Blind Spot,* 318; George Friedman suggests that it was the inability of security officials in the United States to understand how terrorists would solve the problem of guidance that prevented them from conceiving of aircraft as cruise missiles prior to September 11. George Friedman, *America's Secret War: Inside the Hidden Worldwide Struggle between America and Its Enemies* (New York: Doubleday, 2004), 95.

15. Timothy D. Hoyt, "Technology and Security," in *Grave New World: Security Challenges in the 21st Century,* ed. Michael E. Brown (Washington, D.C.: Georgetown University Press, 2003), 26.

16. Steven Johnson, *Where Good Ideas Come From: A Natural History of Innovation* (New York: Riverhead Books, 2010), 16.

17. Quoted in Peter W. Singer, *Wired for War: The Robotics Revolution and Conflict in the Twenty-first Century* (New York: Penguin Press, 2009), 62.

18. Nasra Hassan, "An Arsenal of Believers: Talking to the 'Human Bombs,' " *New Yorker,* November 19, 2001, 38.

19. Reuven Paz, "Programmed Terrorists? Analysis of the Letter of Instructions Found in the September 11th Attack," PRISM (Project for the Research of Islamist Movements), www.e-prism.org/projectsandproducts.html.

20. Martin van Crevald, *Technology and War: From 2000 B.C. to the Present,* rev. ed. (New York: Free Press, 1991), 232.

21. Understanding technology as the embodiment of progress has characterized the interaction of Western states and the non-Western world since the colonialism of the 1800s. Michael Adas, *Machines as the Measure of Men: Science, Technology, and Ideologies of Western Dominance* (Ithaca, N.Y.: Cornell University Press, 1989); Daniel R. Headrick, *The Tools of Empire: Technology and European Imperialism in the Nineteenth Century* (New York: Oxford University Press, 1981), esp. 130.

22. Naim Qassem, *Hizbullah: The Story from Within,* trans. Dalia Khalil (London: Saqi, 2005), 50; Barbara Victor, *Army of Roses: Inside the World of Palestinian Women Suicide Bombers* (New York: Rodale, 2003), 185.

23. Leo Marx, "Technology: The History of a Hazardous Concept," *Technology and Culture* 51, no. 3 (July 2010): esp. 576.

24. Eric Schatzberg, "*Technik* Comes to America: Changing Meanings of *Technology* before 1930," *Technology and Culture* 47, no. 3 (June 2006): 488–90.

25. Harvey Brooks, "Technology, Evolution, and Purpose," *Daedalus* 109, no. 1 (1980): 65.

26. Peter F. Drucker, *Technology, Management, and Society* (New York: Harper Colophon, 1977), 45.

27. Joel Mokyr, *The Gifts of Athena: Historical Origins of the Knowledge Economy* (Princeton, N.J.: Princeton University Press, 2002), 2–3.

28. Thomas P. Hughes, *American Genesis: A Century of Innovation and Technological Enthusiasm* (New York: Viking, 1989), 6 (emphasis in the original).

29. Everett M. Rogers, *Diffusion of Innovations*, 5th ed. (New York: Free Press, 2003), 13 (emphasis in the original).

30. Arnold Pacey, *The Culture of Technology* (Cambridge, Mass.: MIT Press, 1983), 4–7; also see Arnold Pacey, *Meaning in Technology* (Cambridge, Mass.: MIT Press, 1999), 6–11.

31. Pacey, *Culture of Technology*, 4–7, quote from 6.

32. Robert A. Pape, *Dying to Win: The Strategic Logic of Suicide Bombing* (New York: Random House, 2005); Robert A. Pape and James K. Feldman, *Cutting the Fuse: The Explosion of Global Suicide Terrorism and How to Stop It* (Chicago: University of Chicago Press, 2010).

33. Assaf Moghadam, "Suicide Terrorism, Occupation, and the Globalization of Martyrdom: A Critique of *Dying to Win*," *Studies in Conflict and Terrorism* 29, no. 6 (August 2006): 713–16; Assaf Moghadam, *The Globalization of Martyrdom: Al Qaeda, Salafi Jihad, and the Diffusion of Suicide Attacks* (Baltimore: Johns Hopkins University Press, 2008). Also see Robert J. Brym and Bader Araj, "Suicide Bombing as Strategy and Interaction: The Case of the Second Intifada," *Social Forces* 84, no. 4 (June 2006): 1973.

34. Thomas Hegghammer, "Apostates vs. Infidels: Explaining Differential Use of Suicide Bombings by Jihadist Groups" (paper presented at the conference "Understanding Jihadism: Origins, Evolution, and Future Perspectives," Oslo, March 19–21, 2009).

35. John H. Lienhard, *How Invention Begins: Echoes of Old Voices in the Rise of New Machines* (New York: Oxford University Press, 2006), 137.

36. W. Brian Arthur, *The Nature of Technology: What It Is and How It Evolves* (New York: Free Press, 2009), 19.

37. Mohammed M. Hafez, *Suicide Bombers in Iraq: The Strategy and Ideology of Martyrdom* (Washington, D.C.: United States Institute of Peace Press, 2007), 18.

38. Donald MacKenzie and Judy Wajcman, "Introductory Essay: The Social Shaping of Technology," in *The Social Shaping of Technology*, ed. Donald MacKenzie and Judy Wajcman (Philadelphia: Open University Press, 1985), 3–27.

39. Ariel Merari, "The Readiness to Kill and Die: Suicidal Terrorism in the Middle East," in *Origins of Terrorism: Psychologies, Ideologies, Theologies, States of Mind*, ed. Walter Reich (Washington, D.C.: Woodrow Wilson Center Press, 1998), 194–95.

40. Yoram Schweitzer, "Palestinian *Istishhadia*: A Developing Instrument," *Studies in Conflict and Terrorism* 30, no. 8 (2007): 670.

41. Ariel Merari, "Social, Organizational, and Psychological Factors in Suicide Terrorism," in *Root Causes of Terrorism: Myths, Reality, and Ways Forward*, ed. Tore Bjørgo (London: Routledge, 2005), 71.

42. Michael Thad Allen and Gabrielle Hecht, "Introduction: Authority, Political Machines, and Technology's History," in *Technologies of Power: Essays in Honor of Thomas Park Hughes and Agatha Chipley Hughes*, ed. Michael Thad Allen and Gabrielle Hecht (Cambridge, Mass.: MIT Press, 2001), 1–24.

43. Alan Beyerchen, "Rational Means and Irrational Ends: Thoughts on the Technology of Racism in the Third Reich," *Central European History* 30, no. 3 (1997): 386–402; for a striking example, see Michael J. Neufeld, *The Rocket and the Reich: Peenemünde and the Coming of the Ballistic Missile Era* (New York: Free Press, 1995), 278; also see David Noble, *The Religion of Technology: The Divinity of Man and the Spirit of Invention* (New York: Alfred A. Knopf, 1997).

44. Van Crevald, *Technology and War*, 77.

45. Quoted in Donald Cardwell, *Wheels, Clocks, and Rockets: A History of Technology* (New York: W. W. Norton and Company, 1995), 18.

46. Beyerchen, "Rational Means and Irrational Ends."

47. David Alan Grier, *When Computers Were Human* (Princeton, N.J.: Princeton University Press, 2005), 5.

48. James R. Beniger, *The Control Revolution: Technological and Economic Origins of the Information Society* (Cambridge, Mass.: Harvard University Press, 1986), esp. 390–425.

49. Quoted in David A. Mindell, *Between Human and Machine: Feedback, Control, and Computing before Cybernetics* (Baltimore: Johns Hopkins University Press, 2002), 283–84.

50. Stephen B. Johnson, *Secret of Apollo: Systems Management in American and European Space Programs* (Baltimore: Johns Hopkins University Press, 2002), 125.

51. Slava Gerovitch, "Human-Machine Issues in the Soviet Space Program," in *Critical Issues in the History of Spaceflight*, ed. Steven J. Dick and Roger D. Launius (Washington, D.C.: NASA Office of External Relations, 2006), 122.

52. Gregory J. E. Rawlins, *Slaves of the Machine: The Quickening of Computer Technology* (Cambridge, Mass.: MIT Press, 1997), 112–13, and Singer, *Wired for War*, 76–77.

53. Arthur, *Nature of Technology*, 28.

54. Norbert Wiener, *The Human Use of Human Beings: Cybernetics and Society* (Boston: Houghton Mifflin, 1950), 16.

CHAPTER 1. MARTYRDOM AS INNOVATION: THE INVENTION OF SUICIDE BOMBING IN IMPERIAL RUSSIA

1. This account of Alexander's assassination is drawn from Franco Venturi, *Roots of Revolution: A History of the Populist and Socialist Movements in Nineteenth Century Russia*, trans. Francis Haskell (New York: Alfred A. Knopf, 1964); Avraham Yarmolinsky, *Road to Revolution: A Century of Russian Radicalism* (New York: Collier, 1962), 268–71; and Edvard Radzinsky, *Alexander II: The Last Great Tsar*, trans. Antonia W. Bouis (New York: Free Press, 2005), 410–17.

2. Quoted in Yarmolinksy, *Road to Revolution*, 266.

3. Edward Constant, "Recursive Practice and the Evolution of Technological Knowledge," in *Technological Innovation as an Evolutionary Process*, ed. John Ziman (Cambridge: Cambridge University Press, 2000), 219–33.

4. W. Brian Arthur, *The Nature of Technology: What It Is and How It Evolves* (New York: Free Press, 2009), 19; George Basalla, *The Evolution of Technology* (Cambridge: Cambridge University Press, 1988), 45, 135.

5. Constant, "Recursive Practice," 220; Arthur, *Nature of Technology*, 38; James Fleck, "Artefact-Activity: The Coevolution of Artifacts, Knowledge, and Organization" in Ziman, *Technological Innovation*, 248–66.

6. See Paul G. Gillespie, *Weapons of Choice: The Development of Precision Guided Munitions* (Tuscaloosa: University of Alabama Press, 2006), 6. Gillespie defines precision-guided munitions as "conventional bombs that are interactively guided to terminal impact."

7. Michael S. Sherry, *The Rise of American Air Power: The Creation of Armageddon* (New Haven, Conn.: Yale University Press, 1987), 49–57, esp. 53; Conrad C. Crane, *Bombs, Cities, and Civilians* (Lawrence: University Press of Kansas, 1993), 11–20.

8. Gillespie, *Weapons of Choice*, 69–72, 87–89, 109–12; Barry D. Watts, *Six Decades of Guided Munitions and Battle Networks: Progress and Prospects* (Washington, D.C.: Center for Strategic and Budgetary Assessments, 2007), 179–203.

9. Michael Russell Rip and James M. Hasik, *The Precision Revolution: GPS and the Future of Aerial Warfare* (Annapolis, Md.: Naval Institute Press, 2002), 202–21.

10. Ibid., 219.

11. "Martyr," s.v. *Catholic Encyclopedia*, vol. 9, www.newadvent.org/cathen/09736b.htm.

12. Emile Durkheim, *Suicide: A Study in Sociology*, trans. John A. Spaulding (New York: Free Press, 1951), 217–23.

13. Ibid., 225–26.

14. Ibid., 227.

15. David Cook, *Martyrdom in Islam* (Cambridge: Cambridge University Press, 2007), 1–2.

16. Eugene Weiner and Anita Weiner, *The Martyr's Conviction* (Atlanta: Scholar's Press, 1990), 25.

17. Jeffrey Sluka, "From Graves to Nations: Political Martyrdom and Irish Nationalism," in *Martyrdom and Political Resistance Movements: Essays on Asia and Europe*, ed. Joyce Pettigrew (Amsterdam: VU University Press, 1997), 35–60.

18. See David Kertzer, *Ritual, Politics, and Power* (New Haven, Conn.: Yale University Press, 1997), 66, for a discussion of the way that veneration of the fallen contributes to civil religion in the United States through such holidays as Memorial Day.

19. David Beresford, *Ten Men Dead: The Story of the 1981 Irish Hunger Strike* (New York: Atlantic Monthly Press, 1987), 25.

20. Michael Barkun, "Appropriated Martyrs: The Branch Davidians and the Radical Right," *Terrorism and Political Violence* 19, no. 1 (2007): 120; also see Cook, *Martyrdom in Islam*, 3, and Weiner and Weiner, *Martyr's Conviction*, 25.

21. Mohammed M. Hafez, "Rationality, Culture, and Structure in the Making of Suicide Bombers: A Preliminary Theoretical Synthesis and Illustrative Case Study," *Studies in Conflict and Terrorism* 29, no. 2 (2006): 177 (emphasis in the original).

22. Ehud Sprinzak, "Rational Fanatics," *Foreign Policy*, September/October 2000, 68.

23. Farhad Khosrokhavar, *Suicide Bombers: Allah's New Martyrs*, trans. David Macey (London: Pluto Press, 2005), 5–9; Hugh Barlow, *Dead for Good: Martyrdom and the Rise of the Suicide Bomber* (London: Paradigm, 2007), 45.

24. St. Bonaventure, *The Soul's Journey into God / The Tree of Life / The Life of St. Francis*, trans. Ewart Cousins (Mahwah, N.J.: Paulist Press, 1978), 266–71.

25. Cook, *Martyrdom in Islam*, 23–28.

26. Bernard Lewis, *The Assassins: A Radical Sect in Islam* (New York: Oxford University Press, 1967).

27. Louise Richardson, *What Terrorists Want: Understanding the Enemy, Containing the Threat* (New York: Random House, 2006), 26.

28. Ariel Merari, "Social, Organizational, and Psychological Factors in Suicide Terrorism," in *Root Causes of Terrorism: Myths, Reality, and Ways Forward,* ed. Tore Bjørgo (London: Routledge, 2005), 72.

29. Richardson, *What Terrorists Want,* 21–23.

30. Bruce Hoffman, "Terrorist Targeting: Tactics, Trends, and Potentialities," *Terrorism and Political Violence* 5, no. 2 (1993), 13.

31. Bruce Hoffman, "Aviation Security and Terrorism: An Analysis of the Potential Threat to Air Cargo Integrators," *Terrorism and Political Violence* 10, no. 3 (1998), 66; J. Bowyer Bell, *IRA Tactics and Targets* (Dublin: Poolberg Press, 1990), 24–25.

32. Richard Bach Jensen, "Daggers, Rifles, and Dynamite: Anarchist Terrorism in Nineteenth Century Europe," *Terrorism and Political Violence* 16, no. 1 (2004): 116–53; Martin A. Miller, "The Intellectual Origins of Modern Terrorism in Europe," in *Terrorism in Context,* ed. Martha Crenshaw (University Park: Pennsylvania State University Press, 1995), 27–62.

33. Karl Heinzen, "Murder," in *Voices of Terror,* ed. Walter Laqueur (New York: Reed Press, 2004), 57–67; also see the discussion in Benjamin Grob-Fitzgibbon, "From the Dagger to the Bomb: Karl Heinzen and the Evolution of Political Terror," *Terrorism and Political Violence* 16, no. 1 (2004): 97–115.

34. For a history of the People's Will, see Venturi, *Roots of Revolution,* especially chapter 21, "Narodnaya Volya," 633–708; Philip Pomper, "Russian Revolutionary Terrorism," in Crenshaw, *Terrorism in Context,* 63–101; and Norman M. Naimark, "Terrorism and the Fall of Imperial Russia," *Terrorism and Political Violence* 2, no. 2 (1990): 171–92. For an eyewitness account, see Vera Figner, *Memoirs of a Revolutionist* (Dekalb: Northern Illinois University Press, 1991).

35. Quoted in James Billington, *Fire in the Minds of Men: Origins of the Revolutionary Faith* (New Brunswick, N.J.: Transaction Publishers, 1999), 388.

36. The phrasing here is indebted to Richard Dawkins' insight: "However many ways there may be of being alive, it is certain that there are vastly more ways of being dead." *Oxford Dictionary of Quotations,* rev. ed. (Oxford: Oxford University Press, 1996), 232.

37. Hoffman, "Aviation Security and Terrorism," 66.

38. Yarmolinsky, *Road to Revolution,* 264.

39. Jared Diamond, *Guns, Germs, and Steel: The Fates of Human Societies* (New York: W. W. Norton and Company, 1997), 242–43.

40. Richard Pipes, *The Degaev Affair: Terror and Treason in Tsarist Russia* (New Haven, Conn.: Yale University Press, 2003), 27–28.

41. Fyodor Dostoevsky, *The Possessed,* trans. Constance Garnet (New York: Modern Library, 1936); Irina Paperno, *Suicide as a Cultural Institution in Dostoevsky's Russia* (Ithaca, N.Y.: Cornell University Press, 1997), 74–77.

42. See discussion in Paperno, *Suicide as a Cultural Institution*, 123–25, 143–51.

43. Quoted in Venturi, *Roots of Revolution*, 635; also see Figner, *Memoirs of a Revolutionist*, 205.

44. Michael Burleigh, *Earthly Powers: The Clash of Religion and Politics in Europe from the French Revolution to the Great War* (New York: Harper Perennial, 2005), 276–310; Billington, *Fire in the Minds of Men*, 4–8, and chap. 14.

45. Radzinsky, *Alexander II*, 291–95, quote from 295.

46. Yarmolinsky, *Road to Revolution*, 246, 274–75.

47. Figner, *Memoirs of a Revolutionist*, app. I, 308.

48. See Norman M. Naimark, *Terrorists and Social Democrats: The Russian Revolutionary Movement under Alexander III* (Cambridge, Mass.: Harvard University Press, 1983).

49. Anna Geifman, *Thou Shalt Kill: Revolutionary Terrorism in Russia, 1904–1917* (Princeton, N.J.: Princeton University Press, 1993), 45–83; Naimark, "Terrorism and the Fall of Imperial Russia."

50. Boris Savinkov, *Memoirs of a Terrorist*, trans. by Joseph Shaplen (New York: Albert and Charles Boni, 1931), 75.

51. Geifman, *Thou Shalt Kill*, 48–49.

52. Savinkov, *Memoirs of a Terrorist*, 48.

53. Ibid., 60–61.

54. Ibid., 104.

55. Ibid., quotes from 110 and 116, respectively.

56. Pomper, "Russian Revolutionary Terrorism," 91. Kaliayev's case was fictionalized in Albert Camus' play *Les Justes* (The just assassins). Also see the case of Evstiliia Rogozinnikkova, discussed in Geifman, *Thou Shalt Kill*, 168.

57. Geifman, *Thou Shalt Kill*, 57, 69.

58. Paul Avrich, *The Russian Anarchists* (Princeton, N.J.: Princeton University Press, 1967), 46.

59. Geifman, *Thou Shalt Kill*, 74.

60. Ibid., 168–72.

CHAPTER 2. THE WEAPON OF MARTYRDOM: LEBANON, 1981–1985

1. Naim Qassem, *Hizbullah: The Story from Within*, trans. Dalia Khalil (London: Saqi, 2005), 49. There is no generally accepted way of transliterating "Party of God" into English. See discussion in Robin Wright, *Dreams and Shadows: The Future of the Middle East* (New York: Penguin, 2008), 173.

2. "Bomb Razes Iraqi Embassy; 25 Die," *Chicago Tribune*, December 16, 1981, A3. The final tally of sixty-one deaths was reported the following month. "Rescue Efforts End in Beirut," *New York Times*, January 12, 1982, A3; Chris

Quillen, "Mass Casualty Bombings Chronology," *Studies in Conflict and Terrorism* 25, no. 5 (2002): 295.

3. Rodger Shanahan, "Shi'a Political Development in Iraq: The Case of the Islamic Da'wa Party," *Third World Quarterly* 25, no. 5 (2004): 944–46.

4. According to Leonard Weinberg, an undetermined number of suicide attacks and no-escape missions accompanied Viet Cong violence against U.S. forces in Vietnam in the 1960s. Leonard Weinberg, "Suicide Terrorism for Secular Causes," in *Root Causes of Suicide Terrorism: The Globalization of Martyrdom*, ed. Ami Pedahzur (New York: Routledge, 2006), 108–22. Also see Adam Dolnik, *Understanding Terrorist Innovation: Technology, Tactics and Global Trends* (New York: Routledge, 2007), 43.

5. Peter Hill, "Kamikaze, 1943–5," in *Making Sense of Suicide Missions*, ed. Diego Gambetta (Oxford: Oxford University Press, 2005), 1–41, and Emiko Ohnuki-Tierney, *Kamikaze, Cherry Blossoms, and Nationalisms: The Militarization of Aesthetics in Japanese History* (Chicago: University of Chicago Press, 2002).

6. Ohnuki-Tierney, *Kamikaze, Cherry Blossoms, and Nationalisms*, 160; Hill, "Kamikaze," 6–8.

7. John W. Dower, *War Without Mercy: Race and Power in the Pacific War* (New York: Pantheon, 1986), 215–16, 231–32. For the contributions of Zen Buddhism to Japanese militarism, see Brian Victoria, *Zen at War* (New York: Weatherhill, 1997).

8. Translated and quoted in Emiko Ohnuki-Tierney, *Kamikaze Diaries: Reflections of Japanese Student Soldiers* (Chicago: University of Chicago Press, 2006), 163; Ohnuki-Tierney, *Kamikaze, Cherry Blossoms, and Nationalisms*, 300 (emphasis in the original).

9. Translated and quoted in Ohnuki-Tierney, *Kamikaze Diaries*, 84; translated and quoted in Christoph Reuter, *My Life Is a Weapon: A Modern History of Suicide Bombing*, trans. Helena Ragg-Kirkby (New Haven, Conn.: Yale University Press, 2004), 130–31.

10. Paul Carell, *Hitler Moves East, 1941–1943*, trans. Ewald Osers (New York: Ballantine Books, 1971), 134–36.

11. James H. Capshew, "Engineering Behavior: Project Pigeon, World War II, and the Conditioning of B. F. Skinner," *Technology and Culture* 34, no. 4 (1993): 835–57.

12. Quoted in Capshew, "Engineering Behavior," 840.

13. Ibid., 840–43, quote from 853. The idea was to release the bats, who would then seek to roost in the attics and cellars of Japan's highly flammable buildings, at which point timers would detonate the bats' payload, igniting thousands of fires. Michael S. Sherry, *The Rise of American Airpower: The Creation of Armageddon* (New Haven, Conn.: Yale University Press, 1988), 226.

14. Skinner quoted in Capshew, "Engineering Behavior," 842; *Guided Missiles and Techniques*, Summary Technical Report of Division 5, National Defense

Research Committee, vol. 1 (Washington, D.C., 1946), 198–201, quote from 201.

15. Barnaby Rogerson, *The Heirs of the Prophet Muhammad and the Roots of the Sunni-Shia Schism* (London: Little, Brown, 2006), 340–43; Mahmoud Ayoub, *Redemptive Suffering in Islam: A Study of the Devotional Aspects of Ashura in Twelver Shi'ism* (The Hague: Mouton Publishers, 1978).

16. Ervand Abrahimian, *The Iranian Mojehedin* (New Haven and London: Yale University Press, 1989) 35, 152, 218–22. Quote from 99.

17. Saskia Gieling, *Religion and War in Revolutionary Iran* (London: I. B. Tauris, 1999), 44–45, 82, 115.

18. Ibid., 54–55; Vali Nasr, *The Shia Revival: How Conflicts within Islam Will Shape the Future* (New York: W. W. Norton and Company, 2006), 132–33.

19. Robin Wright, *In the Name of God: The Khomeini Decade* (New York: Simon and Schuster, 1989), 87.

20. Ian Brown, *Khomeini's Forgotten Sons: The Story of Iran's Boy Soldiers* (London: Grey Seal, 1990).

21. Ibid., 88–89.

22. Reuter, *My Life Is a Weapon*, 35.

23. Joyce M. Davis, *Martyrs: Innocence, Vengeance, and Despair in the Middle East* (New York: Palgrave MacMillan, 2003), 49; Gieling, *Religion and War in Revolutionary Iran*, 120.

24. Qods, ed., *In Memory of Our Martyrs*, trans. M. Ebrahimi (Tehran: Ministry of Islamic Guidance, 1982), 7.

25. Martin Kramer, "Hizbullah: The Calculus of Jihad," in *Fundamentalisms and the State: Remaking Politics, Economies, and Militance*, ed. Martin E. Marty and R. Scott Appleby (Chicago: University of Chicago Press, 1993), 539–56.

26. Fouad Ajami, *The Vanished Imam: Musa al Sadr and the Shia of Lebanon* (Ithaca, N.Y.: Cornell University Press, 1986), 141–43.

27. For the history of Amal, see Augustus Richard Norton, *Amal and the Shi'a: Struggle for the Soul of Lebanon* (Austin: University of Texas Press, 1987), esp. 37–58.

28. Amad Nizar Hamzeh, *In the Path of Hizbullah* (Syracuse, N.Y.: Syracuse University Press, 2004), 22–23; for details and possible reasons for al-Sadr's disappearance, see Norton, *Amal and the Shi'a*, 52–56.

29. Roschanack Shaery-Eisenlohr, *Shi'ite Lebanon: Transnational Religion and the Making of National Identities* (New York: Columbia University Press, 2008), 101–9.

30. Ajami, *Vanished Imam*, 174; Patrick Seale, *Asad: The Struggle for the Middle East* (Berkeley: University of California Press, 1988), 352.

31. Norton, *Amal and the Shi'a*, 68–69.

32. Ze'ev Schiff and Ehud Ya'ari, *Israel's Lebanon War*, ed. and trans. Ina Friedman (New York: Simon and Schuster, 1984), 81, 157.

33. Eugene Rogan, *The Arabs: A History*, 2nd ed. (New York: Basic Books, 2009), 415.

34. Islamic Amal was a splinter of the Amal group that broke away in the early 1980s. Magnus Ranstorp, *Hiz'ballah in Lebanon: The Politics of the Western Hostage Crisis* (New York: St. Martin's Press, 1997), 30–31.

35. Augustus Richard Norton, *Hezbollah: A Short History* (Princeton, N.J.: Princeton University Press, 2007), 31–32, and Faleh A. Jabar, *The Shi'ite Movement in Iraq* (London: Saqi, 2003), 81–98.

36. Patrick Cockburn, *Muqtada al-Sadr and the Future of Iraq* (New York: Scribner, 2008), 37–39.

37. Jabar, *Shi'ite Movement in Iraq*, 227–34.

38. Shaery-Eisenlohr, *Shi'ite Lebanon*, 109–13.

39. Robert Fisk, *Pity the Nation: Lebanon at War*, 3rd ed. (Oxford: Oxford University Press, 2001), 255–57; 277–78.

40. Schiff and Ya'ari, *Israel's Lebanon War*, 232–33.

41. Thomas L. Friedman, *From Beirut to Jerusalem* (New York: Anchor Books, 1995), 163; Fisk, *Pity the Nation*, 390.

42. Schiff and Ya'ari, *Israel's Lebanon War*, 258–59.

43. Qassem, *Hizbullah*, 89; Hala Jaber, *Hezbollah: Born with a Vengeance* (New York: Columbia University Press, 1997), 75–76. For biographical details on Qassir, see Martin Kramer, "Sacrifice and 'Self-Martyrdom' in Shi'ite Lebanon," *Terrorism and Political Violence* 3, no. 3 (1991): 30–47.

44. Robin Wright, *Sacred Rage: The Wrath of Militant Islam* (New York: Simon and Schuster, 1986), 15–16.

45. Robert Baer, *See No Evil: The True Story of a Ground Soldier in the CIA's War on Terrorism* (New York: Three Rivers Press, 2001), 65–67.

46. Wright, *Sacred Rage*, 76–79; Friedman, *From Beirut to Jerusalem*, 200–201.

47. United States Department of Defense, "Report of the DoD Commission on Beirut International Airport Terrorist Act, October 23, 1983," chaired by Admiral Robert Long, December 20, 1983, 40–41, 95–100 (hereafter "Long Commission Report").

48. "Israeli Military HQ Destroyed," *Times* (London), November 5, 1983, A1; William E. Smith, "New Bloodshed, New Hope," *Time*, November 14, 1983, 48–50.

49. Wright, *Sacred Rage*, 112–13.

50. Shanahan, "Shi'a Political Development in Iraq," 949.

51. Ariel Merari, "The Readiness to Kill and Die: Suicide Terrorism in the Middle East," in *Origins of Terrorism: Psychologies, Ideologies, Theologies, States of*

Mind, ed. Walter Reich (Washington, D.C.: Woodrow Wilson Center Press, 1998), 194–96.

52. Account from Fisk, *Pity the Nation*, 561. A misprint in the text has the attack taking place on April 12, 1983, but this is obviously incorrect based on the narrative. Casualty figures are from Ami Pedahzur, *Suicide Terrorism* (Cambridge, U.K., and Malden, Mass.: Polity Press, 2005), 241–42.

53. David Ignatius and Tewfik Mishlawi, "Terrorist Bombing of U.S. Embassy Annex in Beirut Could Again Suck America into Lebanese Quagmire," *Wall Street Journal*, September 21, 1984, 1; also see Baer, *See No Evil*, 107.

54. "Moslem Chief Threatens Israelis—Suicide Attacks Directed at Invasion Forces," *Chicago Tribune*, September 10, 1984, A3; Merari, "The Readiness to Kill and Die," 204–5. Martin Kramer argues that Amal's decision to begin using suicide attackers was at least partially motivated by a need to compete with Hizballah for the allegiance of the Shiite community. Kramer, "Sacrifice and 'Self-Martyrdom,' " 33.

55. "Car Bomb Kills 2 Israelis," *New York Times*, April 10, 1985, A10. It is possible that Sanaa Muhaidily was not the first female suicide bomber. Amir Taheri asserts that this distinction belongs to Sumayah Sa'ad, who on March 10, 1985, killed twelve Israeli soldiers and wounded fourteen others. He believes that the Israeli government concealed the details of the attack to hide the fact that the bomber had been a woman. See Amir Taheri, *Holy Terror: The Inside Story of Islamic Terrorism* (London: Hutchinson, 1987), 116–17.

56. Jaber, *Hezbollah*, 91–92.

57. Joyce M. Davis, "The Woman as Soldier-Martyr and Suicide Bomber: Loula Abboud," in *Martyrs: Innocence, Vengeance, and Despair in the Middle East*, (New York: Palgrave MacMillan, 2003), 67–84.

58. Nikki R. Keddie and Farah Monian note that "recent scholarship has indicated that Husayn's martyrdom was not, until the late 1970s, generally taken as a model for rebellion or assassinations but rather as an occasion to ask for his intervention with God." "Militancy and Religion in Contemporary Iran," in Marty and Appleby, *Fundamentalisms and the State*, 512.

59. Daniel Byman, *Deadly Connections: States That Sponsor Terrorism* (Cambridge: Cambridge University Press, 2005), 93 n. 49; Shaery-Eisenlohr, *Shi'ite Lebanon*, 104–10.

60. Kramer, "Sacrifice and 'Self-Martyrdom,' " 7–8.

61. Shaery-Eisenlohr, *Shi'ite Lebanon*, 108–15.

62. Norton, *Amal and the Shia*, 106.

63. Qassem, *Hizbullah*, 44 (emphasis in the original).

64. Ibid., 70.

65. Martin Kramer, "The Oracle of Hizbullah: Sayyid Muhammad Husayn Fadlallah," in *Spokesmen for the Despised: Fundamentalist Leaders of the Middle East*, ed. R. Scott Appleby (Chicago: University of Chicago Press, 1997), 83–181.

66. Quoted in Kramer, "Hizbullah: The Calculus of Jihad," 550.

67. Kramer, "The Moral Logic of Hizbullah," in Reich, *Origins of Terrorism*, 148.

68. Qassem, *Hizbullah*, 50.

69. In addition, such was the power of the 1983 blast that the FBI determined that significant casualties would have occurred even if the bomb had detonated outside the perimeter of the base, 330 feet from the operations building. "The Post-Mortem Goes On," *Time*, November 14, 1983, 50; "Long Commission Report," 99.

70. "Long Commission Report," 86, quote from 123.

71. Qassem, *Hizbullah*, 50.

72. Qassem, *Hizbullah*, 93, credits the attacks against the MNF to the Islamic Jihad Organization (but does not mention the embassy).

73. Storer Rowley and Raymond Coffey, "Iran Main Suspect in Bombing, U.S. Says," *Chicago Tribune*, December 14, 1983, A13; Baer, *See No Evil*, 264; Timothy J. Geraghty, "25 Years Later: We Came in Peace," *Proceedings* 134, No. 10 (October 2008).

74. As noted above, the identity of the U.S. embassy bomber is still unknown. According to Robin Wright, U.S. authorities eventually identified (though not by name) the bomber of the Marine barracks as a devout young Shiite who was trained in Baalbek by Iran's Revolutionary Guards. Wright, *In the Name of God*, 122–23.

75. Jaber, *Hezbollah*, 115–20; Carl Anthony Wege, "Iran's Terrorist Asset: A History of Imad Mugniyah," *Terrorism Monitor*, September 8, 2006.

76. Also see interpretations by Kramer, "Moral Logic of Hizbullah," 136, and Wright, *Sacred Rage*, 84–86.

77. Jaber, *Hezbollah*, 80–84.

78. Ariel Merari, *Driven to Death: Psychological and Social Aspects of Suicide Terrorism* (New York: Oxford University Press, 2010), 30.

79. Ibid., 31.

80. Krista E. Wiegand, "Reformation of a Terrorist Group: Hezbollah as a Lebanese Political Party," *Studies in Conflict and Terrorism* 32 (2009): 669–80.

81. Kramer, "Moral Logic of Hizbullah," 146–48.

CHAPTER 3. MARTYRDOM AND CONTROL: THE REINVENTION OF SUICIDE BOMBING BY THE LIBERATION TIGERS OF TAMIL EELAM

1. Shashi Ahluwalia and Meenakshi Ahluwalia, *Assassination of Rajiv Gandhi* (New Delhi: Mittal Publications, 1991), 1–26; Rajeev Sharma, *Beyond the Tigers: Tracking Rajiv Gandhi's Assassination* (New Delhi: Kaveri Books, 1998), 16–27; Rohan Gunaratna, *Indian Intervention in Sri Lanka: The Role of India's Intelligence Agencies* (Colombo: South Asian Network on Conflict Research, 1993), 464.

2. Manoj Joshi, "On the Razor's Edge: The Liberation Tigers of Tamil Eelam," *Studies in Conflict and Terrorism* 19, no. 1 (1996): 30–33.

3. Amy Waldman, "Masters of Suicide Bombing: Tamil Guerrillas of Sri Lanka," *New York Times*, January 14, 2003.

4. For first use of suicide belts, see Sharma, *Beyond the Tigers*, 35–36. The LTTE carried out more than forty boat attacks. Brian A. Jackson et al., *Breaching the Fortress Wall: Understanding Terrorist Efforts to Overcome Defensive Technologies* (Santa Monica, Calif.: RAND, 2007), 67.

5. Rohan Gunaratna, "The LTTE and Suicide Terrorism," *Frontline*, February 5–8, 2000; Bruce Hoffman and Gordon H. McCormick, "Terrorism, Signaling, and Suicide Attack," *Studies in Conflict and Terrorism* 27, no. 4 (2004): 261–62.

6. BBC News Online, "Tamil Rebels Commit Suicide," March 11, 2000.

7. Ami Pedahzur, *Suicide Terrorism* (Cambridge, U.K., and Malden, Mass.: Polity Press, 2005), app., 241–53; National Counterterrorism Center, Worldwide Incidents Tracking System, wits.nctc.gov, accessed September 24, 2009. Also see Stephen Hopgood, "Tamil Tigers, 1987–2002," in *Making Sense of Suicide Missions*, ed. Diego Gambetta (Oxford: Oxford University Press, 2005), 44.

8. David Edgerton, *The Shock of the Old: Technology and Global History since 1900* (Oxford: Oxford University Press, 2007), 187; Eric von Hippel, *Democratizing Innovation* (Cambridge, Mass.: MIT Press, 2005), 33.

9. Mia Bloom, *Dying to Kill: The Allure of Suicide Terrorism* (New York: Columbia University Press, 2005), 46–48; Dagmar Hellmann-Rajanayagam, *The Tamil Tigers: Armed Struggle for Identity* (Stuttgart: Franz Steiner Verlag, 1994), 86–91.

10. Robert I. Rotberg, "Sri Lanka's Civil War: From Mayhem toward Diplomatic Resolution," in *Creating Peace in Sri Lanka: Civil War and Reconciliation*, ed. Robert I. Rotberg (Washington, D.C.: Brookings Institution Press, 1999), 5–6.

11. Neil DeVotta, *Blowback: Linguistic Nationalism, Institutional Decay, and Ethnic Conflict in Sri Lanka* (Stanford, Calif.: Stanford University Press, 2004), esp. chap. 4, "The Official Language Act of 1956," 73–91, and chap. 5, "Institutional Decay: Consequences of the Official Language Act, 1956–77," 92–142; H. P. Chattopadhyaya, *Ethnic Unrest in Modern Sri Lanka: An Account of Tamil-Sinhalese Race Relations* (New Delhi: M. D. Publications, 1994), 17–25.

12. DeVotta, *Blowback*, 140–42; also see Jagath P. Senaratne, *Political Violence in Sri Lanka, 1977–1990: Riots, Insurrections, Counter-insurgencies, Foreign Intervention* (Amsterdam: VU University Press, 1997), 38.

13. M. R. Narayan Swamy, *Inside an Elusive Mind: Prabhakaran, The First Profile of the World's Most Ruthless Guerrilla Leader* (Colombo: Vijitha Yapa Publications, 2003), 60.

14. Ibid., 29–39.

15. John Richardson, *Paradise Poisoned: Learning about Conflict, Terrorism, and Development from Sri Lanka's Civil Wars* (Kandy, Sri Lanka: International Centre for Ethnic Studies, 2005), 493–98; Barnett Rubin, *Cycles of Violence: Human Rights in Sri Lanka since the Indo-Sri Lanka Agreement* (Washington, D.C., Asia Watch, 1987).

16. S. J. Tambiah, *Sri Lanka: Ethnic Fratricide and the Dismantling of Democracy* (Chicago: University of Chicago Press, 1986), 19–20.

17. Swamy, *Inside an Elusive Mind*, 4–9.

18. Tambiah, *Ethnic Fratricide*, 20–22; Chattopadhyaya, *Ethnic Unrest in Modern Sri Lanka*, 68–69; and Neelan Tiruchelvam, "Devolution and the Elusive Quest for Peace," in Rotberg, *Creating Peace in Sri Lanka*, 189–202.

19. DeVotta, *Blowback*, 170.

20. Rubin, *Cycles of Violence*, 31–40.

21. Swamy, *Inside an Elusive Mind*, 126–30. For the LTTE perspective, see Adele Balasingham, *The Will to Freedom: An Inside View of the Tamil Resistance* (Mitcham, U.K.: Fairfax, 2001), 100–101.

22. Barbara Crossette, "Survivors of Attack in Sri Lanka Talk of 'Calm, Disciplined' Killers," *New York Times*, April 20, 1987; Barbara Crossette, "105 Sri Lankans Die as Bomb Rips into Bus Station," *New York Times*, April 22, 1987.

23. Rohan Gunaratna, *War and Peace in Sri Lanka* (Colombo: Institute of Fundamental Studies, 1987), 27, 68; Michael Roberts, "Pragmatic Action and Enchanted Worlds: A Black Tiger Rite of Commemoration," *Social Analysis* 50, no. 1 (2006): 80.

24. The phrase "predatory rationalization" is from Senaratne, *Political Violence in Sri Lanka*, 85; also see Swamy, *Inside an Elusive Mind*, 132–38, 151, and 174.

25. M. R. Narayan Swamy, *Tigers of Lanka: From Boys to Guerrillas*, updated ed. (Colombo: Vijitha Yapa Publications, 2004), 86–87; Anita Pratrap, *Island of Blood: Frontline Reports from Sri Lanka, Afghanistan, and Other South Asian Flashpoints* (New York: Penguin Books, 2001), 100–106; Daya Somasundaram, *Scarred Minds: The Psychological Impact of War on Sri Lankan Tamils* (New Delhi: Sage Publications, 1998), 66–67.

26. Rajan Hoole et al., *The Broken Palmyrah: The Tamil Crisis in Sri Lanka—An Inside Account*, rev. ed. (Claremont, Calif.: Sri Lanka Studies Institute, 1990). Thirinigama was murdered in 1989. See the second preface, ibid., x–xv.

27. Quoted in Jannie Lilja, "Trapping Constituents or Winning Hearts and Minds? Rebel Strategies to Attain Constituent Support in Sri Lanka," *Terrorism and Political Violence* 21, no. 2 (2009): 314.

28. Swamy, *Inside an Elusive Mind*, 19–28. Interviews with Prabhakaran, "The Eye of the Tiger" (1986), "How I Became a Freedom Fighter" (April 1994), are from the website EelamWeb, http://www.eelamweb.com (accessed July 2007, but no longer operational).

29. Balasingham, *Will to Freedom*, 80.

30. Swamy, *Inside an Elusive Mind*, 29.

31. Peter Schalk, "Resistance and Martyrdom in the Process of State Formation of Tamililam," in *Martyrdom and Political Resistance Movements: Essays on Asia and Europe*, ed. Joyce Pettigrew (Amsterdam: VU University Press, 1997), 74–75.

32. Hellmann-Rajanayagam, *Tamil Tigers*, 67; newspaper account cited in Edgar O'Balance, *The Cyanide War: Tamil Insurrection in Sri Lanka, 1973–1988* (London: Brassey's, 1989), 111.

33. Gunaratna, *Indian Intervention in Sri Lanka*, 48–49, 407.

34. Steven R. Weisman, "India Airlifts Aid to Tamil Rebels," *New York Times*, June 5, 1987; Rajesh Kadian, *India's Sri Lanka Fiasco* (New Delhi: Vision Books, 1990), 9–11.

35. For favorable responses of the Tamil people, see Hoole et al., *Broken Palmyrah*, 143. According to William Clarence, radical Sinhalese were so opposed to the agreement that they called for the assassination of the president of Sri Lanka. *Ethnic Warfare in Sri Lanka and the UN Crisis* (Ann Arbor, Mich.: Pluto Press, 2007), 49. When Rajiv Gandhi arrived in Colombo to promote the accord, thousands protested. The Sri Lankan police used deadly force to pacify the crowds, killing five people. Kadian, *India's Sri Lanka Fiasco*, 14.

36. Seth Mydens, "Leader Says Tamils Will Turn in Arms," *New York Times*, August 5, 1987; Gunaratna, *War and Peace in Sri Lanka*, 6–9.

37. Kadian, *India's Sri Lanka Fiasco*, 13, 24–25; "A Tamil Separatist Leader Dies in Protest Fast," *New York Times*, September 27, 1987.

38. Gunaratna, *Indian Intervention in Sri Lanka*, 235–36.

39. K. M. de Silva, *Regional Powers and Small State Security: India and Sri Lanka, 1977–1990* (Baltimore: Johns Hopkins University Press, 1995), 267–323.

40. Sharma, *Beyond the Tigers*, 119–20.

41. Casualty figures for the attack vary significantly. Contemporary newspaper reports varied between twenty and forty fatalities. The figure of twenty-seven is from the START Global Terrorism Database, http://www.start.umd.edu/gtd (accessed March 23, 2008).

42. Schalk, "Resistance and Martyrdom in the Process of State Formation of Tamililam," 77; Liam Pleven, "Secrets of Their Success: Politics, Not Faith, Fuel the Suicide Bombers of Sri Lanka," Newsday.com, July 18, 2005; Amantha Perera, "Suicide Bombers Feared and Revered," *Asia Times Online*, July 17, 2003.

43. Chris Smith, "South Asia's Enduring War," in Rotberg, *Creating Peace in Sri Lanka*, 26.

44. Discussed in Pratrap, *Island of Blood*, 99.

45. START Global Terrorism Database, http://www.start.umd.edu/gtd (accessed April 28, 2011); Associated Press, "Blast Kills 60 in Sri Lanka; 1,400 Injured," *New York Times,* February 1, 1996.

46. V. S. Sambandan, "Living Through the Bombs," *Frontline,* December 25, 1999–January 7, 2000.

47. BBC News, "Sri Lanka Attack Causes Carnage," October 16, 2006; "Suicide Bombing Kills More Than 100 Sri Lankan Sailors," *Times* [London] *Online,* October 16, 2006.

48. D. B. S. Jeyaraj, "Another Human Bomb," *Frontline,* June 19–July 2, 1999.

49. V. S. Sambandan, "Peace-maker as Terrorist Target," and D. B. S. Jeyaraj, "Trails of the Tigers," *Frontline,* August 14–27, 1999.

50. Hoole, et al., *Broken Palymyrah,* 134–35. For Prabhakaran's public admission, see Swamy, *Inside an Elusive Mind,* 233.

51. Arjuna Gunawardena, "Female Black Tigers: A Different Breed of Cat?" in *Female Suicide Bombers: Dying for Equality?* ed. Yoram Schweitzer (Tel Aviv: Jaffee Center for Strategic Studies, 2006), 81; for details on training, see Jackson et al., *Breaching the Fortress Wall,* 63–68.

52. Miranda Alison, "Cogs in the Wheel? Women in the Liberation Tigers of Tamil Eelam," *Civil Wars* 6, no. 4 (Winter 2003): 37–54; Alisa Stack-O'Connor, "Lions, Tigers, and Freedom Birds: How and Why the Liberation Tigers of Tamil Eelam Employs Women," *Terrorism and Political Violence* 19, no. 1 (2007): 45.

53. Pratrap, *Island of Blood,* 98; Swamy, *Inside an Elusive Mind,* 227, 234–35.

54. Somasundaram, *Scarred Minds,* 51.

55. From http://www.eelamweb.com (accessed October 2007, but no longer operational).

56. Michael Roberts, "Tamil Tiger 'Martyrs': Regenerating Divine Potency?" *Studies in Conflict and Terrorism* 28, no. 6 (2005): 494–95.

57. Peter Schalk, "The Revival of Martyr Cults among Illavar," *Temenos* 33 (1997): 151–90.

58. Balasingham, *Will to Freedom,* 249, and 54 for details on the death of Shankar; on the ritual celebration of Great Heroes' Day, see Roberts, "Pragmatic Action and Enchanted Worlds," 84–93.

59. Schalk, "Revival of Martyr Cults among Illavar," sec. 2, 3–5.

60. Christiana Natali, "Building Cemeteries, Constructing Identities: Funerary Practices and Nationalist Discourse among the Tamil Tigers of Sri Lanka," *Contemporary South Asia* 16, no. 3 (2008): 297–99; Rohan Gunaratna suggests that LTTE cadres do believe that dying for the cause will confer immortality upon them. *International and Regional Security Implications of the Sri Lankan Tamil Insurgency* (United Kingdom: International Foundation of Sri Lankans, 1987), 104.

61. Translations of Prabhakaran's Great Heroes' Day speeches are from http:// www.eelamweb.com (accessed October 2007, but no longer operational).

62. Schalk, "Revival of Martyr Cults among Illavar."

63. For example, see Pleven, "Secrets of Their Success."

64. Anthony W. Marx, *Faith in Nation: Exclusionary Origins of Nationalism* (New York: Oxford University Press, 2003), 3–32.

65. Liah Greenfeld, *Nationalism and the Mind: Essays on Modern Culture* (Oxford: Oneworld, 2006), 93–114; Michael Burleigh, *Earthly Powers: The Clash of Religion and Politics in Europe, from the French Revolution to the Great War* (New York: Harper Perennial, 2003), 1–22.

66. Dale Van Kley, *The Religious Origins of the French Revolution* (New Haven, Conn.: Yale University Press, 1996), 367.

67. James H. Billington, *Fire in the Minds of Men: Origins of the Revolutionary Faith* (Brunswick, N.J.: Transaction Publishers, 1999), 4–5.

68. Also see Mia Bloom, "Dying to Kill: Motivations for Suicide Terrorism," in *Root Causes of Suicide Terrorism: The Globalization of Martyrdom*, ed. Ami Pedahzur (New York: Routledge, 2006), 29.

69. Rohan Gunaratna, "The LTTE and Suicide Terrorism," *Frontline*, February 5–8, 2000; Swamy, *Inside an Elusive Mind*, 272.

70. Pape writes that "the logic of religious difference" and "[f]ear of religious persecution . . . largely accounts for the pervasive use of suicide terrorism in this case." Robert A. Pape, *Dying to Win: The Strategic Logic of Suicide Bombing* (New York: Random House, 2005), 140, and also see 146–51. For his explanation of the lack of suicide attacks during India's occupation, see ibid., 151–54.

71. David Rohde, "Tamil Suicide Bomber Kills 4 Policemen in Capital of Sri Lanka," *New York Times*, July 8, 2004.

72. Hellmann-Rajanayagam, *Tamil Tigers*, 119–25.

73. Gunaratna, *Indian Intervention in Sri Lanka*, 411.

74. Crossette, "Survivors of Attack in Sri Lanka Talk of 'Calm, Disciplined' Killers"; Crossette, "105 Sri Lankans Die as Bomb Rips into Bus Station."

75. For example, Balasingham, in *The Will to Freedom*, 126, writes that Miller's attack was part of a "major counter-offensive" and that the attack killed "hundreds" of troops, both of which are patently false statements.

76. One other high-ranking member of the LTTE, S. P. Tamilselvan, chief negotiator (killed in 2007), denied that Miller's attack had been inspired by the attacks in Lebanon. Tamilselvan, quoted in Pleven, "Secrets of Their Success," 3.

77. Hoffman and Horowitz argue that Hizballah played a major role in the spread of suicide bombing to the LTTE, but this author disagrees. Bruce Hoffman, *Inside Terrorism*, 2nd ed. (New York: Columbia University Press, 2006), 141; Michael C. Horowitz, *The Diffusion of Military Power: Causes*

and *Consequences for International Politics* (Princeton, N.J.: Princeton University Press, 2010), 196–97.

78. G. P. V. Somaratne, "Sri Lanka's Relations with Israel," in *External Compulsions of South Asian Politics,* ed. Shelton U. Kodikkara (New Delhi: Sage Publications, 1993), 194–225. Also see Gunaratna, *Indian Intervention in Sri Lanka,* 131, and Swamy, *Tigers of Lanka,* 97–102.

79. Hoole et al., *Broken Palmyrah,* xi.

80. Shawn Teresa Flanigan, "Nonprofit Service Provision by Insurgent Organizations: The Cases of Hizballah and the Tamil Tigers," *Studies in Conflict and Terrorism* 31, no. 6 (2008): 503–4, 507–8, 511; also see Lilja, "Trapping Constituents or Winning Hearts and Minds?" 314–15.

81. Human Rights Watch, "Living in Fear: Child Soldiers and the Tamil Tigers in Sri Lanka," New York, November 2004, 6, 17, 27–28.

82. Hoffman and McCormick, "Terrorism, Signaling, and Suicide Attack," 245–47.

83. United Nations, "Report of the Secretary General's Panel of Experts on Accountability in Sri Lanka," March 31, 2011, ii–iii; Niel A. Smith, "Understanding Sri Lanka's Defeat of the Tamil Tigers," *Joint Forces Quarterly,* no. 59 (October 2010): 40–44.

CHAPTER 4. TRIAL RUNS: THE PROVISIONAL IRA AND THE WORKERS' PARTY OF KURDISTAN

1. The Provisional IRA is usually referred to simply as the IRA in Northern Ireland and the Republic of Ireland, so all references to the IRA in this book can be taken to refer to the Provisional IRA unless otherwise noted.

2. Jamie Dettmer and Edward Gorman, "Seven Dead in IRA 'Human Bomb' Attacks," *Times* (London), October 25, 1990; David McKittrick, "IRA's New Tactic Breaches Security Forces' Defenses," *Independent* (London), October 25, 1990.

3. Dettmer and Gorman, "Seven Dead in IRA 'Human Bomb Attacks'"; Kevin Fulton, the assumed name of a former British agent in the IRA, claims that he was part of the team that held McEvoy's family hostage (and refers to him as Colman McAvoy); Kevin Fulton, with Jim Nally and Ian Gallagher, *Unsung Hero: How I Saved Dozens of Lives as a Secret Agent inside the IRA* (London: John Blake, 2006), 122–29.

4. David McKittrick, "SDLP Leader Denounces IRA 'Cowards,' " *Independent* (London), October 26, 1990.

5. Ibid.

6. This is the primary argument of Robert A. Pape, *Dying to Win: The Strategic Logic of Suicide Bombing* (New York: Random House, 2005).

7. Jonathan Zeitlin and Gerry Herrigel, eds., "Introduction," in *Americanization and Its Limits: Reworking US Technology and Management in Post-War*

Europe and Japan (Oxford: Oxford University Press, 2000), 2–3; Joel Mokyr, *The Gifts of Athena: Historical Origins of the Knowledge Economy* (Princeton, N.J.: Princeton University Press, 2002), 16–21, and see chapter 6, "Political Economy of Knowledge: Innovation and Resistance in Economic History," 218–93.

8. Everett M. Rogers, *Diffusion of Innovations,* 5th ed. (New York: Free Press, 2003), 5, 14.

9. Rogers, *Diffusion of Innovations,* 258–91. For the value of suicide bombing as a demonstrative act, or "signaling game," see Bruce Hoffman and Gordon H. McCormick, "Terrorism, Signaling, and Suicide Attack," *Studies in Conflict and Terrorism* 27 (2004): 243–81.

10. Rogers, *Diffusion of Innovations,* 257–58.

11. Ibid., 229.

12. Ibid., 233.

13. Ibid., 241, 243, 246–47.

14. Sean MacStiofain, *Revolutionary in Ireland* (Edinburgh: Gordon Cremonisi, 1975), 138–39.

15. J. Bowyer Bell, *IRA Tactics and Targets* (Dublin: Poolbeg, 1990), 48–49; Brian A. Jackson et al., *Aptitude for Destruction,* vol. 2, *Case Studies of Organizational Learning in Five Terrorist Groups* (Santa Monica, Calif.: RAND Corporation, 2007), 113.

16. Green Book content is from Tim Pat Coogan, *The IRA* (New York: Palgrave 2002), 555.

17. The fifth part of the strategy consisted of "defending the war of liberation by punishing criminals, collaborators, and informers." Ibid.

18. Bell, *IRA Tactics and Targets,* 107–11. The tension between the IRA's urban and rural branches is discussed in James Dingley, "The Bombing of Omagh, 15 August 1998: The Bombers, Their Tactics, Strategy, and Purpose behind the Incident," *Studies in Conflict and Terrorism* 24, no. 6 (2001): 456–57, and Eamon Collins, with Mick McGovern, *Killing Rage* (London: Granta Books, 1997). The emphasis on armed struggle over politics is the subject of M.L.R. Smith, *Fighting for Ireland: The Military Strategy of the Irish Republican Movement* (London and New York: Routledge, 1997) esp. 219–20.

19. A. R. Oppenheimer suggests that the term "IED" should be the acronym for Irish Explosive Device given the centrality of such weapons to the republican cause from the late 1800s to the late 1900s. A. R. Oppenheimer, *IRA: The Bombs and the Bullets. A History of Deadly Ingenuity* (Dublin: Irish Academic Press, 2009), 8; also see MacStiofain, *Revolutionary in Ireland,* 330–31.

20. Oppenheimer, *IRA,* 204–5; Toby Harnden, *Bandit Country: The IRA and South Armagh* (London: Hodder and Stoughton, 1999), 19; J. Bowyer Bell, *The Secret Army: The IRA,* rev. 3rd ed. (New York: Transaction Publishers, 1997), 453.

21. Oppenheimer, *IRA*, 206–10.

22. Bruce Hoffman, "Terrorist Targeting: Tactics, Trends, and Potentialities," *Terrorism and Political Violence* 5, no. 2 (1993): 19–21, and Oppenheimer, *IRA*, chaps. 6 and 9.

23. Collins, *Killing Rage*, 162. It has become clear in recent years that by the 1980s the IRA was riddled with informers, who also contributed significantly to the organization's numerous operational failures.

24. As told to Bob Perin, *Bombs Have No Pity: My War against Terrorism* (London: William Luscombe, 1975), 62, 122.

25. Tony Geraghty, *The Irish War: The Hidden Conflict between the IRA and British Intelligence* (Baltimore: Johns Hopkins University Press, 2000), 204; Martin van Crevald, *The Changing Face of War: Lessons of Combat from the Marne to Iraq* (New York: Presidio Press, 2006), 234–35.

26. Quoted in Coogan, *IRA*, 555.

27. Oppenheimer, *IRA*, 70.

28. Harnden, *Bandit Country*, 197–216; Oppenheimer, *IRA*, 112–15; Bell, *Secret Army*, 449–55.

29. Chris Ryder, *A Special Kind of Courage: 321 EOD Squadron—Battling the Bombers*, rev. ed. (London: Methuen, 2006), 236; Oppenheimer, *IRA*, 85.

30. For an introduction to the literature regarding nationalism as a modern religion, see Liah Greenfeld, *Nationalism and the Mind: Essays on Modern Culture* (Oxford: Oneworld, 2006), especially chapter 5, "The Modern Religion," 93–114; Adrian Hastings, *The Construction of Nationhood: Ethnicity, Religion, and Nationalism* (Cambridge: Cambridge University Press, 1997); and Anthony D. Smith, *National Identity* (Reno: University of Nevada Press, 1991).

31. Robert Kee, *The Green Flag: A History of Irish Nationalism* (London: Penguin Books, 2000), 143–45; Richard English, *Irish Freedom: The History of Nationalism in Ireland* (London: MacMillan, 2006), 102–11.

32. Padraic H. Pearse, *Political Writings and Speeches* (Dublin: Talbot Press, 1966), 53, 65–66.

33. R. F. Foster, *Modern Ireland, 1600–1972* (London: Allen Lane, 1988), 477–87, "theology of insurrection," from p. 483. While in prison awaiting execution for his part in the Easter Rising, Pearse wrote to his mother that he did "not hope or even desire to live" and in a poem made an explicit comparison between himself and Jesus Christ. Quoted in Kevin Toolis, *Rebel Hearts: Journeys within the IRA's Soul* (New York: St. Martin's Griffin, 1995), 340; also see Kee, *Green Flag*, 503, 531, 568–73; English, *Irish Freedom*, 145, 190–91, 274–75; Conor Cruise O'Brien, *Ancestral Voices: Religion and Nationalism in Ireland* (Chicago: University of Chicago Press, 1994), 99–113.

34. Sean O'Callaghan wrote that his own upbringing was just such a fusion of Catholicism and nationalism: "Padraig Pearse and the other rebel leaders executed by the British after the Easter Rising of 1916 were painstakingly

interwoven with images of Christ and Catholic martyrs into a seamless mix of blood sacrifice." Sean O'Callaghan, *The Informer: The Real Life Story of One Man's War against Terrorism* (New York: Bantam Press, 1998), 17.

35. Stathis Kalyvas and Ignacio Sanchez-Cuenca, "Killing without Dying: The Absence of Suicide Missions," in *Making Sense of Suicide Missions*, ed. Diego Gambetta (Oxford: Oxford University Press, 2005), 213–23; Mia Bloom, *Dying to Kill: The Allure of Suicide Terrorism* (New York: Columbia University Press, 2005), 134–37.

36. Mia Bloom and John Horgan, "Missing Their Mark: The IRA's Proxy Bomb Campaign," *Social Research* 75, no. 2 (2008): 596.

37. The second rule was "never underestimate your enemy, but never overestimate him either." Collins, *Killing Rage*, 18–19; O'Callaghan, *The Informer*, 69. Martin McGartland, an informer from the Belfast area, wrote that he was instructed not to risk his life or the possibility of arrest. His commander told him, "We can always get more arms and Semtex but we can't afford to lose valuable members." Martin McGartland, *Fifty Dead Men Walking* (Norwalk, Conn.: Hastings House, 1997), 179.

38. Padraig O'Malley, *Biting at the Grave: The Irish Hunger Strikes and the Politics of Despair* (Boston: Beacon Press, 1990), 19.

39. For background on the prison protest, see Tim Pat Coogan, *On the Blanket: The Inside Story of the IRA Prisoners' "Dirty" Protest* (New York: Palgrave MacMillan, 2002), 62–65, 83–94.

40. Brendan Hughes, interviewed in Ed Moloney, *Voices from the Grave: Two Men's War in Ireland* (New York: Public Affairs, 2010), 214.

41. Ibid., 213.

42. For prisoner accounts of the escalation of the struggle, see Brian Campbell, Laurence McKeown, and Felim O'Hagan, eds., *Nor Meekly Serve My Time: The H-Block Struggle, 1976–1981* (Belfast: Beyond the Pale, 1994). Also see Coogan, *On the Blanket*, 94.

43. Richard O'Rawe, *Blanketmen: An Untold Story of the H-Block Hunger Strike* (Dublin: New Island, 2005), 36–37.

44. Campbell, McKeown, and O'Hagan, *Nor Meekly Serve My Time*, 70, 84, quote from 90.

45. Ibid., 106–9.

46. Hughes, recollection in Moloney, *Voices from the Grave*, 235–40.

47. Hughes, interviewed in ibid., 229; David Beresford, *Ten Men Dead: The Story of the 1981 Irish Hunger Strike* (New York: Atlantic Monthly Press, 1987), 37.

48. Hughes, interviewed in Moloney, *Voices from the Grave*, 244; O'Rawe, *Blanketmen*, 121.

49. Quoted in O'Malley, *Biting at the Grave*, 85.

50. Beresford, *Ten Men Dead*, 69–88.

51. Robert W. White, *Ruari O Bradaigh: The Life and Politics of an Irish Revolutionary* (Bloomington: Indiana University Press, 2006), 283–307; Liam Clarke, *Broadening the Battlefield: The H-Blocks and the Rise of Sinn Fein* (Dublin: Gill and Macmillan, 1987).

52. Anthony McIntyre, *Good Friday: The Death of Irish Republicanism* (New York: Ausubo Press, 2008), 264.

53. "Comms" (prison communications) from McFarlane quoted in O'Rawe, *Blanketmen*, 138, 168.

54. Quoted in O'Malley, *Biting at the Grave*, 82.

55. Beresford, *Ten Men Dead*, 285.

56. Martin Dillon, *God and the Gun: The Church and Irish Terrorism* (New York: Routledge, 1999), 88–91, quote from 91.

57. I am greatly indebted to Monsignor Frank Lane for helping me to understand the internal dimension of martyrdom in the Catholic tradition and other faiths.

58. O'Malley, *Biting at the Grave*, 171–89.

59. Beresford, *Ten Men Dead*, 103.

60. Ibid., 238, 315.

61. Van Crevald, *Changing Face of War*, 229–35; Sir Alistair Irwin and Mike Mahoney, "The Military Response," in *Combating Terrorism in Northern Ireland*, ed. James Dingley (New York: Routledge, 2009), esp. 213–23; John Newsinger, *British Counter Insurgency: From Palestine to Northern Ireland* (New York: Palgrave, 2002), 179–90; and Sir Rupert Smith, *The Utility of Force: The Art of War in the Modern World* (New York: Alfred A. Knopf, 2007), 302.

62. Sir Rupert Smith, who as a young officer served (and was wounded by a IRA bomb) in Northern Ireland, wrote, "The IRA, who see themselves and to a large measure run themselves as an army, have been very careful to operate below the threshold of utility of the British Army's weapon systems, and the army, in turn, has been careful not to introduce those systems into the Irish theatre." Smith, *Utility of Force*, 302.

63. Van Crevald, *Changing Face of War*, 234–35.

64. Bloom and Horgan, "Missing Their Mark," 581, 610–11. Members of the IRA seem to have understood that the use of proxy bombers was a risky one. Some told John Horgan that they anticipated a possible backlash, but believed that the impact of the attacks would be worthwhile (p. 599).

65. Joost Hiltermann, *A Poisonous Affair: America, Iraq, and the Gassing of Halabja* (Cambridge: Cambridge University Press, 2007).

66. Aliza Marcus, *Blood and Belief: The PKK and the Kurdish Fight for Independence* (New York: New York University Press, 2007); Nur Bilge Criss, "The Nature of PKK Terrorism in Turkey," *Studies in Conflict and Terrorism* 18, no. 1 (1995): 17–37.

67. Marcus, *Blood and Belief,* 30–40, 196.

68. Dogu Ergil, "Suicide Terrorism in Turkey: The Workers' Party of Kurdistan," in *Countering Suicide Terrorism: An International Conference February 20–23, 2000 Herzliya, Israel* (Herzliya: International Policy Institute for Counter-Terrorism, 2001), 107.

69. Bloom, *Dying to Kill,* 110–11; Marcus, *Blood and Belief,* 204–5.

70. Marcus, *Blood and Belief,* 93–95, 135–38.

71. Ibid., 67. Also see Michael Biggs, "Dying without Killing: Self-Immolations, 1963–2002," in Gambetta, *Making Sense of Suicide Missions,* 173–208.

72. Ami Pedahzur, *Suicide Terrorism* (Cambridge, U.K., and Malden, Mass.: Polity Press, 2005), 243.

73. Bloom, *Dying to Kill,* 106–7.

74. Marcus, *Blood and Belief,* 244.

75. Pedahzur, *Suicide Terrorism,* 88, asserts that there was much more debate among the upper ranks of the PKK regarding suicide bombing than there had been in the LTTE, where the decision was Prabhakaran's alone.

76. Ergil, "Suicide Terrorism in Turkey," 123.

77. Marcus, *Blood and Belief,* 243–44.

78. Ergil, "Suicide Terrorism in Turkey," 122.

79. Leyla Kaplan made a brief audiotape in which she said that she was giving her life for the cause, but this was the extent of the internal publicity generated by the suicide bombings of the PKK. Ergil, "Suicide Terrorism in Turkey," 124.

80. Ergil, "Suicide Terrorism in Turkey," 118–20.

81. Lawrence E. Cline, "From Ocalan to al Qaida: The Continuing Terrorist Threat in Turkey," *Studies in Conflict and Terrorism* 27, no. 4 (2004): 326.

CHAPTER 5. MANAGING MARTYRDOM, PART I: PALESTINIAN SUICIDE BOMBING IN THE 1990s

1. Yoram Schweitzer, "Palestinian *Istishhadia*: A Developing Instrument," *Studies in Conflict and Terrorism* 30, no. 8 (2007): 671–72; Ami Pedahzur, Arie Perliger, and Leonard Weinberg, "Altruism and Fatalism: The Characteristics of Palestinian Suicide Terrorists," *Deviant Behavior* 24, no. 4 (2003): 405–23.

2. According to Ariel Merari, there were two unplanned instances of suicide attacks carried out by Palestinian groups in the early 1970s. Ariel Merari, *Driven to Death: Psychological and Social Aspects of Suicide Terrorism* (New York: Oxford University Press, 2010), 32–33.

3. Samuel Katz, *The Hunt for the Engineer: The Inside Story of How Israel's Counterterrorist Forces Tracked and Killed the Hamas Master Bomber* (Guilford, Conn.: Lyons Press, 1999), 74–75.

4. Said K. Aburish, *Arafat: From Defender to Dictator*, rev. ed. (New York: Bloomsbury, 2004), 197–206; Sari Nusseibeh, with Anthony David, *Once Upon a Country: A Palestinian Life* (New York: Farrar, Straus, and Giroux, 2007), 351.

5. Thomas Friedman, *From Beirut to Jerusalem* (New York: Anchor Books, 1995), 326.

6. The word "intifada" means "rising up" or "shaking off." In addition to Friedman, *From Beirut to Jerusalem*, chapters 13 and 14, and Nusseibeh, *Once Upon a Country*, chapters 18 through 21, this account of the intifada is also drawn from Benny Morris, *Righteous Victims: A History of the Zionist-Arab Conflict, 1881–2001* (New York: Vintage Books, 2001), chapter 12.

7. Dennis Ross, *The Missing Peace: The Inside Story of the Fight for Middle East Peace* (New York: Farrar, Straus, Giroux, 2004); Nusseibeh, *Once Upon a Country*, chaps. 22–25; Shlomo Ben-Ami, *Scars of War, Wounds of Peace: The Arab-Israeli Tragedy* (New York: Oxford University Press, 2006), chaps. 9 and 10; Morris, *Righteous Victims*, chaps. 13 and 14; and Aburish, *Arafat*, 244–59.

8. Ilan Pappe, *A History of Modern Palestine: One Land, Two Peoples* (New York: Cambridge University Press, 2004), 243.

9. Ross, *Missing Peace*, 766; Ben-Ami, *Scars of War, Wounds of Peace*, 190–93; Aburish, *Arafat*, 244.

10. Richard P. Mitchell, *The Society of the Muslim Brothers* (Oxford: Oxford University Press, 1969), esp. 230; Brynjar Lia, *The Society of the Muslim Brothers in Egypt: The Rise of an Islamic Mass Movement, 1928–1942* (Reading, U.K.: Ithaca Press, 1998).

11. Khaled Hroub, *Hamas: Political Thought and Practice* (Washington, D.C.: Institute for Palestine Studies, 2000), 11–23; Ziad Abu-Amr, *Islamic Fundamentalism in the West Bank and Gaza: Muslim Brotherhood and Islamic Jihad* (Bloomington: Indiana University Press, 1994), 4–5, 18–19; and Meir Hatina, *Islam and Salvation in Palestine: The Islamic Jihad Movement* (Tel Aviv: Moshe Dayan Center for Middle Eastern and African Studes, 2001), 18–19.

12. Hroub, *Hamas*, 25–27; Abu-Amr, *Islamic Fundamentalism in the West Bank and Gaza*, 43.

13. Hroub, *Hamas*, 36–37; Shaul Mishal and Avraham Sela, *The Palestinian Hamas: Vision, Violence, and Coexistence*, 2nd ed. (New York: Columbia University Press, 2006), 36; and Abu-Amr, *Islamic Fundamentalism in the West Bank and Gaza*, 63–68.

14. Laetitia Bucaille, *Growing Up Palestinian: Israeli Occupation and the Intifada Generation* (Princeton, N.J.: Princeton University Press, 2004), 15–16.

15. Cited in Mishal and Sela, *Palestinian Hamas*, 51.

16. Eli Berman, *Radical, Religious, and Violent: The New Economics of Terrorism* (Cambridge. Mass.: MIT Press, 2009), 121–32; Hroub, *Hamas*, 60–64.

17. Azzam Tamimi, *Hamas: A History from Within* (Northampton, Mass.: Olive Branch Press, 2007), 43–44; Human Rights Watch, *Erased in a Moment:*

Suicide Bombing Attacks against Israeli Civilians (New York, 2002), 71–77; Hroub, *Hamas*, 78, 87; also see Matthew Levitt, *Hamas: Politics, Charity, and Terrorism in the Service of Jihad* (New Haven, Conn.: Yale University Press, 2006), 25–26.

18. Bernard Wasserstein, *Divided Jerusalem: The Struggle for the Holy City*, 2nd ed. (New Haven, Conn.: Yale University Press, 2002), esp. 1–13; Jessica Stern, *Terror in the Name of God: Why Religious Militants Kill* (New York: Harper Collins, 2003), 85–106.

19. Wasserstein, *Divided Jerusalem*, 337; Morris, *Righteous Victims*, 584–85.

20. Mishal and Sela, *Palestinian Hamas*, 57.

21. Zaki Chehab, *Inside Hamas: The Untold Story of the Islamic Resistance Movement* (New York: Nation Books, 2007), 39–41; Abu-Amr, *Islamic Fundamentalism in the West Bank and Gaza*, 98; Ian S. Lustick, "Terrorism in the Arab-Israeli Conflict: Targets and Audiences," in *Terrorism in Context*, ed. Martha Crenshaw (University Park: Pennsylvania State University Press, 1995), 533–36.

22. Morris, *Righteous Victims*, 585.

23. Tamimi, *Hamas: A History from Within*, 64–66.

24. Levitt, *Hamas: Politics, Charity, and Terrorism*, 11; Chehab, *Inside Hamas*, 31–34.

25. Brynjar Lia, *A Police Force without a State: A History of the Palestinian Security Forces in the West Bank and Gaza* (Reading, U.K.: Ithaca Press, 2006), 58. Also see Anne Marie Oliver and Paul Steinberg, *The Road to Martyr's Square: A Journey into the World of the Suicide Bomber* (New York: Oxford University Press, 2005), 35, 95–96.

26. Cited in Lia, *Police Force without a State*, 59–68, 72. Also see the B'Tselem website, www.btselem.org/English/index.asp.

27. Jeroen Gunning, *Hamas in Politics: Democracy, Religion, Violence* (New York: Columbia University Press, 2008), 128.

28. Mishal and Sela, *Palestinian Hamas*, 67.

29. Joel Greenberg, "Mideast Accord: The Opposition: 4 Israelis and 3 Palestinians Killed in Guerilla Attacks," *New York Times*, September 13, 1993.

30. Clyde Haberman, "30 Israelis Hurt by Suicide Bomber," *New York Times*, October 5, 1993.

31. Mohammed M. Hafez, *Manufacturing Human Bombs: The Making of Palestinian Suicide Bombers* (Washington, D.C.: United States Institute of Peace Press, 2006), app. I, 79.

32. Hafez, *Manufacturing Human Bombs*, 18; Mishal and Sela, *Palestinian Hamas*, 65–6.

33. Hafez, *Manufacturing Human Bombs*, 19; Schweitzer, "Palestinian Istishhadia," 673.

34. Ami Pedahzur and Arie Perliger, *Jewish Terrorism in Israel* (New York: Columbia University Press, 2009), 69–77.

35. Clyde Haberman, "Israelis' Faith in Peace Is Put under Strain by Bombing and New Attack," *New York Times,* April 8, 1994; Clyde Haberman, "5 Killed in Israel as Second Bomber Blows Up a Bus," *New York Times,* April 14, 1994.

36. Clyde Haberman, "Attack in Israel: The Overview—20 Killed in Terrorist Bombing of Bus in Tel Aviv; 48 Are Hurt," *New York Times,* October 20, 1994; Clyde Haberman, " 'Living Martyr' Leaves Taped Statement," *New York Times,* October 21, 1994. According to Hafez, twenty-two people eventually died and forty-eight were injured. Hafez, *Manufacturing Human Bombs,* app. A, 79–86.

37. Ibid.

38. Clyde Haberman, "Palestinian Police Rounding up Radicals," *New York Times,* November 15, 1994.

39. Sara Roy, *Hamas and Civil Society in Gaza: Engaging the Islamist Social Sector* (Princeton, N.J.: Princeton University Press, 2011), 36.

40. Clyde Haberman, "Suicide Bombs Kill 19 in Israel; Shadow Cast over Peace Talks," *New York Times,* January 23, 1995.

41. Mishal and Sela, *Palestinian Hamas,* 72–73.

42. Hatina, *Islam and Salvation in Palestine,* 102.

43. Serge Schmemann, "Palestinian Believed to be Bombing Mastermind Is Killed," *New York Times,* January 6, 1996; also see Katz, *Hunt for the Engineer,* 241–70.

44. Serge Schmemann, "Killing of Bomb 'Engineer' Unites Palestinian Factions," *New York Times,* January 10, 1996.

45. Serge Schmemann, "Bombings in Israel: The Overview: 2 Suicide Bombings in Israel Kill 25 and Hurt 77, the Highest Such Toll," *New York Times,* February 26, 1996.

46. Andrew Kydd and Barbara Walter, "Sabotaging the Peace: The Politics of Extremist Violence," *International Organization* 56, no. 2 (Spring 2002): 263–96.

47. Quote from Chehab, *Inside Hamas,* 106; also see Gunning, *Hamas in Politics,* 207–20.

48. Hafez, *Manufacturing Human Bombs,* app. I, 79.

49. Mia Bloom, *Dying to Kill: The Allure of Suicide Terrorism* (New York: Columbia University Press, 2005), 25.

50. Robert A. Pape, *Dying to Win: The Strategic Logic of Suicide Terrorism* (New York: Random House, 2005), 50, table 8.

51. Everett M. Rogers, *Diffusion of Innovations,* 5th ed. (New York: Free Press, 2003), chap. 9, esp. 366.

52. Haberman, " 'Living Martyr' Leaves Taped Statement." See Chapter 6 on the importance of these tapes for sustaining and legitimizing suicide bombing.

53. Hafez, *Manufacturing Human Bombs*, 18; Haberman, "Attack in Israel."

54. David Cook, *Martyrdom in Islam* (Cambridge: Cambridge University Press, 2007), chap. 8; Iris Jean Klein, "Palestinian Militancy, Martyrdom, and Nationalist Communities in the West Bank during the Intifada," in *Martyrdom and Political Resistance Movements: Essays on Asia and Europe*, ed. Joyce Pettigrew (Amsterdam: VU University Press, 1997), 85–109.

55. Bucaille, *Growing Up Palestinian*, 22–23.

56. Oliver and Steinberg, *Road to Martyr's Square*, 60–81; Julie Peteet, "The Writing on the Walls: The Graffiti of the Intifada," *Cultural Anthropology* 11, no. 2 (1996): 139–59.

57. Hatina, *Islam and Salvation in Palestine*, 123–26.

58. Daphne Burdman, "Education, Indoctrination, and Incitement: Palestinian Children on Their Way to Martyrdom," *Terrorism and Political Violence* 15, no. 1 (2003), 96–123; Levitt, *Hamas: Politics, Charity, and Terrorism*, 105–42.

59. Levitt, *Hamas: Politics, Charity, and Terrorism*, 126–27.

60. Chehab, *Inside Hamas*, 43.

61. Bloom, *Dying to Kill*, 23.

62. Michael Horowitz argues that younger groups use suicide bombing because they are more open to technological innovation than are older, bureaucratically rigid organizations. I find this explanation implausible for numerous reasons. See Michael C. Horowitz, *The Diffusion of Military Power: Causes and Consequences for International Politics* (Princeton, N.J.: Princeton University Press, 2010), 166–207.

CHAPTER 6. MANAGING MARTYRDOM, PART II: PALESTINIAN SUICIDE BOMBING IN THE SECOND INTIFADA AND AFTER, 2000–2010

1. Joel Brinkley, "Bomb Kills At Least 19 in Israel as Arabs Meet over Peace Plan," *New York Times*, March 28, 2002; Matthew Levitt, *Hamas: Politics, Charity, and Terrorism in the Service of Jihad* (New Haven, Conn.: Yale University Press, 2006), 2–3.

2. Quoted in Brinkley, "Bomb Kills At Least 19"; also see Serge Schmemann, "Dire Day: Trying to See Beyond Sure Revenge," *New York Times*, March 28, 2008.

3. Benny Morris, *Righteous Victims: A History of the Zionist-Arab Conflict, 1881–2001* (New York: Vintage Books, 2001), 653.

4. Shlomo Ben-Ami, *Scars of War, Wounds of Peace: The Arab-Israeli Tragedy* (New York: Oxford University Press, 2006), 212–13. Also see Sari Nusseibeh, with Anthony David, *Once Upon a Country: A Palestinian Life* (New York: Farrar, Straus and Giroux, 2007), 393.

5. Laetitia Bucaille, *Growing Up Palestinian: Israeli Occupation and the Intifada Generation* (Princeton, N.J.: Princeton University Press, 2004), 70–71; Nusseibeh, *Once Upon a Country*, 402–7.

6. Said K. Aburish, *Arafat: From Defender to Dictator*, rev. ed. (New York: Bloomsbury, 2004), 276–80; Farhad Khosrokhavar, *Suicide Bombers: Allah's New Martyrs*, trans. David Macey (Ann Arbor, Mich.: Pluto Press, 2005), 123.

7. Morris, *Righteous Victims*, 658–59; also see Benny Morris, "Camp David and After: An Exchange. (1. An Interview with Ehud Barak)," *New York Review of Books*, June 13, 2002.

8. According to Shlomo Ben-Ami, when he met with Arafat in summer 2000, Arafat spoke admiringly of Hizballah, referring to its members as his disciples. Ben-Ami, *Scars of War, Wounds of Peace*, 265.

9. Ami Pedahzur and Arie Perliger, *Jewish Terrorism in Israel* (New York: Columbia University Press, 2009), 39.

10. Gilles Kepel, *The War for Muslim Minds: Islam and the West*, trans. Pascale Ghazaleh (Cambridge, Mass.: Harvard University Press, 2004), 14–15.

11. During the scuffle, Sheikh Faisal, the highest-ranking religious official of the al-Aqsa mosque, lost his turban, a symbol of his religious status. Palestinian clerics perceived this indignity to be a deliberate insult, contributing to the heightened tensions.

12. Nusseibeh, *Once Upon a Country*, 432–35. Controversy later arose over whether al-Dura had actually been shot or whether the events filmed were staged. See James Fallows, "Who Shot Muhammad al-Dura?" *Atlantic Monthly*, June 2003, www.theatlantic.com/magazine/archive/2003/06/who-shot-mohammed-al-dura/2735.

13. Isabel Kershner, *Barrier: The Seam of the Israeli-Palestinian Conflict* (New York: Palgrave MacMillan, 2005), 89; Morris, *Righteous Victims*, 665.

14. This is Barak's interpretation of Arafat's behavior. Dennis Ross, *The Missing Peace: The Inside Story of the Fight for Middle East Peace* (New York: Farrar, Straus Giroux, 2004), 730, and Morris, "Camp David and After."

15. Human Rights Watch, *Erased in a Moment: Suicide Bombing Attacks against Israeli Civilians* (New York, 2002), 114–15, 139–40.

16. Shaul Mishal and Avraham Sela, *The Palestinian Hamas: Vision, Violence, and Coexistence*, 2nd ed. (New York: Columbia University Press, 2006), xiv.

17. There is still significant variation among leading studies of suicide bombing by Palestinians as to how many attacks were carried out and by which groups during this time period. See Mohammad M. Hafez, *Manufacturing Human Bombs: The Making of Palestinian Suicide Bombers* (Washington, D.C.: United States Institute of Peace Press, 2006), 80–81; Ami Pedahzur, *Suicide Terrorism* (Cambridge, U.K., and Malden, Mass.: Polity Press, 2005), 245; Robert A. Pape, *Dying to Win: The Strategic Logic of Suicide Terrorism* (New York: Random House, 2005), 260; and Human Rights Watch, *Erased in a Moment*, 141–12.

18. Gal Luft, "The Palestinian H-Bomb: Terror's Winning Strategy," *Foreign Affairs* 81, no. 4 (July/August 2002): 3.

19. Joel Greenberg, "Immigrants Bury Their Friends, but Hopes Live On," *New York Times*, June 4, 2001.

20. Kershner, *Barrier*, 2.

21. Hafez, *Manufacturing Human Bombs*, chart 2, p. 20.

22. Avi Jorisch, *Beacon of Hatred: Inside Hizballah's Al Manar Television* (Washington, D.C.: Washington Institute for Near East Policy, 2004); Mia Bloom, *Dying to Kill: The Allure of Suicide Terror* (New York: Columbia University Press, 2005), 28–30.

23. Ariel Merari et al., "Making Palestinian 'Martyrdom Operations' / 'Suicide Attacks': Interviews with Would-Be Perpetrators and Organizers," *Terrorism and Political Violence* 22, no. 1 (2010): 105.

24. Human Rights Watch, *Erased in a Moment*, 79–87.

25. Yoram Schweitzer, "Palestinian *Istishhadia*: A Developing Instrument," *Studies in Conflict and Terrorism* 30, no. 8 (2007): 680–83. Also see Bader Araj, "Harsh State Repression as a Cause of Suicide Bombing: The Case of the Palestinian Israeli Conflict," *Studies in Conflict and Terrorism* 31, no. 4 (2008): 295.

26. Details on Wafa Idris' attack are from Barbara Victor, *Army of Roses: Inside the World of Palestinian Women Suicide Bombers* (New York: Rodale, 2003), 19–27. Victor is unclear on whether the attack was an accident, while Yoram Schweitzer asserts that Idris' death was unplanned. Yoram Schweitzer, "Palestinian Female Suicide Bombers: Reality vs. Myth," in *Female Suicide Bombers: Dying for Equality?* ed. Yoram Schweitzer (Tel Aviv: Jaffee Center for Strategic Studies, 2006), 25.

27. Victor, *Army of Roses*, 19–20.

28. Rivka Yadin, "Female Martyrdom: The Ultimate Embodiment of Islamic Existence?" in Schweitzer, *Female Suicide Bombers*, 60 n. 7.

29. Bloom, *Dying to Kill*, 144; also see Avi Issacharoff, "The Palestinian and Israeli Media on Female Suicide Terrorists," in Schweitzer, *Female Suicide Bombers*, 43–50.

30. It was not until 1996 that conservative, non-extremist Sunni clerics issued fatwas in support of suicide missions against Israeli targets. Gilles Kepel, *Beyond Terror and Martyrdom: The Future of the Middle East*, trans. Pascale Ghazaleh (Cambridge, Mass.: Harvard University Press, 2008), 93–94.

31. Yassin later explained this inconsistency by saying that he had initially been misquoted. Zaki Chehab, *Inside Hamas: The Untold Story of the Islamic Resistance Movement* (New York: Nation Books, 2007), 88–89.

32. Victor, *Army of Roses*, 96–97, 110–13; Bloom, *Dying to Kill*, 147–53, Yassin quote from 151. The first female Hamas suicide bomber, Reem al-Riashi, killed herself at an Israeli checkpoint on January 14, 2004, killing four Israelis.

Justin Huggler, " 'God Gave Me Two Children and I Loved Them So Much'; The Suicide Message of a Mother Who Left Home To Kill," *Independent*, January 15, 2004.

33. Schweitzer, "Palestinian Female Suicide Bombers," 26.

34. Issacharoff, "Palestinian and Israeli Media."

35. Karen Jacques and Paul L. Taylor, "Male and Female Suicide Bombers: Different Sexes, Different Reasons?" *Studies in Conflict and Terrorism* 31, no. 4 (2008): esp. 315–16.

36. Victor, *Army of Roses*, 233–34; Bloom, *Dying to Kill*, 164; Schweitzer, "Palestinian Female Suicide Bombers," 40.

37. Hafez, *Manufacturing Human Bombs*, 54–55.

38. Hafez, *Manufacturing Human Bombs*, 58; Ben-Ami, *Scars of War, Wounds of Peace*, 267.

39. Nusseibeh, *Once Upon a Country*, 479; also see Araj, "Harsh State Repression," 290, 294–96.

40. Bloom, *Dying to Kill*, 23.

41. Kershner, *Barrier*, 136–40.

42. Ariel Merari, *Driven to Death: Psychological and Social Aspects of Suicide Terrorism* (New York: Oxford University Press, 2010), 39–42.

43. Ibid., 40; Scott Atran, *Talking to the Enemy: Faith, Brotherhood, and the (Un) Making of Terrorists* (New York: HarperCollins, 2010), 362.

44. Steven Erlanger, "Israeli and Palestinian Leaders Pledge to Halt Attacks," *New York Times*, February 8, 2005.

45. Greg Myre, "Bomber Kills 3 Israelis as Hamas Takes Power," *New York Times*, March 31, 2006.

46. By one estimate, as many as a thousand rocket attacks took place between 2001 and 2006, with the pace of attacks increasing in 2006. Ben Wedeman, "Reporter's Dangerous Trip To Secret Rocket Factory," CNN.com, June 1, 2006; also see Tony Karon, "The Homemade Rocket That Could Change the Mideast," *Time*, February 11, 2002.

47. Robin Wright, *Dreams and Shadows: The Future of the Middle East* (New York: Penguin, 2008), 59–63.

48. Human Rights Watch, *Deprived and Endangered: Humanitarian Crisis in the Gaza Strip* (New York, January 2009).

49. BBC News Online, "Just Married and Determined to Die," October 13, 2008.

50. Abdul Hameed Bakier, "Gaza's 'Ghost' Suicide Bombers—More Rhetoric than Threat?" *Terrorism Focus*, January 21, 2009.

51. Jack Khoury, " 'Watch Your Step,' Barak Warns Hamas Over Renewed Gaza Rocket Fire," www.miftah.org, January 12, 2010.

52. Daniel Byman, "How to Handle Hamas," *Foreign Affairs* 89, no. 5 (September/October 2010): 56.

53. Merari, *Driven to Death*, 261; also see Assaf Moghadam, "Palestinian Suicide Terrorism in the Second Intifada: Motivations and Organizational Aspects," *Studies in Conflict and Terrorism* 26, no. 2 (March 2003): 65–92; Assaf Moghadam, "Roots of Suicide Terrorism: A Multi-causal Approach," in *Root Causes of Suicide Terrorism: The Globalization of Martyrdom*, ed. Ami Pedahzur (New York: Routledge, 2006), 81–107; Ami Pedahzur and Arie Perliger, "The Changing Nature of Suicide Attacks: A Social Network Perspective," *Social Forces* 94, no. 4 (June 2006); and Mohammed M. Hafez, *Suicide Bombers in Iraq: The Strategy and Ideology of Martyrdom* (Washington, D.C.: United States Institute of Peace Press, 2007), 16.

54. Max Taylor and John Horgan, "A Conceptual Framework for Addressing Psychological Process in the Development of the Terrorist," *Terrorism and Political Violence* 18, no. 4 (2006): esp. 591.

55. Hafez, *Manufacturing Human Bombs*, 25.

56. Anat Berko, *The Path to Paradise: The Inner World of Suicide Bombers and Their Dispatchers*, trans. Elizabeth Yuval (Westport, Conn.: Praeger Security International, 2007), 27, 29, 34, 110; Merari, *Driven to Death*, 151–53, 171.

57. Ami Pedahzur, Arie Perliger, and Leonard Weinberg, "Altruism and Fatalism: The Characteristics of Palestinian Suicide Terrorists," *Deviant Behavior* 24, no. 4 (2003): 405–23; also see Jacques and Taylor, "Male and Female Suicide Bombers," 321.

58. Levitt, *Hamas: Politics, Charity, and Terrorism*, 59–60; Merari, *Driven to Death*, 112–19.

59. Merari, *Driven to Death*, 112–19.

60. Pedahzur, Perliger, and Weinberg, "Altruism and Fatalism," 420.

61. Israel Orbach, "Terror Suicide: How Is It Possible?" *Archives of Suicide Research* 8, no. 1 (2004): 118.

62. Anne Marie Oliver and Paul Steinberg, *The Road to Martyr's Square: A Journey into the World of the Suicide Bomber* (New York: Oxford University Press, 2005), 75.

63. Christoph Reuter, *My Life Is a Weapon: A Modern History of Suicide Bombing*, trans. Helena Ragg-Kirkby (New Haven: Yale University Press, 2004), 128.

64. Raphael Israeli, "Islamikaze and Their Significance," *Terrorism and Political Violence* 9, no. 3 (1997): 105.

65. Ariel Merari, "The Readiness To Kill and Die: Suicidal Terrorism in the Middle East," in *Origins of Terrorism: Psychologies, Ideologies, Theologies, States of Mind*, ed. Walter Reich (Washington, D.C.: Woodrow Wilson Center Press, 1990), 195.

66. Merari, *Driven to Death*, 163.

67. Atran, *Talking to the Enemy*, 27, 222–23.

68. Nasra Hassan, "An Arsenal of Believers: Talking to the 'Human Bombs,' " *New Yorker*, November 19, 2001.

69. Taylor and Horgan, "A Conceptual Framework," 594.

70. Oliver and Steinberg, *Road to Martyr's Square*, 130–31, 153–54. Merari cautions that the impact of the tapes in this respect should not be overstated, because he found that many of the bombers who voluntarily abandoned their missions did so even after they had recorded their testimonial. Merari, *Driven to Death*, 168–69.

71. This is particularly noteworthy because Merari's research shows that most Palestinian suicide attackers did not display many of the characteristics of predisposed individuals more generally. Merari, *Driven to Death*, 218–21.

72. Thomas Joiner, *Why People Die by Suicide* (Cambridge, Mass.: Harvard University Press, 2005), 49–58, quote from 81–82.

73. David P. Phillips, "The Influence of Suggestion on Suicide: Substantive and Theoretical Implications of the Werther Effect," *American Sociological Review* 39, no. 3 (1974), 340–54; Nicholas A. Christakis and James H. Fowler, *Connected: The Surprising Power of Our Social Networks and How They Shape Our Lives* (New York: Little, Brown, and Company, 2009), 121–29.

74. Elmar Etzersdorfer and Gernot Sonneck, "Preventing Suicide by Influencing Mass-Media Reporting. The Viennese Experience, 1980–1996," *Archives of Suicide Research* 4, no. 1 (1998): 67–74.

75. Graham Martin, "Media Influence to Suicide: The Search for Solutions," *Archives of Suicide Research* 4, no. 4 (1998): 59.

76. Phillips, "Werther Effect," 351–52.

77. Quoted in Hafez, *Manufacturing Human Bombs*, 26.

78. Merari, *Driven to Death*, 99–100; Atran, *Talking to the Enemy*, 407.

79. Reuter, *My Life Is a Weapon*, 72.

80. Chehab, *Inside Hamas*, 93–97, quote from 96.

81. Merari, *Driven to Death*, 101.

82. Quote from Azzam Tamini, *Hamas: A History from Within* (Northampton, Mass.: Olive Branch Press, 2007), 180–81; also see Meir Hatina, *Islam and Salvation in Palestine: The Islamic Jihad Movement* (Tel Aviv: Moshe Dayan Center for Middle Eastern and African Studies, 2001), 119.

83. Merari, *Driven to Death*, 163–64, 156.

84. Hafez, *Manufacturing Human Bombs*, 33–45, quote from 33.

85. Merari, *Driven to Death*, 133, 145.

CHAPTER 7. GLOBALIZED MARTYRDOM: THE JIHADI MOVEMENT AND SUICIDE BOMBING AFTER 9/11

1. Dexter Filkins and Richard A. Oppel Jr., "Top Aid Officials Are Among 17 Killed," *New York Times*, August 19, 2003; George Packer, *The Assassins' Gate: America in Iraq* (New York: Farrar, Straus and Giroux, 2005), 217–18.

2. Jarrett Brachman, *Global Jihadism: Theory and Practice* (New York: Routledge, 2009), 5; Thomas Hegghammer, *Jihad in Saudi Arabia: Violence*

and Pan-Islamism since 1979 (New York: Cambridge University Press, 2010), 222–24; Nelly Lahoud, *The Jihadis' Path to Self-Destruction* (New York: Columbia University Press, 2010), 18–19.

3. Brian A. Jackson, "Groups, Networks, or Movements: A Command-and-Control Driven Approach to Classifying Terrorist Organizations and Its Application to Al Qaeda," *Studies in Conflict and Terrorism* 29, no. 3 (2006): esp. 253–56.

4. Lahoud, *Jihadis' Path*, xix, 97; Brachman, *Global Jihadism*, 12–14; Mohammed M. Hafez, *Suicide Bombers in Iraq: The Strategy and Ideology of Martyrdom* (Washington, D.C.: United States Institute of Peace Press, 2007); Ami Pedahzur and Arie Perliger, "The Changing Nature of Suicide Attacks: A Social Network Perspective," *Social Forces* 94, no. 4 (June 2006): 1,987–2,008.

5. Sayyid Qutb, *Milestones* (New Delhi: Millat Book Centre, n.d.); for context, see John Calvert, *Sayyid Qutb and the Origins of Radical Islamism* (New York: Columbia University Press, 2010), 189–95 and 197–227.

6. David C. Rapoport, "Sacred Terror: A Contemporary Example from Islam," in *Origins of Terrorism: Psychologies, Ideologies, Theologies, States of Mind*, ed. Walter Reich (Washington, D.C.: Woodrow Wilson Center Press, 1998), 103–30; Jean-Pierre Filiu, "The Brotherhood vs. Al Qaeda: A Moment of Truth?" *Current Trends in Islamist Ideology* 9 (2009): 18–25; Lahoud, *Jihadis' Path*, 120–27.

7. Thomas Hegghammer, "Abdallah Azzam: The Imam of Jihad," in *Al Qaeda in Its Own Words*, ed. Gilles Kepel and Jean-Pierre Milelli, trans. Pascale Ghazaleh (Cambridge Mass.: Harvard University Press, 2008), 81–101, esp. 98–101; Lahoud, *Jihadis' Path*, 127–31.

8. See excerpts from Azzam's "Join the Caravan," 119, and "Morals and Jurisprudence of Jihad," 132–35, in Kepel and Milelli, *Al Qaeda in Its Own Words*.

9. Lawrence Wright, *The Looming Tower: Al Qaeda and the Road to 9/11* (New York: Alfred A. Knopf, 2006), 99–120; Hegghammer, *Jihad in Saudi Arabia*, 38–48.

10. Olivier Roy, *Globalized Islam: The Search for a New Ummah* (New York: Columbia University Press, 2004), 24–25.

11. Wright, *Looming Tower*, 121–44.

12. Quote from Kepel and Milelli, *Al Qaeda in Its Own Words*, 49; also see Assaf Moghadam, *The Globalization of Martyrdom: Al Qaeda, Salafi Jihad, and the Diffusion of Suicide Attacks* (Baltimore: Johns Hopkins University Press, 2008), 80–83.

13. Roy, *Globalized Islam*, 10–11, 165.

14. Daniel Benjamin and Steve Simon, *The Next Attack: The Failure of the War on Terror and a Strategy for Getting It Right* (New York: Times Books, 2005), 56.

15. Hegghammer, *Jihad in Saudi Arabia*, 28.

16. Yoram Schweitzer and Sari Goldstein Ferber, "Al-Qaeda and the Internationalization of Suicide Terrorism," Memorandum no. 78, Jaffee Center for Strategic Studies, Tel Aviv University, November 2005, 26, quote from 33.

17. Marc Sageman, *Leaderless Jihad: Terror Networks in the Twenty-First Century* (Philadelphia: University of Pennsylvania Press, 2008), 42; Rohan Gunaratna, *Inside Al Qaeda: Global Network of Terror* (New York: Columbia University Press, 2002), 195–98.

18. Joshua Teitelbaum, *Holier Than Thou: Saudi Arabia's Islamic Opposition* (Washington, D.C.: Washington Institute for Near East Policy, 2000), 73–77.

19. For the Egyptian embassy bombing, see Wright, *Looming Tower*, 217–18, and Zawahiri's own discussion of the attack, Ayman al Zawahiri, *His Own Words: Translation and Analysis of the Writings of Dr. Ayman al Zawahiri*, trans. Laura Mansfield (n.p.: TLG Publications, 2006), 43–45.

20. Brigitte L. Nacos, *Mass Mediated Terrorism: The Central Role of the Media in Terrorism and Counterterrorism* (New York: Rowman and Littlefield, 2002), 49–50; Louise Richardson, *What Terrorists Want: Understanding the Enemy, Containing the Threat* (New York: Random House, 2006), 77; Wright, *Looming Tower*, 246.

21. Albert Bandura, "Mechanisms of Moral Disengagement," in Reich, *Origins of Terrorism*, 164.

22. For general background to the conflict, see Norman M. Naimark, *Fires of Hatred: Ethnic Cleansing in Twentieth-Century Europe* (Cambridge, Mass.: Harvard University Press, 2001), chap. 3, and John B. Dunlop, *Russia Confronts Chechnya: Roots of a Separatist Conflict* (Cambridge: Cambridge University Press, 1998).

23. Gordon M. Hahn, *Russia's Islamic Threat* (New Haven, Conn.: Yale University Press, 2007), 36–54; James Hughes, *Chechnya: From Nationalism to Jihad* (Philadelphia: University of Pennsylvania Press, 2007), 97–107; Matthew Evangelista, *The Chechen Wars: Will Russia Go the Way of the Soviet Union?* (Washington, D.C.: Brookings Institution Press, 2002), 71–73.

24. Moshe Gammer, *The Lone Wolf and the Bear: Three Centuries of Chechen Defiance of Russian Rule* (Pittsburgh: University of Pittsburgh Press, 2006), 210; Hughes, *Chechnya*, 125.

25. Anna Politkovskaya, *A Small Corner of Hell: Dispatches from Chechnya*, trans. Alexander Burry and Tatiana Tulchinsky (Chicago: University of Chicago Press, 2003), 81–82.

26. Quoted in Hughes, *Chechnya*, 155.

27. Anne Speckhard and Khapta Ahkmedova, "The Making of a Martyr: Chechen Suicide Terrorism," *Studies in Conflict and Terrorism* 29, no. 5 (2006): 451–52, 484–86.

28. Hahn, *Russia's Islamic Threat*, 40–41, 49–54.

29. Speckhard and Ahkmedova, "Making of a Martyr," 431.

30. Steven Lee Myers, "Russians Find Explosives on Second Plane," *New York Times,* August 29, 2004.

31. Steven Lee Myers, "Suicide Bomber Kills 9 at Moscow Subway Station," *New York Times,* September 1, 2004.

32. Alexander Knysh, "The Caucasus Emirate: Between Reality and Virtuality," Keyman Program in Turkish Studies Working Paper Series Working Paper no. 09–001, Northwestern University, June 2009.

33. Center for Strategic and International Studies, Human Rights and Security Initiative, "Violence in the North Caucasus: 2009: A Bloody Year," January 2010.

34. Steven Lee Myers, "From Dismal Chechnya, Women Turn to Bombs," *New York Times,* September 10, 2004; Anne Nivat, "The Black Widows: Chechen Women Join the Fight for Independence—and Allah," *Studies in Conflict and Terrorism* 28, no. 5 (2005): 413–19.

35. Scott Atran, *Talking to the Enemy: Faith, Brotherhood, and the (Un) Making of Terrorists* (New York: HarperCollins, 2010), 138–49; Moghadam, *Globalization of Martyrdom,* 168–70.

36. Worldwide Incidents Tracking System, National Counterterrorism Center, wits.nctc.gov (accessed December 12, 2010).

37. Atran, *Talking to the Enemy,* 155–67.

38. Brachman, *Global Jihadism,* 17–19; Moghadam, *Globalization of Martyrdom,* 189–91.

39. Jack Kalpakian, "Building the Human Bomb: The Case of the 16 May 2003 Attacks in Casablanca," *Studies in Conflict and Terrorism* 28, no. 2 (2005): 113–27; Rogelio Alonso and Fernando Reinares, "Maghreb Immigrants Becoming Suicide Terrorists," in *Root Causes of Suicide Terrorism: The Globalization of Martyrdom,* ed. Ami Pedahzur (New York: Routledge, 2006), 179–97; Rogelio Alonso and Marcos Garcia Rey, "The Evolution of Jihadist Terrorism in Morocco," *Terrorism and Political Violence* 19, no. 4 (2007): 571–92.

40. Alonso and Rey, "Evolution of Jihadist Terrorism in Morocco," 474–75.

41. Kalpakian, "Building the Human Bomb," 115–16.

42. Craig Whitlock, "Suicide Bombers Strike N. Africa Again," *Washington Post,* April 15, 2007; Ian Fisher, "Bombings Leave Moroccans Both Worried and Confused," *New York Times,* April 21, 2007.

43. Joseph Felter and Brian Fishman, "Becoming a Foreign Fighter: A *Second* Look at the Sinjar Records," in *Bombers, Bleedout, and Bank Accounts: Al-Qa'ida's Road in and out of Iraq,* ed. Brian Fishman (West Point, N.Y.: Combating Terrorism Center, 2008), 35, 56.

44. Kalpakian, "Building the Human Bomb, 118–23; Javier Jordan and Fernando M. Mañas, "Strengths and Weaknesses of Grassroot Jihadist Networks: The Madrid Bombings," *Studies in Conflict and Terrorism* 31, no. 1 (2008): 25; Atran, *Talking to the Enemy,* 195–210.

45. Craig Whitlock, "Odyssey of an Al Qaeda Operative," *Washington Post*, May 2, 2005; Craig Whitlock, "In Morocco's 'Chemist,' A Glimpse of Al Qaeda," *Washington Post*, July 7, 2007; Moghadam, *Globalization of Martyrdom*, 177.

46. Alison Pargeter, *The New Frontiers of Jihad: Radical Islam in Europe* (Philadelphia: University of Pennsylvania Press, 2008), 115–39, 175–79; Atran, *Talking to the Enemy*, 173–94.

47. Thomas Hegghammer, "Deconstructing the Myth about al-Qaʿida and Khobar," *CTC Sentinel* 1, no. 3 (February 2008): 20–22.

48. Hegghammer, *Jihad in Saudi Arabia*, 152–77.

49. Douglas Jehl and David Johnston, "U.S. and Saudis Sensed Attacks Were Imminent," *New York Times*, May 14, 2003.

50. Steven R. Weisman, "Toll in Saudi Arabia Rises to at Least 20, U.S. Official Says," *New York Times*, May 13, 2003; Neil MacFarquhar, "Saudis Link 4 in Bomb Plot to Qaeda Cell," *New York Times*, May 19, 2003.

51. Neil MacFarquhar, "Four Killed and 148 Wounded in a Suicide Bombing in Riyadh," *New York Times*, April 22, 2004.

52. Christopher Boucek, "Saudi Security and the Islamist Insurgency," *Terrorism Monitor*, January 26, 2006.

53. Thomas Hegghammer, "Terrorist Recruitment and Radicalization in Saudi Arabia," *Middle East Policy* 13, no. 4 (2006): 39–60; Hegghammer, *Jihad in Saudi Arabia*, chap. 9.

54. Christopher Boucek, "Extremist Re-education and Rehabilitation in Saudi Arabia," in *Leaving Terrorism Behind: Individual and Collective Disengagement*, ed. Tore Bjørgo and John Horgan (London: Routledge, 2009), 212–23.

55. Hegghammer, *Jihad in Saudi Arabia*, 217–23.

56. Murad Batal al-Shishani, "An Assessment of the Anatomy of al-Qaeda in Yemen: Ideological and Social Factors," *Terrorism Monitor*, March 5, 2010, 6–8.

57. BBC News Online, "Profile: Al-Qaeda in the Arabian Peninsula," January 4, 2010; Dominic Kennedy, "Abdulmutallab's Bomb Plans Began with Classroom Defence of 9/11," *Times* (London), December 28, 2009.

58. Sam Dagher, "2 Blasts Expose Security Flaws in the Heart of Iraq," *New York Times*, August 20, 2009.

59. Worldwide Incidents Tracking System, National Counterterrorism Center, wits.nctc.gov (accessed November 12, 2009).

60. Hafez, *Suicide Bombers in Iraq*, 94.

61. Associated Press, Brian Murphy, "106 Shiite Pilgrims Killed by Bombers; Nine U.S. Soldiers Slain on Monday, Military Announces," March 7, 2007.

62. John Ward Anderson and Salih Dehima, "Offensive Targets Al Qaeda in Iraq," *Washington Post*, June 20, 2007.

63. Stephen Farrell, "Around 150, Death Toll in Iraq among War's Worst," *New York Times*, July 9, 2007; Damien Cave and James Glanz, "Toll Rises above 500 in Iraq Bombings," *New York Times*, August 22, 2007.

64. Hafez, *Suicide Bombers in Iraq*, 104.

65. Thomas E. Ricks, *Fiasco: The American Military Adventure in Iraq* (New York: Penguin Press, 2006), 145–46.

66. Violence was an integral instrument in holding Iraq's fragmented national community together during the relatively brief history of the state. Charles Tripp, *A History of Iraq* (Cambridge: Cambridge University Press, 2000), 6–7.

67. Nir Rosen, *In the Belly of the Green Bird: The Triumph of the Martyrs in Iraq* (New York: Free Press, 2006), 1; for Kurdish autonomy in the aftermath of the American invasion, see Peter W. Galbraith, *The End of Iraq: How American Incompetence Created a War without End* (New York: Simon and Schuster, 2006), 158–71.

68. Hafez, *Suicide Bombers in Iraq*, 35–56.

69. Ahmed S. Hashim, *Insurgency and Counter-Insurgency in Iraq* (Ithaca, N.Y.: Cornell University Press, 2006), 131.

70. Joseph Felter and Brian Fishman, *Al-Qa'ida's Foreign Fighters in Iraq: A First Look at the Sinjar Records* (West Point, N.Y.: Combating Terrorism Center, 2007), 6.

71. David Kilcullen, *The Accidental Guerilla: Fighting Small Wars in the Midst of a Big One* (New York: Oxford University Press, 2009), basic idea of the "accidental guerilla," 28–38, and application to Iraq, 127–28.

72. James William Gibson, *The Perfect War: Technowar in Vietnam*, 2nd ed. (New York: Atlantic Monthly Press, 2000), 322–41.

73. Martin van Crevald, *Technology and War: From 2000 B.C. to the Present*, rev. ed. (New York: Free Press, 1991), 70–72.

74. Patrick Cockburn, *Muqtada al-Sadr and the Battle for the Future of Iraq* (New York: Scribner, 2008), 136.

75. Kilcullen, *Accidental Guerilla*, 127.

76. Brian Fishman, *Dysfunction and Decline: Lessons Learned from Inside Al-Qa'ida in Iraq* (West Point, N.Y.: Combating Terrorism Center, 2009), 2.

77. Jean-Charles Brisard, with Damien Martinez, *Zarqawi: The New Face of Al-Qaeda* (New York: Other Press, 2005), 12–13, 24–25, 30, 44, 56–57, 88; Bruce Riedel, *The Search for Al Qaeda: Its Leadership, Ideology, and Future* (Washington, D.C.: Brookings Institute Press, 2008), 85–115.

78. Brisard, *Zarqawi*, 150–51, 203.

79. Riedel, *Search for al Qaeda*, 101.

80. Richard A. Oppel Jr., "Foreign Fighters in Iraq Are Tied to Allies of U.S.," *New York Times*, November 22, 2007; Felter and Fishman, "Becoming a Foreign Fighter."

81. Felter and Fishman, *Al-Qa'ida's Foreign Fighters in Iraq*, 7–9, 16–18; Felter and Fishman, "Becoming a Foreign Fighter," 58. For detail on one particularly striking case, see Dexter Filkins, *The Forever War* (New York: Alfred A. Knopf, 2008), 175–78.

82. Quoted in Hafez, *Suicide Bombers in Iraq*, 75–76 and 78.

83. Zawahiri, *His Own Words*, 250–79, esp. 258–60; see discussion in Riedel, *Search for Al Qaeda*, 104–5.

84. James J. F. Forest, Jarret Brachman, and Joseph Felter, eds., *Harmony and Disharmony: Exploiting al-Qa'ida's Organizational Vulnerabilities* (West Point, N.Y.: Combating Terrorism Center, 2006), 34–36.

85. Robin Wright, *Dreams and Shadows: The Future of the Middle East* (New York: Penguin, 2008), 5.

86. BBC News Online, "Zarqawi 'Replaced as Unrest Head,' " March 4, 2006.

87. Felter and Fishman, *Al-Qa'ida's Foreign Fighters in Iraq*, 5–6; Fishman, *Dysfunction and Decline*, 4.

88. Kilcullen, *Accidental Guerilla*, 171–83; Fishman, *Dysfunction and Decline*, 10.

89. Letter from Zawahiri to Zarqawi, October 11, 2005, in Zawahiri, *His Own Words*, quote from 273, also see 259, 261–63.

90. Steven R. Hurst, "2 Mentally Disabled Women Blown Up," Associated Press, February 2, 2008.

91. Ernesto Londoño, "Al Qaeda in Iraq Regaining Strength," *Washington Post*, November 22, 2009.

92. Timothy Williams, "Bombings in Iraq, Deadliest Since 2007, Raise Security Issue," *New York Times*, October 26, 2009.

93. Londoño, "Al Qaeda in Iraq Gaining Strength."

94. "Scores Die as Car Bombs Rock Baghdad," CNN.com, December 9, 2009; Steven Lee Myers and Marc Santora, "Election Date Set in Iraq as Bombs Kill Scores," *New York Times*, December 9, 2009.

95. Roger Hardy, "Iraq: The Violence Returns," BBC News Online, December 11, 2009.

96. Everett M. Rogers, *Diffusion of Innovations*, 5th ed. (New York: Free Press, 2003), 389.

97. A jihadi in the Afghanistan-Pakistan region admitted that the sacrifice of the first few suicide attackers would make the recruitment of future attackers easier. Ahmed Rashid, *Descent into Chaos: The United States and the Failure of Nation Building in Pakistan, Afghanistan, and Central Asia* (New York: Viking, 2008), 366.

CHAPTER 8. THE BUSINESS OF MARTYRDOM

1. Jarret M. Brachman, *Global Jihadism: Theory and Practice* (New York: Routledge, 2009), 40.

2. Ralph Joseph, "40 Killed in Attack on Tribal Assembly," *Washington Times*, March 3, 2008.

3. Carlotta Gall, "Old Line Taliban Commander Is Face of Rising Threat," *New York Times*, June 17, 2008; Imtiaz Ali, "The Haqqani Network and Cross-Border Terrorism in Afghanistan," *Terrorism Monitor*, March 24, 2008.

4. Elizabeth Rubin, "In the Land of the Taliban," *New York Times Magazine*, October 22, 2006; Carlotta Gall and Ismail Khan, "Taliban and Allies Tighten Grip in North of Pakistan," *New York Times*, December 11, 2006.

5. BBC News Online, "Bomb Rocks India Embassy in Kabul," July 7, 2008; Abdul Waheed Wafa and Alan Cowell, "Suicide Car Blast Kills 41 in Afghan Capital," *New York Times*, July 8, 2008; for allegations of Pakistani complicity, see "Pointing a Finger at Islamabad," *Economist*, July 12, 2008, and Mark Mazzetti and Eric Schmitt, "Pakistanis Aided Attack in Kabul, U.S. Officials Say," *New York Times*, August 1, 2008.

6. Antonio Giustozzi, *Koran, Kalishnikov, and Laptop: The Neo-Taliban Insurgency in Afghanistan* (New York: Columbia University Press, 2008), 120–22, 138–39.

7. Gall, "Old Line Taliban Commander."

8. Steve Coll, *Ghost Wars: The Secret History of the CIA, Afghanistan, and bin Laden, from the Soviet Invasion to September 10, 2001* (New York: Penguin Press, 2004), 567–76.

9. Ahmed Rashid writes that in 1992 Maulvi Jamil-ur Rehman, a Saudi-backed warlord, was killed by a suicide attacker in Afghanistan. Ahmed Rashid, *Descent into Chaos: The United States and the Failure of Nation Building in Pakistan, Afghanistan, and Central Asia* (New York: Viking, 2008), 366.

10. Ibid, 133–35, 195, 218.

11. Peter Bergen and Katherine Tiedemann, "Does Killing Afghan Civilians Keep Us Safe?" *Los Angeles Times*, September 12, 2008.

12. Human Rights Watch, " 'Troops in Contact' Airstrikes and Civilian Deaths in Afghanistan," September 2008, 13–14; United Nations Assistance Mission to Afghanistan (UNAMA), Human Rights Unit, "Afghanistan: Annual Report on the Protection of Civilians in Armed Conflict, 2008," January 2009, 16; UNAMA, Human Rights Unit, "Afghanistan: Mid Year Bulletin on Protection of Civilians in Armed Conflict, 2009," July 2009, 10.

13. David Kilcullen, *The Accidental Guerilla: Fighting Small Wars in the Midst of a Big One* (New York: Oxford University Press, 2009), chap. 2; Tom Coghlan, "The Taliban in Helmand: An Oral History," in *Decoding the New Taliban: Insights from the Afghan Field*, ed. Antonio Giustozzi (New York: Columbia University Press, 2009), esp. 126.

14. Coghlan, "Taliban in Helmand," 142. Also see Kilcullen, *Accidental Guerilla*, 48–49.

15. Thomas Ruttig, "Loya Paktia's Insurgency: (I) The Haqqani Network as Autonomous Entity," in Giustozzi, *Decoding the New Taliban*, 57–100; David Rohde, "Inside the Islamic Emirate," *New York Times*, October 19, 2009.

16. Assaf Moghadam, *The Globalization of Martyrdom: Al Qaeda, Salafi Jihad, and the Diffusion of Suicide Attacks* (Baltimore: Johns Hopkins University Press, 2008), 133–41; Anne Stenersen, "Foreign Fighters in Afghanistan and Pakistan after 9/11" (paper presented at the conference "Understanding Jihadism: Origins, Evolution, and Future Perspectives," Oslo, March 19–21, 2009).

17. Claudio Franco, "The Tehrik-e Taliban in Pakistan," in Giustozzi, *Decoding the New Taliban*, 269–91; also see Mukhtar A. Khan, "Pakistan's Most Wanted: A Profile of Tehrik-e-Taliban Leader Baitullah Mahsud," *Terrorism Monitor*, April 24, 2009; Carlotta Gall, "Pakistan and Afghan Taliban Close Ranks," *New York Times*, March 27, 2009; and Imtiaz Gul, *The Most Dangerous Place: Pakistan's Lawless Frontier* (New York: Viking, 2010), 21–24, 38–42.

18. For the anti-technology stance of the original Taliban, see Ahmed Rashid, *Taliban: Militant Islam, Oil, and Fundamentalism in Central Asia* (New Haven, Conn.: Yale University Press, 2000), 115; for the development of communications capabilities by the Neo-Taliban, see Joanna Nathan, "Reading the New Taliban," in Giustozzi, *Decoding the New Taliban*, 23–42.

19. Brian Glyn Williams, "Mullah Omar's Missiles: A Field Report on Suicide Bombers in Afghanistan," *Middle East Policy* 15, no. 4 (Winter 2008): 30.

20. Ibid, 31–32.

21. Quotes from Rashid, *Descent into Chaos*, 366; Gul, *Most Dangerous Place*, 130.

22. Franco, "Tehrik-E Taliban in Pakistan," 283; Williams, "Mullah Omar's Missiles," 32–44.

23. United Nations Assistance Mission to Afghanistan (UNAMA), "Suicide Attacks in Afghanistan, 2001–2007," September 2007, 29, 95.

24. Ibid., 61; Williams, "Mullah Omar's Missiles," 35–36; Brian Glyn Williams, "The Taliban Fedayeen: The World's Worst Suicide Bombers?" *Terrorism Monitor*, July 19, 2007.

25. Williams, "Mullah Omar's Missiles," 38–39; UNAMA, "Suicide Attacks in Afghanistan," 75, 11, 50.

26. Williams, "Mullah Omar's Missiles," 40–41; Atia Abawi, "Teen Trained To Be Suicide Bomber Feels Tricked," CNN.com, January 2, 2009; Nic Robertson, "Pakistan: Taliban Buying Children for Suicide Attacks," CNN.com, July 7, 2009; for analysis of some of the literature used to indoctrinate and recruit children, see Qanteel Siddique, "Child Martyrs," www.jihadica.com, March 11, 2009.

27. Dexter Filkins, *The Forever War* (New York: Alfred A. Knopf, 2008), 17–18.

28. Rashid, *Descent into Chaos,* 374–79; for the bombing of the Marriott in Islamabad, see Asif Shahzad, "At Least 60 Die as Suicide Bombers Hit Pakistan Hotel," *Independent,* September 21, 2008.

29. Barnett R. Rubin, "Saving Afghanistan," *Foreign Affairs* 86, no. 1 (January/February 2007): 57–78; Rashid, *Descent into Chaos,* 29–33, 91–93, 147, 241; Bruce Riedel, *Deadly Embrace: Pakistan, America, and the Future of Global Jihad* (Washington, D.C.: Brookings Institution Press, 2011), 68–70.

30. Rohde, "Inside the Islamic Emirate."

31. Franco, "Tehrik-e Taliban in Pakistan"; Gul, *Most Dangerous Place,* 21–24, 185, 206–7.

32. BBC News Online, "Pakistani Soldiers Storm Mosque," July 10, 2007; Syed Shoaib Hasan, "Profile: Islamabad's Red Mosque," BBC News Online, July 27, 2007; Rashid, *Descent into Chaos,* 381–83.

33. Moghadam, *Globalization of Martyrdom,* 183.

34. Animesh Roul, "Terrorism's Trojan Horse: Vehicle-Borne Suicide Attacks Give Taliban Upper Hand in Pakistan," *Terrorism Monitor,* November 6, 2009, 6–8.

35. Dan Edge, "Children of the Taliban," *PBS Frontline,* August 14, 2009, quoted in Kalsoom Lakhani, "Indoctrinating Children: The Making of Pakistan's Suicide Bombers," *CTC Sentinel* 3, no. 6 (June 2010): 11–13.

36. BBC News, " 'Dozens Killed' in Algerian Blasts," December 11, 2007; Katrin Bennhold, "A Grandfather's Suicide Bombing Puzzles Algerians," *New York Times,* December 18, 2007; Katrin Bennhold, "Privation and Despair Colored an Algiers Bomber's Life," *New York Times,* December 14, 2007.

37. Martin Evans and John Phillips, *Algeria: Anger of the Dispossessed* (New Haven, Conn.: Yale University Press, 2007), xiv.

38. Camille Tawil, *Brothers in Arms: The Story of al-Qa'ida and the Arab Jihadists,* trans. Robin Bray (London: Saqi, 2010), 67–87.

39. Al Qaeda strategist Abu Musab al-Suri served as liaison to Algeria during the 1990s and also published a newsletter for the militants. Brynjar Lia, *Architect of Global Jihad: The Life of Al-Qaida Strategist Abu Mus'ab al-Suri* (New York: Columbia University Press, 2008), 126–27, 153; International Crisis Group, "Islamism, Violence, and Reform in Algeria: Turning the Page," ISG Middle East Report no. 29, Cairo/Brussels, July 30, 2004, esp. 10–17.

40. Michael Moss, "Ragtag Insurgency Gains a Lifeline from al Qaeda," *New York Times,* July 1, 2008; Kathryn Haahr, "GSPC Joins al-Qaeda and France Becomes Top Enemy," *Terrorism Focus,* September 26, 2006; Andrew Black, "The Reconstituted Al-Qaeda Threat in the Maghreb," *Terrorism Monitor,* February 21, 2007; Paul Cruickshank, "Al Qaida's Expanding Franchise," *Guardian,* December 12, 2007.

41. Jean-Pierre Filiu, "The Local and Global Jihad of al-Qa'ida in the Islamic Maghrib," *Middle East Journal* 63, no. 2 (Spring 2009): 221–23.

42. Craig Whitlock, "Suicide Attacks Mark Turn in Algeria," *Washington Post*, April 13, 2007; Andrew Black, "AQIM Employs Martyrdom Operations on Algeria," *Terrorism Focus*, September 20, 2007.

43. BBC News, "Deadly Bombings Hit Algerian Town," August 20, 2008.

44. Andrew Black, "The Ideological Struggle over al-Qaeda's Suicide Tactics in Algeria," *Terrorism Monitor*, February 11, 2008; Filiu, "Local and Global Jihad," 225.

45. Hanna Rogan, "Violent Trends in Algeria Since 9/11," *CTC Sentinel* 1, no. 12 (November 2008): 16–19; Worldwide Incidents Tracking System, National Counterterrorism Center, wits.nctc.gov (accessed August 3, 2010, and April 1, 2011).

46. BBC News Online, "Somalia Suicide Bombing Arrests," September 28, 2006; "8 Die in Suicide Attack in Somalia," *Los Angeles Times*, December 1, 2006.

47. David H. Shinn, "Somalia's New Government and the Challenge of Al-Shabab," *CTC Sentinel* 2, no. 3 (March 2009): 1–5; Leah Farrall, "How al Qaeda Works," *Foreign Affairs* 90, no. 2 (March/April 2011): 136–37.

48. Mohammad Ibrahim and Jeffrey Gettleman, "5 Suicide Bomb Attacks Hit Somalia," *New York Times*, October 30, 2008; Edmund Sanders, "Suicide Bomber Kills 11 Soldiers in Somalia," *Los Angeles Times*, February 23, 2009; Mohammad Ibrahim, "Somalia Fighting Kills at Least 15," *New York Times*, February, 25, 2009; Alisha Ryu, "Suicide Bombing in Somalia Raises Concerns about Foreign Support," VOAnews.com, May 26, 2009; Mohammad Ibrahim, "Somali Minister Killed in Bombing," *New York Times*, June 19, 2009; Andrew McGregor, "Suicide Bombing Kills Somali Security Minister as Islamists Mount Assault on Mogadishu," *Terrorism Monitor*, June 25, 2009; Reuters AlertNet, "Suicide Car Bombers Hit Main AU Base in Somalia," September 17, 2009; BBC News Online, "AU Urges More Weapons for Somalia," September 18, 2009.

49. BBC News Online, "Somali Ministers Killed by Bomb," December 3, 2009; Tim Pippard, "Al-Shabab's Agenda in the Wake of the Kampala Suicide Attacks," *CTC Sentinel* 3, no. 7 (July 2010): 4–6.

50. Christopher Anzalone, "From 'Martyrdom' Videos to *Jihadi* Journalism in Somalia: The Rapid Evolution of *Harakat al-Shabab al-Mujahideen*'s Multimedia," www.juancole.com, August 25, 2010.

51. David Axe and John Masato Ulmer, "Somali 'Travelers': The Holiest Gang," parts I and II, worldpoliticsreview.com; Raffaello Pantucci, "American Jihad: New Details Emerge about al-Shabaab Recruitment in North America," *Terrorism Monitor*, December 3, 2009; Jean-Pierre Filiu, "Eid News from the Shabab," www.jihadica.com, September 21, 2009.

52. Brachman, *Global Jihadism*, 178.

53. Alison Pargeter, *The New Frontiers of Jihad: Radical Islam in Europe* (Philadelphia: University of Pennsylvania Press, 2008), 140–52.

54. Gilles Kepel, *The War for Muslim Minds: Islam and the West,* trans. Pascale Ghazaleh (Cambridge, Mass.: Belknap Press, 2004), 242.

55. Brachman, *Global Jihadism,* 174–77.

56. Aidan Kirby, "The London Bombers as 'Self-Starters': A Case Study in Indigenous Radicalization and the Emergence of Autonomous Cliques," *Studies in Conflict and Terrorism* 30, no. 5 (2007): quote from 416.

57. Bruce Hoffman, "Radicalization and Subversion: Al Qaeda and the 7 July 2005 Bombings and the 2006 Airline Bombing Plot," *Studies in Conflict and Terrorism* 32, no. 12 (2009): esp. 1102; James Brandon, "Al-Qaʾidaʾs Involvement in Britain's 'Homegrown' Terrorist Plots," *CTC Sentinel* 2, no. 3 (March 2009): 10–12.

58. Hoffman, "Radicalization and Subversion," 1102–4.

59. Marc Sageman, *Understanding Terror Networks* (Philadelphia: University of Pennsylvania Press, 2004), esp. 139–51, and Marc Sageman, *Leaderless Jihad: Terror Networks in the Twenty-First Century* (Philadelphia: University of Pennsylvania Press, 2008), esp. 120–33, 145.

60. The ideas in this section were first explored in Jeffrey W. Lewis, "Precision Terror: Suicide Bombing as Control Technology," *Terrorism and Political Violence* 19, no. 2 (2007): 223–45.

61. Gregory J. E. Rawlins, *Slaves of the Machine: The Quickening of Computer Technology* (Cambridge, Mass.: MIT Press, 1997), 72.

62. G. J. Mulgan, *Communication and Control: Networks and the New Economies of Communication* (New York: Guilford Press, 1991), 4, 54; Peter McMahon, *Global Control: Information Technology and Globalization since 1845* (Northampton, Mass.: Edward Elgar, 2000), 2–4.

63. John W. Dower, *Embracing Defeat: Japan in the Wake of World War II* (New York: W. W. Norton and Company, 1999).

64. Mette Eilstrup-Sangiovanni and Calvert Jones, "Assessing the Dangers of Illicit Networks: Why al-Qaeda May Be Less Threatening Than Many Think," *International Security* 33, no. 2 (Fall 2008): 12–13. For a different interpretation, see Jonathan Kennedy and Gabriel Weimann, "The Strength of Weak Terrorist Ties," *Terrorism and Political Violence* 23, no. 2 (2011): 201–12.

65. Jessica Stern, *Terror in the Name of God: Why Religious Militants Kill* (New York: Harper Collins, 2003), 147–71.

66. For an introduction, see Ilya Prigogine with Isabelle Stengers, *Order Out of Chaos: Man's New Dialogue with Nature* (New York: Bantam, 1984), esp. 13–18, 140–53.

67. Steven Johnson, *Emergence: The Connected Lives of Ants, Brains, Cities and Software* (New York: Scribner, 2004), esp. 18–21; Stuart Kaufmann, *At Home in the Universe: The Search for the Laws of Self-Organization and Complexity* (New York: Oxford University Press, 1995), esp. 71–93; for the application of emergence specifically to militant groups, see John Robb,

Brave New War: The Next Stage of Terrorism and the End of Globalization (Hoboken, N.J.: John Wiley and Sons, 2007), 125–27.

68. Mulgan, *Communication and Control*, 57.

69. Ayman al Zawahiri, *His Own Words: Translation and Analysis of the Writings of Dr. Ayman al Zawahiri*, trans. Laura Mansfield (n.p.: TLG Publications, 2006), 207.

70. Ayman al Zawahiri, "Loyalty and Separation," quoted in Gilles Kepel and Jean-Pierre Milelli, eds., *Al Qaeda in Its Own Words*, trans. Pascale Ghazaleh (Cambridge Mass.: Harvard University Press, 2008), 234 (emphasis in the original).

71. Lia, *Architect of Global Jihad*, 7–10; also see the discussion of Suri in Gilles Kepel, *Beyond Terror and Martyrdom: The Future of the Middle East*, trans. Pascale Ghazaleh (Cambridge, Mass.: Harvard University Press, 2008), 160–69.

72. Translated and quoted in Lia, *Architect of Global Jihad*, 421–23, quote from 422 (emphasis in the original).

73. Brigitte L. Nacos, *Mass Mediated Terrorism: The Central Role of the Media in Terrorism and Counterterrorism* (New York: Rowman and Littlefield, 2002), 13–14.

74. Marc Lynch, *Voices of the New Arab Public: Iraq, Al-Jazeera, and Middle East Politics Today* (New York: Columbia University Press, 2006).

75. Gabriel Weimann, *Terror on the Internet: The New Arena, the New Challenges* (Washington, D.C.: U.S. Institute of Peace, 2006), 5.

76. Sageman, *Leaderless Jihad*, 117–20.

77. Audrey Kurth Cronin, "Cyber-Mobilization: The New *Levée en Masse*," *Parameters* (Summer 2006): 84. Sageman notes that in the post-9/11 wave of jihadi terrorism, recruits are far more likely to be poorly educated and have criminal backgrounds than in previous waves. Sageman, *Leaderless Jihad*, 140.

78. Brachman, *Global Jihadism*, 19.

79. Stephen L. Talbott, *The Future Does Not Compute: Transcending the Machines in Our Midst* (Sebastopol, Calif.: O'Reilly and Associates, 1995), 74–75.

80. Nicholas A. Christakis and James H. Fowler, *Connected: The Surprising Power of Our Social Networks and How They Shape Our Lives* (New York: Little, Brown, and Company, 2009), 31, 185, 283–84, quote from 185. For the significance of social isolation for the jihadi movement in particular, see Adam Lankford, *Human Killing Machines: Systematic Indoctrination in Iran, Nazi Germany, al Qaeda, and Abu Ghraib* (New York: Lexington, 2010), 23–25, 76–79, 148–50.

81. Olivier Roy, *Globalized Islam: The Search for a New Ummah* (New York: Columbia University Press, 2004), 275–76.

82. Evan F. Kohlman, "Al-Qa'ida's 'MySpace': Terrorist Recruitment on the Internet," *CTC Sentinel* 1, no. 2 (January 2008): 8–9.

83. Anne Stenersen, *Al-Qaida's Quest for Weapons of Mass Destruction: The History Behind the Hype* (Saarbrücken: Verlag Dr. Müller AG, 2008).

84. Michael Kenney, "Organizational Learning and Islamic Militancy" (paper submitted to the National Institute of Justice, Office of Justice Programs, U.S. Department of Justice, September 29, 2008), award no. 2006-IJ-CX-0025, 75–79, quote from 127; for the Glasgow bombings, see Michael Kenney, "Beyond the Internet: *Mētis, Techne,* and the Limitations of Online Artifacts for Islamist Terrorists," *Terrorism and Political Violence* 22, no. 2 (2010): 187.

85. Peter Bergen, *Holy War, Inc.: Inside the Secret World of Osama bin Laden* (New York: Free Press, 2002); Christoph Reuter, *My Life Is a Weapon: A Modern History of Suicide Bombing,* trans. Helena Ragg-Kirkby (Princeton, N.J.: Princeton University Press, 2004), 16.

86. Aaron Zelinsky and Martin Shubik, "Research Note: Terrorist Groups as Business Firms: A New Typological Framework," *Terrorism and Political Violence* 21, no. 2 (2009): 327–36; Alex Gallo, "Understanding Al-Qa'ida's Business Model," *CTC Sentinel* 4, no. 1 (January 2011): 15–18. Gallo describes al Qaeda as pursuing a professional services/consultancy model.

87. Susan Strasser, *Satisfaction Guaranteed: The Making of the American Mass Market,* rev. ed. (Washington, D.C.: Smithsonian Institution Press, 1989), 27.

88. Mukul Pandya, "A Good Brand Is Hard to Buy," *Wall Street Journal,* June 9, 2000, quoted in James R. Gregory, with Jack G. Wiechmann, *Branding across Borders: A Guide to Global Brand Marketing* (New York: McGraw Hill, 2002).

89. Douglas B. Holt, *How Brands Become Icons: The Principles of Cultural Branding* (Boston: Harvard Business School Press, 2004), quote from 8, also see 27–28, 211–12.

90. Ibid, 221.

91. Discussed in Thomas Hegghammer, *Jihad in Saudi Arabia: Violence and Pan-Islamism since 1979* (New York: Cambridge University Press, 2010), 227.

92. Vance Packard, *The Hidden Persuaders,* rev. ed. (New York: Pocket Books, 1980), 2, 68–78.

93. Michael J. Mazarr, *Unmodern Men in the Modern World: Radical Islam, Terrorism, and the War on Modernity* (Cambridge: Cambridge University Press, 2007), 49–52, 71; Benjamin Barber, *Jihad vs. McWorld: Terrorism's Challenge to Democracy* (New York: Ballantine Books, 2001), esp. 155–68.

94. Moghadam, *Globalization of Martyrdom,* 105.

95. Nelly Lahoud, *The Jihadis' Path to Self-Destruction* (New York: Columbia University Press, 2010), xix.

96. Ibid., esp. 245, 252, 196, 18–19.

CONCLUSION: AUTHENTIC MARTYRDOM

1. Translated and quoted in Emiko Ohnuki-Tierney, *Kamikaze Diaries: Reflections of Japanese Student Soldiers* (Chicago: University of Chicago Press, 2006), 84.

2. Norbert Wiener, *The Human Use of Human Beings: Cybernetics and Society* (Boston: Houghton Mifflin, 1950), 16.

3. Worldwide Incidents Tracking System, National Counterterrorism Center, wits.nctc.gov (accessed on April 1, 2011).

4. Magnus Ranstorp, "Terrorist Awakening in Sweden?" *CTC Sentinel* 4, no. 1 (January 2011): 1–5.

5. Siobhan Gorman, Anand Gopal, and Yochi J. Dreazen, "CIA Blast Blamed on Double Agent," *Wall Street Journal*, January 5, 2009; Richard A. Oppel Jr., Mark Mazzetti, and Souad Mekhennet, "Behind Afghan Bombing, an Agent with Many Loyalties," *New York Times*, January 5, 2009.

6. For details on al-Balawi's online activities, see Vahid Brown, "CIA Bomber a Jihadi Blogger?" jihadica.com, January 4, 2009; Joas Wagemakers, "From the Pen to the Sword," jihadica.com, January 3, 2011; for details on the entire incident, see Joby Warrick, *The Triple Agent: The al-Qaeda Mole Who Infiltrated the CIA* (New York: Doubleday, 2011).

7. Vahid Brown, "Al-Qa'ida Central and Local Affiliates," in *Self-Inflicted Wounds: Debates and Divisions within al-Qa'ida and Its Periphery*, ed. Assaf Moghadam and Brian Fishman (West Point, N.Y.: Combating Terrorism Center, 2010), 70.

8. Kim Cragin, "Al Qaeda Confronts Hamas: Divisions in the Sunni *Jihadi* Movement and Its Implications for U.S. Policy," *Studies in Conflict and Terrorism* 32 (2009): 576–90; Yoram Cohen and Matthew Levitt, with Becca Wasser, "Deterred but Determined: Salafi-Jihadi Groups in the Palestinian Area," Policy Focus no. 99, Washington Institute for Near East Policy, Washington, D.C., January 2010; Nelly Lahoud, *The Jihadis' Path to Self-Destruction* (New York: Columbia University Press, 2010), 165–70.

9. Leah Farrall, "Hotline to the Jihad," *Australian*, December 7, 2009. For the failure of the jihadi message to resonate in the Islamic world more generally, especially in light of the so-called Arab Spring of 2011, see Robin Wright, *Rock the Casbah: Rage and Rebellion across the Islamic World* (New York: Simon and Schuster, 2011), esp. chaps. 2 and 3, 41–64 and 65–89.

10. Alexandra Sandels and Patrick J. McDonnell, "Indictment Issued in Killing of Ex-Lebanese Leader Rafik Hariri," *Los Angeles Times*, July 1, 2011; additional information can be found on the website of the UN Special Tribunal for Lebanon at www.stl-tsl.org; for background on the assassination, see Nicholas Blanford, *Killing Mr. Lebanon: The Assassination of Rafik Hariri and Its Impact on the Middle East* (London: I. B. Tauris, 2006), 11–12, 141–44, 150–52.

11. Thanassis Cambanis, *A Privilege to Die: Inside Hezbollah's Legions and Their Endless War against Israel* (New York: Free Press, 2010), 164–66.

12. Mohammad M. Hafez, *Suicide Bombers in Iraq: The Strategy and Ideology of Martyrdom* (Washington, D.C.: United States Institute of Peace Press, 2007), 78.

13. Quoted in Toby Harnden, *Bandit Country: The IRA and South Armagh* (London: Hodder and Stoughton, 1999), 367.

14. Spencer Ackerman and Adam Rawnsley, "Wheelbarrow Rockets, Remote-Control Suicide Vests and Captured Drones: Wikileaks Eposes Insurgent Tech," *Wired,* http://www.wired.com/dangerroom/2010/10/wheelbarrow-rockets-remote-control-suicide-vests-and-captured-drones-wikileaks-exposes-insurgent-tech.

15. Thomas X. Hammes, *The Sling and the Stone: On War in the 21st Century* (St. Paul, Minn.: Zenith Press, 2004), 204–9.

16. Martin van Crevald, *Technology and War: From 2000 B.C. to the Present,* rev. ed. (New York: Free Press, 1991), 304.

17. Franklin C. Spinney, *Defense Facts of Life: The Plans/Reality Mismatch,* ed. James Clay Thompson (Boulder: Westview Press, 1985), 37.

18. Che Guevara, *Guerilla Warfare* (New York: Monthly Review Press, 1961), 27–29.

19. Charles Kenny, *Getting Better: Why Global Development Is Succeeding—and How We Can Improve the World Even More* (New York: Basic Books, 2011), 40–41.

20. Adrian R. Lewis, *The American Culture of War: The History of U.S. Military Force from World War II to Operation Iraqi Freedom* (New York: Routledge, 2007), 443.

21. Declan Walsh, "Pakistan Suicide Bomb Kills 80 as Taliban Seeks Revenge for Bin Laden," *Guardian,* May 13, 2011.

22. Bruce Hoffman, "Bin Ladin's Killing and Its Effect on al-Qa'ida: What Comes Next?" *CTC Sentinel* 4, no. 5 (2011): 1–2.

23. Will McCants, "Zawahiri Speaks," *Foreign Policy,* June 9, 2011, www.foreign-policy.com.

24. Nelly Lahoud, "Bin Ladin's Death through the Lens of al-Qa'ida's Confidential Secretary," *CTC Sentinel* 4, no. 5 (2011): 12–15.

SELECT BIBLIOGRAPHY

WEB RESOURCES ON TERRORISM

Combating Terrorism Center, United States Military Academy (*CTC Sentinel* and Harmony Project reports), www.ctc.usma.edu

Jamestown Foundation (*Terrorism Focus* and *Terrorism Monitor*), www.jamestown .org/programs/gta

Jihadica, www.jihadica.com

National Counterterrorism Center, www.nctc.gov; especially Worldwide Incidents Tracking System, www.nctc.gov/wits/witsnextgen.html

START Global Terrorism Database, www.start.umd.edu/gtd

MEMOIRS, POLITICAL WRITINGS, AND CONTEMPORARY REPORTS

Aaron, David, ed. *In Their Own Words: Voices of Jihad*. Santa Monica, Calif.: RAND, 2008.

Baer, Robert. *See No Evil: The True Story of a Ground Soldier in the CIA's War on Terrorism*. New York: Three Rivers Press, 2001.

Balasingham, Adele. *The Will to Freedom: An Inside View of the Tamil Resistance*. Mitcham, U.K.: Fairfax, 2001.

Ben-Ami, Schlomo. *Scars of War, Wounds of Peace: The Arab-Israeli Tragedy*. New York: Oxford University Press, 2006.

Campbell, Brian, Laurence McKeown, and Felim O'Hagan, eds. *Nor Meekly Serve My Time: The H-Block Struggle, 1976–1981*. Belfast: Beyond the Pale, 1994.

Collins, Eamon, with Mick McGovern. *Killing Rage*. London: Granta Books, 1997.

Figner, Vera. *Memoirs of a Revolutionist*. Introduction by Richard Stites. Dekalb: Northern Illinois University Press, 1991.

Fulton, Kevin, with Jim Nally and Ian Gallagher. *Unsung Hero: How I Saved Dozens of Lives as a Secret Agent inside the IRA*. London: John Blake, 2006.

Guevara, Che. *Guerilla Warfare*. New York: Monthly Review Press, 1961.

Guided Missiles and Techniques. Summary Technical Report of Division 5, National Defense Research Committee. Vol. 1. Washington, D.C., 1946.

Gurney, Peter. *Braver Men Walk Away*. London: HarperCollins Limited, 1993.

Hamas Covenant, 1988. http://avalon.law.yale.edu/20th_century/hamas.asp.

Heinzen, Karl. "Murder." In *Voices of Terror*, edited by Walter Laqueur, 57–67. New York: Reed Press, 2004.

Hoole, Rajan, et al. *The Broken Palmyrah: The Tamil Crisis in Sri Lanka—An Inside Account*. Rev. ed. Claremont, Calif.: Sri Lanka Studies Institute, 1990.

Human Rights Watch. *Deprived and Endangered: Humanitarian Crisis in the Gaza Strip*. New York, January 2009.

———. " 'Troops in Contact' Airstrikes and Civilian Deaths in Afghanistan." New York, 2008.

———. "Living in Fear: Child Soldiers and the Tamil Tigers in Sri Lanka." New York, November 2004.

———. *Erased in a Moment: Suicide Bombing Attacks against Israeli Civilians*. New York, 2002.

International Crisis Group. *Islamism, Violence, and Reform in Algeria: Turning the Page*. ISG Middle East Report no. 29. Cairo and Brussels: International Crisis Group, 2004.

Kepel, Gilles, and Jean-Pierre Milelli, eds. *Al Qaeda in Its Own Words*. Translated by Pascale Ghazaleh. Cambridge, Mass.: Harvard University Press, 2008.

Khomeini, Imam. *Islam and Revolution: Writings and Declarations of Imam Khomeini*. Translated and annotated by Hamid Algar. North Haledon, N.J.: Mizan Press, 1981.

MacStiofain, Sean. *Revolutionary in Ireland*. Edinburgh: Gordon Cremonisi, 1975.

McGartland, Martin. *Fifty Dead Men Walking*. Norwalk, Conn.: Hastings House, 1997.

McIntyre, Anthony. *Good Friday: The Death of Irish Republicanism*. New York: Ausubo Press, 2008.

Nasrallah, Sayyed Hassan. *The Voice of Hezbollah: The Statements of Sayyed Hassan Nasrallah*. Edited by Nicholas Noe. Translated by Ellen Khouri. London: Verso, 2007.

The 9/11 Commission Report: Final Report of the National Commission on Terrorist Attacks upon the United States. Authorized ed. New York: W. W. Norton and Company, 2004.

Nusseibeh, Sari, with Anthony David. *Once Upon a Country: A Palestinian Life*. New York: Farrar, Straus and Giroux, 2007.

O'Callaghan, Sean. *The Informer: The Real Life Story of One Man's War Against Terrorism*. New York: Bantam Press, 1998.

O'Doherty, Shane. *The Volunteer: A Former IRA Man's True Story*. London: Fount, 1993.

"Open Letter Addressed by Hizb'allah to the Downtrodden in Lebanon and in the World." In *Amal and the Shia: Struggle for the Soul of Lebanon*, by Augustus Richard Norton, app. II, 167–87. Austin: University of Texas Press, 1987.

O'Rawe, Richard. *Blanketmen: An Untold Story of the H-Block Hunger Strike*. Dublin: New Island, 2005.

Pearse, Padraic H. *Political Writings and Speeches*. Reprint, Dublin: Talbot Press, 1966.

Qassem, Naim. *Hizbullah: The Story from Within*. Translated by Dalia Khalil. London: Saqi, 2005.

Qods, ed. *In Memory of Our Martyrs*. Translated by M. Ebrahimi. Tehran: Ministry of Islamic Guidance, 1982.

Qutb, Sayyid. *Milestones*. New Delhi: Millat Book Centre, n.d.

Ross, Dennis. *The Missing Peace: The Inside Story of the Fight for Middle East Peace*. New York: Farrar, Straus Giroux, 2004.

Savinkov, Boris. *Memoirs of a Terrorist*. Translated by Joseph Shaplen. New York: Albert and Charles Boni, 1931.

Styles, George, as told to Bob Perin. *Bombs Have No Pity: My War against Terrorism*. London: William Luscombe, 1975.

United Nations Assistance Mission to Afghanistan (UNAMA), Human Rights Unit. "Afghanistan: Mid Year Bulletin on Protection of Civilians in Armed Conflict, 2009." New York, July 2009.

———. "Afghanistan: Annual Report on the Protection of Civilians in Armed Conflict, 2008." New York, January 2009.

———. "Suicide Attacks in Afghanistan, 2001–2007." New York, September 2007.

United States Department of Defense. "Report of the DoD Commission on Beirut International Airport Terrorist Act, October 23, 1983." Washington, D.C., December 20, 1983.

al Zawahiri, Ayman. *His Own Words: Translation and Analysis of the Writings of Dr. Ayman al Zawahiri*. Translated by Laura Mansfield. N.p.: TLG Publications, 2006.

BOOKS AND ARTICLES

Abrahimian, Ervand. *The Iranian Mojehedin*. New Haven and London: Yale University Press, 1989.

Abu-Amr, Ziad. *Islamic Fundamentalism in the West Bank and Gaza: Muslim Brotherhood and Islamic Jihad*. Bloomington: Indiana University Press, 1994.

Aburish, Said K. *Arafat: From Defender to Dictator*. Rev. ed. New York: Bloomsbury, 2004.

Adas, Michael. *Machines as the Measure of Men: Science, Technology, and Ideologies of Western Dominance*. Ithaca, N.Y.: Cornell University Press, 1989.

Ahluwalia, Shashi and Meenakshi Ahluwalia. *Assassination of Rajiv Gandhi*. New Delhi: Mittal Publications, 1991.

Ajami, Fouad. *The Vanished Imam: Musa al Sadr and the Shia of Lebanon*. Ithaca, N.Y.: Cornell University Press, 1986.

Ali, Imtiaz. "The Haqqani Network and Cross-Border Terrorism in Afghanistan." *Terrorism Monitor*, March 24, 2008.

Alison, Miranda. "Cogs in the Wheel? Women in the Liberation Tigers of Tamil Eelam." *Civil Wars* 6, no. 1 (2003): 37–54.

Allen, Michael Thad. *The Business of Genocide: The SS, Slave Labor, and the Concentration Camps*. Chapel Hill: University of North Carolina Press, 2002.

Allen, Michael Thad, and Gabriel Hecht, eds. *Technologies of Power: Essays in Honor of Thomas Parke Hughes and Agatha Chipley Hughes.* Cambridge, Mass.: MIT Press, 2001.

Alonso, Rogelio, and Fernando Reinares. "Maghreb Immigrants Becoming Suicide Terrorists." In *Root Causes of Suicide Terrorism: The Globalization of Martyrdom,* edited by Ami Pedahzur, 179–97. New York: Routledge, 2006.

Alonso, Rogelio, and Marcos Garcia Rey. "The Evolution of Jihadist Terrorism in Morocco." *Terrorism and Political Violence* 19, no. 4 (2007): 571–92.

Araj, Bader. "Harsh State Repression as a Cause of Suicide Bombing: The Case of the Palestinian-Israeli Conflict." *Studies in Conflict and Terrorism* 31, no. 4 (2008): 284–303.

Arthur, W. Brian. *The Nature of Technology: What It Is and How It Evolves.* New York: Free Press, 2009.

Atran, Scott. *Talking to the Enemy: Faith, Brotherhood, and the (Un)Making of Terrorists.* New York: HarperCollins, 2010.

Avrich, Paul. *The Russian Anarchists.* Princeton, N.J.: Princeton University Press, 1967.

Ayoub, Mahmoud. *Redemptive Suffering in Islam: A Study of the Devotional Aspects of Ashura in Twelver Shi'ism.* The Hague: Mouton Publishers, 1978.

Bakier, Abdul Hameed. "Gaza's 'Ghost' Suicide Bombers—More Rhetoric Than Threat?" *Terrorism Focus,* January 21, 2009, 2–3.

Bandura, Albert. "Mechanisms of Moral Disengagement." In *Origins of Terrorism: Psychologies, Ideologies, Theologies, States of Mind,* edited by Walter Reich, 161–91. Washington, D.C.: Woodrow Wilson Center Press, 1998.

Barber, Benjamin. *Jihad vs. McWorld: Terrorism's Challenge to Democracy.* 2nd ed. New York: Ballantine Books, 2001.

Barkun, Michael. "Appropriated Martyrs: The Branch Davidians and the Radical Right." *Terrorism and Political Violence* 19, no. 1 (2007): 117–24.

Barlow, Hugh. *Dead for Good: Martyrdom and the Rise of the Suicide Bomber.* London: Paradigm, 2007.

Basalla, George. *The Evolution of Technology.* Cambridge: Cambridge University Press, 1988.

Bell, J. Bowyer. *The Secret Army: The IRA.* Rev. 3rd ed. New York: Transaction Publishers, 1997.

———. *IRA Tactics and Targets.* Dublin: Poolberg Press, 1990.

Beniger, James R. *The Control Revolution: Technological and Economic Origins of the Information Society.* Cambridge, Mass.: Harvard University Press, 1986.

Benjamin, Daniel, and Steve Simon. *The Next Attack: The Failure of the War on Terror and a Strategy for Getting It Right.* New York: Times Books, 2005.

Beresford, David. *Ten Men Dead: The Story of the 1981 Irish Hunger Strike.* New York: Atlantic Monthly Press, 1987.

Bergen, Peter. *Holy War, Inc.: Inside the Secret World of Osama bin Laden.* New York: Free Press, 2002.

Berko, Anat. *The Path to Paradise: The Inner World of Suicide Bombers and Their Dispatchers.* Translated by Elizabeth Yuval. Westport, Conn.: Praeger Security International, 2007.

Berman, Eli. *Radical, Religious, and Violent: The New Economics of Terrorism.* Cambridge, Mass.: MIT Press, 2009.

Beyerchen, Alan. "Rational Means and Irrational Ends: Thoughts on the Technology of Racism in the Third Reich." *Central European History* 30, no. 3 (1997): 386–402.

Biggs, Michael. "Dying without Killing: Self-Immolations, 1963–2002." In *Making Sense of Suicide Missions,* edited by Diego Gambetta, 173–208. Oxford: Oxford University Press, 2005.

Billington, James. *Fire in the Minds of Men: Origins of the Revolutionary Faith.* 2nd ed. New Brunswick, N.J.: Transaction Publishers, 1999.

Black, Andrew. "The Ideological Struggle over al-Qaeda's Suicide Tactics in Algeria." *Terrorism Monitor,* February 11, 2008.

———. "AQIM Employs Martyrdom Operations on Algeria." *Terrorism Focus,* September 20, 2007.

———. "The Reconstituted al-Qaeda Threat in the Maghreb." *Terrorism Monitor,* February 21, 2007.

Blanford, Nicholas. *Killing Mr. Lebanon: The Assassination of Rafik Hariri and Its Impact on the Middle East.* London: I. B. Tauris, 2006.

Bloom, Mia M. "Dying to Kill: Motivations for Suicide Terrorism." In *Root Causes of Suicide Terrorism: The Globalization of Martyrdom,* edited by Ami Pedahzur, 25–53. New York: Routledge, 2006.

———. *Dying to Kill: The Allure of Suicide Terrorism.* New York: Columbia University Press, 2005.

Bloom, Mia M., and John Horgan. "Missing Their Mark: The IRA's Proxy Bomb Campaign." *Social Research* 75, no. 2 (2008): 579–61.

St. Bonaventure. *The Soul's Journey into God / The Tree of Life / The Life of St. Francis.* Translated by Ewart Cousins. Mahwah, N.J.: Paulist Press, 1978.

Boucek, Christopher. "Extremist Re-education and Rehabilitation in Saudi Arabia." In *Leaving Terrorism Behind: Individual and Collective Disengagement,* edited by Tore Bjørgo and John Horgan, 212–23. London: Routledge, 2009.

———. "Saudi Security and the Islamist Insurgency." *Terrorism Monitor,* January 26, 2006.

Brachman, Jarret. *Global Jihadism: Theory and Practice.* New York: Routledge, 2009.

Brandon, James. "Al-Qa'ida's Involvement in Britain's 'Homegrown' Terrorist Plots." *CTC Sentinel* 2, no. 3 (March 2009): 10–12.

Brisard, Jean-Charles, with Damien Martinez. *Zarqawi: The New Face of al-Qaeda.* New York: Other Press, 2005.

Brooks, Harvey. "Technology, Evolution, and Purpose." *Daedalus* 109, no. 1 (1980): 65–81.

Brown, Ian. *Khomeini's Forgotten Sons: The Story of Iran's Boy Soldiers.* London: Grey Seal, 1990.

Brown, Vahid. "Al-Qa'ida Central and Local Affiliates." In *Self-Inflicted Wounds: Debates and Divisions within al-Qa'ida and Its Periphery*, edited by Assaf Moghadam and Brian Fishman, 69–99. Harmony Project. West Point, N.Y.: Combating Terrorism Center, 2010.

Brym, Robert J., and Bader Araj. "Suicide Bombing as Strategy and Interaction." *Social Forces* 84, no. 4 (2006): 1,969–86.

Bucaille, Laetitia. *Growing Up Palestinian: Israeli Occupation and the Intifada Generation*. Princeton, N.J.: Princeton University Press, 2004.

Burdman, Daphne. "Education, Indoctrination, and Incitement: Palestinian Children on Their Way to Martyrdom." *Terrorism and Political Violence* 15, no. 1 (2003): 96–123.

Burke, Jason. *Al Qaeda: Casting a Shadow of Terror*. New York: I. B. Tauris, 2003.

Burleigh, Michael. *Sacred Causes: The Clash of Religion and Politics, From the Great War to the War on Terror*. New York: HarperCollins, 2007.

———. *Earthly Powers: The Clash of Religion and Politics in Europe, from the French Revolution to the Great War*. New York: HarperCollins, 2005.

Byman, Daniel. "How to Handle Hamas." *Foreign Affairs* 89, no. 5 (September/October 2010): 45–62.

———. *Deadly Connections: States That Sponsor Terrorism*. Cambridge: Cambridge University Press, 2005.

Calvert, John. *Sayyid Qutb and the Origins of Radical Islamism*. New York: Columbia University Press, 2010.

Cambanis, Thanassis. *A Privilege to Die: Inside Hezbollah's Legions and Their Endless War against Israel*. New York: Free Press, 2010.

Capshew, James H. "Engineering Behavior: Project Pigeon, World War II, and the Conditioning of B. F. Skinner." *Technology and Culture* 34, no. 4 (1993): 835–57.

Cardwell, Donald. *Wheels, Clocks, and Rockets: A History of Technology*. New York: W. W. Norton and Company, 1995.

Carell, Paul. *Hitler Moves East, 1941–1943*. Translated by Ewald Osers. London: George G. Harrap and Company, 1964. Reprint, New York: Ballantine Books, 1971.

Chattopadhyaya, H. P. *Ethnic Unrest in Modern Sri Lanka: An Account of Tamil-Sinhalese Race Relations*. New Delhi: M. D. Publications, 1994.

Chehab, Zaki. *Inside Hamas: The Untold Story of the Islamic Resistance Movement*. New York: Nation Books, 2007.

Christakis Nicholas A., and James H. Fowler. *Connected: The Surprising Power of Our Social Networks and How They Shape Our Lives*. New York: Little, Brown, and Company, 2009.

Clarence, William. *Ethnic Warfare in Sri Lanka and the UN Crisis*. Ann Arbor, Mich.: Pluto Press, 2007.

Clarke, Liam. *Broadening the Battlefield: The H-Blocks and the Rise of Sinn Fein*. Dublin: Gill and Macmillan, 1987.

Cline, Lawrence E. "From Ocalan to al Qaida: The Continuing Terrorist Threat in Turkey." *Studies in Conflict and Terrorism* 27, no. 4 (2004): 321–35.

Cockburn, Patrick. *Muqtada al-Sadr and the Battle for the Future of Iraq.* New York: Scribner, 2008.

Coghlan, Tom. "The Taliban in Helmand: An Oral History." In *Decoding the New Taliban: Insights from the Afghan Field,* edited by Antonio Giustozzi, 119–53. New York: Columbia University Press, 2009.

Cohen, Stephen Philip. *The Idea of Pakistan.* Washington, D.C.: Brookings Institution Press, 2004.

Cohen, Yoram, Matthew Levitt, and Becca Wasser. "Deterred but Determined: Salafi-Jihadi Groups in the Palestinian Area." Policy Focus no. 99. Washington Institute for Near East Policy, Washington, D.C., January 2010.

Coll, Steve. *Ghost Wars: The Secret History of the CIA, Afghanistan, and bin Laden, from the Soviet Invasion to September 10, 2001.* New York: Penguin Press, 2004.

Constant, Edward. "Recursive Practice and the Evolution of Technological Knowledge." In *Technological Innovation as an Evolutionary Process,* edited by John Ziman, 219–33. Cambridge: Cambridge University Press, 2000.

Coogan, Tim Pat. *The IRA.* New York: Palgrave MacMillan, 2002.

———. *On the Blanket: The Inside Story of the IRA Prisoners' "Dirty" Protest.* Dublin: Wards River Press, 1980. Reprint, New York: Palgrave MacMillan, 2002.

Cook, David. *Martyrdom in Islam.* Cambridge: Cambridge University Press, 2007.

———. *Understanding Jihad.* Berkeley: University of California Press, 2005.

Cook, David, and Olivia Allison. *Understanding and Addressing Suicide Attacks: The Faith and Politics of Martyrdom Operations.* Westport, Conn.: Praeger Security International, 2007.

Cragin, Kim. "Al Qaeda Confronts Hamas: Divisions in the Sunni Jihadist Movement and Its Implications for U.S. Policy." *Studies in Conflict and Terrorism* 32, no. 7 (2009): 576–90.

Crane, Conrad C. *Bombs, Cities, and Civilians.* Lawrence: University Press of Kansas, 1993.

Criss, Nur Bilge. "The Nature of PKK Terrorism in Turkey." *Studies in Conflict and Terrorism* 18, no. 1 (1995): 17–37.

Cronin, Audrey Kurth. "Cyber-Mobilization: The New Levée en Masse." *Parameters* 36 (2006): 77–87.

Davis, Joyce M. *Martyrs: Innocence, Vengeance, and Despair in the Middle East.* New York: Palgrave MacMillan, 2003.

De Silva, K. M. *Regional Powers and Small State Security: India and Sri Lanka, 1977–1990.* Baltimore: Johns Hopkins University Press, 1995.

DeVotta, Neil. *Blowback: Linguistic Nationalism, Institutional Decay, and Ethnic Conflict in Sri Lanka.* Stanford, Calif.: Stanford University Press, 2004.

Diamond, Jared. *Guns, Germs, and Steel: The Fates of Human Societies.* New York: W. W. Norton and Company, 1997.

Dillon, Martin. *God and the Gun: The Church and Irish Terrorism.* New York: Routledge, 1999.

Dingley, James. "The Bombing of Omagh, 15 August 1998: The Bombers, Their Tactics, Strategy, and Purpose Behind the Incident." *Studies in Conflict and Terrorism* 24, no. 6 (2001): 451–65.

Dolnik, Adam. *Understanding Terrorist Innovation: Technology, Tactics and Global Trends.* New York: Routledge, 2007.

Dostoevsky, Fyodor. *The Possessed.* Translated by Constance Garnet. New York: Modern Library, 1936.

Dower, John W. *Embracing Defeat: Japan in the Wake of World War II.* New York: W. W. Norton and Company, 1999.

———. *War without Mercy: Race and Power in the Pacific War.* New York: Pantheon, 1986.

Drucker, Peter F. *Technology, Management, and Society.* New York: Harper Colophon, 1977.

Dunlop, John B. *Russia Confronts Chechnya: Roots of a Separatist Conflict.* Cambridge: Cambridge University Press, 1998.

Durkheim, Emile. *Suicide: A Study in Sociology.* Translated by John A. Spaulding. New York: Free Press, 1951.

Edgerton, David. *The Shock of the Old: Technology and Global History since 1900.* Oxford: Oxford University Press, 2007.

Eilstrup-Sangiovanni, Mette, and Calvert Jones. "Assessing the Dangers of Illicit Networks: Why al-Qaeda May Be Less Threatening Than Many Think." *International Security* 33, no. 2 (2008): 7–44.

English, Richard. *Irish Freedom: The History of Nationalism in Ireland.* London: MacMillan, 2006.

———. *Armed Struggle: The History of the IRA.* New York: Oxford University Press, 2003.

Ergil, Dogu. "Suicide Terrorism in Turkey: The Workers' Party of Kurdistan." In *Countering Suicide Terrorism: An International Conference February 20–23, 2000 Herzliya, Israel,* 105–28. Herzliya, Israel: The International Policy Institute for Counter-Terrorism, 2001.

Etzersdorfer, Elmar, and Gernot Sonneck. "Preventing Suicide by Influencing Mass-Media Reporting. The Viennese Experience, 1980–1996." *Archives of Suicide Research* 4, no. 1 (1998): 67–74.

Evangelista, Matthew. *The Chechen Wars: Will Russia Go the Way of the Soviet Union?* Washington, D.C.: Brookings Institution Press, 2002.

Evans, Martin, and John Phillips. *Algeria: Anger of the Dispossessed.* New Haven, Conn.: Yale University Press, 2007.

Fandy, Mamoud. *Saudi Arabia and the Politics of Dissent.* New York: St. Martin's Press, 1999.

Farrall, Leah. "How al Qaeda Works." *Foreign Affairs* 90, no. 2 (March/April 2011): 128–38.

Felter, Joseph, and Brian Fishman. "Becoming a Foreign Fighter: A Second Look at the Sinjar Records." In *Bombers, Bleedout, and Bank Accounts: Al-Qa'ida's*

Road in and out of Iraq, edited by Brian Fishman, 32–65. Harmony Project. West Point, N.Y.: Combating Terrorism Center, 2008.

Felter, Joseph, and Brian Fishman. *Al-Qa'ida's Foreign Fighters in Iraq: A First Look at the Sinjar Records*. Harmony Project. West Point, N.Y.: Combating Terrorism Center, 2007.

Filiu, Jean-Pierre. "The Brotherhood vs. al Qaeda: A Moment of Truth?" *Current Trends in Islamist Ideology* 9 (2009): 18–25.

———. "The Local and Global Jihad of al-Qa'ida in the Islamic Maghrib." *Middle East Journal* 63, no. 2 (2009): 213–26.

Filkins, Dexter. *The Forever War*. New York: Alfred A. Knopf, 2008.

Fishman, Brian. *Dysfunction and Decline: Lessons Learned from Inside al-Qa'ida in Iraq*. Harmony Project. West Point, N.Y.: Combating Terrorism Center, 2009.

Fisk, Robert. *Pity the Nation: Lebanon at War*. 3rd ed. Oxford: Oxford University Press, 2001.

Flanigan, Shawn Teresa. "Nonprofit Service Provision by Insurgent Organizations: The Cases of Hizballah and the Tamil Tigers." *Studies in Conflict and Terrorism* 31, no. 6 (2008): 499–519.

Fleck, James. "Artefact ←→ Activity: The Coevolution of Artifacts, Knowledge, and Organization." In *Technological Innovation as an Evolutionary Process*, edited by John Ziman, 248–66. Cambridge: Cambridge University Press, 2000.

Forest, James J. F., Jarret Brachman, and Joseph Felter, eds. *Harmony and Disharmony: Exploiting al-Qa'ida's Organizational Vulnerabilities*. Harmony Project. West Point, N.Y.: Combating Terrorism Center, 2006.

Foster, R. F. *Modern Ireland, 1600–1972*. London: Allen Lane, 1988.

Franco, Claudio. "The Tehrik-e Taliban in Pakistan." In *Decoding the New Taliban: Insights from the Afghan Field*, edited by Antonio Giustozzi, 269–91. New York: Columbia University Press, 2009.

Friedman, George. *America's Secret War: Inside the Hidden Worldwide Struggle between America and Its Enemies*. New York: Doubleday, 2004.

Friedman, Thomas L. *From Beirut to Jerusalem*. New York: Anchor Books, 1995.

Fromkin, David. *A Peace to End All Peace: Creating the Modern Middle East, 1914–1922*. New York: Henry Holt, 1989.

Galbraith, Peter W. *The End of Iraq: How American Incompetence Created a War without End*. New York: Simon and Schuster, 2006.

Gallo, Alex. "Understanding al-Qa'ida's Business Model." *CTC Sentinel* 4, no. 1 (2011): 15–18.

Gammer, Moshe. *The Lone Wolf and the Bear: Three Centuries of Chechen Defiance of Russian Rule*. Pittsburgh: University of Pittsburgh Press, 2006.

Geifman, Anna. *Thou Shalt Kill: Revolutionary Terrorism in Russia, 1904–1917*. Princeton, N.J.: Princeton University Press, 1993.

Geraghty, Timothy J. "25 Years Later: We Came in Peace." *Proceedings* 134, no. 10 (2008).

Geraghty, Tony. *The Irish War: The Hidden Conflict between the IRA and British Intelligence*. Baltimore: Johns Hopkins University Press, 2000.

Gerovitch, Slava. "Human-Machine Issues in the Soviet Space Program." In *Critical Issues in the History of Spaceflight*, edited by Steven J. Dick and Roger D. Launius, 107–40. Washington, D.C.: NASA Office of External Relations, 2006.

Gibson, James William. *The Perfect War: Technowar in Vietnam*. 2nd ed. New York: Atlantic Monthly Press, 2000.

Gieling, Saskia. *Religion and War in Revolutionary Iran*. London: I. B. Tauris, 1999.

Gillespie, Paul G. *Weapons of Choice: The Development of Precision Guided Munitions*. Tuscaloosa: University of Alabama Press, 2006.

Giustozzi, Antonio. *Koran, Kalishnikov, and Laptop: The Neo-Taliban Insurgency in Afghanistan*. New York: Columbia University Press, 2008.

Greenfeld, Liah. *Nationalism and the Mind: Essays on Modern Culture*. Oxford: Oneworld, 2006.

Gregory, James R., with Jack G. Wiechmann. *Branding across Borders: A Guide to Global Brand Marketing*. New York: McGraw Hill, 2002.

Grier, David Alan. *When Computers Were Human*. Princeton, N.J.: Princeton University Press, 2005.

Grob-Fitzgibbon, Benjamin. "From the Dagger to the Bomb: Karl Heinzen and the Evolution of Political Terror." *Terrorism and Political Violence* 16, no. 1 (2004): 97–115.

Grossman, Dave. *On Killing: The Psychological Cost of Learning to Kill in War and Society*. Rev. ed. New York: Back Bay Books, 2009.

Gul, Imtiaz. *The Most Dangerous Place: Pakistan's Lawless Frontier*. New York: Viking, 2010.

Gunaratna, Rohan. *Inside al Qaeda: Global Network of Terror*. New York: Columbia University Press, 2002.

———. "The LTTE and Suicide Terrorism." *Frontline*, February 5–18, 2000.

———. *Indian Intervention in Sri Lanka: The Role of India's Intelligence Agencies*. Colombo: South Asian Network on Conflict Research, 1993.

———. *International and Regional Security Implications of the Sri Lankan Tamil Insurgency*. United Kingdom: International Foundation of Sri Lankans, 1987.

———. *War and Peace in Sri Lanka*. Colombo: Institute of Fundamental Studies, 1987.

Gunawardena, Arjuna. "Female Black Tigers: A Different Breed of Cat?" In *Female Suicide Bombers: Dying for Equality?* edited by Yoram Schweitzer, 81–91. Tel Aviv: Jaffee Center for Strategic Studies, 2006.

Gunning, Jeroen. *Hamas in Politics: Democracy, Religion, Violence*. New York: Columbia University Press, 2008.

Haahr, Kathryn. "GSPC Joins al-Qaeda and France Becomes Top Enemy." *Terrorism Focus*, September 26, 2006.

Hafez, Mohammed M. "Martyrdom Mythology in Iraq: How Jihadists Frame Suicide Terrorism in Videos and Biographies." *Terrorism and Political Violence* 19, no. 1 (2007): 95–115.

———. *Suicide Bombers in Iraq: The Strategy and Ideology of Martyrdom.* Washington, D.C.: United States Institute of Peace Press, 2007.

———. "Dying to Be Martyrs: The Symbolic Dimensions of Suicide Terrorism." In *Root Causes of Suicide Terrorism: The Globalization of Martyrdom,* edited by Ami Pedahzur, 54–80. New York: Routledge, 2006.

———. *Manufacturing Human Bombs: The Making of Palestinian Suicide Bombers.* Washington, D.C.: United States Institute of Peace Press, 2006.

———. "Rationality, Culture, and Structure in the Making of Suicide Bombers: A Preliminary Theoretical Synthesis and Illustrative Case Study." *Studies in Conflict and Terrorism* 29, no. 2 (2006): 165–85.

Hahn, Gordon M. *Russia's Islamic Threat.* New Haven, Conn.: Yale University Press, 2007.

Hammes, Thomas X. *The Sling and the Stone: On War in the 21st Century.* St. Paul, Minn.: Zenith Press, 2004.

Hamzeh, Amad Nizar. *In the Path of Hizbullah.* Syracuse, N.Y.: Syracuse University Press, 2004.

Harnden, Toby. *Bandit Country: The IRA and South Armagh.* London: Hodder and Stoughton, 1999.

Hashim, Ahmed S. *Insurgency and Counter-Insurgency in Iraq.* Ithaca, N.Y.: Cornell University Press, 2006.

Hassan, Nasra. "An Arsenal of Believers: Talking to the 'Human Bombs.' " *New Yorker,* November 19, 2001.

Hastings, Adrian. *The Construction of Nationhood: Ethnicity, Religion, and Nationalism.* Cambridge: Cambridge University Press, 1997.

Hatina, Meir. *Islam and Salvation in Palestine: The Islamic Jihad Movement.* Tel Aviv: Moshe Dayan Center for Middle Eastern and African Studies, 2001.

Hayes, Peter. *From Complicity to Cooperation: Degussa in the Third Reich.* Cambridge: Cambridge University Press, 2004.

Headrick, Daniel R. *The Tools of Empire: Technology and European Imperialism in the Nineteenth Century.* New York: Oxford University Press, 1981.

Hegghammer, Thomas. *Jihad in Saudi Arabia: Violence and Pan-Islamism since 1979.* New York: Cambridge University Press, 2010.

———. "Apostates vs. Infidels: Explaining Differential Use of Suicide Bombings by Jihadist Groups." Paper presented at the conference "Understanding Jihadism: Origins, Evolution, and Future Perspectives," Oslo, March 19–21, 2009.

———. "Abdallah Azzam: The Imam of Jihad." In *Al Qaeda in Its Own Words,* edited by Gilles Kepel and Jean-Pierre Milelli, translated by Pascale Ghazaleh, 81–101. Cambridge, Mass.: Harvard University Press, 2008.

———. "Deconstructing the Myth about al-Qaʿida and Khobar," *CTC Sentinel* 1, no. 3 (2008): 20–22.

————. "Terrorist Recruitment and Radicalization in Saudi Arabia." *Middle East Policy* 13, no. 4 (2006): 39–60.

Hellmann-Rajanayagam, Dagmar. *The Tamil Tigers: Armed Struggle for Identity.* Stuttgart: Franz Steiner Verlag, 1994.

Hill, Peter. "Kamikaze, 1943–5." In *Making Sense of Suicide Missions,* edited by Diego Gambetta, 1–41. Oxford: Oxford University Press, 2005.

Hiltermann, Joost. *A Poisonous Affair: America, Iraq, and the Gassing of Halabja.* Cambridge: Cambridge University Press, 2007.

Hoffer, Eric. *The True Believer: Thoughts on the Nature of Mass Movements.* New York: Harper and Row, 1951. Reprint, New York: Perennial Classics, 2002.

Hoffman, Bruce. "Bin Ladin's Killing and Its Effect on al-Qa'ida: What Comes Next?" *CTC Sentinel* 4, no. 5 (2011): 1–2.

————. "Radicalization and Subversion: Al Qaeda and the 7 July 2005 Bombings and the 2006 Airline Bombing Plot." *Studies in Conflict and Terrorism* 32, no. 12 (2009): 1100–16.

————. *Inside Terrorism.* 2nd ed. New York: Columbia University Press, 2006.

————. "The Logic of Suicide Terrorism." In *Homeland Security and Terrorism: Readings and Interpretations,* edited by Russell D. Howard, James J. F. Forest, and Joanne C. Moore, 59–70. New York: McGraw Hill, 2006.

————. "Aviation Security and Terrorism: An Analysis of the Potential Threat to Air Cargo Integrators." *Terrorism and Political Violence* 10, no. 3 (1998): 54–69.

————. "Terrorist Targeting: Tactics, Trends, and Potentialities." *Terrorism and Political Violence* 5, no. 2 (1993): 12–29.

Hoffman, Bruce, and Gordon H. McCormick. "Terrorism, Signaling, and Suicide Attack." *Studies in Conflict and Terrorism* 27, no. 4 (2004): 243–81.

Holt, Douglas B. *How Brands Become Icons: The Principles of Cultural Branding.* Boston: Harvard Business School Press, 2004.

Hopgood, Stephen. "Tamil Tigers, 1987–2002." In *Making Sense of Suicide Missions,* edited by Diego Gambetta, 43–74. Oxford: Oxford University Press, 2005.

Horowitz, Michael C. *The Diffusion of Military Power: Causes and Consequences for International Politics.* Princeton, N.J.: Princeton University Press, 2010.

Hoyt, Timothy D. "Technology and Security." In *Grave New World: Security Challenges in the 21st Century,* edited by Michael E. Brown, 17–37. Washington, D.C.: Georgetown University Press, 2003.

Hroub, Khaled. *Hamas: Political Thought and Practice.* Washington, D.C.: Institute for Palestine Studies, 2000.

Hughes, James. *Chechnya: From Nationalism to Jihad.* Philadelphia: University of Pennsylvania Press, 2007.

Hughes, Thomas P. *Human-Built World: How to Think about Technology and Culture.* Chicago: University of Chicago Press, 2004.

————. *American Genesis: A Century of Innovation and Technological Enthusiasm.* New York: Viking, 1989.

Irwin, Alistair, and Mike Mahoney. "The Military Response." In *Combating Terrorism in Northern Ireland,* edited by James Dingley, 198–226. New York: Routledge, 2009.

Israeli, Raphael. "Islamikaze and Their Significance." *Terrorism and Political Violence* 9, no. 3 (1997): 96–121.

Issacharoff, Avi. "The Palestinian and Israeli Media on Female Suicide Terrorists." In *Female Suicide Bombers: Dying for Equality?* edited by Yoram Schweitzer, 43–50. Tel Aviv: Jaffee Center for Strategic Studies, 2006.

Jabar, Faleh A. *The Shi'ite Movement in Iraq.* London: Saqi, 2003.

Jaber, Hala. *Hezbollah: Born with a Vengeance.* New York: Columbia University Press, 1997.

Jackson, Brian A. "Groups, Networks, or Movements: A Command-and-Control Driven Approach to Classifying Terrorist Organizations and Its Application to al Qaeda." *Studies in Conflict and Terrorism* 29, no. 3 (2006): 241–62.

Jackson, Brian A., et al. *Breaching the Fortress Wall: Understanding Terrorist Efforts to Overcome Defensive Technologies.* Santa Monica, Calif.: RAND, 2007.

Jackson, Brian A., et al. *Aptitude for Destruction.* Vol. 2: *Case Studies of Organizational Learning in Five Terrorist Groups.* Santa Monica, Calif.: RAND, 2007.

Jacques, Karen, and Paul L. Taylor. "Male and Female Suicide Bombers: Different Sexes, Different Reasons?" *Studies in Conflict and Terrorism* 31, no. 4 (2008): 304–26.

Jarecki, Eugene. *The American Way of War: Guided Missiles, Misguided Men, and a Republic in Peril.* New York: Free Press, 2008.

Jensen, Richard Bach. "Daggers, Rifles, and Dynamite: Anarchist Terrorism in Nineteenth Century Europe." *Terrorism and Political Violence* 16, no. 1 (2004): 116–53.

Jeyaraj, D. B. S. "The Trails of the Tigers." *Frontline,* August 14–27, 1999.

———. "Another Human Bomb." *Frontline,* June 19–July 2 1999.

Johnson, Stephen B. *Secret of Apollo: Systems Management in American and European Space Programs.* Baltimore: Johns Hopkins University Press, 2002.

Johnson, Steven. *Where Good Ideas Come From: A Natural History of Innovation.* New York: Riverhead Books, 2010.

———. *Emergence: The Connected Lives of Ants, Brains, Cities and Software.* New York; Scribner, 2004.

Joiner, Thomas. *Why People Die by Suicide.* Cambridge, Mass.: Harvard University Press, 2005.

Jordan, Javier, and Fernando M. Mañas. "Strengths and Weaknesses of Grassroot Jihadist Networks: The Madrid Bombings." *Studies in Conflict and Terrorism* 31, no. 1 (2008): 17–39.

Jorisch, Avi. *Beacon of Hatred: Inside Hizballah's al Manar Television.* Washington, D.C.: Washington Institute for Near East Policy, 2004.

Joshi, Manoj. "On the Razor's Edge: The Liberation Tigers of Tamil Eelam." *Studies in Conflict and Terrorism* 19, no. 1 (1996): 19–42.

Kadian, Rajesh. *India's Sri Lanka Fiasco.* New Delhi: Vision Books, 1990.

Kalpakian, Jack. "Building the Human Bomb: The Case of the 16 May 2003 Attacks in Casablanca." *Studies in Conflict and Terrorism* 28, no. 2 (2005): 113–27.

Kalyvas, Stathis, and Ignacio Sanchez-Cuenca. "Killing without Dying: The Absence of Suicide Missions." In *Making Sense of Suicide Missions*, edited by Diego Gambetta, 209–32. Oxford: Oxford University Press, 2005.

Katz, Samuel. *The Hunt for the Engineer: The Inside Story of How Israel's Counterterrorist Forces Tracked and Killed the Hamas Master Bomber.* Guilford, Conn.: Lyons Press, 1999.

Kaufmann, Stuart. *At Home in the Universe: The Search for the Laws of Self-Organization and Complexity.* New York: Oxford University Press, 1995.

Keddie, Nikki R., and Farah Monian. "Militancy and Religion in Contemporary Iran." In *Fundamentalisms and the State: Remaking Polities, Economies, and Militance*, edited by Martin E. Marty and R. Scott Appleby, 511–38. Chicago: University of Chicago Press, 1993.

Kee, Robert. *The Green Flag: A History of Irish Nationalism.* London: Penguin Books, 2000.

Kennedy, Jonathan, and Gabriel Weimann. "The Strength of Weak Terrorist Ties." *Terrorism and Political Violence* 23, no. 2 (2011): 201–12.

Kenny, Charles. *Getting Better: Why Global Development Is Succeeding—and How We Can Improve the World Even More.* New York: Basic Books, 2011.

Kenney, Michael. "Beyond the Internet: *Mētis, Techne*, and the Limitations of Online Artifacts for Islamist Terrorists." *Terrorism and Political Violence* 22, no. 2 (2010): 177–97.

———. *From Pablo to Osama: Trafficking and Terrorist Networks, Government Bureaucracies, and Competitive Adaptation.* University Park: University of Pennsylvania Press, 2007.

Kepel, Gilles. *Beyond Terror and Martyrdom: The Future of the Middle East.* Translated by Pascale Ghazaleh. Cambridge, Mass.: Harvard University Press, 2008.

———. *The War for Muslim Minds: Islam and the West.* Translated by Pascale Ghazaleh. Cambridge, Mass.: Belknap Press, 2004.

Kershner, Isabel. *Barrier: The Seam of the Israeli-Palestinian Conflict.* New York: Palgrave MacMillan, 2005.

Kertzer, David. *Ritual, Politics, and Power.* New Haven, Conn.: Yale University Press, 1997.

Khalidi, Rashid. *The Iron Cage: The Story of the Palestinian Struggle for Statehood.* Boston: Beacon Press, 2007.

———. *Palestinian Identity: The Construction of Modern National Consciousness.* New York: Columbia University Press, 1997.

Khan, Mukhtar A. "Pakistan's Most Wanted: A Profile of Tehrik-e-Taliban Leader Baitullah Mahsud." *Terrorism Monitor*, April 24 2009, 6–9.

Khosrokhavar, Farhad. *Suicide Bombers: Allah's New Martyrs*. Translated by David Macey. London: Pluto Press, 2005.

Kilcullen, David. *The Accidental Guerilla: Fighting Small Wars in the Midst of a Big One*. New York: Oxford University Press, 2009.

King, Mary Elizabeth. *A Quiet Revolution: The First Palestinian Intifada and Nonviolent Resistance*. New York: Nation Books, 2007.

Kirby, Aidan. "The London Bombers as 'Self-Starters': A Case Study in Indigenous Radicalization and the Emergence of Autonomous Cliques." *Studies in Conflict and Terrorism* 30, no. 5 (2007): 415–28.

Klein, Iris Jean. "Palestinian Militancy, Martyrdom, and Nationalist Communities in the West Bank during the Intifada." In *Martyrdom and Political Resistance Movements: Essays on Asia and Europe*, edited by Joyce Pettigrew, 85–109. Amsterdam: VU University Press, 1997.

Kloppenburg Jr., Jack Ralph. *First the Seed: The Political Economy of Plant Biotechnology, 1492–2000*. New York: Cambridge University Press, 1988.

Knysh, Alexander. "The Caucasus Emirate: Between Reality and Virtuality." Keyman Program in Turkish Studies Working Paper Series, Working Paper no. 09-001, Northwestern University, June 2009.

Kohlman, Evan. F. "Al-Qa'ida's 'MySpace': Terrorist Recruitment on the Internet." *CTC Sentinel* 1, no. 2 (2008): 8–9.

Kramer, Martin. "Suicide Terrorism: Origins and Response. Martin Kramer on Robert Pape's Thesis." From a Washington Institute for Near East Policy Special Policy Forum, November 8, 2005, www.geocities.com/martinkramerorg/PapeKramer.htm.

———. "The Moral Logic of Hizballah." In *Origins of Terrorism: Psychologies, Ideologies, Theologies, States of Mind*, edited by Walter Reich, 131–57. Washington, D.C.: Woodrow Wilson Center Press, 1998.

———. "The Oracle of Hizbullah: Sayyid Muhammad Husayn Fadlallah." In *Spokesmen for the Despised: Fundamentalist Leaders of the Middle East*, edited by R. Scott Appleby, 83–181. Chicago: University of Chicago Press, 1997.

———. "Hizbullah: The Calculus of Jihad." In *Fundamentalisms and the State: Remaking Polities, Economies, and Militance*, edited by Martin E. Marty and R. Scott Appleby, 539–56. Chicago: University of Chicago Press, 1993.

———. "Sacrifice and 'Self-Martyrdom' in Shi'ite Lebanon." *Terrorism and Political Violence* 3, no. 3 (1991): 30–47.

Kydd, Andrew, and Barbara Walter. "Sabotaging the Peace: The Politics of Extremist Violence." *International Organization* 56, no. 2 (2002): 263–96.

Lahoud, Nelly. "Bin Ladin's Death through the Lens of al-Qa'ida's Confidential Secretary." *CTC Sentinel* 4, no. 5 (2011): 12–15.

———. *The Jihadis' Path to Self-Destruction*. New York: Columbia University Press, 2010.

Lakhani, Kalsoom. "Indoctrinating Children: The Making of Pakistan's Suicide Bombers." *CTC Sentinel* 3, no. 6 (2010): 11–13.

Lankford, Adam. *Human Killing Machines: Systematic Indoctrination in Iran, Nazi Germany, al Qaeda, and Abu Ghraib.* New York: Lexington, 2010.

Levitt, Matthew. *Hamas: Politics, Charity, and Terrorism in the Service of Jihad.* New Haven, Conn.: Yale University Press, 2006.

Lewis, Adrian R. *The American Culture of War: The History of U.S. Military Force from World War II to Operation Iraqi Freedom.* New York: Routledge, 2007.

Lewis, Bernard. *The Assassins: A Radical Sect in Islam.* New York: Oxford University Press, 1967.

Lewis, Jeffrey W. "Self-Sacrifice as Innovation: The Strategic and Tactical Utility of Martyrdom." *Dynamics of Asymmetric Conflict* 1, no. 1 (2008): 66–87.

———. "Precision Terror: Suicide Bombing as Control Technology." *Terrorism and Political Violence* 19, no. 2 (2007): 223–45.

Lia, Brynjar. *Architect of Global Jihad: The Life of al-Qaida Strategist Abu Mus'ab al-Suri.* New York: Columbia University Press, 2008.

———. *A Police Force without a State: A History of the Palestinian Security Forces in the West Bank and Gaza.* Reading, U.K.: Ithaca Press, 2006.

———. *The Society of the Muslim Brothers in Egypt: The Rise of an Islamic Mass Movement, 1928–1942.* Reading, U.K.: Ithaca Press, 1998.

Lienhard, John H. *How Invention Begins: Echoes of Old Voices in the Rise of New Machines.* New York: Oxford University Press, 2006.

Lilja, Jannie. "Trapping Constituents or Winning Hearts and Minds? Rebel Strategies to Attain Constituent Support in Sri Lanka." *Terrorism and Political Violence* 21, no. 2 (2009): 306–26.

Luft, Gal. "The Palestinian H-Bomb: Terror's Winning Strategy." *Foreign Affairs* 81, no. 4 (July/August 2002): 2–7.

Lustick, Ian S. "Terrorism in the Arab-Israeli Conflict: Targets and Audiences." In *Terrorism in Context*, edited by Martha Crenshaw, 514–52. University Park: Pennsylvania State University Press, 1995.

Lynch, Marc. *Voices of the New Arab Public: Iraq, al-Jazeera, and Middle East Politics Today.* New York: Columbia University Press, 2006.

MacKenzie, Donald, and Judy Wajcman. "Introductory Essay: The Social Shaping of Technology." In *The Social Shaping of Technology*, edited by Donald MacKenzie and Judy Wajcman, 3–27. Philadelphia: Open University Press, 1985.

Mahnken, Thomas G. *Technology and the American Way of War since 1945.* New York: Columbia University Press, 2008.

Marcus, Aliza. *Blood and Belief: The PKK and the Kurdish Fight for Independence.* New York: New York University Press, 2007.

Martin, Graham. "Media Influence To Suicide: The Search for Solutions." *Archives of Suicide Research* 4, no. 4 (1998): 51–66.

Marx, Anthony W. *Faith in Nation: Exclusionary Origins of Nationalism.* New York: Oxford University Press, 2003.

Marx, Leo. "Technology: The History of a Hazardous Concept." *Technology and Culture* 51, no. 3 (2010): 561–77.

Mazarr, Michael J. *Unmodern Men in the Modern World: Radical Islam, Terrorism, and the War on Modernity.* Cambridge: Cambridge University Press, 2007.

McGregor, Andrew. "Suicide Bombing Kills Somali Security Minister as Islamists Mount Assault on Mogadishu." *Terrorism Monitor,* June 25, 2009, 5–6.

McMahon, Peter. *Global Control: Information Technology and Globalization since 1845.* Northampton, Mass.: Edward Elgar, 2000.

McShane, Clay, and Joel A. Tarr. *The Horse in the City: Living Machines in the Nineteenth Century.* Baltimore: Johns Hopkins University Press, 2007.

Merari, Ariel. *Driven to Death: Psychological and Social Aspects of Suicide Terrorism.* New York: Oxford University Press, 2010.

———. "Social, Organizational, and Psychological Factors in Suicide Terrorism." In *Root Causes of Terrorism: Myths, Reality, and Ways Forward,* edited by Tore Bjørgo, 70–86. London: Routledge, 2005.

———. "The Readiness To Kill and Die: Suicidal Terrorism in the Middle East." In *Origins of Terrorism: Psychologies, Ideologies, Theologies, States of Mind,* edited by Walter Reich, 192–207. Washington, D.C.: Woodrow Wilson Center Press, 1998.

Merari, Ariel, et al. "Personality Characteristics of 'Self-Martyrs' / 'Suicide Bombers' and Organizers of Suicide Attacks." *Terrorism and Political Violence* 22, no. 1 (2010): 87–101.

Merari, Ariel, et al. "Making Palestinian 'Martyrdom Operations' / 'Suicide Attacks': Interviews with Would-Be Perpetrators and Organizers." *Terrorism and Political Violence* 22, no. 1 (2010): 102–19.

Miles, Hugh. *Al-Jazeera: The Inside Story of the Arab News Channel That Is Challenging the West.* New York: Grove Press, 2005.

Miller, Joseph C. *Way of Death: Merchant Capitalism and the Angolan Slave Trade, 1730–1830.* Madison: University of Wisconsin Press, 1988.

Miller, Martin A. "The Intellectual Origins of Modern Terrorism in Europe." In *Terrorism in Context,* edited by Martha Crenshaw, 27–62. University Park: Pennsylvania University Press, 1995.

Mindell, David A. *Between Human and Machine: Feedback, Control, and Computing before Cybernetics.* Baltimore: Johns Hopkins University Press, 2002.

Mishal, Shaul, and Avraham Sela. *The Palestinian Hamas: Vision, Violence, and Coexistence.* 2nd ed. New York: Columbia University Press, 2006.

Mitchell, Richard P. *The Society of the Muslim Brothers.* Oxford: Oxford University Press, 1969.

Moghadam, Assaf. *The Globalization of Martyrdom: Al Qaeda, Salafi Jihad, and the Diffusion of Suicide Attacks.* Baltimore: Johns Hopkins University Press, 2008.

———. "Roots of Suicide Terrorism: A Multi-causal approach." In *Root Causes of Suicide Terrorism: The Globalization of Martyrdom,* edited by Ami Pedahzur, 81–107. New York: Routledge, 2006.

———. "Suicide Terrorism, Occupation, and the Globalization of Martyrdom: A Critique of *Dying to Win.*" *Studies in Conflict and Terrorism* 29, no. 6 (2006): 707–29.

———. "Palestinian Suicide Terrorism in the Second Intifada: Motivations and Organizational Aspects." *Studies in Conflict and Terrorism* 26, no. 1 (2003): 65–92.

Mokyr, Joel. *The Gifts of Athena: Historical Origins of the Knowledge Economy.* Princeton, N.J.: Princeton University Press, 2002.

Moloney, Ed. *Voices from the Grave: Two Men's War in Ireland.* New York: Public Affairs, 2010.

———. *A Secret History of the IRA.* 2nd ed. London: Penguin Books, 2007.

Morris, Benny. *Righteous Victims: A History of the Zionist-Arab Conflict, 1881–2001.* New York: Vintage Books, 2001.

Mulgan, G. J. *Communication and Control: Networks and the New Economies of Communication.* New York: Guilford Press, 1991.

Nacos, Brigitte L. *Mass Mediated Terrorism: The Central Role of the Media in Terrorism and Counterterrorism.* New York: Rowman and Littlefield, 2002.

Naftali, Timothy. *Blind Spot: The Secret History of American Counterterrorism.* New York: Basic Books, 2005.

Naimark, Norman M. *Fires of Hatred: Ethnic Cleansing in Twentieth-Century Europe.* Cambridge, Mass.: Harvard University Press, 2001.

———. "Terrorism and the Fall of Imperial Russia." *Terrorism and Political Violence* 2, no. 2 (1990): 171–92.

———. *Terrorists and Social Democrats: The Russian Revolutionary Movement under Alexander III.* Cambridge, Mass.: Harvard University Press, 1983.

Nasr, Vali. *The Shia Revival: How Conflicts within Islam Will Shape the Future.* New York: W. W. Norton and Company, 2006.

Natali, Christiana. "Building Cemeteries, Constructing Identities: Funerary Practices and Nationalist Discourse among the Tamil Tigers of Sri Lanka." *Contemporary South Asia* 16, no. 3 (2008): 287–301.

Nathan, Joanna. "Reading the New Taliban." In *Decoding the New Taliban: Insights from the Afghan Field,* edited by Antonio Giustozzi, 23–42. New York: Columbia University Press, 2009.

Neufeld, Michael J. *The Rocket and the Reich: Peenemünde and the Coming of the Ballistic Missile Era.* New York: Free Press, 1995.

Newsinger, John. *British Counter Insurgency: From Palestine to Northern Ireland.* New York: Palgrave, 2002.

Nivat, Anne. "The Black Widows: Chechen Women Join the Fight for Independence—and Allah." *Studies in Conflict and Terrorism* 28, no. 5 (2005): 413–19.

Noble, David. *The Religion of Technology: The Divinity of Man and the Spirit of Invention.* New York: Alfred A. Knopf, 1997.

Norton, Augustus Richard. *Hezbollah: A Short History.* Princeton, N.J.: Princeton University Press, 2007.

———. *Amal and the Shi`a: Struggle for the Soul of Lebanon*. Austin: University of Texas Press, 1987.

Nye, David E. *Technology Matters: Questions to Live With*. Cambridge, Mass.: MIT Press, 2006.

O'Balance, Edgar. *The Cyanide War: Tamil Insurrection in Sri Lanka, 1973–1988*. London: Brassey's, 1989.

O'Brien, Conor Cruise. *Ancestral Voices: Religion and Nationalism in Ireland*. Chicago: University of Chicago Press, 1994.

O'Malley, Padraig. *Biting at the Grave: The Irish Hunger Strikes and the Politics of Despair*. Boston: Beacon Press, 1990.

Ohnuki-Tierney, Emiko. *Kamikaze Diaries: Reflections of Japanese Student Soldiers*. Chicago: University of Chicago Press, 2006.

———. *Kamikaze, Cherry Blossoms, and Nationalisms: The Militarization of Aesthetics in Japanese History*. Chicago: University of Chicago Press, 2002.

Oliver, Anne Marie, and Paul Steinberg. *The Road to Martyr's Square: A Journey into the World of the Suicide Bomber*. New York: Oxford University Press, 2005.

Oppenheimer, A. R. *IRA: The Bombs and the Bullets: A History of Deadly Ingenuity*. Dublin: Irish Academic Press, 2009.

Orbach, Israel. "Terror Suicide: How Is It Possible?" *Archives of Suicide Research* 8, no. 1 (2004): 115–30.

Pacey, Arnold. *Meaning in Technology*. Cambridge, Mass.: MIT Press, 1999.

———. *The Culture of Technology*. Cambridge, Mass.: MIT Press, 1983.

Packard, Vance. *The Hidden Persuaders*. Rev. ed. New York: Pocket Books, 1980.

Packer, George. *The Assassins' Gate: America in Iraq*. New York: Farrar, Straus and Giroux, 2005.

Pantucci, Raffaello. "American Jihad: New Details Emerge about al-Shabaab Recruitment in North America." *Terrorism Monitor*, December 3, 2009.

Pape, Robert A. *Dying to Win: The Strategic Logic of Suicide Bombing*. New York: Random House, 2005.

Pape Robert A., and James K. Feldman. *Cutting the Fuse: The Explosion of Global Suicide Terrorism and How To Stop It*. Chicago: University of Chicago Press, 2010.

Paperno, Irina. *Suicide as a Cultural Institution in Dostoevsky's Russia*. Ithaca, N.Y.: Cornell University Press, 1997.

Pappe, Ilan. *A History of Modern Palestine: One Land, Two Peoples*. New York: Cambridge University Press, 2004.

Pargeter, Alison. *The New Frontiers of Jihad: Radical Islam in Europe*. Philadelphia: University of Pennsylvania Press, 2008.

Paz, Reuven. "Programmed Terrorists? Analysis of the Letter of Instructions Found in the September 11th Attack." PRISM (Project for the Research of Islamist Movements). http://www.e-prism.org/projectsandproducts.html

Pedahzur, Ami. *Suicide Terrorism*. Cambridge, U.K., and Malden, Mass.: Polity Press, 2005.

Pedahzur, Ami, and Arie Perliger. *Jewish Terrorism in Israel*. New York: Columbia University Press, 2009.

———. "The Changing Nature of Suicide Attacks: A Social Network Perspective." *Social Forces* 94, no. 4 (2006): 1987–2008.

Pedahzur, Ami, Arie Perliger, and Leonard Weinberg. "Altruism and Fatalism: The Characteristics of Palestinian Suicide Terrorists." *Deviant Behavior* 24, no. 4 (2003): 405–23.

Peteet, Julie. "The Writing on the Walls: The Graffiti of the Intifada." *Cultural Anthropology* 11, no. 2 (1996): 139–59.

Phillips, David P. "The Influence of Suggestion on Suicide: Substantive and Theoretical Implications of the Werther Effect." *American Sociological Review* 39, no. 3 (1974): 340–54.

Pipes, Richard. *The Degaev Affair: Terror and Treason in Tsarist Russia*. New Haven, Conn.: Yale University Press, 2003.

Pippard, Tim. "Al-Shabab's Agenda in the Wake of the Kampala Suicide Attacks." *CTC Sentinel* 3, no. 7 (2010): 4–6.

Politkovskaya, Anna. *A Small Corner of Hell: Dispatches from Chechnya*. Translated by Alexander Burry and Tatiana Tulchinsky. Chicago: University of Chicago Press, 2003.

Pomper, Phillip. "Russian Revolutionary Terrorism." In *Terrorism in Context*, edited by Martha Crenshaw, 63–101. University Park: Pennsylvania University Press, 1995.

Pratrap, Anita. *Island of Blood: Frontline Reports from Sri Lanka, Afghanistan, and Other South Asian Flashpoints*. New York: Penguin Books, 2001.

Prigogine, Ilya, with Isabelle Stengers. *Order Out of Chaos: Man's New Dialogue with Nature*. New York: Bantam, 1984.

Quillen, Chris. "Mass Casualty Bombings Chronology." *Studies in Conflict and Terrorism* 25, no. 5 (2002): 293–302.

Radzinsky, Edvard. *Alexander II: The Last Great Tsar*. Translated by Antonia W. Bouis. New York: Free Press, 2005.

Ranstorp, Magnus. "Terrorist Awakening in Sweden?" *CTC Sentinel* 4, no. 1 (2011): 1–5.

———. *Hiz'ballah in Lebanon: The Politics of the Western Hostage Crisis*. New York: St. Martin's Press, 1997.

Rapoport, David C. "Sacred Terror: A Contemporary Example from Islam." In *Origins of Terrorism: Psychologies, Ideologies, Theologies, States of Mind*, edited by Walter Reich, 103–30. Washington, D.C.: Woodrow Wilson Center Press, 1998.

Rashid, Ahmed. *Descent into Chaos: The United States and the Failure of Nation Building in Pakistan, Afghanistan, and Central Asia*. New York: Viking, 2008.

———. *Taliban: Militant Islam, Oil, and Fundamentalism in Central Asia*. New Haven, Conn.: Yale University Press, 2000.

Rawlins, Gregory J. E. *Slaves of the Machine: The Quickening of Computer Technology*. Cambridge, Mass.: MIT Press, 1997.

Reuter, Christoph. *My Life Is a Weapon: A Modern History of Suicide Bombing*. Translated by Helena Ragg-Kirkby. New Haven, Conn.: Yale University Press, 2004.

Richardson, John. *Paradise Poisoned: Learning about Conflict, Terrorism, and Development from Sri Lanka's Civil Wars*. Kandy, Sri Lanka: International Centre for Ethnic Studies, 2005.

Richardson, Louise. *What Terrorists Want: Understanding the Enemy, Containing the Threat*. New York: Random House, 2006.

Ricks, Thomas E. *Fiasco: The American Military Adventure in Iraq*. New York: Penguin Press, 2006.

Riedel, Bruce. *Deadly Embrace: Pakistan, America, and the Future of Global Jihad*. Washington, D.C.: Brookings Institution Press, 2011.

———. *The Search for al Qaeda: Its Leadership, Ideology, and Future*. Washington, D.C.: Brookings Institution Press, 2008.

Rip, Michael Russell, and James M. Hasik. *The Precision Revolution: GPS and the Future of Aerial Warfare*. Annapolis, Md.: Naval Institute Press, 2002.

Robb, John. *Brave New War: The Next Stage of Terrorism and the End of Globalization*. Hoboken, N.J.: John Wiley and Sons, 2007.

Roberts, Michael. "Pragmatic Action and Enchanted Worlds: A Black Tiger Rite of Commemoration." *Social Analysis* 50, no. 1 (2006): 73–102.

———. "Tamil Tiger 'Martyrs': Regenerating Divine Potency?" *Studies in Conflict and Terrorism* 28, no. 6 (2005): 493–514.

Rogan, Eugene. *The Arabs: A History*. 2nd ed. New York: Basic Books 2009.

Rogan, Hanna. "Violent Trends in Algeria since 9/11." *CTC Sentinel* 1, no. 12 (2008): 16–19.

Rogers, Everett M. *Diffusion of Innovations*. 5th ed. New York: Free Press, 2003.

Rogerson, Barnaby. *The Heirs of the Prophet Muhammad and the Roots of the Sunni-Shia Schism*. London: Little, Brown, 2006.

Rosen, Nir. *In the Belly of the Green Bird: The Triumph of the Martyrs in Iraq*. New York: Free Press, 2006.

Rotberg, Robert I. "Sri Lanka's Civil War: From Mayhem toward Diplomatic Resolution." In *Creating Peace in Sri Lanka: Civil War and Reconciliation*, edited by Robert I. Rotberg, 1–16. Washington, D.C.: Brookings Institution Press, 1999.

Rougier, Bernard. *Everyday Jihad: The Rise of Militant Islam among Palestinians in Lebanon*. Cambridge, Mass.: Harvard University Press, 2007.

Roul, Animesh. "Terrorism's Trojan Horse: Vehicle-Borne Suicide Attacks Give Taliban Upper Hand in Pakistan." *Terrorism Monitor* 8, no. 33 (2009): 6–8.

Roy, Olivier. *Globalized Islam: The Search for a New Ummah*. New York: Columbia University Press, 2004.

Roy, Sara. *Hamas and Civil Society in Gaza: Engaging the Islamist Social Sector*. Princeton, N.J.: Princeton University Press, 2011.

Rubin, Barnett R. "Saving Afghanistan," *Foreign Affairs* 86, no. 1 (2007): 57–78.

———. *The Fragmentation of Afghanistan: State Formation and Collapse in the International System.* 2nd ed. New Haven, Conn.: Yale University Press, 2002.

———. *The Search for Peace in Afghanistan: From Buffer State to Failed State.* New Haven, Conn.: Yale University Press, 1995.

———. *Cycles of Violence: Human Rights in Sri Lanka since the Indo-Sri Lanka Agreement.* Washington, D.C.: Asia Watch, 1987.

Ruttig, Thomas. "Loya Paktia's Insurgency: (I) The Haqqani Network as Autonomous Entity." In *Decoding the New Taliban: Insights from the Afghan Field,* edited by Antonio Giustozzi, 57–100. New York: Columbia University Press, 2009.

Ryder, Chris. *A Special Kind of Courage: 321 EOD Squadron—Battling the Bombers.* Rev. ed. London: Methuen, 2006.

Sageman, Marc. *Leaderless Jihad: Terror Networks in the Twenty-First Century.* Philadelphia: University of Pennsylvania Press, 2008.

———. *Understanding Terror Networks.* Philadelphia: University of Pennsylvania Press, 2004.

Sambandan, V. S. "Living Through the Bombs." *Frontline,* December 25, 1999–January 7, 2000.

———. "Peace-maker as terrorist target." *Frontline,* August 14–27, 1999.

Schalk, Peter. "Resistance and Martyrdom in the Process of State Formation of Tamililam." In *Martyrdom and Political Resistance Movements: Essays on Asia and Europe,* edited by Joyce Pettigrew, 61–84. Amsterdam: VU University Press, 1997.

———. "The Revival of Martyr Cults among Ilavar." *Temenos* 33 (1997): 151–90.

Schatzberg, Eric. "Technik Comes to America: Changing Meanings of Technology before 1930." *Technology and Culture* 47, no. 3 (2006): 486–512.

Schiff, Ze'ev, and Ehud Ya'ari. *Israel's Lebanon War.* Edited and translated by Ina Friedman. New York: Simon and Schuster, 1984.

Schweitzer, Yoram. "Palestinian *Istishhadia*: A Developing Instrument." *Studies in Conflict and Terrorism* 30, no. 8 (2007): 667–89.

———. "Palestinian Female Suicide Bombers: Reality vs. Myth." In *Female Suicide Bombers: Dying for Equality?* edited by Yoram Schweitzer, 25–42. Tel Aviv: Jaffee Center for Strategic Studies, 2006.

Schweitzer, Yoram, and Sari Goldstein Ferber. "Al-Qaeda and the Internationalization of Suicide Terrorism." Jaffee Center for Strategic Studies, Tel Aviv University, Memorandum no. 78, November 2005.

Seale, Patrick. *Asad: The Struggle for the Middle East.* Berkeley: University of California Press, 1988.

Senaratne, Jagath P. *Political Violence in Sri Lanka, 1977–1990: Riots, Insurrections, Counter-insurgencies, Foreign Intervention.* Amsterdam: VU University Press, 1997.

Shaery-Eisenlohr, Roschanack. *Shi'ite Lebanon: Transnational Religion and the Making of National Identities*. New York: Columbia University Press, 2008.

Shanahan, Rodger. "Shi'a Political Development in Iraq: The Case of the Islamic Da'wa Party." *Third World Quarterly* 25, no. 5 (2004): 943–54.

Sharma, Rajeev. *Beyond the Tigers: Tracking Rajiv Gandhi's Assassination*. New Delhi: Kaveri Books, 1998.

Sherry, Michael S. *The Rise of American Air Power: The Creation of Armageddon*. New Haven, Conn.: Yale University Press, 1987.

Shinn, David H. "Somalia's New Government and the Challenge of al-Shabab." *CTC Sentinel* 2, no. 3 (2009): 1–4.

Al-Shishani, Murad Batal. "An Assessment of the Anatomy of al-Qaeda in Yemen: Ideological and Social Factors." *Terrorism Monitor* 8, no. 9 (2010): 6–8.

Singer, Peter W. *Wired for War: The Robotics Revolution and Conflict in the Twenty-first Century*. New York: Penguin Press, 2009.

Sluka, Jeffrey. "From Graves to Nations: Political Martyrdom and Irish Nationalism." In *Martyrdom and Political Resistance Movements: Essays on Asia and Europe*, edited by Joyce Pettigrew, 35–60. Amsterdam: VU University Press, 1997.

Smith, Anthony D. *National Identity*. Reno: University of Nevada Press, 1991.

Smith, Chris. "South Asia's Enduring War." In *Creating Peace in Sri Lanka: Civil War and Reconciliation*, edited by Robert I. Rotberg, 17–40. Washington, D.C.: Brookings Institution Press, 1999.

Smith, M. L. R. *Fighting for Ireland: The Military Strategy of the Irish Republican Movement*. London and New York: Routledge, 1997.

Smith, Niel A. "Understanding Sri Lanka's Defeat of the Tamil Tigers." *Joint Force Quarterly*, no. 59 (October 2010): 40–44.

Smith, Rupert. *The Utility of Force: The Art of War in the Modern World*. New York: Alfred A. Knopf, 2007.

Somaratne, G. P. V. "Sri Lanka's Relations with Israel." In *External Compulsions of South Asian Politics*, edited by Shelton U. Kodikkara, 194–225. New Delhi: Sage Publications, 1993.

Somasundaram, Daya. *Scarred Minds: The Psychological Impact of War on Sri Lankan Tamils*. New Delhi: Sage Publications, 1998.

Speckhard, Anne, and Khapta Ahkmedova. "The Making of a Martyr: Chechen Suicide Terrorism." *Studies in Conflict and Terrorism* 29, no. 5 (2006): 429–92.

Spinney, Franklin C. *Defense Facts of Life: The Plans/Reality Mismatch*. Edited by James Clay Thompson. Boulder, Colo.: Westview Press, 1985.

Sprinzak, Ehud. "Rational Fanatics." *Foreign Policy*, September/October 2000.

Stack-O'Connor, Alisa. "Lions, Tigers, and Freedom Birds: How and Why the Liberation Tigers of Tamil Eelam Employs Women." *Terrorism and Political Violence* 19, no. 1 (2007): 43–63.

Stenersen, Anne. "Foreign Fighters in Afghanistan and Pakistan after 9/11." Paper presented at the conference "Understanding Jihadism: Origins, Evolution, and Future Perspectives," Oslo, March 19–21, 2009.

———. *Al-Qaida's Quest for Weapons of Mass Destruction: The History behind the Hype.* Saarbrücken: Verlag Dr. Müller AG, 2008.

Stern, Jessica. *Terror in the Name of God: Why Religious Militants Kill.* New York: Harper Collins, 2003.

Strasser, Susan. *Satisfaction Guaranteed: The Making of the American Mass Market.* Rev. ed. Washington, D.C.: Smithsonian Institution Press, 1989.

Swamy, M. R. Narayan. *Tigers of Lanka: From Boys to Guerrillas.* 2nd ed. Colombo: Vijitha Yapa Publications, 2004.

———. *Inside an Elusive Mind: Prabhakaran, The First Profile of the World's Most Ruthless Guerrilla Leader.* Colombo: Vijitha Yapa Publications, 2003.

Taheri, Amir. *Holy Terror: The Inside Story of Islamic Terrorism.* London: Hutchinson, 1987.

Talbott, Stephen L. *The Future Does Not Compute: Transcending the Machines in Our Midst.* Sebastopol, Calif.: O'Reilly and Associates, 1995.

Tambiah, S. J. *Sri Lanka: Ethnic Fratricide and the Dismantling of Democracy.* Chicago: University of Chicago Press, 1986.

Tamimi, Azzam. *Hamas: A History from Within.* Northampton, Mass.: Olive Branch Press, 2007.

Tawil, Camille. *Brothers in Arms: The Story of al-Qa'ida and the Arab Jihadists.* Translated by Robin Bray. London: Saqi, 2010.

Taylor, Max, and John Horgan. "A Conceptual Framework for Addressing Psychological Process in the Development of the Terrorist." *Terrorism and Political Violence* 18, no. 4 (2006): 585–601.

Teitelbaum, Joshua. *Holier Than Thou: Saudi Arabia's Islamic Opposition.* Washington, D.C.: Washington Institute for Near East Policy, 2000.

Tiruchelvam, Neelan. "Devolution and the Elusive Quest for Peace." In *Creating Peace in Sri Lanka: Civil War and Reconciliation,* edited by Robert I. Rotberg, 189–202. Washington, D.C.: Brookings Institution Press, 1999.

Toolis, Kevin. *Rebel Hearts: Journeys within the IRA's Soul.* New York: St. Martin's Griffin, 1995.

Tripp, Charles. *A History of Iraq.* Cambridge: Cambridge University Press, 2000.

Van Crevald, Martin. *The Changing Face of War: Lessons of Combat from the Marne to Iraq.* New York: Presidio Press, 2006.

———. *Technology and War: From 2000 B.C. to the Present.* Rev. ed. New York: Free Press, 1991.

Van Kley, Dale. *The Religious Origins of the French Revolution.* New Haven, Conn.: Yale University Press, 1996.

Venturi, Franco. *Roots of Revolution: A History of the Populist and Socialist Movements in Nineteenth Century Russia.* Translated by Francis Haskell with an introduction by Isaiah Berlin. New York: Alfred A. Knopf, 1960.

Victor, Barbara. *Army of Roses: Inside the World of Palestinian Women Suicide Bombers.* New York: Rodale, 2003.

Victoria, Brian. *Zen at War*. New York: Weatherhill, 1997.

Von Hippel, Eric. *Democratizing Innovation*. Cambridge, Mass.: MIT Press, 2005.

Warrick, Joby. *The Triple Agent: The al-Qaeda Mole Who Infiltrated the CIA*. New York: Doubleday, 2011.

Wasserstein, Bernard. *Divided Jerusalem: The Struggle for the Holy City*. 2nd ed. New Haven, Conn.: Yale University Press, 2002.

Watts, Barry D. *Six Decades of Guided Munitions and Battle Networks: Progress and Prospects*. Washington, D.C.: Center for Strategic and Budgetary Assessments, 2007.

Wege, Carl Anthony. "Iran's Terrorist Asset: A History of Imad Mugniyah." *Terrorism Monitor*, September 8, 2006.

Weimann, Gabriel. *Terror on the Internet: The New Arena, the New Challenges*. Washington: U.S. Institute of Peace Press, 2006.

Weinberg, Leonard. "Suicide Terrorism for Secular Causes." In *Root Causes of Suicide Terrorism: The Globalization of Martyrdom*, edited by Ami Pedahzur, 108–22. New York: Routledge, 2006.

Weiner, Eugene, and Anita Weiner. *The Martyr's Conviction*. Atlanta, Ga.: Scholar's Press, 1990.

White, Robert W. *Ruari O Bradaigh: The Life and Politics of an Irish Revolutionary*. Bloomington: Indiana University Press, 2006.

Wiegand, Krista E. "Reformation of a Terrorist Group: Hezbollah as a Lebanese Political Party." *Studies in Conflict and Terrorism* 32, no. 8 (2009): 669–80.

Wiener, Norbert. *The Human Use of Human Beings: Cybernetics and Society*. Boston: Houghton Mifflin, 1950.

Wigle, John. "Introducing the Worldwide Incident Tracking System (WITS)." *Perspectives on Terrorism* 4, no. 1 (2010): 3–23.

Williams, Brian Glyn. "Mullah Omar's Missiles: A Field Report on Suicide Bombers in Afghanistan." *Middle East Policy* 15, no. 4 (2008): 26–46.

———. "The Taliban Fedayeen: The World's Worst Suicide Bombers?" *Terrorism Monitor*, July 19, 2007.

Wright, Lawrence. *The Looming Tower: Al Qaeda and the Road to 9/11*. New York: Alfred A. Knopf, 2006.

Wright, Robin. *Rock the Casbah: Rage and Rebellion across the Islamic World*. New York: Simon and Schuster, 2011.

———. *Dreams and Shadows: The Future of the Middle East*. New York: Penguin, 2008.

———. *In the Name of God: The Khomeini Decade*. New York: Simon and Schuster, 1989.

———. *Sacred Rage: The Wrath of Militant Islam*. New York: Simon and Schuster, 1986.

Yadin, Rivka. "Female Martyrdom: The Ultimate Embodiment of Islamic Existence?" In *Female Suicide Bombers: Dying for Equality?* edited by Yoram Schweitzer, 51–62. Tel Aviv: Jaffee Center for Strategic Studies, 2006.

Yarmolinsky, Avraham. *Road to Revolution: A Century of Russian Radicalism.* New York: Collier, 1962.

Zeitlin Jonathan, and Gerry Herrigel, eds. *Americanization and Its Limits: Reworking US Technology and Management in Post-War Europe and Japan.* Oxford: Oxford University Press, 2000.

Zelinsky, Aaron, and Martin Shubik. "Research Note: Terrorist Groups as Business Firms: A New Typological Framework." *Terrorism and Political Violence* 21, no. 2 (2009): 327–36.

INDEX

Names beginning with al and al- are alphabetized under the main element of the name. For example, al Qaeda is alphabetized under Q.

ABOUT THE AUTHOR

Jeffrey W. Lewis received his bachelor's degree from Case Western Reserve University and both his master's degree and doctorate from Ohio State University. He is the recipient of a Fulbright Hays Grant for doctoral research as well as a research grant from the German Academic Exchange Service (DAAD). He has been a guest scholar of Germany's Max Planck Society for the Advancement of Science and in 2007–2008 was a postdoctoral researcher at the START Center (Studies on Terrorism and Responses to Terrorism) located at the University of Maryland. Since 2003 he has been teaching in the Undergraduate International Studies Program at Ohio State University focusing on international security issues.

The Naval Institute Press is the book-publishing arm of the U.S. Naval Institute, a private, nonprofit, membership society for sea service professionals and others who share an interest in naval and maritime affairs. Established in 1873 at the U.S. Naval Academy in Annapolis, Maryland, where its offices remain today, the Naval Institute has members worldwide.

Members of the Naval Institute support the education programs of the society and receive the influential monthly magazine *Proceedings* or the colorful bimonthly magazine *Naval History* and discounts on fine nautical prints and on ship and aircraft photos. They also have access to the transcripts of the Institute's Oral History Program and get discounted admission to any of the Institute-sponsored seminars offered around the country.

The Naval Institute's book-publishing program, begun in 1898 with basic guides to naval practices, has broadened its scope to include books of more general interest. Now the Naval Institute Press publishes about seventy titles each year, ranging from how-to books on boating and navigation to battle histories, biographies, ship and aircraft guides, and novels. Institute members receive significant discounts on the Press's more than eight hundred books in print.

Full-time students are eligible for special half-price membership rates. Life memberships are also available.

For a free catalog describing Naval Institute Press books currently available, and for further information about joining the U.S. Naval Institute, please write to:

Member Services
The Naval Institute Press
291 Wood Road
Annapolis, MD 21402-5034
Telephone: (800) 233-8764
Fax: (410) 571-1703
Web address: www.usni.org